PRACTICAL PROFESSIO

PRACTICAL PROFESSIONAL CATERING

H.L. Cracknell, F.H.C.I.M.A.

R.J. Kaufmann, M.H.C.I.M.A.

G. Nobis, B.A.(Hons), M.H.C.I.M.A.

MACMILLAN EDUCATION

First published 1983
Reprinted (with corrections) 1985

Published by
MACMILLAN EDUCATION LTD
Houndmills, Basingstoke, Hampshire RG21 2XS
and London
Companies and representatives
throughout the world

Printed and bound in Great Britain at
The Camelot Press Ltd, Southampton

ISBN 0-333-36075-3 (hard cover)
ISBN 0-333-22565-1 (paper cover)

PREFACE

In common with many other industries, the catering industry is becoming increasingly efficient in the way it operates and this has been brought about by means of technological developments which now put it alongside those industries which have adapted to the changing needs of the times.

From being an industry which clung tenaciously to traditional methods of operation designed to give the customer what it thought he needed rather than what he actually wanted, catering has now largely transformed itself into one where advanced practices and entrepreneurial expertise are well in advance of consumers' demands. It has accepted, perhaps not always without struggle, the need for research and experimentation into its many different activities and it is now more ready than ever to adapt itself to new ideas, and to seek to improve its image both to the customer and to its employees. In the pathway towards increased efficiency, however, there lie many pitfalls, and despite the present high standards of operation, problems and complaints can still arise. These frequently occur because, by its very nature, catering is a service industry which employs people rather than machines to carry out most of its functions; it is the failure of staff to adhere to sound operating procedure which so often leads to problems and complaints. And it is the calibre of staff and the way they are trained that is so important in what is still a labour-intensive industry.

With customers becoming more discerning and demanding, caterers have learnt that, provided the great traditions of hospitality are not lost sight of, changes of demand have to be met and innovations of operation implemented. Not to recognise the need for change is to deny that any advancement is necessary.

It is against this background of continued progress that this book is presented as a textbook for students following catering courses and of which Food and Beverage Operations and Management is a required study.

To underpin the various practical activities peculiar to a catering operation with valid principles requires, first, an understanding of how these activities inter-relate one with the other, and second, an identification of those principles which can be common to all sectors of the industry.

It is our earnest hope that our attempt in this book to do this will make it a useful basis for all Food and Beverage studies in colleges of catering education as well as becoming an additional source of information and assistance for those engaged in the industry.

H. L. C.
R. J. K.
G. N.

CONTENTS

Planning – Planning Methods – Allocation of Space for the Dining Room, Customer Amenity Areas, Kitchen Areas, Staff Facilities and Offices – Planning the Dining Room, Visual, Thermal and Auditory – Types of Dining Rooms – Planning of Customer Amenities, Bars and Cloakrooms – Planning the Dispense Bar and Cellar, Staff Facilities and Offices – Planning the Kitchen – Detailed Planning of the Kitchen Areas.

Centres – Vending – Leisure Catering – Motorway Catering – Railway
Catering – Catering at Sea – Airline Catering – Catering in HM Forces –
Holiday Camps Catering – Kosher Catering – Banqueting – Receptions –
Outdoor Catering.

LIST OF FIGURES

INTRODUCTION

This book attempts to identify the many diverse aspects of catering in all its differing sectors, and thus of necessity covers a very wide expanse. It would be impossible to treat each sector as a separate entity and describe all their peculiar diversifications in any one book, but there is, however, one factor that is common to catering in all its many branches and that is its cycle of operations. All forms of catering undertaken in both the commercial and non-commercial or welfare sectors follow this cycle, either completely or in part and knowingly or unknowingly, because it relates to every aspect of their functioning.

The cycle commences with the formation of a new enterprise or an emerging one that stems from a previous undertaking, and follows from its inception, through the various stages of planning and operation to the actual practicalities of serving and satisfying customers as efficiently and, in the case of the commercial sector, as profitably as possible. The chapters of this book follow these stages, those which cover a very wide field being given two or more chapters in order to encompass the relevant information.

Much effort, however, has gone into attempting to identify those principles which are fundamental to each part of the cycle of operations and to build a framework of ideas upon which the reader can enlarge. It is hoped then that this will provide a stimulus to read more widely, and to this end a Select Bibliography has been prepared and can be found at the end of the book. It is prepared under section headings and each relates to a subject dealt with in the book.

The title of the book has been chosen carefully to match its contents because, although much of the work can be thought of as being theoretical, an emphasis has been laid on the practical aspects of catering. It demonstrates procedures and attempts to answer problems in as simple and straightforward a manner as possible. These two aspects interlock to give a basis for individual interpretation and thus will allow for some original thinking and expansion on the content matter.

The authors recognise that this work has been prepared primarily for students following catering courses in college and they hope that they will be provided with sufficient depth of study to enable them to meet successfully the demands of Food and Beverage syllabuses.

1 THE CATERING INDUSTRY

Historical Background – The Great Chefs – The Great Restaurants and Restaurateurs – Hotels – Staff – Extent of the Industry – The War Years – Tourism – Holidays – Associations – Professional Bodies – Trade Associations – The Training Board – Catering Education – The Future.

The providing of refreshment, in the form of food and drink is a very old and honourable trade, as old as civilisation itself. Almost always its end result is the bodily comfort and well being of the individual and for this reason alone, if for nothing else it can be seen as one of the most important facets of today's highly organised and complex society. The business activity which is concerned in the providing of this refreshment is carried on by the 'catering industry', a fairly loose term which is commonly bracketed with that of hotel keeping – thus the hotel and catering industry; but for most purposes and particularly for that of this book, the terms catering and catering industry relate specifically to the pro-vision of food and drink away from the home, it being provided by people who work in the industry following a career, and taking place in a wide variety of premises ranging in extent from a mobile snack bar to a de luxe restaurant.

It is often said that the past can be a mirror for the future; knowing some-thing of the history of catering may enable us to discern some of the problems faced by our predecessors and to learn from them how to face the social and technological changes that are affecting the industry today. The history of catering in this country is very closely related to that of hotels and to travel and tourism in general and it was inevitable that they developed in close association with one another. Whilst dwelling mainly on the provision of refreshment the following pages cannot avoid reference to that of shelter since they so often complement one another.

HISTORICAL BACKGROUND

The need for people to go on journeys for business or pilgrimage gave rise to the need for refreshment and shelter along the way; thus it was that as long ago as the time of the Druids an order called the Bryghnibhs provided these facilities and could be likened to the motorway caterers of those days.

Whilst the Romans were here they built good roads and set up posting houses which were in fact inns that provided overnight shelter. Each town also had its ale-house as well as taverns which sold food; so catering really began in taverns rather than in the inns. After the Romans left Britain the roads and inns fell into decay and consequently when people travelled they had to stay at the nearest castle or monastery. In the sixth century monks combined the jobs of taverner and innkeeper by offering food, drink and accommodation in return for a donation to the monastery. It was very democratic as all travellers had to sit down at the same table and all shared a dormitory, whether nobleman, pauper or pilgrim.

By medieval times commerce began to flourish and there were many more people travelling the roads going about their business, or on their way to visit religious shrines. There was not sufficient room in the monasteries to accommodate all, so the church built and ran separate lodgings which were in fact secular inns. The monks of those days used colourings and spices perhaps even more than their successors do today. The new manor houses also started to take in travellers making them welcome without charge and the standard of food provided was good with much imported produce being used.

When Henry III decided to tax the owners of the manor houses some of them gave their reply by hanging a sign outside so transforming their homes into commercial inns with themselves becoming professional landlords.

The dissolution of the monasteries in 1536 under Henry VIII and the decline of manor houses during the same time meant that inns regained their importance; in the reign of Elizabeth I more foreign tourists came to Britain and made good use of them. In 1551 statutory reference was made to distinguish an inn from a tavern; the former being for use by travellers to rest on the journey whilst a tavern offered food and drink but no accommodation. The first stage coaches began running in 1555 so the larger inns in every major town and city took on the additional job of posting house where the horses were changed and passengers fed before continuing their journey. The inns, or post houses, installed four-poster beds in place of the truckle kind previously used; there were mattresses and linen sheets, carpets and tapestries in the rooms and servants to light fires, clean guests' boots, and wait at table. Under James I innkeepers were bound to provide beds for travellers, and the ale-houses too were allowed to offer accommodation to travellers, but not the taverns. Food was plentiful for those with the money and the cooks who had now replaced the monks cooking in the monasteries commanded good salaries, but the job was not a very congenial one as the work had to be carried out over an open fire that gave off fumes, and with pans made of lead or iron.

There were no great changes over the succeeding decades but a steady though patchy improvement in the standard of accommodation and catering was evident. A greater interest in cooking led to the publication of many cookery books and these in their turn influenced the organisation and quality of the kitchen and service.

During the latter half of the eighteenth century and the early part of the nineteenth the growth of commerce again led to a great increase in travel and tourism; it was the heyday of coach travel and the inn was thus the most important place in each town, the innkeeper as 'mine host' being a person of some eminence in the community.

The inn became the social centre of the town where travellers and local clubs met; it often housed the council's meetings and was the centre of activity at election time, as well as catering for public dinners and balls. Inns started to change their name to hotel which gave customers the impression of being in a more superior class of establishment with better facilities than that offered by the common inn.

The first railway train ran in 1826 and by the middle of the century the roads were carrying fewer vehicles and the inns alongside them began to decline; the condition of the roads deteriorated as traffic switched from stagecoach to train. The railway companies saw the need to provide accommodation and refreshment for their passengers, and so provided restaurants and bars operated by themselves, or by firms of caterers, at each main terminus and on dining cars for meals en route. Railway catering became renowned for its high standard.

As the inns changed their titles and became hotels so the word inn became more associated with taverns which were the forerunners of our public houses. In turn the name tavern lost some of its meaning and in time indicated an eating house or restaurant.

To a certain extent the precursor of the restaurant, however, was the club which in its early days offered bar and dining room facilities to its members; the more sumptuous club of Victorian times also provided accommodation. The famous clubs of the nineteenth century could offer very exclusive and select facilities at modest prices because of the income from the annual membership subscription. The standard of cooking and service was exemplary and club secretaries prided themselves on the extent of their club's cellar. These clubs, which

3

at one time were numerous in every town, had in turn grown out of the coffee houses of the seventeenth and eighteenth centuries, which were places not only famous for the drinking of coffee but also for business and intrigue – to such an extent that Charles II had them closed down. Clubs were open only to male membership because it was accepted that the woman's place was in the home helping to bring up the large number of children favoured by most families.

In those days even the most modest household could afford servants, which meant that the family could dine in style at home on the food produced by their own cook and served by the maid. In the larger houses there was a proper hierarchy of servants and below stairs each rank insisted on guarding its particular privileges. When people travelled they took their personal servant with them, the very wealthy taking a whole retinue including the coachman, footman, valet and lady's maid; when they stayed in a hotel these took their meals in the special room set aside and were waited on by hotel staff!

In the same way that the ranks of private servants held on to their privileges, so was there a tradition of staff status in catering particularly in hotels where some staff exerted as much influence as the manager himself, and even considered themselves his equal.

It was not until the 1880s that women began to assert their right to eat in public, and in 1890 they received valuable support from César Ritz when he took over the management of the Savoy Hotel in London and made it accepted that they could patronise its restaurants without being frowned on by society. Restaurants became more than just a place to eat and drink; they were given a setting that would act as a frame of female charm and elegance. Women persuaded their husbands to take them out to dine. But not all were luxurious palaces at this time; there was a demand for women to take jobs in other than the limited, traditional careers of becoming nurses, nannies, teachers and servants, and they started to work in offices and factories. This brought a need for modest, popular establishments such as tea-shops that could cater for the lower-middle and working classes for meal breaks and for relaxation at other times. This need was fulfilled by the Aerated Bread Company which started to form a chain of popular restaurants in 1883, and by J. Lyons, in 1894, who opened tea-shops and later a number of restaurants called Corner Houses. These offered luxury surroundings for different styles of restaurants at reasonable prices.

The pattern of meals also underwent many changes over the years; the draughty, uncomfortable rooms of the monasteries and castles, where the diners shared trenchers and satisfied their appetites with one plainly cooked but abundant meal a day at lunchtime, changed drastically when Richard II came to the throne. England was then very much a part of Europe and his court was renowned for its standard of food, hospitality and meals at his table were a magnificent ceremony of the utmost distinction. At this time there were two or more main courses, the entrée and the remove each being a full menu in itself with a wide variety of dishes arranged in a formal pattern on the table so that guests could help themselves to those nearest to them. It was not until about

4

1850 that the serving of courses separately was introduced. The carving was done either in the kitchen or at the sideboard and diners were thus able to eat their meal without having to get up for the table to be relaid. This was known as service *à la Russe* as it was copied from the type of service prevalent in the houses of the Russian nobility.

THE GREAT CHEFS

The catering industry in this country has always been, and still continues to be a cosmopolitan one which attracts people wishing to promote and enhance it by their knowledge and prowess. Great Britain has always acknowledged that chefs from France have much to offer and has accepted them and their methods of operation, merging them into our way of operating.

During the early part of the nineteenth century many chefs came here from France primarily to work in the households of the nobility and royalty. However, when the grand hotels and restaurants began to open it was very often a French head chef who was brought over to take charge, and gradually the larger and more important kitchens became staffed almost entirely by foreign craftsmen. Naturally, a French chef would write his menu in his own language and as menu French does not readily translate into English in a concise manner French had to become the language of a significant part of catering in this country, as well as in many other countries where there was a strong French influence.

This influence, on the whole, has been a useful and improving one and we cannot be but grateful for famous chefs who have come to work here, many of them becoming very Anglophile and remaining in England after retirement. The books written by these chefs have been of great benefit and whilst many were for professional use only, others, such as those written by Alexis Soyer and Auguste Escoffier, had and continue to have a great influence on domestic catering.

Perhaps the greatest chef ever to come to these shores was Antonin Carême (1783-1833) who worked briefly for the Prince Regent and who was to have a profound influence on succeeding generations of chefs both here and abroad. Charles Elmé Francatelli (1805-76) was chef to Queen Victoria for many years. Jules Gouffé (1807-77) was one of Carême's commis and his brother, Alphonse Gouffé, also worked for Queen Victoria. Alexis Soyer (1809-58) first worked here in private service and was then appointed chef of the Reform Club; he became well known mainly because of the many books he wrote and also because of his flamboyant personality. During the Crimean War he went to Scutari and reorganised the feeding of the troops in hospital, and during the famine in Ireland opened soup kitchens to feed the starving population.

Urbain Dubois wrote many books and from his experience in several European countries helped by codifying the culinary repertoire and laying the foundations of the modern kitchen. He particularly popularised service *à la Russe*.

5

Prosper Montagné (1865-1948) was a working chef who helped to disseminate the glory of French cooking and indeed the whole world of cookery through his great encyclopaedic *Larousse Gastronomique*, which contains the history that vouches for the authenticity of most of the great dishes of the world and the notable events in culinary history.

Auguste Escoffier (1847-1935) spent nearly thirty years of his life working in London, first at the Savoy Hotel where, with César Ritz, he made it the most fashionable place to eat, then, at a later date, at the Carlton Hotel. He is probably the best known chef of all time because he had such a profound influence on the organisation of the kitchen and restaurant, on the writing of the menu, and on the various methods of service. His book *Le Guide Culinaire* is still the one that sets the standards of professional cookery even although it was written more than eighty years ago.

Since his day many other fine chefs have come to work in the well-known restaurants of this country and are still coming not only from France but also from Italy, Switzerland and Germany. However, since the last war the profession of chef has attracted many highly motivated young Britishers who, because of good training and experience, have shown themselves to be if not better at least equal to their continental counterparts.

THE GREAT RESTAURANTS AND RESTAURATEURS

Just as we welcomed the Swiss to manage our hotels and the French to run the kitchens of top establishments, so have we made welcome Italians to run some of our restaurants. Their able diplomacy and discretion has always been right for the demands of the job. Many have made their name and enjoyed unrivalled popularity in their day though perhaps not so long lasting as that of the chefs.

The word restaurant is derived from the French verb *restaurer* - to restore or refresh - and thus by usage means an establishment that offers food and drink for sale. The restaurateur is the person in charge of the restaurant or dining room and as such has to meet the challenge of stamping it with his own personality. This challenge is to make it a place where people like to eat and to be welcomed personally by him, and this is still a significant feature of any successful eating place. The feeling of importance and well being which it gives the customer is reflected in his patronising an establishment on a regular basis. Such a person was Auguste Oddenino who for years was restaurant manager at the Café Royal until 1901 when he opened his own place nearby and ended up by giving his name to a group of hotels and restaurants. Romano's in the Strand was another successful venture by a waiter, and there are many others too numerous to relate of waiters who saved sufficient capital, or obtained the backing of a prosperous client, to open their own business, knowing they had a following of loyal customers.

Many new hotels opened in major cities in the 1920s, the de luxe ones having restaurants. Each had its own dance band many of which were broadcast on the radio from the hotel ballroom, where cabarets and floor shows were included in the price of the meal. It was the restaurant, however, that represented the hotel and the whole emphasis was on the catering side.

The twenties and thirties was a great era for night clubs and the head waiters and band leaders of many of these became famous people. Ferraro went from the Criterion to Ciro's Club, Naintre went from Ciro's to the Embassy Club. The Kit Cat opened in 1925 with Soso from Ciro's as manager; the Criterion in Piccadilly Circus had an all night restaurant and cabaret. Restaurants complained of loss of business resulting from competition from clubs which operated late night bottle parties to evade the licensing laws. Ferraro was afterwards appointed restaurant manager of the Berkeley Hotel and made it a fashionable place for the young set of those days.

In 1923 the first radio broadcast was made of a restaurant orchestra from Frascati's. Henry Hall was Musical Director, or Band Leader, of the LMS Railways Hotels Dance Orchestra with thirty-two hotel bands under his direction. Carroll Gibbons was the pianist of the Savoy Orpheans under Debroy Somers, then became leader of the dance orchestra and musical director, arranging the cabaret acts for the Savoy Hotel. Charlie Kunz directed the orchestra at the Casani Club; Ambrose played at the Embassy Club and later at the May Fair, the last but one hotel to be opened by the Gordon Hotels group when Sir Francis Towle was its Managing Director. Roy Fox was at the Kit Cat Club and Café de Paris; Lew Stone was with Roy Fox when he played at the Monseigneur and took over when he left. Jack Payne landed a contract to organise the dance music at the Hotel Cecil. This hotel was opened in 1896 but was never a success and was closed in 1929 to be demolished, but proved to be so well built that it caused difficulties when being razed.

The development of high-class restaurants continued into the depression of the early thirties, and although catering mainly for the more affluent they continued to promote the habit of eating out and guiding the public towards an alternative form of entertainment from the established ones of enjoying an evening out at the theatre, opera or cinema. To this end a number of hotels and restaurants feature dinner dances so as to extend the idea of a complete evening's entertainment. After the war years of 1939-45 this practice was maintained and gradually it became accepted by almost everyone that eating out was an experience to be enjoyed by itself, and as such a form of diversion from everyday activities and responsibilities.

The increasing preparation of food in front of the customer became an emerging feature of the first-class restaurant where the waiters were provided with opportunities to do a considerable amount of work at the table; also this was a feature of the more modest type of operations such as Pizza Houses and Steak Houses where the dishes were baked or grilled in front of the customer.

With eating out becoming more of a socially accepted practice and the standard of living rising, the caterer needed to enlarge his area of operation to all members of the community. Because different social groups have different requirements the early 1960s were marked by the development of restaurant chains operating speciality houses which catered for groups seeking not only diversion but value for money.

The same period is also remembered for the adolescent revolution, when young people strived to create an identity of their own, in style of living, attire and social habits. The catering industry responded with the creation of·Espresso coffee bars, serving up dishes in a manner which dispensed with conventions of etiquette such as sitting at the table and using knives and forks.

This movement is still the predominant feature of mass catering, enjoying the name of fast food. Thus the catering industry responded as always to the changing social scene by providing products which were easily identifiable with the trends and needs of the period. This cannot be viewed in isolation but the caterer to be successful must be cognisant of social change and direction.

HOTELS

The word hotel is derived from hostel or hospice which was a residence for a group pursuing a particular aim, and from hostelry which means an inn. In France apartments or rooms were let by the week in buildings that were known as *hotels-garni*, a hotel being a large house and the garni being a furnished room in it. The *hôte* or host was the landlord or innkeeper and the hostess was the landlady.

The Hotel Proprietors' Act of 1956 embodies a legal definition of an hotel as 'an establishment held out by the proprietor as offering food, drink, and, if so required, sleeping accommodation, without special contract, to any traveller presenting himself and who appears able and willing to pay a reasonable sum for the services provided and who is in a fit state to be received'. This distinguishes the difference between an hotel and a private hotel, as in the latter the proprietor has no obligation to receive and offer his facilities to anyone.

Hotels are as much a part of the catering industry as is any other section and in this country, almost without exception, they serve meals in their dining rooms and drinks in their bars. The vast majority still offer room service though the charge for serving meals in the guests' rooms can be extremely high.

From the time of the opening of the first railway hotel at Euston in 1838 there was a steady increase in the number of hotels built in Britain to take care of the affluent middle class and the well-to-do. Great Britain became increasingly wealthy and with the vast range of developing manufacturing industries travel within this country and abroad on business and pleasure created a demand for particular types of hotel. The last quarter of the nineteenth century saw the advent of the luxury hotel and the large hotel companies.

Lyons & Co. opened their first hotel, the Strand Palace, in 1909, the Regent

8

Palace Hotel opened during the First World War and the first Corner House in 1915. The company continued to expand in all branches of the industry until 1977 when it diversified.

The Savoy Hotel in London was opened by Richard d'Oyly Carte in 1889 as the most luxurious hotel of the day having seventy bathrooms, electric lighting and a lift. It did not prosper so the next year d'Oyly Carte enticed César Ritz (1850-1918) and Auguste Escoffier to take over the management and kitchens respectively; they remained at the Savoy for only eight years then Ritz went on to form the Ritz Hotel Company and Escoffier went as head chef to the Carlton Hotel, London, when it opened in 1899. The Ritz Hotel, London, opened in 1906 but César Ritz had already retired two years earlier from a mental breakdown. He died in Switzerland in 1918.

The Savoy Hotel bought Claridges Hotel and rebuilt it before re-opening it in 1899 then went on to acquire the Berkeley Hotel, Connaught Hotel, and Simpson's in the Strand.

At this time the only really large hotel chains were in the USA and some European countries. The nearest thing to a chain here was Trust Houses which began as a trust to preserve licenced houses which, in 1903, were still in the doldrums. The aim was to offer the best accommodation and service of its kind anywhere at reasonable prices, and at the time of the merger with Fortes it had over 183 large and small hotels including Brown's Hotel, the St Georges Hotel and a number of motor hotels, as well as the Reina Cristina at Algeciras in Spain. It owned Gardner Merchant, the biggest industrial catering contract company; British Automatic, the largest vending machine company; Travelodge, the Australian hotel company; and Travelodge International which operates motels in America. It also owned the Little Chef cafes and when it merged with Forte Holdings in 1970 the number of hotels in the joint company was 224. At that time the two companies had another 13,000 rooms under construction.

Two previous groups that were taken over were the Gordon Hotels group, which was acquired by Grand Metropolitan Hotels in 1965 and the Frederick Hotels groups which was taken over by Fortes in 1967. The Gordon Hotels was founded by Frederick Gordon and in 1890 was the largest hotel organisation in the world with fifteen hotels, five in London, the rest at south coast resorts and three in France. Mr Gordon was a director of the Frederick Hotels group which owned seven hotels and which was the creation of Sir Blundell Maple, owner of the drapery, carpet and furniture stores.

The May Fair Hotel was opened in 1927 and so was the Park Lane Hotel. Grosvenor House in Park Lane opened in 1929 and originally had an ice-skating rink, but five years later this was converted into a banqueting room, the largest in Europe and able to hold 2,000 people for a ball. In 1931 the Dorchester Hotel was opened as a joint venture by Gordon Hotels and McAlpine who were the builders. The Cumberland Hotel was opened by Lyons with 1,000 bedrooms each with private bathroom in 1933, and the Mount Royal next door to it in 1934 with 750 service flats.

The Hilton Group was founded by Conrad Hilton who bought his first hotel in Texas in 1920 at the age of thirty-three and went on to create a chain of hotels that circled the world. The first London Hilton opened in 1963 and is Britain's tallest hotel; other Hilton's opened later at Stratford-upon-Avon and at Holland Park, London. In 1954 Hilton paid 111 million dollars for the Statler Hotels Group and in 1949 bought the Waldorf-Astoria; the group is now owned by Trans-World Airlines.

It was in 1946 that Maxwell Joseph first entered the hotel industry by taking over the Mandeville Hotel. In 1950 he took over and modernised the Washington Hotel, then in 1954 he bought Honywood Hotels followed by two more hotels the following year. In 1957 he bought Mount Royal for £1 million, and in 1958 he acquired the Royal Palace, St Ermin's Hotel and Dolphin Square, a block of flats. The company's name was changed to Grand Metropolitan Hotels Ltd in 1962 when there were sixteen hotels in London and six in Scotland. In 1964 it opened its first new hotel, the Europa in Grosvenor Square, and bought control of the last two of the Gordon Hotels – the May Fair in London and the Metropole in Monte Carlo. By 1970 Grand Metropolitan had taken over Levy and Franks, Berni Inns and Mecca, making it worth £135 million. Brewery companies including Trumans and Watney Mann were taken over as well as Express Dairies and many other companies. In 1981 it bought the Intercontinental Hotels Group from Pan-Am airline.

At this point, what must be fully appreciated in this survey of catering is that there has been this move by entrepreneurs, who shaped the industry, to expand and bring more units under their control. The purpose of this movement has been not only to amass wealth but also, through good direction and management, to ensure the long-term survival and soundness of the company which they own. What is being effectively observed in these expansionist movements is the application of the so-called theory of 'economics of scale', which, it is suggested, should contribute to the increased competitiveness of the organisation. For example, in the past most major hotels had a number of their own specialised departments such as sales or marketing, purchasing, personnel, audit or accounts and maintenance control, but now a single company can have similar departments for its entire organisation which can be much larger and more sophisticated. Thus by controlling the marketing of a large number of hotels of comparable standard throughout Europe, the central company can operate a centralised reservation system across the continent, and at the same time it can make savings by not having to pay commission to travel agents. Likewise the printing of brochures can effectively be done for the group rather than for a single unit, therefore ensuring a wider coverage at the same cost as for a single brochure. What is also important is that by having a considerable number of rooms available in major cities the company can enter into direct agreement with the carrier or transport operator to promote special price packages which can increase room occupancy and, in turn, profits.

Similarly with purchasing, the buying power of the company can be greatly increased and lead to major discounts, indeed the company's other outlets may be put to good use for the benefit of the whole organisation, such as a brewery or retail chain.

By concentrating their functions in a centralised fashion, these companies have also, in recent years, opened up a new perspective for the caterer - that of the functional specialist. A caterer can thus specialise mainly in one activity either in purchasing, marketing or control for the total organisation, and setting specific standards throughout the company.

Looking at the other side of the coin, the small independent operator has now been placed at a distinct disadvantage by the larger company. Fortunately the most enlightened independents have joined forces themselves by merging as co-operatives, called consortiums, to gain the same advantage as the larger firms. The effect of all this is increased sophistication in operation and a move towards common standards within various levels of the hotel and catering industry.

STAFF

The staffing of catering establishments still presents a problem, as even in periods of high unemployment there are not enough keen and dedicated people coming forward to fill the vacancies. The Manpower Services Commission indicated, in a major survey in 1974, that the catering industry still had one of the worst staff turnovers by comparison with any other industry. Later reports seem to show that a similar situation still exists. There is no clear evidence that this has been remedied at the present time. One of the main problems, other than unsocial hours, appears to be in finding ways and means to improve overall performance and increasing total output in monetary terms to generate the means for offering higher wages. This it is hoped will be achieved by implementing new technological advances in the production area which would permit a more effective use of staff time, and by finding new methods of food service which are less staff intensive.

However, the dispersed nature of catering establishments is such that in the majority of cases this will never be achieved unless and until the food manufacturing industry makes available an acceptable range of products which would enable better use to be made of manpower.

There is no doubt that the present method of work organisation can be improved so as to increase staff flexibility and make better use of time. This should result in greater profitability and in turn result in higher wages.

Working conditions in the industry have not always been ideal and this has perhaps been partially responsible for the occurrence of short periods of unrest and some measure of legislation. In 1913 there was a series of lightning strikes by hotel and restaurant staff; the strikes were unsuccessful as they were largely in 1946 when a strike began at the Savoy Hotel and spread to others in the group. It was called off after the British Hotels and Restaurants Association had agreed to recognise the National Union of General and Municipal Workers as the trade union for catering workers, but there were further strikes shortly after which later lead to Mr A. H. Jones, the Managing Director of Grosvenor House in

11

Park Lane leaving the BHRA after he had expressed his disagreement with them. In the late 1940s he became the first hotelier to introduce straight shift working for kitchen staff in a hotel, something only enjoyed up to then by some restaurant staff. He died in 1966 at the early age of fifty-nine.

The Catering Wages Act, to regulate the wages and conditions of employment, was placed on the Statute Book in 1943 and was followed soon after by the establishment of the Catering Wages Commission, and the following year the first of the five wages boards was set up for industrial and staff canteens. In 1945 three more were established and the last one, for unlicensed residential hotels, in 1946.

The regulations enforced minimum wage rates for all workers and were imposed one by one, although that for unlicensed residential hotels was abolished before its proposals were made law. The matter of tips gave the Commission some difficulty and it advised the wages boards to ignore them, until in 1954 they were taken into account. In 1952 after much criticism of the way it operated the Catering Wages Act was abolished and the wages boards were converted into wages councils under a more flexible Wages Council Act, but in 1958 it was itself abolished. The wages councils consist of equal numbers of members representing the employers and members representing workers with not more than three independent members, one of whom acts as a chairman and one as his deputy. A wages council has power to submit proposals for the fixing of minimum remuneration and holidays and may also make recommendations in respect of any matters concerning the employment, health, welfare and industrial conditions affecting workers.

Tipping still plays a large part in the running of catering establishments and the Catering Wages Commissions do take account of this practice in arriving at minimum wage levels. Even though the customer's bill will have VAT and a service charge of up to 15 per cent added, the habit of giving a tip to the waiter for his good service still prevails. The service charge is usually administered by the management for distribution amongst all catering staff, whereas tips given to the dining room staff in large establishments will often be pooled and distributed by the head waiter, with the assistance of a small committee, to his staff. This is done on a points system which makes a distinction according to status and responsibility. This system for the distribution of tips received by waiting staff is traditionally known as the *Tronc*. Although the *Tronc* is distributed without deduction of income tax the restaurant manager has to keep proper accounts and staff have to declare their tips. In 1975 a head waiter was jailed and fined for defrauding the Inland Revenue over tips, and more recently the authorities have clamped down on tax avoidance by casual waiting staff who were signing their pay claim forms with a different fictitious name each time. In 1977 wages inspectors reported that of 520 caterers interviewed 153 were paying less than the legal minimum wage rates. It was alleged at this time that many foreign staff were working without work permits which placed them at the mercy of the staff manager, despite the fact that until this time the industry had always been short of skilled people in the kitchen and restaurant and the catering industry has always employed a high percentage of overseas workers.

THE EXTENT OF THE INDUSTRY

The entire catering industry in this country gives employment to more than 2 million people with approximately 70 per cent of them in the commercial sector. Of these nearly half work only part time and there are a further 150,000 who are classed as seasonal workers.

The percentages of staff employed is as follows: hotels and guest houses 25 per cent, restaurants and cafes 16 per cent, clubs and public houses 27.7 per cent, hospitals and local authorities 23.1 per cent, and industrial catering 8.2 per cent. In the hotels sector nearly half the workers are employed in establishments that have at least fifty staff on the payroll whereas in restaurants nearly 50 per cent work in places that have fewer than twenty at work. Of course, small guest houses are usually run by the proprietors and do not employ other staff and many public houses are run on similar lines. Of the total staff employed in hotels it can be reckoned that up to 70 per cent are engaged in the areas directly related to the provision of food and drink.

There are 340,000 hospital catering staff and 242,000 in canteens of whom 41,000 work for catering contractors.

The total number of establishments involved in catering exceeds 200,000 of which approximately 23,500 are hotels, 12,000 guest houses, 43,700 restaurants and cafes, 47,000 public houses, 30,000 canteens, 38,000 colleges and schools, 3,000 hostels, and 110 holiday camps – this is without including hospitals and nursing homes. The total number of beds exceeds 450,000 and the number of meals served in canteens exceeds 8 million per day.

These few stark statistics give only a slight insight into this great and vital industry which does so much for the benefit of mankind in so many different ways, as perhaps exemplified by its contribution during the last war.

THE WAR YEARS 1939-45

In 1939 the government commandeered hundreds of hotels and holiday camps to which civil servants from London were evacuated. Nearly 2,700 hotels were requisitioned and during the war nearly 24,000 hotels and licenced premises were destroyed or damaged. The big seaside hotels were all closed and those that were allowed to remain open were rationed for meat, fats and sugar. Over 2,000 British Restaurants were opened as emergency feeding centres run by the local authority and over 100 canteens were being opened each month in 1941 to feed factory workers. The manpower shortage meant that the help-yourself cafeteria system had to be introduced; the Savoy had to employ waitresses; the Nippy's in Lyon's tea shops went and help-yourself service was substituted. Meals in restaurants were limited to three courses and a maximum price of 5 shillings – 25p.; charges for service, dancing and cabaret, and a house charge were permitted but the prices of whisky, gin and beer served with meals were

13

controlled. The only area where there was expansion was industrial catering and the government passed several orders whereby every factory employing 250 or more was obliged to provide a meal service and by the end of hostilities there were 25,000 of them.

The immediate post-war years were difficult ones for all branches of the industry; rationing went on until 1954, building licences were difficult to obtain and there was much bomb damage to repair. This meant that it was almost impossible to open a new catering business at that time and because of the lack of progress, due mainly to scarcity, the industry had difficulty in regaining its previous standards. The new generation had not had the advantage of pre-war experience which itself had, however, managed to survive the set-backs of the First World War.

TOURISM

As stated at the outset of this chapter travel and tourism have always been closely interlinked with the need for refreshment in the form of food and drink, with either one or the other setting the pace which the other immediately seeks to support. The effect of modern tourism on the catering industry is two-fold; first, the tourist in his own country is exposed to a variety of foods prepared and served in various ways, particularly at those times when he is psychologically ready to enjoy things the most. At these times he is willing to extend his interest in food, and discover the acceptability of new dishes. Secondly, the tourist from abroad will seek and wish to be understood not only verbally but also in his eating habits by the host country. The caterer must therefore make a conscious effort to be part of this international movement and cater for the demands created by mass tourism.

Tourism began to assume some importance after the last war when the government supported the industry by advertising Britain abroad in an attempt to attract more visitors; it felt the need for new forms of income to help pay the debts incurred in fighting the war. Other countries traditionally spent a great deal of money on advertising their attractions and tourism for them was a major industry; up to the Second World War Britain did not really consider it as such and it contributed relatively little to the balance of payments.

It was in 1947 that Britain set out to rehabilitate and expand its tourist and holiday business with the setting up of a board which developed into the British Travel and Holiday's Association, formed by merging the British Tourist and Holidays Board with the Travel Association of Great Britain. By 1951 tourism had become Britain's biggest dollar earner and by 1956 there were over 1 million overseas visitors which then doubled by 1963. It was estimated that they spent £97 million in hotels and restaurants in this country. By 1968 the number of visitors was 4 million and they spent £375 million here, but in the same year

14

5 million Britons spent £320 million on holidays abroad. The figures for overseas visitors began to be of some importance.

In 1969 the Development of Tourism Bill was given Royal Assent and implemented a hotel grants and loan scheme to give £1,000 per room, up to a maximum of £100,000 for new hotels and extensions for work begun after 31 March 1968 and to be completed by 31 March 1973. In January 1971 there were thirty-three new hotels being built and by the closing date 2,195 applications for grants had been received by the English Tourist Board, representing 66,400 new bedrooms. By 1973 the Board estimated that 33,726 new bedrooms would be opening and there were forty-eight new hotels due to open during that year.

Britons spent £7,700 million on holidays in 1980, £4,550 million of it at home and £3,150 million abroad; this was the third successive rise. The number of bed nights at home was 550 million against 170 million spent abroad. Great Britain received 12,393,000 foreign tourists and earned £3,760 million in foreign currency; tourism supported up to $1\frac{1}{2}$ million jobs. This income was £613 million more than in 1977 which was Silver Jubilee Year.

The figures for 1981 were expected to be 12 million visitors spending £40,000 million, including fares paid to British carriers, and the forecast for 1985 is for 15 million overseas visitors to come to Britain who could spend £6,000 million at current prices, plus the cost of fares paid to British carriers.

People are taking more holidays at home – the traditional fortnight by the sea is no longer the pattern which is now for shorter breaks with some emphasis on bargain week-ends. But at the same time more people are going abroad for their holidays and are spending longer at the resorts.

In 1980 UK residents' expenditure on holidays at home was £828 million which included £175 million on caravans and camping equipment. Overseas visitors spent £402 million.

HOLIDAYS

World travel increased towards the end of the nineteenth century when shipping companies built steamships for passengers only, offering several classes of accommodation and meals. In cabin class the standard was much higher than that to be found in any hotel and this led to the building of luxury hotels for the well-to-do and then to the chains of hotels in capital cities, major seaside resorts and spas. An annual summer holiday was part of the British way of life and the resorts expanded with the building of boarding houses, private hotels and other kinds of hotels many of which were as large and luxurious as those in the cities. These differed from French hotels by allocating plenty of space for lounge, reading and writing rooms, billiard rooms, bars, and an emphasis on food served in various public restaurants and in private rooms. This led to a hotel's reputation being based on the quality of food it served as being more important to some extent than the standard of accommodation.

15

The motor car and motor cycle brought increased business to hotels, guest houses and restaurants that were not within easy reach of the railways, and coaches and steamers took holidaymakers to seaside resorts. Holidays abroad were for the well-to-do although the cost of staying in a hotel on the Continent was not necessarily all that expensive, just that it was considered too adventurous to take the family across the Channel and travel by air was just becoming popular when the Second World War put an end to it. The seaside resorts benefited when holidays with pay were introduced and people stayed a week or fortnight at one establishment, often going back to the same place year after year while the children were growing up.

Holiday camps, where an informal kind of holiday with all sorts of entertainment included in the price, opened at several resorts and proved very popular for families with children. The second of Butlin's holiday camps was opened at Clacton in 1938 built to cater for 2,000 people. Butlins now have eight holiday camps, nine centres and six hotels which they operate in the style of camps. This is a popular form of holiday because it offers full board and entertainment on the site at a competitive price.

ASSOCIATIONS

The catering industry is served by many organisations which set out to bring caterers of a like mind together to further a common purpose or to give professional status to various sectors.

A professional body is usually an organisation that accepts only persons into membership who qualify either by examination or by knowledge and experience at a suitably high level, and who conform to a code of conduct that means they are persons of integrity who will uphold the ideals of the body.

A trade association can be either a national or a local one, or the local one may be a branch of the national one; its purpose is to speak for its members with one voice on any topic concerning them, perhaps to protect members' interest against proposed legislation that will affect them. Membership is of the establishment rather than the owners and the only condition of joining is to pay the annual subscription. The establishment will often announce its membership by displaying the logo of the association outside its premises thus indicating to prospective customers that it offers a standard which satisfies the association.

Professional Bodies

In 1944 the Catering Trades Education Committee was formed to survey educational and training needs for the industry for when the war ended, and in 1946 the Ministry of Education urged local authorites to provide facilities in colleges

16

for training 12,000 recruits each year and by 1948 courses were available in over forty towns.

The CTEC became the Hotel and Catering Institute in 1949 – the professional body for caterers, which announced in 1951 that there were then 5,000 catering students following courses in colleges. Fifteen years later this number increased to 18,000. In 1971 the HCI merged with the Institutional Management Association – a body mainly of women engaged in school meals and other large-scale catering establishments formed in 1938 – to create a new professional body called the Hotel Catering and Institutional Management Association.

The HCIMA carries out many services for its members including salary surveys, an industrial experience scheme for catering teachers, a corpus of knowledge, national and local conferences and meetings, seminars, careers advice, various prizes and awards including scholarships. It publishes a monthly journal and holds an annual general meeting as well as branch meetings. Membership at the end of 1980 was 20,799 of which 6,437 were student members. Entrance is usually by examination only.

Other related professional bodies include the Royal Society of Health which conducts examinations in nutrition and hygiene, The British Dietetic Association, The British Institute of Management, The Industrial Society and The Nutrition Society.

Trade Associations

In 1907 the National Hotel-Keepers Association was formed which merged in 1910 with the Incorporated Association of Hotels and Restaurants to form what was to become the British Hotels and Restaurants Association. The first President was the Earl of Bessborough, Chairman of Gordon Hotels and the Vice-President and Chairman was Sir George Reeves-Smith, Managing Director of the Savoy until his death in 1941. In 1972 the Caterers Association of Great Britain, founded in 1917, merged with the BHRCA to become the British Hotels, Restaurants and Caterers Association, a powerful trade association.

The BHRCA has a national membership of both hoteliers and restaurateurs and represents more than 25,000 establishments. Members may affix the association's sign to their premises which means that the establishment is run by a professional person.

The association acts as a representative with the government so that members have some say in any legislation laid before Parliament which may affect them. Its services to members include information, legal advice, a hotels' guide, bulk buying, statutory notices, meetings, and recruitment of staff from overseas. The *Stagiare* exchange scheme whereby a young person engaged in the catering industry may have the benefit of experience abroad, whilst overseas staff may come to work in this country, is operated by the BHRCA.

There are many other associations connected with the catering industry: these include the British Tourist Authority; the Catering Equipment Manufacturer's Association of Great Britain; the Catering Teacher's Association; the Civic Catering Authorities Association; the College Caterer's Association; the Cookery and Food Association; the Craft Guild of Chefs; Association Culinaire Française; the Food and Beverage Manager's Association; the Guild of Sommelier's and Friends of Bacchus; the Hospital Caterers' Association; the Hotel Purchasing Managers' Association; the Industrial Catering Association; the Institute of Marketing; the International Hotel Association; the International Wine and Food Society; the National Association of Toastmasters; the National Catering Federation; the National Union of Licensed Victuallers; the Restaurateurs Association of Great Britain; the Society of Catering Consultants; the Takeaway and Fast Food Federation (UK); the United Kingdom Bartenders Guild; and the Wine and Spirit Association of Great Britain.

These associations are open to persons engaged in that particular section of the industry without examination and membership is by subscription.

THE TRAINING BOARD

The catering industry has its own training board which began work in 1967 as the Hotel and Catering Industry Training Board to improve the quality and quantity of training for all branches of the industry. In fact, it deals mainly with the commercial side, but catering at sea, in the air, in hospitals, at all government catering centres such as staff canteens and prisons, clubs, schools and college catering are outside of the board's scope.

Training is covered for all levels from commis chefs to managers and is financed by a levy on the payroll. Joint City and Guilds and HCITB certificates are awarded to staff who pass the CG 706/1 and CG 706/2 examinations; on-the-job instructor's certificates are awarded to supervisory level staff who attend instructor courses with a view to devoting time to their trainees whilst attending college on a part-time or block release arrangement.

There are group training schemes in which a number of employers in a particular area, such as Central London, can share the services of a group training officer to help small firms achieve the benefits of a large company, most of whom, of course, have their own training division.

The board's other activities include conferences on many topics such as improving staff productivity, management education, development awards to take courses at business schools, courses in marketing and sales, specialised training to assist personnel managers, staff selection techniques, scholarships and awards, development programmes for training specialists, guides and training aids, careers leaflets and conventions, research reports, computer advice, and exhibitions.

The HCITB works closely with the Manpower Services Commission which meets part of the board's operating costs. The MSC offers the Training Opportunities Schemes, known as TOPS courses, for persons who have been working in other careers and who wish to take a college course retraining them for a job in the catering industry. The full cost and a grant for living expenses is payable. It also offers the Youth Opportunities Programme and Unified Vocation Preparation programme of training.

CATERING EDUCATION

No survey of catering, no matter how brief, would be complete without some reference to the role of the colleges in preparing young people for a career in this industry. With so many of today's managers having commenced their studies as young aspirants in a college it shows the influence wielded by these institutes on the industry as a whole. The first college to offer courses for potential chefs and head waiters was opened in 1910; there were already several well established domestic science colleges, but for thirty-five years Westminster College was on its own in the field of catering education. In 1944 the Education Act gave local authorities the go-ahead to offer courses in catering at technical colleges and in 1946 made the necessary cash resources available. The Catering Trades Education Committee was set up in 1943 to plan the manpower needs for when the Second World War ended and as to how staff should be educated for the jobs. The Catering Wages Commission looked at apprenticeships which had long been a common feature, and at colleges and various forms of on-the-job training.

It was not long before every city and big town in the British Isles had a department of catering at its local technical college with the majority of them offering full-time courses leading to City and Guilds of London Institute certificate examinations, and a minority offering part-time courses on either day release or as evening class only. The City and Guilds Institute's examinations were really designed for part-time courses but as there was no suitable alternatives colleges adopted them for full-time work submitting students for the CG 150 at the end of one year and CG 151 at the end of the two-year course. For part-time students it was a two-year stint to obtain the CG 150 followed by the CG 151 at the end of four years. Then, if they wished, these part-time students could go on to devote a further two years of intense study for the CG 152 which is now renumbered as CG 706/3. Some colleges such as Westminster continued to offer their own diploma whilst others followed regional examining board syllabuses. Entrance to these courses was by motivation rather than on academic ability and it was not until 1959 that academic passes were necessary; this was when the National Diploma in Hotel-Keeping and Catering was introduced with entry at four 'O' level passes. This course was displaced in 1969 with a similar set-up as for other disciplines – the Ordinary and Higher National Diploma courses, the first having the same entrance qualifications as the old National Diploma and the second requiring one 'A' level pass. For all these courses there was a national outline syllabus but it was left to each college to define the actual content within the guide-lines and recommended hours of study. The Ordinary Diploma was expected to turn out technicians, the Higher Diploma the technologists.

A different examining body had been brought into existence when the Catering Trades Education Committee changed its title, first to the National Council for Hotel and Catering Education, then, in November 1949, to the Hotel and Catering Institute which, although really the professional body for caterers, conducted examinations in waiting. The City and Guilds examinations had begun in 1947 and by 1949 1,000 students took CG and HCI examinations in seventeen colleges offering full-time courses, and fifty where only part-time courses were held. In 1982 there were 200 departments of catering in colleges of further and higher education and at least a dozen degree courses in catering subjects, many of them at honours level, three of them being in universities.

Apprenticeships are not a significant feature of this industry but some young people prefer to go straight into it from school and they get on-the-job training, allied to day or block release to attend college to obtain the joint City and Guilds and Hotel and Catering Industrial Training Board Certificates. The HCIMA introduced its own examinations by which candidates could become members. It set a very high standard with students having to pass four papers in Part 1 and six in the final membership examination, but before embarking on it they had to have CG 151 or be attending this course.

THE FUTURE

The prospects for catering always look good if only because for the foreseeable future people will need to eat and drink in much the same way as they do today. The accelerating social trends which are resulting in earlier retirement on good pensions, the shorter working week and longer holidays and leisure time means more business for the tourist industry at home and abroad. All over the world people are taking up the idea of having several holidays each year – the number of people from overseas coming to this country on holiday will continue to increase each year. To meet this demand new holiday and tourism resorts are being developed in those countries with a viable tourist trade. All these trends can only result in an expanding and healthy catering industry. Sport will continue to increase in popularity not only for the spectator, and leisure parks with various sporting activities will lead to a demand for residential accommodation on site. Adventure holidays will also help to keep people fit by providing challenging situations instead of total relaxation and sightseeing. The size of central hotel rooms will be considerably reduced as visitors use them for only a few hours during which time they are mostly asleep, so that spartan amenities at a cheap rate will satisfy most guests.

Customers will possibly become more nutrition conscious and the demand to know the calorie value of menu items, could mean that all levels of catering staff would have to study this subject to a certain depth. The micro-chip will control much in the way of equipment and machinery in the catering department and this could ultimately be total, leaving little room for errors on the part of staff. This type of control could lead to a single standard of production so that little or nothing would go wrong with dishes since the human element has been largely removed. Fuel will be rigidly controlled so as to conserve or even ration it, at the same time cutting production costs by ensuring that none is ever wasted.

The possibility of the kitchen and restaurant operation becoming largely computerised and thus rigidly controlled by the standards fed into it may be an acceptable part of mass catering. But the already noticeable reaction against standardisation and the forcing of people into particular moulds decided by the planners and behavioural psychologists may result in more and more units devoted to individual needs. The future will indeed continue to be rosy for those who choose to work in the industry, certainly for those whose concern will be the satisfaction and comfort of the customer.

The leisure industry will undoubtedly continue to grow substantially and there will always be opportunities for those entrepreneurs who can so satisfy their customers that they return again and again. The main problem has always been in attracting and retaining the right calibre of staff although a lot is now being done to develop those who are in the right job, but management will need to learn now to motivate staff and obtain more flexible working so as to reduce costs and turnover of staff. Even greater progress will be made in marketing and selling with the difference that caterers will sell the public what they want, not what they think they ought to have; operators will have to become even more professional and adopt all the management techniques that are used in the more efficient industries.

The future presents a challenge but the catering industry will surely meet this as it has always done in the past. So important is this industry as an underpinning of modern society that anything less than a successful solving of its problems would diminish the whole fabric and quality of life.

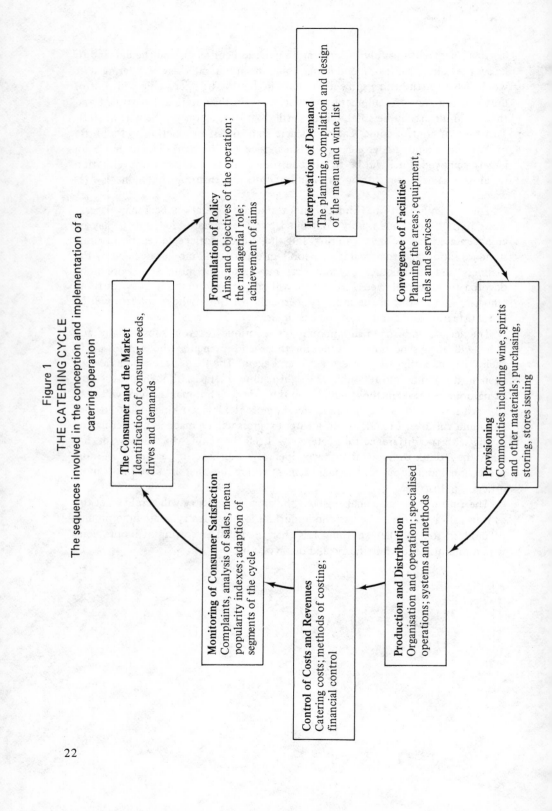

Figure 1
THE CATERING CYCLE
The sequences involved in the conception and implementation of a catering operation

The Consumer and the Market Identification of consumer needs, drives and demands

Formulation of Policy Aims and objectives of the operation; the managerial role; achievement of aims

Interpretation of Demand The planning, compilation and design of the menu and wine list

Convergence of Facilities Planning the areas; equipment, fuels and services

Provisioning Commodities including wine, spirits and other materials; purchasing, storing, stores issuing

Production and Distribution Organisation and operation; specialised operations; systems and methods

Control of Costs and Revenues Catering costs; methods of costing; financial control

Monitoring of Consumer Satisfaction Complaints, analysis of sales, menu popularity indexes; adaption of segments of the cycle

2 THE CATERING CYCLE

Definition – The Segments of the Cycle – Segment Responsibilities and
Involvement

A catering cycle can be defined as being the total of a number of organised
decision making and practical activities which take place within a catering
establishment and comprise the whole operation. It has as its starting point the
identification of the consumer, his needs, his drives and his demands, these are
met by a logical sequence of activities where an identification of these needs,
policy decisions as to how to meet and satisfy them, and the planning that is
necessary to fulfil them, are all carefully worked out. The cycle continues
through a series of closely related segments until it reaches the point where it is
possible to monitor the success, or otherwise, of the business by ascertaining the
degree of customer satisfaction obtained.

After this the cycle recommences, taking into account any alterations or
improvements as brought to light by the monitoring procedure.

Responsibility for organising the actual operations contained within the cycle
and ensuring that each part of it runs smoothly and efficiently is delegated to
management, whether as an employee of an owning company or the actual
owner of a small business. At one level management may carry out the policy

23

decisions as laid down by the head office of a company; at other levels management may also be responsible for determining policy itself. In the case of an owner he will still consciously, or subconsciously, follow the cycle albeit with modifications and adaptations as seen fit. In a similar way, the cycle may differ in detail and operation from one business enterprise to another – there can be one for an existing business, one for setting up an entirely new business, and yet another for adapting an existing business to a new concept, deriving from an emerging change of demand. The segments and sequence of the cycle applicable in each of these cases will vary but whatever the type of establishment be it a snack bar or luxury restaurant, all of them are used at one time or the other.

The cycle will define the resources, finance, materials, manpower and machinery needed for management's disposition and it is its duty to allocate them so as to bring about the best possible result in terms of customer satisfaction, which in turn should give the desired profit margins.

Fig. 1 shows in diagrammatic form the Catering Cycle as a number of sequences involved in the conception and implementation of a catering operation; the following paragraphs deal more fully with these segments and identify their content and extent.

THE CONSUMER AND THE MARKET

When setting up a new catering business or adapting an existing one there are several alternatives in deciding how to go about it. The owner may want to open his doors to a particular type of clientele who will beat a path to his establishment because they know it caters for their requirements and that they will encounter similar people to themselves there. The owner may select a location because of the people who live or work in the vicinity and set out to cater for what he believes they require. He can make his place play a dual role either by having a different style of operation from lunch to dinner, or by combining two kinds of catering in the same premises by means of two entrances and a division. If the new business is a branch of a company the pattern of catering will have been set at head office and be identical with all the other units in the chain. Whatever the operation, it is necessary to have an understanding of customers' needs and to know something of the different aspects of customer motivation before attempting to identify a demand for any particular type of catering service.

For example, the caterer in the large-scale field of feeding, say students, may assume that his customers want cheap snack-type meals with chips or salad. Should he decide to do some market research, even of a very elementary kind, he may be surprised to find there is a demand for vegetarian meals or even gourmet meals that is sufficiently large to make it a viable alternative even though the prices are higher. In hospitals, it was shown years ago that patients want a choice of popular dishes of the kind they are used to at home or work.

This segment of the cycle then is concerned with man's needs and driving forces, his place in society and from this what he demands and needs from a business which purports to offer and provide refreshment in the form of food and drink. By using various techniques including market research the caterer should thus be able to perceive a potential market and be in a position to plan how this would best be catered for.

FORMULATION OF POLICY

This originates from the analysis of a possible market, or the alteration of an existing operation in the light of an emerging demand, or from discerning a new market need in an existing operation. The aim will be to set up guide-lines to which the whole operation will adhere and the objective will help create a successful and therefore profitable business. For this the policy must be directly related to demand.

The policy will in effect determine the type and level of operation as well as the resources to be made available. The responsibility for determining policy should be in the hands of professionally qualified persons working alone or in the form of a team, according to the size and type of enterprise envisaged. A team could consist of general management plus department managers such as the food and beverage manager, chef and dining room supervisor or head waiter.

INTERPRETATION OF DEMAND

A catering establishment needs to interpret its perceived demand first through the broad framework of its formulated policy and then through the means with which it seeks to satisfy this demand. These means take form initially in the shape of a list of food and/or drink offered, either for sale as in a commercial enterprise or chosen by persons who do not pay for it as in a hospital or some areas of industrial catering. This list, whether written in chalk on the window of a small backstreet cafe or presented in the shape of an expensive and artistically produced card, is the menu. Where necessary this is complemented by a separate wine list but can be combined in a single presentation with the menu.

Every catering firm or operation no matter how large or small, or in whatever sector of the industry, uses the menu and wine list as a means of giving information about itself to its customers. A menu provides the consumer with much in the way of information and is an outward reflection of their demands showing how the establishment sets out to meet those demands. As far as management is concerned it also reflects the level of skills needed and controls the professional ability at all levels of the staff employed. It is the silent salesman of the operation

25

and as such must reflect it exactly. If it is pretentious and the food and drink does not live up to the expectations created by the menu, customers will be deterred. An unpretentious menu and a modest wine list that show the flair of the caterer are much more preferable than a lengthy one with too many dishes that may fail to attract customers.

In the compilation of a menu an inbuilt capacity of modification according to taste and demand, is of value providing it can be done without altering the image of the operation. An emerging demand may have a direct effect upon the basic concept of a menu so leading to a reconsideration or re-orientation of the overall operation; some allowance can be made for this.

The menu and wine list then are a reflection of the professional ability of the person or persons who compiled them and responsibility for compilation can be in the hands of various people. At the level of a large company with a chain of fast food outlets the menu will be decided at head office level and is usually the work of a qualified team. In other instances it can be left in the hands of the catering supervisor, the chef, the food and beverage manager, the manager or again a team effort on the part of two or more of the foregoing.

CONVERGENCE OF FACILITIES

Once a policy has been established and a particular kind of menu is seen as a perceived demand or possible market, a planning stage is necessary to translate these into an operational reality. This may mean the erection of purpose-built premises, the alteration or adaption of an existing operation to meet a new policy or making an existing operation more efficient.

In all cases the planning will include the best use to be made of the available space for the production, service and ancillary areas and in relation to the sequence of activities to be carried out in them; it will require decisions to be taken on the installation of equipment or re-equipping, and also regarding the choice of fuels, power and other services needed.

According to the implication of the policy there will possibly be the need for consultation with various experts such as an architect, engineer or equipment specialist and with local or national offices concerned with planning or fire regulations.

PROVISIONING

This segment of the cycle relates to the procurement of foodstuffs in the form of commodities or in prepared form, according to the policy of the operation; drink in the form of alcoholic and non-alcoholic liquor for use in bar and restaurant; cleaning materials; small equipment; and expendable goods such as paper and china, etc. The ordering of all these is determined by the menu and wine list which act as the blueprint for the requisitioning of goods and the subsequent processing of them. With this goes the knowledge of the demand which must be predicted as regards quantity and quality. Unless the demand is known fairly accurately no allocation of space for storage of goods can be estimated.

The ordering of goods is done in accordance with this anticipated demand and several people can be involved in this important operation. A very large business could employ a buying team for food commodities – these would be well informed on the state of the market and be respected figures in their own particular field. In many cases the head chef or food and beverage manager will have authority to order perishable foodstuffs. In the purchasing of wines and spirits there can be a buyer who has authority to procure the best available and endeavour to ensure adequate supplies.

All this obviously depends upon the size and type of establishment. In a small business there could be one person only combining the duties of buyer, store-keeper and possibly delivery man, bringing the goods from a cash and carry warehouse.

The duties of store-keeper and cellarman which include the receipt and issue of goods and the security of these whilst in their care, together with the relevant paperwork, contribute greatly to the profitable operation of the business.

PRODUCTION AND DISTRIBUTION

The production and distribution or service, of food and drink, are at the core of the entire catering operation and are the results of the previous segments brought to bear upon the end-product. This end-product is the food, prepared in accordance with the laid down policy, together with drink, and made ready for distribution to the consumer. The raw materials are made into the dishes as defined by the menu to the standard as determined for the type of business, and a check has to be made on the standard and quality of these products to ensure they conform to the consumer's expectations and meet his demands.

The organisation and staffing of the departments in a catering operation create hierarchies and the inter-relationships of these is both complex and finely balanced. The systems and methods used in the multiplicity of establishments are all based to some extent on traditional division of labour concepts but how traditional they are depends largely on the type of operation. Many of the new concepts of organisation are the result of meeting the new demands of standardisation and quick turnover.

There are many grades of personnel involved and their titles alter according to the area of their involvement or the size and type of the establishment, but the overall responsibility for the whole food and beverage area lies with the manager who may actually be a catering manager, chef-manager or superintendent in other spheres. Then there are the heads of each of the separate departments – the chef in charge of production, the restaurant manager or head waiter in charge of distribution, and the head cellarman and head sommelier responsible for the distribution of drink.

CONTROL OF COSTS AND REVENUES

This refers to the ingoings and outgoings of money on a day to day basis, not necessarily at head office or company level but at departmental level. This ensures that the departments run profitably and that there is a control which can deter pilfering and other malpractices, control waste and profligacy and institute correct procedures of accounting for everything that takes place. It commences with the pricing policy as established and what the customer is going to be charged to keep the enterprise solvent; it embraces the kitchen percentage, restaurant or dining room control and takings, and keeps records of business done. The day's takings, checks, stocktaking and customers' bills all have to balance; if they do then the income and expenditure will be correctly related.

The persons involved can be at management or supervisory level in certain types of operation; in a large operation there can be audit and control clerks, a cashier in the dining room and a chief cashier to reconcile the information.

MONITORING OF CONSUMER SATISFACTION

This entails the measurement of performance of the entire operation so as to ascertain whether it is meeting the consumer's demands. There are various ways of doing this – in a small establishment the owner or manager will circulate amongst customers in bar and restaurant to ask each guest personally if everything is to their satisfaction, noting any complaints or criticisms. Acting as mine host he builds a close customer relationship that keeps him aware of consumer reaction to his products. The head waiter in a luxury restaurant can do this but may not take any action if a customer is dissatisfied. In fact, it is not always easy to discover if consumers are satisfied. Information can be obtained by means of questionnaires, analysis of sales, noting plate waste, and examining trends.

Complaints can arise from many quarters, not just poor quality food or poor service. If a complaint is not handled seriously and an explanation or apology not given it will be aggravated and custom lost.

It may become necessary to alter the entire concept and reorganise the business on different lines, involving the re-identification of customers' and consumer demand, resulting in a new and different product being offered.

28

The personnel responsible for monitoring are the manager and, where applicable, his heads of department, in particular the head waiter or restaurant supervisor who is in close contact with the customer.

The Catering Cycle can be seen then as a complete inter-related series of activities which are always ongoing and in a state of flux and modification. The following chapters will look at each segment in more detail and will attempt to give the reader an understanding of the complexities of catering and how the various facets can link together to form the whole.

It should be noted that some of the segments of the cycle have more than one chapter devoted to them; this is because of the scope of the information they contain.

3 THE CONSUMER AND THE MARKET

Man's Needs and Driving Forces – Micro Aspects of the Consumer –
Nutritional Needs – Homeostasis – The Consumer's Senses – General
Properties of the Senses – Macro Aspects of the Consumer – Man and
Society – Market Segments – Market Research

In attempting to identify the consumer or customer of a catering establishment
and to lay down the foundations needed to obtain an understanding of the consumer, it is first of all necessary to look at his special needs, drives and motives
as related to food and drink. It is important that these psychological aspects are
considered prior to the investigation of a market demand and the identification
of a possible market, these being the factors on which the whole operational
cycle of catering is built.

Each purposeful activity in man has an intended outcome – each intelligent
action attempts to influence the reaction that should follow; the caterer in
supplying food to man should be in the position to assess the amount of satisfaction that his services are going to provide. Yet in order to be able to measure
the amount of satisfaction provided he must be aware of the natural or essential

needs of the customer as well as those imposed by society and the customer's place in society. Because of the difficulties involved in this assessment, the areas of consumer behaviour and market orientation have until recently received only superficial treatment by the catering industry and to a certain extent this is still a fairly vague area.

So far, two major approaches have been noted in this area: in one the caterer has frequently been accused of being totally self-centred in determining at what level of standard he will operate and which products he will make available to his customer; in the second the caterer has placed the consumer at the top of his priorities for operational decision-making and has adopted the maxim 'the customer is always right'

As we now know, neither of these approaches can be absolutely correct. in fact most professional caterers have always made an honest, almost intuitive effort to find out who his customers are, what they need, and how these can be most effectively satisfied. It is only necessary to read Marie Ritz's book about her husband, *César Ritz – Host to the World*, to find out how this comes about and to place it into context. It becomes clear that Ritz set out to work his way across Europe in order to identify the habits, needs, and whims of the users of the grand hotels of that time; also to discover what would be his way of satisfying them when the time came. The hackneyed statement 'the customer is always right' is over-simplified because it fails to make explicit which customer and under what circumstances he may be right. As an example, a soldier lost in the desert without food for three weeks would derive great pleasure from a mouthful of camel meat but it would not be the same for someone where cooked camel was being served to him for the third time that day! In the second case, the need to satisfy a severe weight loss does not exist and although such extremes are perhaps uncommon, they form a suitable premise from which to observe the relationships to catering of some concepts of the disciplines of nutrition, physiology, psychology and sociology.

MAN'S NEEDS AND DRIVING FORCES

Man's needs can be examined at several different levels as well as in an hierarchical structure; to an extent the food and beverage manager finds himself in a position to adopt Maslow's theory of motivation as a means of explaining the consumer's needs.

Abraham Maslow was a leader in the development of humanistic psychology and he indicated a fascinating way of classifying human motives. He adopted the premise that a hierarchy of motives ascend from the basic biological needs present at birth to the more complex order of needs that become important after the basic needs have been met, and he went on to suggest that the needs at one level must at least be partially satisfied before those at the next level become important in determining future effort to achieve them.

A similar situation exists in the study of patterns of eating habits with the added complication that the eating pattern of a society derives not only from the attempt to satisfy basic biological needs but also to some extent from inter-linked psychological concepts which in turn can adversely affect the benefit to be gained from certain foods. This means that eating behaviour must always be studied at two different levels – the micro level, and the macro level. The micro level refers in this context to the individual, and the macro level refers to his place in society.

MICRO ASPECTS OF THE CONSUMER

Nutritional Needs

Man's needs at this level lie in satisfying basic physiological demands although there is, as already stated, a constant interaction with psychological needs. Like any other living creature, man requires food for growth, repair and energy and his body is like a sophisticated machine in constant need of fuel to keep it going. Since the body is in constant motion the faster it goes the greater is its need for an intake of fuel as well as more lubricant for maintenance. Furthermore, what makes this machine more perfect than any invented by man is that it has the ability to store any surplus energy and possesses a regular mechanism which indicates any deficiencies in the internal system.

The following then is a very brief outline of man's nutritional requirements. Man needs food to satisfy his requirements for growth, repair and maintenance and these are provided by the protein foods. They are composed of amino acids and in the main are obtained from animal sources, pulse vegetables and cereals. The arrangement of the amino acids varies considerably between foods and because of this it is necessary to consume proteins from the various available sources; it does, however, appear that the body can manufacture certain amino acids to suit its needs. The average daily need for a man is 120 g of protein: if more is consumed than is required, then part is converted into glucose and if not used as energy, is stored as fat.

Carbohydrates are the main energy source and the daily requirement varies according to the activity and size of the individual. Carbohydrate sources provide sugar, starch, cellulose and in many cases, certain vitamins and mineral salts. A balance of the first three makes the best mix with sugar and starch providing energy, and cellulose providing roughage.

Fats are broken down by digestion into fatty acids; in its various forms, fat provides energy and heat and the protection of the body's organs. Natural fat is a source of vitamins and the main supply in the diet is from animal and vege-table fats such as lard, dripping, oil, margarine, bacon and butter.

Vitamins are essential chemical substances vital to good health and found in

32

small quantities in certain foods. They perform a number of functions and are involved in growth, protection against infections and skin diseases, and are present in many foods in their natural form but are also added artificially to staple foods such as margarine and breakfast cereals.

Minerals are an important requirement in the diet and the function of each is different ranging from bone formation to the functioning of certain glands and the nervous system; a deficiency of minerals in the body is rare.

Water is of great importance in the diet and it performs many essential functions such as lubrication. This brief outline can thus provide a background to the physical functioning of man with specific reference to eating behaviour.

Homeostasis

Man's physical body is composed of millions of minute cells with each cell housing a complex mechanism in itself. Most cells are distinctive in structure and effect, that is, muscle cells, nerve cells, bone cells, fat cells, blood cells and others. Some of the specific cells are joined into tissues and the tissues form organs of the body thus giving the organic system.

The various systems within the human frame work in close co-operation rather as in a community where there is a division of labour amongst the population, but where all activity and progress is programmed by a central committee and closely monitored by it. Each group or system communicates its requirements to the central control point so that an appropriate balance of activity is maintained at peak efficiency. Where a balance exists within the functioning of an organism and where an optimum condition is maintained, this ideal state is called **homeostasis** or equilibrium. Homeostasis operates in all organisms and is essential for the survival of complex organisms, and is thus involved in maintaining normal body temperature, heart beat and blood pressure. The total process is controlled at the higher cognitive centre, namely the brain, by a small structure called the **hypothalamus** which, although extremely small, governs all the primary drives in both man and beast such as the basic needs of drinking, eating and sexual behaviour. The bodily needs are communicated to the hypothalamus which in turn sets out to satisfy them. It controls other activities in the body such as temperature, reaction to fear, and stress, but our interest in this connection is primarily with eating and drinking behaviour.

By stimulating the hypothalamus with a mild electric current, pleasurable sensations are created; in the same way patterns of eating and drinking can be brought out. Going on a little further, it has been observed that removal of the hypothalamus from animals causes them to lose control of their eating behaviour with possible resulting obesity. Since the hypothalamus receives internal messages concerning the state of well-being of the body, it can equally well channel the animal's effort towards the satisfaction or replenishment of a tissue deficiency.

Experimental evidence indicates that mammals from which the adrenal glands have been removed thus causing a deficiency in sodium ions, intuitively prefer to drink a salt water solution in preference to plain or sweetened water. In this way they make good their tissue deficiency and maintain homeostatic balance. From this it can be indicated that a basic mechanism in man guides him towards a balance of nutrients essential for his well-being and the satisfaction of his basic biological needs.

The Consumer's Senses

The senses of sight, hearing, taste, smell and touch all combine to produce various experiences, and each of them plays an important role in how the external world is perceived. The word perceived is used to call attention to a very complex and important psychological phenomena – perception. Perception refers to the way in which incoming information from the external world is received, processed and given a meaning. The senses are not what we believe them to be but appear to require some development in order to give stability to the external world. Without this stability the human mind would be in a state of total confusion and be completely incapable of discriminating amongst the continuous bombardment of incoming stimuli. We continually structure all incoming information according to a developed internal framework.

Perception is closely interconnected with another psychological concept – motivation, which refers to an internal state of arousal which energises man's activities towards certain goals. So what we often perceive is not what is actually there but is what we want to see, integrated without internal framework, and it is in this context that the saying 'beauty is in the eye of the beholder' comes into its own.

General Properties of the Senses

Before a spot of light in a dark room can be seen it must reach a certain level of intensity; before a sound can be heard it must be emitted at a certain level; before a particular flavour can be described it must reach a certain level of concentration. These levels of perception are described as the threshold levels and although they vary from one individual to another, the following estimates as indicated by the work of Galanter give a fair picture of them.

SENSE	THRESHOLD
Vision	a candle flame seen at 45 km on a dark clear night
Hearing	the tick of a watch at 7 metres, in quiet conditions
Taste	a teaspoon of sugar in 9 litres of water
Smell	one drop of perfume diffused throughout a 6-room bungalow
Touch	the wing of a fly at 1 cm distance from the cheek

From this, it follows that man is endowed with a complicated method of assessing and monitoring various properties and characteristics of materials. It can be seen that both sensory thresholds and homeostasis are important determinants and motivators of choice and thus by extension, consumer choice, they interlink with perception, or the sum of previous experience, to guide individual action.

MACRO ASPECTS OF THE CONSUMER

Man and Society

Man, as an organism, needs to survive, procreate and progress in order to acquire a better control over his environment. To an extent the human being, more than any other organism, if he wants to progress is totally dependant on the sharing of collective effort and division of activities which are regulated by necessity, the stage of development of that particular community, and the customs, rules and institutions which form a society. Society also needs stability and this can only be achieved through an established order which allocates certain tasks to the various individuals in order to maintain continuity and equilibrium. The reward that these individuals receive is mainly the outcome of the value that society places on the individual's role and efforts in his task. Normally the more complex or sophisticated the role, the higher the reward; within this reward system individuals are placed into certain categories and certain social positions and this, in turn, determines the consumer purchasing power. In addition to this, his role and the compensation he receives will expose man to various social experiences and pressures and these will form the basis of his expectations.

These facts are recognised by leading institutions and the foremost organisations in every country of the world; with minor modifications it takes the following form of classification.

CLASSIFICATION OF THE VARIOUS GROUPS IN A STRUCTURED SOCIETY

Group	Definition	Approx. % of population
A	diplomats, doctors, barristers, solicitors, university professors and lecturers, heads of public schools, senior executives, bishops.	3
B	vicars, college lecturers, executives in medium-sized businesses, headmasters, veterinary surgeons, bank managers.	8
C1	civil servants, teachers, bank clerks, library assistants, clerks, supervisors.	18

Group	Definition	Approx. % of Population
C2	skilled manual workers – mechanics, electricians, plumbers, tool setters, chefs, policemen, miners.	35
D	semi-skilled workers – postmen, bus drivers, typists, clerical workers, farm workers.	30
E	unskilled manual workers – labourers, cleaners, porters.	6

Disposable income varies considerably from one of the above groups to another and although it appears that the amount spent on meals away from home, on average over the year, does not vary very much from groups A and B to the groups C and D, the choice sought and expectations differ considerably.

Market Segments

Marketing practitioners tend to isolate the various groups into more uniform aggregations of individuals who have similar expectations, similar purposes and similar backgrounds. These groups are referred to as market segments and this concept of market segmentation has been noted from the early days of marketing literature. In 1912 in the US Quarterly Journal of Economics, Archy W. Shaw indicated that effective demand stems not only from buying power but also from the education, habits and environment of the individual. He suggested that different people have different needs because influences vary greatly from person to person and that the market separates according to the various income levels which he called **market contours**, suggesting that each contour or segment splits into a different market problem.

It is indicated then that individuals, because of their physiological make-up, their environmental experiences, their education and eating habits, have differing requirements; these requirements are expressed not only in the type of food demanded but also in terms of the service and environment.

Within catering there is a further subdivision of the market segment that needs to be considered and that is the consumer's need and purpose. For example if food needs to be taken for the purpose of fuel whilst an individual is out shopping, does this need differ considerably between a member of one social level and another? If a person requires a meal at his place of work would the expectations of service and surroundings differ greatly from one group to another? In terms of calorie intake it is well known that the requirements of active people are different from those carrying out sedentary jobs, but when people are involved in a similar environment do their expectations change markedly so as to warrant more than one dining area? For example, is an executive or supervisory dining area needed that is separate from that for manual workers.

36

To summarise, it might be useful to consider market segments under the following headings:

THE INDIVIDUAL	THE SITUATION NEEDS	THE PURPOSE
Age, sex, religion, socio-economic status, ethnic origin, spending power, education, family circumstances, expectations.	Free choice, semi-captive e.g. choice at firm's restaurant, paid for. Captive e.g. restricted choice at work's canteen not paid for.	Pleasure or domestic substitute.

At this stage the physical needs become integrated with the psychological needs; many forms of food as fuel could be used but what are the conditions that make one form more agreeable than another? Eating habits seem to evolve continuously yet some regional variation in climate and other probable causes such as patterns of jobs cannot explain, for example, why both Scotland and the south-west of England have the highest consumption of suet and dripping in the country. Of course, the caterer must be aware of this regional variation in considering his customers because the body seems to become accustomed to certain patterns of food intake and the consumer, almost unconsciously, often attempts to satisfy body demands. People's eating habits appear to be very consistent in terms of basic nutrient intake though the method of preparing food can be changed continuously. Thus it can be seen that an understanding of the consumer's needs and drives are of prime importance if we are to identify the need for a particular type of catering operation.

How can an understanding of these be achieved then? Resources of finance, skills and materials are not unlimited but if they were freely available and a market need identified then an attempt could be made to satisfy this market need completely. Unfortunately this ideal state is not often achieved so a reconciliation between the consumer's needs and what can be done to satisfy them, at a price he can afford, has to be considered. In a catering business, management must be aware of the continual change in the consumer's needs, as an example, this may be that an emphasis on serving lunches should change to that on dinners. Whilst at present most people consider lunch as more of a utilitarian meal, dinner appears to be more of an occasion with the factors of environment, atmosphere and standard of service being of an equal importance as value for money and the quality of the food; when associated with speed of service these can be major reasons for choosing to patronise a particular restaurant. Many successful businesses having an excellent choice of menu items and a very sophisticated atmosphere have frequently failed to attract a good steady luncheon trade. The main reason has not always been the price charged nor even the menu items or speed of service, but that the customer does not wish to be slowed down by a too relaxing environment; this is more likely to be wished for at the end of a strenuous day. It is then that the senses need to absorb fewer cues thus

37

reducing the amount of mental processing; no firm indication of this interpretation exists but it would appear to have a genuine and logical basis.

So the nature of a catering operation must be seen in relation to the market need and with serious consideration being given to the consumer's particular requirements at specific periods of the day. The determination of these particular needs greatly influences the choice and siting of an establishment, if for example, the aim is to attract people out shopping in the high street, then the location would best be in the proximity of a supermarket, or even a hypermarket. If, alternatively, the proposed venture also attempts to attract workers from nearby offices and local business men, then some compromise may be relevant. However, if a restaurateur wants to create a high-class restaurant with a theme or decor that concentrates on eating out as an occasion, then an important consideration might be that it be set up in a well-known position such as a beauty spot; the point to remember is that one aspect is seldom compatible with the other. Specialised catering activities as, for example, a carvery, need a high concentration of business men and visitors in the area to keep it viable, in addition to being in the centre of a good residential area.

Market Research

Once the location for setting up a catering operation has been selected, or the decision to change the nature of an existing but failing one, has been taken, and once a clear perspective of the type of consumer living in or frequenting this location has been acquired, a market survey can be carried out in order to ascertain certain characteristics. For this purpose, a questionnaire may be compiled to include such topics as (i) User likes and dislikes in terms of service and environment; open-ended questions such as 'if we were to open a new restaurant in this area, what would you like it to be like?' can be used. It may be that the interviewee will model his answers on another establishment in the area or one he has used whilst on holiday, but it is still a good starting point. Reaction to self-service as against waiter service needs to be included in the list of questions. (ii) Menu choice – which items would the interviewee like to see on the menu and the choice of starters, intermediate and main courses; would he discriminate between the use of fresh as against convenience foods, etc.? (iii) The time allowed for eating – this would have an effect on the opening hours and the consequent kitchen organisation. (iv) The price a potential customer would wish to pay; depending on the method of food costing this may have an effect upon the available choices. (v) The size of portion expected by this type of customer – a skilful interviewer may be able to assess at this stage what a customer considers to be value for money. (vi) Any ideas on colour schemes, general decor – this tends to indicate the sort of atmosphere likely to be sought by customers. (vii) The subject of drinks – whether the customer is likely to require an aperitif before a meal. A point to note on this subject is that consumption of alcohol tends to inhibit the higher cognitive centre or, as it is termed, the function of the hypothalamus, as well as stimulating the flow of gastric juices so that, to an extent, the pattern of eating changes. For instance, a young woman who had an aperitif would tend possibly to select something more substantial than a fruit juice to start the meal. (viii) If the majority of the people interviewed were male is it likely that they would sometimes visit the restaurant in the company of a lady, if so then the operation should express the female touch and feature suitable menu items that meet the femine self-image. (ix) The age of the people interviewed – although this can be a delicate question age is important not only in determining spending power but in pitching the entire tone of the operation. (x) Entertainment – is background music of a particular type required and would dinner-dances find favour.

Once these points have been established it is necessary to try to assess the frequency of usage according to the **existing demand** together with a forecast on **displaced demand** plus the **created demand** so as to determine the total turnover. Existing demand is the demand found to exist as a result of the market survey; displaced demand is the demand from customers who are prepared to move to the new restaurant because it seems a more attractive proposition than the place they have been used to; created demand means the special features that may attract new custom that does not normally exist.

The total demand is then broken down into takings for food and for drink and for lunch and for dinner; this can then be used to construct a **market feasibility** study which is the expected average revenue over a period set against the budgeted expenditure. Often precise standards of operation cannot be determined until this exercise has been carried out, since compromises may have to be made in operating costs to provide the customer with the right services at a price that attracts him. At this stage rule of thumb guide-lines may also have to be used to arrive at fair approximations of, for example, setting the percentage of drink to food on total revenue at 25 per cent for lunch and $33\frac{1}{3}$ per cent for dinner.

Take, for instance, a company intending to expand its operations into a new area; the company is of good standing and is creditworthy. It establishes that there is a market gap in a city centre where there are a number of commercial enterprises which will mean a high-class business turnover at lunchtime and a good sophisticated clientele for the evening trade. Assume that the demand is identified for a 100-seater restaurant, the company will then have to acquire the premises in the location and this may turn out to be quite expensive. It then has to furnish the premises at a standard acceptable to the clientele it hopes to attract. The total costs of setting up the operation may come to a very high figure and entail the borrowing of a substantial sum of money. The question to be answered is what amount of turnover will be needed in order to be able to repay this loan within a brief period and at the same time reap some reward for the time and expertise spent on the project? The breakdown of such an exercise will be based then on certain assumptions as follows: (i) the expected return as a percentage in terms of net profit; (ii) the expected spending on average for lunch and for dinner per person and (iii) taking the minimum average for the ongoing expenses against the expected minimum seat turnover for lunch and for dinner.

A fall in this occupancy rate would mean that the amount allocated for materials for food and for drinks would need to be decreased, in which case the value for money passed on to the customer may fall below acceptable standards. Savings could be made in other areas but would the restaurant still attract the same kind and amount of business? A market feasibility study will serve the purpose of finding the best compromise between demand and resource allocation.

4 FORMULATION OF POLICY

Aims and Objectives – Operational Objectives – The Role of Policies –
Policy Formulation – Examples of Specific Policy Applications.

Once the possible market has been analysed and the demand identified, or an
emerging demand suggests possible alterations to an existing operation, it is then
necessary to formulate a policy which will act as a set of guide-lines to which
close adherence of the operation is necessary for it to become successful.

Integral to the formulation of policy is the question of aims and objectives
and what form these should take in relation to the envisaged practical operations.
These will be seen to be vital steps in the development and formulation of a
policy.

AIMS AND OBJECTIVES

The possible market having been identified, a caterer then needs to transform
the research carried out into a plan of action.

At this stage he must outline the methods and techniques he will use to satisfy

41

the demand that he has found to exist, and inform his colleagues or any interested parties of his intentions as to how he will go about fulfilling it.

He is, in effect, making a statement of the aims and objectives of his business; the aims can be understood as being the result of the long-term planning and the ideal conditions in which it hopes to operate in the future. For example, the broad aim could be couched in such terms as 'this firm aims to achieve a market penetration of 10 per cent of the de luxe restaurant business, and to maintain that share by means of continuous market satisfaction'. Having defined the long-term aims of the firm, management will then lay down operational objectives for each area of activities of the proposed establishment in keeping with those aims, and emphasising and supporting the expected results with figures wherever possible.

The objectives as then seen in this context are precise statements of the performance expected by that particular department or unit in the framework of the total operation. In his book *Management by Objectives and Self-Control*, Peter Drucker writes, 'Each manager, from the "big boss" down to the production foreman or chief clerk needs clearly spelled-out objectives. These objectives should lay out what performance the man's own managerial unit is supposed to produce.'

Seen in this light the objectives are precisely quantifiable achievements in terms of output or revenue earning. Normally, in order to establish realistic objectives, it is necessary to seek the co-operation of key staff so as to establish their departmental objectives and ensure the achievement of the desired performance. At the same time when the objectives are being established, all available resources must be considered so as to ensure that targets are realistic.

OPERATIONAL OBJECTIVES

There are a number of areas for which objectives can be established and it is the function of management to interpret the objective to the subordinate member of staff. The following examples are some of the aspects which have to be considered.

1. Rate of turnover in financial terms.
2. Overall space usage per department – bars, restaurant, function rooms, to be calculated in terms of floor space per person.
3. Occupancy rate – which is the occupancy rate that will ensure the best cost distribution in these departments?
4. Minimum number of meals at specific times – e.g. lunch or dinner, or minimum throughput of meals at self-service counters per hour.
5. Kitchen – minimum amount of production in relation to labour and demand; can a ratio be established between the number of customers and labour hours?
6. Dining room – ratio of waiting or serving staff to customers according to style or service.

42

7. Gross profit – precise ratio of return although flexibility should be allowed in order to ensure optimum use of space.
8. Average spending per customer – is there a desired minimum expected for each occupied seat in the various departments and, if so, when are alternatives of usage to be sought e.g. change from a function suite to a conference room or canteen to a dinner and dance function?
9. Hours of business – when will the establishment be open for business, how long will it be open for a specific mealtime, will it be closed on any day or open continuously?

The same objectives as above and if applicable can be applied, albeit in a modified form, to the areas concerned with the sales of beverages. Objectives can also be established in quantitative terms as follows:

1. The quality of the food – measured through complaints records.
2. Material utilisation – through food waste records.
3. Standard of service – from complaints received.

Once objectives have been set the policy will indicate their implementation.

THE ROLE OF POLICIES

In attempting to identify the nature and type of consumer demand the foundation of the policy formulation framework has been laid. What is meant by policy? In general terms policy is understood to be a set of rules or guide-lines which direct management action under certain environmental conditions. Within the policy framework should be found the basis for decision making which should meet with the firm's acceptance.

Policies have an important role to play in an organisation and in order for them to be effective they must be simple and realistic and based on current information; simple policy that is understood by employees can make a useful contribution to the smooth running of an organisation. It is therefore important that it is easily understood and communicated to all levels of staff so that they are fully aware of the situation in which they work. It is only possible to achieve the objectives if the policies are clear cut; if they are not, managerial decisions become blurred through uncertainty and can never be fully satisfactory. By their very nature policies can influence decisions, outline areas of responsibility and promote inter-departmental co-operation. There are even instances where policies act as a catalyst, so helping to achieve certain targets as, for example, in an establishment which has a specific rate of turnover forecast from its budgetary policy but may fall short of that target, at which point the overall policy may indicate a particular course of action which will solve the problem.

Some establishments offer their function rooms free of charge at certain periods and even provide a band in order to attract business. Others allow for an automatic increase of the budget for advertising at times when business is slack in the expectation of attracting customers. A highly successful boost to business was the policy decision of a major hotel company to sell drinks at cost price at quiet periods during the week; this had the effect of both attracting outsiders into the bar and keeping in hotel residents, so considerably improving the takings. To operate this kind of sales promotion it is necessary to forecast that profits will be at variance from the norm, yet it is through sales that profit is increased even though in this instance the control method received a setback.

So policies must of necessity be flexible, simple to understand and adaptable to circumstances as they arise; they must also delineate the chain of responsibility. For example, when dealing with maintenance and replacement budgets, is an individual unit manager able to take a decision or is the decision-making process determined by a budget laid down by a head office?

To sum up then the role of a policy is to provide the framework which facilitates decision making, in the knowledge that the decision taken will meet with the approval of those concerned and be supported by the people at the top.

POLICY FORMULATION

Implicit in any policy are the ethics or rules of conduct, also known as codes of practice, which govern managerial actions. Explicit within a policy statement should be the aims of the organisation, indicating in general terms the desired outcome of certain activities; the objectives of the organisation can here be framed in more specific terms as, for example, in the result of a market feasibility study. In it the need to reach a certain level of profitability can be clearly identified so as to meet the firm's commitments; but this profitability must not be at the expense of customer loyalty and goodwill to the organisation. Thus it can be found that certain aims must always appear within the most immediate objectives.

The formulation of policy can also be looked at from two different levels – namely, the micro level, which deals with internal organisation of activities known as operational policies, and the macro level, which deals with the business involvement on the societal plane, both aspects to a certain extent being interlinked but capable of being considered independently. For example, a report prepared for possible investors will be very much connected with the external aims of the organisation, while nothing of the internal organisation activity would appear – this would be of more interest to an operational manager.

In attempting to define a policy role in an organisation it may help if it is viewed in the context of the person actually responsible for the implementation of policy. In any catering business this overall responsibility, which is in effect the running of the food and beverage operation, will be vested in the hands of the catering manager. This title is perhaps the most widely used; in an hotel the title is usually food and beverage manager, in a residential college it might be bursar or manciple, in a club the title is often secretary or steward, and so on. It is he who has the task of putting the policy, as decided by senior management, into day to day operation and to plan the internal organisation so that the several departments under his control work together in close co-operation and complete unanimity. He must be responsible for the design of the operational framework that supports the firm's or institution's policy decision in providing the range of items as reflected in menus and lists. These must be at the prices the customer can afford and of the quality he will expect for his money and in this way he will ensure optimum satisfaction and give maximum enjoyment by fulfilling the customer's demands.

The design of this operational framework must be made in complete awareness of the constraints that impinge upon the operation and of the wider external forces that affect any operation; these external factors that influence the formulation of a policy must be considered and, to a certain extent, superimposed on the organisation. Without this wider perspective the organisation would insulate itself from the external world and tend to operate almost in a vacuum – a state of affairs that would not create the right environment for adaptation and innovation and response to change. The following are some of these external factors grouped under the headings of General Trends, Constraints and Demand.

General Trends
  Population – composition, age, income, family status.
  The changing pattern of consumption.
  The impact of tourism.
  The pace of living.

Constraints
  The raising of capital.
  The availability of labour.
  The scarcity of commodities and equipment.
  The location of the business.
  Government economic policies.

Demand
  The assessment of total demand.
  The selection of a specific market.
  The competition.

Having considered the factors appertaining to the Catering Cycle it is possible to analyse the managerial role. After he has identified the product required according to the demands of the customer he will proceed to develop the product and service required, doing it in the light of those constraints that impinge upon his operation.

In Chapter 5 – Interpretation of Demand, which is concerned with the menu and wine list, there are areas shown which may force the manager to fall short of his ideal in what food or services he wishes to offer; this can be illustrated by means of two examples. In the first, having identified that a customer is prepared to pay a certain amount for a particular dish, say a grilled steak weighing 250 g, it must be considered (i) if a particular type of beef, say Aberdeen Angus, is available, (ii) if supplies can be maintained and a consistent product be procured, (iii) if the equipment for cooking it is on site or being made available, and (iv) if the staff with the skill for doing this is available. Normally such an item does not present major problems.

As a second example, it may be useful to consider a restaurant specialising in traditional pizzas where the planning and organisation is somewhat more complex. First, not all the regional ingredients may be readily available in this country, for instance, real Mozzarella cheese could be unobtainable and the aromatic wood needed to fire the proper type of oven may not be easily come by. Furthermore, the *pizzaiolo*, or specialist pizza-maker with the ability to produce the light dough is not a craftsman in plentiful supply, therefore it is necessary to be aware of the limitations imposed here by such external circumstances. At the same time, because the manager is aware of the consumer requirements he must be able to translate them into a precise form of instructions for his staff. This creates a formal framework within which any member of staff can proceed, knowing exactly what is expected of him.

The next stage is to define precisely how all this is going to be achieved. It should be noted that some of the success of a Fried Chicken operation can be due to the rigidly enforced method of seasoning the chicken then coating and frying it; not only are ingredients specified but also the method of cooking and the equipment required.

Other factors are to specify clearly the method of service and presentation of the product by means of precise information and instructions. Thus it is that a policy of operations can start either, from a general guide-line as an instruction given to a chef to produce certain items of his own choice that are suitable for a specific market, or, from instructions imposed on him regarding the menu choice, recipes to be used, standard portion sizes, and what will be produced on the premises and what bought in ready-made. Many catering concerns are operating successfully by using a variety of prepared ingredients which are assembled in the kitchen and doing without any fresh ingredients requiring preparation.

This decision of how to operate is a very important one and the decision arrived at, and the principles involved, must be clearly explained to all members of staff, especially since the major role of most business activities is the matching of resources to demand. This means the need to find the equilibrium between operating costs and the price acceptable to a customer, a problem solved in some companies by means of a full set of operating instructions issued to employees.

Once the choice of items has been identified and the method of production decided, then the selection of equipment and the space allocation for both production and service areas can be determined. Although a policy must be based on firm findings, an ideal allocation of space per person can be made theoretically, linking it with an indication of the desired rate of customer turnover. At this time also, the policy as regards customers may be drawn up to include such topics as credit facilities, dealing with complaints and special

46

requests and the establishing of good public relations. In addition, the policy will cover the hours of opening both to customers and staff, since when operating on a low profit margin the amount of paid overtime may exceed the gains made by staying open late.

Having now established the method of operation, management will need to set specific cost ceilings against each of the various component parts of the operation. First, budget guide-lines or instructions must be laid down regarding staffing levels in each department and staff costs in relation to the budgets for materials, overheads and maintenance.

It is then necessary to set up a precise procedure for making maximum use of resources; as an example, the firm may decide that throughout the day only freshly prepared food be served, but that after the full staff go off duty convenience foods are served in order to prevent prohibitive payment of overtime. The policy-maker may then decide to implement a precise method of materials and revenue control and this may affect a number of areas. If a firm decides to operate a system of unitary control rather than a gross profit control then each item will have to be specifically purchased in that form, for example, portion-controlled sirloin steaks, lamb chops, and so on. This method has several implications particularly on pricing strategies, and a feedback from the customer to determine satisfaction or otherwise can be obtained by an analysis of plate waste and by questionnaires devised to show their opinion of the food and service provided.

EXAMPLES OF SPECIFIC POLICY APPLICATIONS

Although a policy is concerned with providing guidance for the total cycle of catering, it can also be set for a specific aspect of the organisation as in the following examples:

A policy for purchasing can include:
1. the precise nature of the material by means of a specification,
2. the nominated suppliers,
3. the probable frequency of deliveries,
4. the amount of stock to be carried,
5. the method of payment,
6. the payment of accounts – centralised or decentralised.

A policy on manpower can include:
1. the terms of employment including job specification, wages, whether overtime is payable, holidays, fringe benefits, etc.,
2. the pension arrangements,
3. the trial period of probation,
4. the procedure on dismissals,
5. the provision of meals on duty,

6. the grievances procedure,
7. the promotion prospects; transfers,
8. the training programme within the organisation,
9. the consultation and progress feedback,
10. the health and safety regulations.

A policy for laying down standards of operation can include:
1. value for money, related to gross profit returns,
2. quality of the product and its presentation,
3. standard source of supply,
4. codes of practice, e.g. do the recipes conform to established rules and to menu descriptions?

A policy for governing control procedures can include:
1. the establishment of stock levels,
2. the responsibility for good ordering,
3. the inspection of goods delivered; storage,
4. requisitioning and inter-department transfer,
5. preparation – amounts to be issued,
6. sales records,
7. revenue records,
8. reconciliation,
9. the trading statement.

It can be seen then that a policy may be established for any area of the operation and can lay down a clearly defined set of guide-lines which can act as a control for maintaining standards.

Overall the formulation of policy is related to all segments of the Catering Cycle and can be useful in defining the relationship between the overall management and line or operational management. It can show how each section of the operation should match the others in that the standard of food must match the type of service and other facilities and vice versa – the ultimate objective being to give complete customer satisfaction in keeping with the prices charged. Even in those establishments where meals are provided as an emolument or amenity, They should still meet with the consumer's expectations. This fundamental aspect of a catering operation is the responsibility of the food and beverage manager, or whatever his title may be, and it is he who initiates and controls the operation in accordance with the policy and throughout the whole cycle.

5 INTERPRETATION OF DEMAND

The Menu as a Tool of Marketing – Some Gastronomic Considerations –
Menu Planning and Compilation – Types of Menu – Cost Distribution –
The Language of the Menu – Menu Pricing – Menu Compilation, Guiding
Considerations – The Wine List – Planning and Compilation – Design
and Presentation of the Menu and Wine List – Price Display of Menus
and Wine Lists.

For any catering establishment interpretation of demand refers to that which is
produced and offered for sale to its customers and is directly related to their
needs and demands. These needs and demands take the form of a list of suitable
items of food and can be a printed or handwritten card or booklet, or even a
list of dishes written in chalk on a blackboard. This is the menu or bill of fare.
In many cases the menu includes beverages but in licensed restaurants alcoholic
drinks are usually presented separately as a wine list. In either case the menu and
wine list must reflect the policy decision of the firm.

49

THE MENU

To some people the menu is simply a list of dishes to choose from in a restaurant, but to the professional caterer it assumes a much more empirical role and becomes the outward expression of the entire catering operation of an establishment; at a more personal level it assumes the professional expression of the person who is actually charged with the responsibility for its compilation. At a practical level the menu is the *modus operandi* of the entire food preparation and service section and everybody concerned must work from it, from the buyer to the cashier. In effect, it instructs all staff as to their duties and, knowing exactly how the person in charge requires things to be prepared, they can get on with the work without requiring further detailed instructions. For these reasons the menu must be examined for its multifarious functions from a number of different aspects which, though interlinked, are at the same time independent. These aspects can be grouped into two broad sections though they do come together at times. The first aspect is that of the menu as a tool of marketing, its effect in attracting custom to a particular establishment in a certain location, and its function as a sales aid. The second deals with the mechanics of menu planning and compilation and its effect on the meal experience together with responsibilities for compilation and the attributes of the compiler.

THE MENU AS A TOOL OF MARKETING

The need to undertake a serious investigation of the market in order to identify a particular slice of the market has been dealt with in Chapter 3. It was shown how it was necessary to build a clear profile of the consumer in order to make the offered product acceptable in terms of consumer expectations under particular circumstances and for specific needs. From this, three points emerge:

1. the consumer's needs
2. the occasion
3. the customer's expectations

The Consumer's Needs

Initially the needs of the consumer are determined biologically but are also linked with psychological factors inasmuch as the food drive is promoted in the higher cognitive centres, just like man's other impulses. To place this drive in context a knowledge of how the consumer's needs can be better interpreted and how individual consumers vary in their needs and in their spending power is paramount. For the purpose of an investigation it is necessary to select a section of the market and examine the characteristics of a small homogeneous group from the cultural and socio-economic standpoints. Food habits are instilled into young people from an early age and are the expression of a particular culture evolved over the years by experimentation under a variety of climatic conditions and the resources of their country of birth, together with the guidance gained from certain religious beliefs. These habits are reflected later in life as consumer choices.

Other factors that bear on the socio-economic background of consumers are that well-educated people generally have a more discerning taste, and people who travel abroad frequently are usually more receptive to new dishes. The age of the consumer has some influence since as a person grows older basic metabolism slows down and the need for high calorie meals lessens; the sensitivity of the palate and often the ability to masticate also decrease. The sex of the consumer has the effect that women usually look for delicate dishes of a low calorie type while men prefer heavier dishes. The dishes thus offered by way of the menu must be a reflection of these requirements.

The Occasion

Customers usually expect to be offered a purely functional meal for lunch, just sufficient to keep them going, whereas dinner affords an opportunity to relax and make the meal more of a special event. Work in this field exists which shows that the situational needs of the consumer change his expectations in terms of meal experience and value for money.

The quality of the product is one reason why customers find a restaurant attractive, the more easily the product can be identified with the consumer the greater the number of customers that will be attracted; this is one reason why continental restaurants in this country usually require a much larger catchment area than their British counterparts.

On the other hand it is the uniqueness of the type of product sold that exercises the strongest market pull. For example, if a restaurant specialises in a particular type of food such as high-class French cuisine or seafoods, and its methods of preparation are, or appear to be, superior to that of the competition, then customers seeking that particular meal experience will be prepared to travel a considerable distance in order to satisfy this longing. This is one of the reasons that good food guides and gourmet magazines often report favourably on a restaurant which is far off the beaten track. The merit of such places lies in their individuality and scarcity value together with excellence of preparation and value for money. In this type of operation location is of secondary importance as the market travels to the source of gratification, but it must be appreciated that this is for a total experience and not merely for the satisfaction of a basic

51

need or drive; a high volume of business is seldom a common everyday occurrence. When a high business volume is sought, but for some reason is not readily available in that area, it is advisable to take the service to the public; if the customer will not travel any distance to obtain something that is available nearer home, and when only an 'occasion' will justify the journey, then the product must be located near to the market. For a product that sets out to satisfy the basic needs of consumers, even where it is prepared and served in the most pleasant surroundings, the location must be close to the centre of the demand. As an example, in a shopping centre customers want a quickly prepared meal that gives good value for money but doesn't take long to eat – this means a fast food snack bar that has no pretentions to any sense of occasion but has a pleasing background that does not need exploring.

The more sophisticated an operation the more expensive it will be in terms of resources which means more space, good furnishings and fittings, skilled labour, and good quality commodities; this applies even though the restaurant is situated in a remote area. These costs must be met by the customers and leave a considerable surplus for the financial risk taken and provide a return on this investment. It is the uniqueness of the operation for special occasions that is the principal attraction so it follows that occupancy is never very high because (i) special occasions are comparatively rare events, and (ii) the meal that is an occasion is an elaborate one that takes a long time to get through. For these reasons a de luxe restaurant rarely attains 100 per cent occupancy in proportion to the number of seats available, whilst a fast food eating-house will fill its seats eight to ten times during the course of the day thus giving an occupancy rate of 800–1,000 per cent.

The Customer's Expectations

It is often stated that men prefer hearty, wholesome dishes and that women want light, appetising but interesting ones. The point is subtle and Brillat-Savarin's aphorism, 'Tell me what you eat and I'll tell you what you are,' has direct relevance to identification with the self. One of the major attractions of the classical restaurant is undoubtedly based on the mystique of French cuisine and its terminology. This not only promises higher expectations but assures the customer that he is a partaker of an experience of sophisticated eating comparable to what many great people before him enjoyed; customers of either sex tend to be attracted to a restaurant because the selection of items that it offers directly appeals to their image of the self. They like to identify themselves with, on one hand, graceful living and sophistication and on the other with adventurous travel and love of the exotic, or even with down-to-earth substantial yet practical dishes. It follows that when compiling his menus a caterer must ensure that the dishes he makes available have an appeal to that particular group of customers he wishes to attract, be they gourmets or merely those seeking a meal experience.

52

SOME GASTRONOMIC CONSIDERATIONS

The customer's needs are continuously being modified by the external environment. The environment exerts its influence through the season and climate in determining the selection of food in terms of (i) biological needs, and (ii) cultural ritual. In (i) it is obvious that high calorie dishes are more acceptable in the winter when more energy is expended in keeping the body warm and that light meals are best during summer because the physical activities do not require a high energy output. Under (ii) people seek out dishes as a result of the cultural ritual of their nationality and there are also traditions to be satisfied in the form of turkey at Christmas, pancakes on Shrove Tuesday, and so on. The time of day is another important factor to consider in that food is eaten for pleasure as well as for necessity; it must replenish the energy source so the meal taken at a particular time of day should satisfy the activity that has gone on before. Breakfast should therefore be the lightest meal of the day since only a minimal amount of energy will have been expended while sleeping. Lunch should be the more substantial meal of the day for people doing a manual job and dinner slightly less so, but the occasion on which food is consumed creates certain expectations which have an energising effect on the appetite and this can vary the intake for a particular period of the day.

Quality and Pleasure

An important factor is the concept of food quality allied with pleasure, and this concept indicates that a dish is of a good standard when it is compared with another dish. This is a judgement by comparison which also involves the concept of pleasure. Pleasure is never constant and appears to create differing reactions amongst different individuals, it also changes during the course of the day with peaks of arousal in a person and a continuous change in the attitude to food. The restaurateur therefore needs to try to create or maintain conditions for a favourable reaction to good quality foods. This may be achieved by alerting the senses through an orderly progression of intensity of sensations in the total meal experience and if there is any discordance of flavour, colour, aroma or temperature the pleasure will evaporate and quality be dissipated. This can be exemplified by drinking wines in the reverse order to that accepted, such as a sweet Sauternes followed by a white Burgundy. The second will be found unpleasant and acid which, of course, it would not be when drunk in the correct order.

Food Combinations

The main components of food combination are colour, aroma, flavour and taste, temperature, consistency, texture and shape.

53

Colour Vision as the most efficient of the senses is usually the first to be stimulated. The colour of a food or a dish can create a favourable reaction of pleasure in the consumer; colourless dishes, or where the expected natural colour is not evident or has been destroyed by poor cooking techniques, can create the reverse effect even to that of extreme displeasure.

Aroma The smell of a dish of food is usually related to what it is expected to be – thus it is essential that its aroma should be clean and identifiable and in keeping with the consumer's expectations. The new techniques of using many different wines or liqueurs, or a mixture of different herbs and spices often unrelated in flavour and aroma in the preparation of a single dish, tend to destroy simplicity and elegance – the aroma thus becomes meaningless.

Flavour and taste The four basic flavours are sour, bitter, salt and sweet and all prepared dishes contain a combination of these four basic flavours although very often single flavours predominate, e.g. a sweet dish is expected to be sweet. In some cases flavours are used to enhance, improve, develop, or make more evident the dominant flavour such as adding a pinch of salt to sweet paste.

Highly spiced, strongly flavoured dishes eaten first will tend to destroy the appreciation of a delicately flavoured item which may follow.

The major flavour component of a dish can be from any single basic flavour but it is more usual the balancing of more than one with each complementing the others which gives the greatest satisfaction. The repetition of flavours can lead to taste fatigue, hence the desire for variety in taste and flavour.

Temperature A dish which is accepted as being a hot one will not give the consumer pleasure if it is served other than hot because it does not satisfy his expectations.

The same observation holds good for cold dishes which should be served cold, chilled or iced, as expected. In most cases, serving it at the correct temperature means presenting food in its most pleasurable form.

Savoury dishes which are served cold need more salt in their preparation than does the same dish when served hot, and this also applies to a sweet dish when served cold – it requires more sugar than when served hot if it is to give the same pleasurable sensation of taste. This is because of the anaesthetising effect of extremes of temperature on the palate.

Consistency The consistency of a food refers to its viscosity and density and it applies mainly to soup and sauces. In general terms the expectation is that of smoothness as far as a liquid is concerned but there are obviously cross-sensations as when a sauce contains textured or shaped items. Sauces are useful adjuncts because they retain their own flavour for a longer time than the item they accompany, thus prolonging the pleasure expected and derived from the main item.

Texture This is concerned not only with firmness and tenderness but more often with crispness, crunchiness, rubberiness and chewiness. Food texture involves a degree of mastication and this in itself gives a pleasurable sensation particularly if associated with variations in texture at different points in a meal.

Shape The mouth is a very sensitive part of the body and is able to discriminate

54

between varying shapes even if very small. The roughness of a soup that has been passed through a coarse strainer is immediately noticeable and only tends to spoil the pleasure that would be derived from the same soup if it were served very smooth. The identifiable shape of cooked chicken cut in regular small dice for a chicken cutlet is preferable when compared with the same meat having been passed through a mincer which breaks down the texture and gives no identifiable shape. In this comparison the identifiable feeling of the first method is not only preferable in terms of tactile sensitivity but even appears to taste better.

As far as vision is concerned the even shape of a carefully cut garnish in a clear soup can convey a feeling of uniformity, care and orderliness.

MENU PLANNING AND COMPILATION

In the production of a menu, or bill of fare, as a card or as a list and displayed for the benefit of the customer, there are two distinct phases involved which, however, are very closely related. The first phase embodies the actual planning stages which should be precisely related to the identified demand and its market and which take form in the policy decisions of the firm. The policy decisions in effect will have planned the parameters within which the actual compiler has to work. Planning includes the type of menu, e.g. whether it will be an à la Carte one with each item separately priced, a Table d'Hôte menu with a small variety of dishes at a particular price, or a menu for a particular occasion; the size of the menu, i.e. the number of items or courses to be included; the language to be used; the type of presentation; and such things as cost distribution between courses if applicable. The second stage, menu compilation, refers to the actual compiling or bringing together of those dishes to be featured on any particular menu within the framework of the planning stage.

The selection of dishes for inclusion entails an understanding of the practical considerations which will allow the business to produce attractive dishes in an acceptable order, at a charge which produces the required amount of profit and at the same time obtains the goodwill of the customer.

Menu Planning

The planning of a menu cannot take place without a clear picture of the firm's formulated policy which provides the framework for the particular type of operation envisaged.

Those things to be considered in the formulation of policy are mentioned in Chapter 4 such as the expected occupancy rate of the dining room, maximum number of meals expected, the gross profit return required, and thus the type of business envisaged will determine the type of menu – its size and number of courses or items, and the prices to be charged. This in turn will determine the parameters within which the compiler will have to work in producing the correct menus.

Types of Menu

Every establishment will have its own particular types of menus, having decided when formulating policy what kind, or kinds, of meals it will serve. The policy will say what the opening hours of the business will be and this, to an extent, gives the compiler guidance as to which kinds of menus he must produce. The identified customer's demand will dictate the actual content and extent of each menu needed.

There are two basic types of menu in general used throughout the industry. The first is a set meal usually with a limited choice for each course and referred to as a Table d'Hôte menu. It can be priced or included as part of an hotel's terms. A useful translation of this name is the 'host's table' which derived from the days when a traveller arriving at an inn, partook of a meal prepared by the host or proprietor which was eaten by all his guests who sat down at table together.

The second is a menu that offers a choice of dishes within the range of courses, the extent of these and range of dishes being related to the type of business. Each item is separately priced and the customer can thus make his own selection. For custom and for the sake of convenience this type of menu is referred to as an à la Carte menu, and though not generally called as such in popular and industrial catering the term is used extensively in high-class establishments where the two types of menu can be on offer at the same time. What must be remembered is that basically a Table d'Hôte menu offers a set meal with limited choice and an à la Carte offers individually priced items at the customer's choice.

There is a third category which although it has some relationship with the Table d'Hôte menu differs in a number of important points which suggest that it should be treated separately. This type of menu is a set one sometimes without any choice, sometimes with a limited choice, and sometimes with a wide choice, usually depending upon the actual numbers of guests and the type of occasion. The kind of occasions can be a small party of business associates, a cocktail reception, a wedding breakfast, or a large or small banquet. This type of menu may be referred to as a special function or party menu.

Although it is often suggested that there are many other completely distinct types of menu in reality they can all be related to any or a combination of these three, however, there are a number of these menus which, because of their special nature, warrant more detailed description. The following details are representative of the three basic types of menu as defined above and their most important extensions.

The Table d'Hôte Menu   This is possibly the most common type of menu and is used in both the commercial and welfare sectors. It indicates a set meal usually with a number of choices in each course, sometimes at different prices and the number of courses can vary. The price can be changed in several ways on the same menu, either according to the price of the main course selected with each one on the menu having a different value, or according to the number of courses inclusive in a set price.

In menus with few choices the dishes included must have popular appeal so as to cater for the majority of tastes; at the same time they must be fairly equal in popularity so that they are chosen somewhat equally and thus do not become unavailable a long time before the other dishes on the menu. Table d'Hôte dishes are mostly ready in time for the opening of the dining room with the exception of items such as omelettes or other egg dishes. This means some foods may have to be kept hot for the duration of the service. Obviously some forecast of number of portions likely to be served is required which may be had from such things as advance reservations, the weather and the day's events. The number of customers envisaged needs then to be divided by most of the main courses so as to avoid over-production of any item.

Table d'Hôte menus are used in all large-scale operations as being the best way of feeding large numbers over a limited period of time. The inclusion of some à la Carte dishes, however, is possible. There are several adaptations and extensions of the Table d'Hôte menu over and above the following which illustrate how the two main menus are sometimes combined.

1. A restaurant operating an à la Carte menu may allow customers to select certain specified dishes from it to form a Table d'Hôte meal at an inclusive price – this is usually allowed only at lunchtime.
2. An à la Carte menu could have a set menu selected from it at each meal shown in the form of an inset to the full à la Carte menu.
3. Table d'Hôte and à la Carte menus can be printed on the same paper, either as one each side of a centre fold or inserted in the centre of the à la Carte menu.

Coffee is sometimes included in the prices of a Table d'Hôte menu, in others it is available at an additional charge.

The à la Carte Menu This type of menu consists of a list of dishes that an establishment will provide to order; it indicates that where applicable each item will be cooked especially for the individual customer ordering it.

The use of this menu requires the essentials of well-trained staff, the correct equipment and the right commodities to make for a successful operation. Each dish on the menu will be present in the form of raw commodities and ingredients together with some degree of pre-preparation. The cooking does not start until an order is received in the kitchen, except for some popular items that take a long time to cook such as ducks and chickens which can be held against an order without undue deterioration. Even so the customer knows, or is told, he will have to wait whilst his order is being cooked. In some instances this information is included on the menu card.

Dishes on an à la Carte menu are individually priced except for some large items such as Chateaubriand or pheasant which can only be prepared successfully for two or more portions. The prices shown are in accordance with that of supply and according to the size of portion, which is normally larger than for a Table d'Hôte menu. Prices are inclined to be higher because cooking to order requires proportionately more and usually better staff than for the operation of a Table d'Hôte menu.

There is the usual sequence of courses on this type of menu and a variety, including cold dishes, in keeping with the type and volume of business. A customer may choose as many items as he requires, even only one dish, though there is usually a set minimum charge.

An à la Carte menu is compiled to cover a given period of time and is perhaps in more durable form than the Table d'Hôte one which is usually changed every day. Some establishments change the à la Carte menu only when the season changes, and when fresh products come on the market which can give it a new look.

A la Carte menus are not the prerogative of the high-class sector, they are in daily use in many other businesses such as snack bars, call order units and fast food restaurants which use a permanent menu on which each item is listed and priced.

The Special Function or Party Menu As suggested before, these menus are basically of the same type as the Table d'Hôte menu inasmuch as they are set menus sometimes with limited choice and at a set price. They are usually for a private party of people who all sit down at the same time and all partake of the same meal. The number of people attending is determined by the organiser or host, or by the number of members of the particular society or association who are invited or wish to attend. The size of room available to accommodate the party, once the organiser has selected the menu, is also a determinant of the number of people invited. At small functions it is possible to offer alternatives on the menu usually on the hors-d'oeuvre and soup courses only, but when the numbers attending are large it becomes difficult to ask guests if they want say, thick or clear soup. The only optional dishes made available could be for any vegetarian guests.

Large functions where the guests are all seated and partake of the same meal are usually referred to as banquets. They can be held to celebrate particular occasions such as, annual reunions; for more regular meetings such as dining clubs and gourmet gatherings; after annual general meetings of associations and companies; as 'thank-you' gestures to employees, and many others. As special occasions, in contrast to normal everyday catering activities, these affairs require a menu that is out of the ordinary so that the meal is one to remember and befits the occasion. This indicates that the dishes offered should be outside the usual run of items, yet at the same time should be chosen carefully so that they are likely to please every single guest. The dishes selected should also be those that do not deteriorate quickly as it is not usually possible to cook everything at the last suitable minute, especially when dealing with very large numbers. The larger the number attending the more limited becomes the range of suitable

58

dishes, as in most establishments banqueting is also carried out by the same staff who cater for the other customers.

The way some firms cater for banquets is by showing an organiser the list of menus of various numbers of courses and quality and at a range of prices, letting him make his choice on behalf of the body he represents. In this way the organiser has some say in the choice of food and the onus is passed to him. Obviously the time of day when the banquet is being held has an affect upon the menu with lunch usually being lighter than dinner, this being in accordance with the normal principles of menu compilation.

Breakfast Menus These are of the straightforward Table d'Hôte type as served to people living or lodging in residential accommodation such as hotels and hostels; the number of restaurants serving breakfast are few except in locations where people start work very early in the morning and have time for a breakfast break. In a residential establishment an inclusive charge may be made for bed and breakfast, or it can be part of full board terms.

There are several different kinds of breakfast menus that are applicable to particular establishments, but they are variations of the two main ones which are the full English breakfast and the Continental breakfast. The full English breakfast can include grapefruit or fruit juice to start followed by choice of cereals, egg dishes; fish items such as kippers, smoked haddock, bloaters, fried fish or fish cakes; grilled items such as bacon, ham, sausages, lamb's kidneys often served with fried eggs, grilled tomatoes and mushrooms, and sauté potatoes; cold meats; marmalade, jam or honey, fresh fruit; beverages – coffee, tea and chocolate, and also rolls, croissants or toast, etc. The number of items on this type of menu is, of course, determined by the demand and expectation of the customers.

The Continental breakfast, which is now very popular in the United Kingdom, is much smaller in content than the English breakfast. It can consist of fruit juices; rolls, croissants, brioches or toast with butter and jam; and either tea, coffee or chocolate. Cereals are sometimes included.

In Scotland breakfast includes a selection of the many different kinds of rolls such as baps, girdle scones and potato cakes for which Scottish bakers are famous. Some places offer fried fish, others cold meats, while some even offer Victorian style breakfast dishes of grilled kidneys, kedgeree, etc.

Breakfast menus are usually served at a set price, all main items deemed to be of equal value, although items are sometimes priced individually.

Lunch Menus According to the type of establishment this can be the main meal of the day with dinner being shorter and lighter; but in general, lunch is a more utilitarian meal and less money and time is spent over it by the customer than for dinner. So long as the menu compiler is aware of the weight given to the meal he will have no problem in producing appropriate menus, because he will already be aware of the unwritten rules regarding the suitability of certain items for luncheon.

Stews, braisings, made-up dishes and plain ungarnished roasts are suitable items for lunch – in other words less expensive foods including the vegetables, and uncomplicated garnishes are served for the reasons that lunch is charged less than dinner and less time is taken over it. It would be correct to say that where both a Table d'Hôte and an à la Carte menu are in use less importance would be paid to the latter at lunchtime.

A three- or four-course Table d'Hôte lunch usually suffices for all forms of catering.

Afternoon Tea Menus The menu for teatime is very straightforward and, like breakfast, is the same almost everywhere. It is an informal meal, usually served in the lounge of an hotel rather than the restaurant. The usual menu consists of small triangle- or square-shaped sandwiches of egg and cress, cucumber, tomato, meat spread, sardine paste, it is not usual to serve sliced meat such as ham, tongue or chicken but to use them as a spread. Bread and butter may be served instead of, or in addition to sandwiches and as with these, both brown and white bread can be used and jam or honey served. Small cakes, pastries, sliced fruit cake or sponge sandwich and tea in a pot, either Indian or China, with cold milk or sliced lemon are served.

A Cornish cream tea consists of home-made scones with butter, strawberry jam and clotted cream; other counties have slight variations on this theme.

Other items served at teatime are toasted tea cakes, Sally Lunns and during the winter months, crumpets – all spread with butter and served hot.

High Tea Menus In some establishments where the main meal of the day is deemed to be the lunch, and where the customers retire to bed fairly early, a combined tea and supper is served slightly later than the usual five o'clock meal. It consists of a snack dish together with the normal tea and any cheese and egg dish is admirably suitable for it. Items on toast, poached smoked haddock, cold meat and pickles are other dishes, but it is a more formal repast and must be taken at table.

Dinner Menus Where this is designated as the main meal of the day the compiler has a wider scope than at lunchtime to show his prowess as it can be made more of an occasion. In the commercial sector customers are prepared to pay more for it whilst in the welfare sector the cost distribution between the day's meals will allocate the major part of the allowance to dinner. A hotel offering full board terms may budget as much as 40–45 per cent of the food allowance to the evening meal.

The number of courses at dinner is usually more than for lunch and the dishes can be more elaborate. It is usual to avoid ordinary stews and plain roasts, egg and farinaceous dishes are not the best of dinner dishes. Sweets should be lighter and more elegant than those for lunch – those based on ice-creams and fruits are ideal.

Supper Menus The menu for supper varies considerably according to the kind of place where it is to be served and also at what time of night. The usual places are night clubs, casinos and all-night restaurants, but there are other occasions such as after the first night of a play or film or a charity function where a ball supper is held.

The normal type of supper menu is an à la Carte one featuring both hot and cold dishes which are lighter and less elaborate than those served at dinner. Sandwiches are often a feature of supper menus, these being made of expensive items like smoked salmon; toasted ones such as Club Sandwich are also served and if the establishment stays open until early the following morning, breakfast dishes may also be included.

Cyclical Menus This is a way of compiling a menu to make it cover a given period of time. It consists of a series of set menus suited to the particular establishment and based on a determined period of time; this in effect could be four weeks or even longer. At the end of each four weeks the menus would be used again thus obviating the need to keep compiling new ones. The length of the cycle can be determined, for example, by taking account of the seasons of the year and the different foods available, or the need to alter menus to take account of changes in customer requirements caused by the weather. If a cyclical menu is designed to remain in operation for a fairly lengthy period of time it must be carefully compiled so that it does not have to be changed in any way and the proviso 'subject to alteration' is not appended.

The advantage of being able to operate a cyclical menu is that it removes the daily or weekly chore of compiling menus, although in the light of experience it may be necessary to make some alterations before using them in the next period around. When used in conjunction with a cook-freeze operation it is possible to produce the entire number of portions of each item to last the whole cycle, provided that the standardised recipes are correct in the first place. In this way the cyclical menu can give greater efficiency of time and labour and to an extent can cut down on the number of commodities held in stock.

A possible disadvantage could be that with a captive clientele particular days of the cycle become associated with a particular dish, but this happens only if the cycle is a short one or the menu not planned carefully.

A cyclical menu can be successfully used in any sector of the industry and it does not have to be rigidly fixed so that no alternative dishes are featured. It would consist of Table d'Hôte menus and the usual principles apply when compiling it, giving special regard to balance.

School Meals Menus After nearly forty years of serving traditional meals, the 1980 Education Act removed the statutory obligation of local authorities to provide a school meal service and allowed them to decide for themselves as to the nature, if any, of the menus they would offer. The result of this is that many schools now offer a snack bar meal based on a Table d'Hôte menu; this can be a choice of easy to cook and serve dishes of the kind which appeal to young people. The service must cover all costs as no government subsidy is paid to cover the difference between the total cost and the price paid by the pupil.

The limitation imposed by the mother on the amount she will allow her child dictates the items that constitute today's school meal. In general these are burgers, sausages, filled rolls, sausage rolls, hot dogs, etc. served with chips or baked potatoes, salads, simple sweets and beverages, keeping the menu in balance as far as pupils' choice allows. The aim is to provide sustenance to satisfy hunger rather than a planned meal, and a help-yourself service affords a more mature atmosphere than the take-it-or-leave-it system that previously applied in many schools.

Canteen Menus Meals served to people at their place of work vary considerably in standard and extent from one employer to another and this is mainly the result of the company's outlook on the welfare of its work force. Progressive companies always ensure that their employees are fed very well indeed; some charge for meals, others charge a token sum and are happy to offer meals at a highly subsidised cost, but most canteens charge a price that covers the cost of food and labour with all the other charges being subsidised. In most of these places, whether it is a factory canteen or a head office staff restaurant, the menu is a two or three course limited choice Table d'Hôte with perhaps a call order à la Carte selection at a higher charge.

The food is mainly English with a few well-known foreign dishes for added variety. The meal usually consists of soup, main meat or fish dish with vegetables followed by a sweet, with cold meat or cheese with salad as the alternative.

Fast Food Menus The idea of a fast food restaurant is to serve customers in the quickest possible time with the minimum of fuss and using the minimum of facilities. This does not mean that the menu must be unattractive, on the contrary it should be a well presented and described list, albeit of straightforward snack type dishes. They should always provide value for money. The menu is in effect a very limited à la Carte one which is standardised and only infrequently changed or amended.

Popular menu items in this class of catering are all types of hamburger, hot-dogs, baked potatoes with various fillings, double-decker sandwiches, toasted sandwiches, pizzas, various stuffed pancakes, fruit pies, doughnuts, cheesecake, hot beverages and milk shakes.

Railway Menus Meals served on trains are not a profit-making item for British Rail; it is almost impossible to run this form of catering at a profit because of the many problems connected with cooking on the move for an unknown number of passengers. By tradition railway meals are a target for criticism but given the difficulties of getting supplies and staff on board, the menus offered are reasonable in price and quality especially as it is wages which constitute the major part of the costs of providing the service.

Menus offer traditional British fare with a limited variety of dishes to choose from each course of a Table d'Hôte meal. The facilities are licensed and a limited number of alcoholic drinks are available.

62

On buffet cars the menu consists of snack items, hot and cold beverages and alcoholic drinks.

Breakfast is featured as a substantial meal on traditional British lines with a choice of food on each course.

Motorway Restaurant Menus Catering for motorists at motorway service stations takes many forms. The varying demands of travellers mean that several different kinds of menu have to be made available. For those who are in a hurry it has to be possible to obtain a quick snack and be on the way; for others with more time a more extensive and better class menu has to be made available throughout most of the day. Thus a Table d'Hôte snack menu of popular items both hot and cold, but not full meals, will be needed for one class of customer and a multi-choice Table d'Hôte menu of cooked food for the other. Printed menus can remain in existence for a long period of time, say until prices have to be raised, and any specialities can be added as a daily insert. Menus can be in the form of boards fixed where they can be seen by all on entering the room, using a lettering system or by printed notices that act as sales aids. An à la Carte menu can be offered in addition to the Table d'Hôte one as many sites feature a called order unit where grills are prepared to order.

To cater for an unknown number of customers at odd times means having a back-up supply of prepared food which can be brought into action quickly, therefore the menu would be based mainly on convenience foods and items that do not take over long to cook. This indicates snack dishes which can be quickly shallow or deep fried, grilled or griddled and for which a high degree of skill is not required.

Airline Menus The menus of airline companies take many forms and the standard of meals has long been a source of rivalry between them. The nature of the meal offered depends on the length of the flight and its quality upon the kind of ticket purchased – whether tourist or first class. No cooking can be carried out on an airplane and all the food is put on board ready for serving as a cold meal or for reheating; it is produced in the company's own commissariat or supplied by an airline catering contractor.

The menus are Table d'Hôte, the tourist class one being without choice unless a special diet has been requested in advance, and the first-class menu offering a good quality meal of four or more courses, according to destination, with several choices on each course. Drinks are served with meals, with wine to accompany the meal and hot tea or coffee afterwards. Individual meals are served to tourist passengers each tray holding everything required including condiments; bulk portion packs are used to serve onto plates from a trolley for first-class service. Menus must be planned with the thought that meals are put on board in chilled form and reheated for a specific length of time in electric ovens, so all the dishes must be arranged in exactly the same way, be of the same depth and still look appetising several hours after being prepared.

63

Cost Distribution

In the situation where a catering manager is allocated a certain sum of money per day or week for each person whose meals are included free, or in some large-scale catering situation where there is a fixed charge per meal, it is useful to have some sort of guide on how to allocate the total cost between the number of courses offered. The table in Fig. 2 is given as an example of the way in which money available can be divided between the courses of meals of different lengths; expressed as percentages of the total figures such as these, they can only be a guide since every establishment will have its own parameters within which it must operate. In a high-class establishment it can only be a guide for the Table d'Hôte menu and the allocation must even itself out over the choices offered in each course by ensuring that all the alternatives offered enjoy the same degree of popularity. In compiling special menus for banquets, cost distribution is applicable as each course must be an interesting one that fits into the food cost allocation without the fear that a particularly good course will bring down the quality of the others. It is obvious that because of the high cost of protein foods the main course is usually given the major portion of the allocation. Sensible cost distribution applies in these cases but not for à la Carte menus where the consumer has complete freedom to choose his meal without constraint, and to the price which suits him.

Figure 2
EXAMPLE OF POSSIBLE ALLOCATION OF COSTS BETWEEN COURSES

Course	Dish	Approx. percentage From	to
First	hors-d'oeuvre, soup	7.5	12
Second	fish, meat or poultry	60	45
	vegetables	7.5	10
	potatoes	5	7.5
Third	sweet, cheese or savoury	15	20
Sundries	roll and butter, condiments	5	5.5

The Language of the Menu

As the means of communication between caterer and customer the menu needs to be written in a language which meets with the customer's expectation and is one that he can understand. In high-class catering the menu is usually written in French; ethnic restaurants use mainly their own particular language, and it would be expected that most other restaurants in the British Isles would write the menu in English. Thus at the planning level great care should be taken that the envisaged menu for the particular operation relates to its closely. For example, a top-level restaurant which serves an international clientele should write its menu in French, whilst an industrial canteen would write its menu in English, bearing in mind that of necessity this will include some of the well-known dishes of other countries which will have to be written in their own language. This type of dish would lose its attraction if any attempt at translation was made.

If it is felt necessary a decision can be taken, especially where menus are to be written in a foreign language, to give outline descriptions of the dishes underneath in English. It is advisable, however, that these descriptions should not be too long and flowery but be truthful and written in terms that convey a clear picture of what is being offered.

In all cases, whichever language and technique of communicating details of the menu to the customer is chosen, great care must be taken to see that it is grammatically correct. This obviously can be more difficult if the chosen language should be French and it is not the compiler's first language. Care should be taken to see that genders and plurals are correct, that all accents are properly used and generally that the titles are written as they should be. However, if there should be any doubts, advantage should be taken of any help available, whether it be from a competent individual or one of the many useful books on the subject.

Where writing the menu in French is concerned there are two points worth making, aside from the foregoing observations. These are the bones of contention concerning the use of the definite article, i.e. le, la and les for prefixing menu titles and the use of capital letters. The use of the article is largely outmoded these days and should not be used unless on a very special menu for a private party or banquet where formality and care is an absolute concomitant of every aspect of the meal.

A menu written completely in capitals would appear to be an easy way to ignore some of the grammatical difficulties inherent in the French language as far as the use of capital letters are concerned. But the general appearance of this can be of a too boring uniformity and is not very pleasing to the eye.

It is grammatically correct that the only capitals which should be used in the title of the dish are the first letter of the title and the first letter of the name of a person or place. But if it is accepted that a menu item is indeed the title of a dish, then due emphasis should be given to its salient features by capitalising the first letter of each word except for conjugations, prepositions, adverbs and the definite article when used in the body of the title. A well-presented menu printed in this manner, using an appropriate type face gives a greater aesthetic appeal and scans much better. It is definite as being a title and does not give the reader a feeling of incompleteness and of needing to read further along the line. The following example may allow the reader to judge for himself.

Example

English titling	Best End of Lamb Sarladaise Style
French titling	Carré d'agneau à la sarladaise
French titling (capitalised)	Carré d'Agneau à la Sarladaise

65

Menu Pricing

The range of prices to be charged will be determined as part of policy decision and planning which has decided the type of operation and the menus to be followed. Within this range there should be allowance for higher or lower profit margins on particular commodities and thus menu items according to seasonal fluctuations in prices; these would balance out over a period of time. It is not good business practice to keep altering the price of menus to the annoyance of the customer; a good median line together with a minimal frequency of increases is always more desirable.

For a high-class restaurant operating with a de luxe à la Carte menu and where the price to the customer can be no object, then these prices would not be controlled as part of policy decision making but would reflect only the cost of commodities plus the required level of profit; the selection of dishes would thus not be constrained by the cost of commodities.

It can be seen then that the price of a menu is determined either by (i) the policy of the establishment, which in turn determines the level and quality of items on the menu, or (ii) solely by the cost of dishes plus the required profit.

However, there is another aspect of menu pricing which should be considered in the light of the consumer's expectations which in turn are largely the result of custom and usage. The price on the menu can either increase or reduce the consumer's expectations – the higher it is the greater his expectations. The difference between the price charged for set lunch and dinner menus stems from our view of lunch as being a utilitarian meal to be hurried over, with good but utilitarian dishes and fewer courses on the menu. For most people, going out to dinner is a more complex experience and carries a sense of occasion, enhanced in many cases by some form of entertainment, which is reflected in the price; usually it is also a more relaxed affair. From this it follows that the dishes on a dinner menu should be more sophisticated than those at luncheon so as to satisfy a different urge and also to justify the higher price; it follows on further that the expensive items used at dinner will yield a higher return on sales. So it is important to see that consumer expectations are not found wanting as this will surely lead to loss of custom and poor occupancy. A customer expects to be given value for money so if there is any doubt about the possibility of satisfying his expectations then the prices must be lowered to the level which will provide him with his value and the firm with its right return.

Menu Compilation

The planning stage has laid down the parameters within which the type and nature of menus have to be prepared and it has elucidated which language is to be used, and what the cost distribution among courses can be – the overall price ranges for the envisaged menus will have been previously determined at the policy-making level of the firm. The next phase is the actual compilation of the menu, using the foregoing points as a guide to the selection of dishes which will comply with the guiding considerations of menu compilation.

But initially it may be useful to look at the qualities of the person who is given the responsibility of compilation. It is obvious that it needs to be someone who is or has been closely connected with the actual food and beverage operation, particularly on the production side, and has had sufficient experience to fill a position of responsibility within the firm. It would undoubtedly be done best by the food and beverage manager or the head chef, or a combined effort by both of them; in a small establishment it could possibly be the responsibility of the manager, the supervisor or the proprietor. A chain or franchise operation will serve an identical menu in all its branches which emanates from the head office and which is compiled there, but the actual compilation would be the result of a team effort by qualified experts.

The compiler may need to research the subject in order to compile menus and should know which reference books are most useful as a source of information. He should be resourceful and inventive in his ability to use the correct descriptive terms necessary for the creation of interest in the customer. He should not only have a knowledge of the various foods but also have a feeling for the subtle relationships between them; here the relationship between food and wine would be an essential area of understanding. Nor should the compiler have such tastes and prejudices as would affect his fine judgement in meeting the requirements of the customer.

Finally, it is suggested that the guiding considerations regulating the successful compilation of menus would be part of the compiler's overall body of knowledge and experience. Adherence to the broad outlines of these considerations would thus be an automatic reflex to all the problems of menu writing; it would not take the form of continuous reference to a list of points which needed to be crossed off one by one during compilation.

The Guiding Considerations of Menu Compilation

These considerations should not be thought of as absolute, hard and fast rules which need to be adhered to at all costs. Some are determined by traditional approaches to the subject and are the result of well-tried practices but still leave room for modification and adaptation. Some make good gastronomic sense and are the result of trial and error and keen observation of the way in which certain foods and their combinations can influence the well-being of the human body. Others just make good sense and are the logical approach to what often looks to be a fairly daunting task. In all cases, though, these considerations need to be part and parcel of experience; if the compiler understands their limitations and is prepared to be something less than inflexible, they can provide the necessary framework for success. The guiding considerations are as follows:

1. *The Consumer, the Occasion and the Type of Menu*

As has been said, it is the kind of customer who determines the framework of the type and quality of menus which need to be compiled. At the planning stage such things as the type of business, opening hours, the segment of the public to be catered for, and their possible financial circumstances will have been taken into account. Thus the type of menu required has to be known, whether it is to be Table d'Hôte with its implications of being a fixed menu with some choice and at a fixed price, or à la Carte with all items priced separately, or perhaps a banquet or special function menu with its attendant constraints of numbers, the particular requirements of the occasion and the types of dishes or items best suited to preparation, serving and fitting the occasion.

It is as well to remember that the particular meal to be catered for creates its own special demands in terms of the prices to be charged and the dishes to be selected with their sequence or order of presentation on the menu.

2. *The Sequence of Courses*

There is an established order of succession of courses which by tradition are best followed; new dishes can be featured in the various courses but the sequence should not be changed if customers are not to be confused. The accepted pattern enables the caterer to compile the separate courses on Table d'Hôte and à la Carte menus, and to suggest suitable banquet or special menus with a larger number of courses if needed, putting them in their correct order.

The possible total of courses for lunch and dinner can be as many as twelve or thirteen but in present times this number is very rarely attained. Perhaps for some very special occasion an extended menu would be served but naturally portion sizes would be smaller. The custom today is for set lunches of three or four courses and three, four and sometimes five for dinner.

The sequence of courses for the main meals of the day with some notes on appropriate dishes follow.

LUNCH

HORS-D'OEUVRE

Grapefruit, melon, avocado pears, fruit juice. Fruit and shellfish cocktails. De luxe items such as oysters, caviar, foie gras. Smoked fish. Charcuterie items such as salami and Parma ham. Pâtés, terrines and mousses. Selection of Hors-d'Oeuvre Variés. Sometimes hot or cold vegetables such as asparagus, globe artichoke, corn on the cob.

SOUPS

All types of soups except for Veloutés which are perhaps better for dinner. The more robust potages such as Minestrone are very suitable.

FARINACEOUS DISHES

All pastas such as spaghetti, macaroni, lasagne, noodles. Gnocchi. Risotto and other rice dishes.

EGGS

All types with various garnishes, except boiled and served in the shell.

FISH

All types of fish and shellfish cooked by all methods but not too compli-cated or over garnished. Cold fish would appear in this place when intended as a fish course on a set Table d'Hôte menu. Otherwise it would be found on the Cold Buffet section of an à la Carte menu.

ENTREES

All type of stews, sautés, pies, puddings, hot pots, curries, escalopes, noisettes and offals. Rechauffé dishes and made-up dishes such as bitoks, pojarski and vols-au-vent. Boiled and braised meats.

ROASTS

Joints of butcher's meat. Poultry and game.

GRILLS

Steaks, chops, cutlets of butcher's meat. Poultry. Sometimes venison.

COLD BUFFET – Salads

All cold meats, poultry and game. Pies, terrines, mayonnaises, aspics and mousses. Cold fish and shellfish. Salads.

VEGETABLE DISHES

Hot or cold asparagus, globe artichoke, seakale, corn on the cob.

SAVOURY SOUFFLES

Soufflés of spinach, cheese, lettuce, sweetcorn, etc. can be served in this position. They frequently take the place of the sweet course when not required.

SWEETS

Milk puddings, steamed puddings, creams, etc. Pies, flans, tarts, croûtes, baked rolls, etc. Charlottes, bavarois, jellies, trifles, etc. Pastries, gâteaux, savarins, etc. Fruit dishes, compotes, salad. Various ices and coupes, but not more sophisticated presentations such as bombes and biscuits glacés.

CHEESES

All varieties and types with celery and biscuits.

DESSERT

All fresh fruits.

COFFEE

Observations

From the foregoing it becomes more than obvious that such a large number of courses would be quite inappropriate for the modern lunch. Thus for meals of a lesser number of courses some grouping of suitable sections is indicated.

The usual grouping for a three-course lunch excluding coffee would be: first course – a selection from Hors-d'Oeuvre, Soup, Farinaceous and Egg dishes, second course – a selection as a main dish, from Fish, Entrées, Roasts, Grills and Cold Buffet, in all cases served with vegetables, potatoes and/or salad; third course – a selection from the Sweet dishes or Cheese or, if needed or indicated, Vegetable Dishes or Savoury Soufflés.

For a four-course luncheon menu the grouping would be much the same but with the extra course being Fish, or in some cases a selection from Fish, Farinaceous and Egg Dishes. When in season a vegetable dish such as asparagus is often added as a further course between the main dish and sweet course.

DINNER

HORS-D'OEUVRE

As for lunch but with more emphasis on single de luxe items as far as high-class catering is concerned. The selection of Hors-d'Oeuvre from the trolley is not always suitable for the à la Carte menu.

SOUPS

All types both clear and thick, the lighter and more delicate kind being more suitable. A choice of clear or thick soup should be offered on a Table d'Hôte menu if a separate course.

FISH

All types of quality fish and shellfish dishes both hot and cold and with appropriate fine garnishes and sauces can be offered here. Such fish as cod, whiting and herrings, etc. are best for lunch.

ENTREES

A light dish of meat, poultry, offal, etc. served with a sauce if appropriate and lightly garnished. Would be served with vegetables and potatoes only if served as a main dish.

Tournedos, noisettes, cutlets, escalopes, suprêmes of chicken, sweetbreads, vols-au-vent, hot mousses of chicken or ham, timbales, quails, etc.

RELEVES

A more substantial item in the form of a joint or whole bird cooked by poêling or braising and sometimes roasting. Can be well garnished and should always be accompanied with vegetables and potatoes.

Examples include baron or saddle or lamb, braised ham, sirloin or fillet of beef, cushion or saddle of veal, haunch of venison, chicken, duck and pheasant. Pork other than ham is unsuitable for dinner because of its indigestibility. Cabbage and onions are best not served as an accompanying vegetable.

ROASTS

Poultry and game birds served with a plain or mixed salad. Sometimes a roast of veal or lamb.

COLD DISHES

Chaudfroids of poultry. Mousses, mousselines and soufflés of poultry, ham and game. Foie gras.

VEGETABLE DISHES

Hot asparagus, globe artichokes, seakale, corn on the cob. These can be offered cold if not preceded by a cold dish.

71

SWEETS

Hot and cold soufflés, pancakes, flambéed fruits, Crêpes Suzette. Ice bombes, parfaits, biscuits glacés, coupes, mousses. Cold fruit dishes using strawberries, raspberries, peaches, nectarines, pears, cherries etc. and very often with liqueurs.

SAVOURIES

Toasts, croûtes, canapés, tartelettes, flans, quiches, fondues. Savoury soufflés.

CHEESE

All varieties and types served with celery and biscuits.

DESSERT

Fresh fruits and nuts.

COFFEE

Observations

Here again the large number of possible courses for dinner requires some sort of grouping. That for a three-course dinner menu excluding coffee would be: first course – a selection from Hors-d'Oeuvre, Soup and Fish; second course – a selection as a main dish from Fish, Entrées, Relevé, Roasts and perhaps the Cold Dishes; third course – a selection from Sweet dishes, Savouries and perhaps Cheeses.

For a four-course dinner the grouping would be much the same except for the Fish being best as the second course.

A five-course dinner can be suitable if grouped in the following manner: first course – a selection from Hors-d'Oeuvre and Soups; second course – Fish; third course – Entrée; fourth course – Relevé; fifth course – a selection from Sweet dishes and Savouries.

A six-course dinner menu would be suitable if a Vegetable Dish were to be included between the Cold Dish and Sweet. Alternatively, a Savoury or Savoury Soufflé could be served as the extra course.

Larger menus would mean the addition of a course suitable to the requirements of the meal but taking care to have it placed in its correct order. There is a certain latitude allowed in choosing the particular courses for larger meals but what is essential, however, is to keep a balance between the main commodities. No more than one course should be given over to the Hors-d'Oeuvre, Soup, Fish, Sweet or Savoury but three or four meat dishes in the correct order are always permissible providing that repetition is obviated.

Again it should be noted that coffee by itself is not considered as a course. But if it is served and accompanied with Petits Fours it can be so designated although logically it cannot carry the same weight as the other courses.

The inclusion of a Sorbet, which is a light type of refreshing ice, at the half-way stage of a large, multi-course dinner has become quite popular again after its relative decline after the Second World War. Its purpose is clear – to refresh the palate after a number of courses and prepare it for what is to follow. Its place would be between two naturally balanced parts of a meal being neither too early nor too late in the proceedings. Its ideal placing, therefore, would be between the Entrée and the Relevé and means in effect that it would be quite inappropriate in a dinner menu of less than five courses; the placing of a Sorbet between the fish course and main dish of a four-course menu is thus wrong in principle. The presenting of Russian cigarettes coincident with the Sorbet is to be frowned upon, as smoking at this stage dulls the palate, interferes with digestion and is distasteful to those who do not smoke. A digestive liqueur or spirit may be served instead of a Sorbet.

Traditionally cheese should not usually figure on a dinner menu but it is more commonly offered on the modern menu. In any case, it can be served if requested. Another point concerns the placing of cheese on the menu. In France and for continental customers it is considered correct to serve cheese before the sweet whereas it is the custom to serve it after the sweet on English menus.

Breakfast The traditional English breakfast has an accepted sequence of courses or items on its menu. Although it seems overlong, today's customer still expects it to be correctly compiled even though his own selection may not be extensive. The sequence is: Fruit, such as grapefruit and fruit juices; Cereals; Eggs; Fish; Main dish based on Eggs, Bacon, Sausages, etc.; Cold meats; Preserves – marmalade, jam, etc.; Fresh fruits; Beverages; and finally Bread, Rolls, Toast, etc. The first four or five items would be served in the order as given but the beverages could be served throughout. The preserves or jam could be placed on the table at any time but should be there when the toast is served. Fresh fruit is quite often the last item on this type of menu.

Afternoon Tea Although most items would be available more or less at the same time, a printed menu for afternoon tea would also have its particular sequence. This is – Sandwiches; Hot buns; Bread and butter with jam, etc.; Pastries; and Tea. Each section would give details of the particular items on offer.

Supper Menus particularly designated for supper follow the same sequence and grouping as dinner menus with the dishes themselves being of a much lighter nature and of smaller portions. The number of courses would rarely exceed four at the most.

The à la Carte Menu One well prepared menu giving a balanced choice of items usually suffices for both lunch and dinner and naturally it would feature dishes common to both meals. The listing should be under the main headings of the sequence of courses of which some can be grouped together according to the requirements of the business. The usual headings in their correct sequence are – Hors-d'Oeuvre (popularly called starters); Soups (Potages); Eggs (Oeufs); Farinaceous Dishes (Farineux); Fish (Poissons); Entrees; Roasts (Rôtis); Grills (Grillades); Cold Buffet (Buffet froid); Vegetables (Légumes); Salads (Salades); Sweets (Entremets); Savouries; Cheeses (Fromages); Dessert; Coffees (Cafés).

The Hors-d'Oeuvre, Soups and Farinaceous dishes are frequently grouped together under the heading of starters whilst Entrées, Roasts, Grills and sometimes Fish and Cold meats are sometimes grouped under the heading of main dishes. Again it should be stressed that although some arbitrary groupings can be used because of the demands of the particular operation, nevertheless, the correct sequence or order of dishes should always be adhered to.

3. *The Selection and Balance of a Meal*

The dishes selected for any particular menu require that they be appropriate to that menu in variety, quality, price, value for money and in keeping with the expected customer's needs and expectations. The balance of a meal selected by the customer from an à la Carte menu is largely his own responsibility. Nevertheless, there should be sufficient variety in the range of dishes offered to cover any possible variation in likes and tastes and, furthermore, there should be the same attention paid to the avoidance of repetition as should be found in a set menu.

The selection and balance of a set Table d'Hôte menu or Special Function menu is a very broad and all-embracing consideration which covers the relationship between several important aspects of menu compilation based mainly on avoidance of repetition. These are:

(a) **Colour** The eye provides the first point of contact between the customer and his meal and a pleasing blend of colours can be the start of satisfying his appetite. The colours of cooked food should be natural and not spoilt by overcooking or use of artificial colours. There are enough naturally coloured and appetising foodstuffs to enable attractive meals to be produced without recourse to artificiality.

A good compiler will have a sound knowledge of the colours of various foods and will take these into account when selecting items for menus, and endeavour to prevent repetition. A preponderance of one similar colour throughout the meal can be very boring, in much the same way as some dishes can be if there is no effort made to relieve their overall monotony of tone. Watercress as a garnish for roast meats is a point in case - although pleasant to eat in itself its functions as a reliever of a monotonous brown tone can be very important. Thus it is useful to envisage the colour scheme of a dish and any accompaniments as it will appear on the customer's plate when he has been served. Because of this there is a growing trend in modern catering to serve each complete course on a plate, not

74

because of doubting the ability of waiting staff to serve correctly from dishes, but in order that the food will be presented in the most harmonious and eye-appealing way.

(b) **Texture** This is concerned mainly with the properties of tenderness and firmness of food to the mouth and the amount of mastication required. In a meal, indeed even on the one plate, there should be a variety of different textures including soft, firm, crisp and crunchy, all of which add interest to the act of eating and assist with the flow of saliva and, in its turn, aid digestion. An over-soft diet is a dull one, even to the elderly and very young, and yet it is perfectly feasible to produce interesting meals for people like these without thinking that softness in everything is essential for them. It is quite easy to slip into the error of compiling a menu which is totally devoid of textures and on the other hand one that is totally chewy. This can very often happen where the compiler has insufficient knowledge of the particular textural quality of dishes, or does not feel that this area is worth attention.

(c) **Flavour and Aroma** Flavour comes from the natural taste of food itself which is modified in cooking with the natural seasonings and flavourings of salt and pepper, herbs and spices – or from sugar and spices. Seasonings assist by enhancing the natural flavour without, in most cases, masking or diminishing it and thus rendering it more appetising to the taste. Exceptions to this are highly spiced food such as a curry or some South American dishes; these rely to a greater extent on the flavour and aroma of their sauces than on the main ingredients which are subservient and play only a minor role in flavouring the sauces and imparting aroma.

The aroma or smell of expertly prepared food is well able to excite appetite, providing of course that it relates correctly to the food and the customer's expectations. A clean identifiable smell which is the result of careful cooking is an easily assimilated sensation – that from overcooking, or the use of conflicting herbs, spices and flavourings, or again, the injudicious over-use and mixing of wines and spirits can create a feeling of unease and disinterest.

In the balance of the menu care should be taken not to repeat flavours and aromas but to try to create some sort of harmonious progression. The main dish should usually be the richest in flavour and aroma, in reality the central interest of the meal. The preceding dishes would ideally then lead up to it in order of ascending intensity and fall away afterwards with perhaps a final peak at the end of the meal; the inclusion of a suitable savoury at the end of a dinner is an example of this last point.

(d) **Sauces and Garnishes** Many dishes would be too dry to eat and enjoy properly unless served with a suitable sauce. Sauces can complement or contrast with a dish; they can be thin as with melted butter, of flowing or coating consistency, or hard as with brandy butter. They should, except for a very few exceptions, never totally overpower the natural taste of the food which they accompany. In a complete meal there should be no repetition of the same sauce and ideally when there are several the method of making each should be different.

A well-prepared garnish can add enormously to the quality of a dish. It can allow scope for artistic arrangement thus becoming an eye-catching part of the presentation, it enlarges the basic portion and gives added distinction to the whole. But simplicity and appropriateness should be the watchword; if it takes a long time to arrange the garnish around the dish it follows that it will take equally as long to serve onto the plate, with the danger of it becoming cold for the last customer served. This is especially true when serving a large number of customers at a banquet – the solution is to have another person serving the garnish from another dish.

If at all possible care should be taken to ensure that where a number of different garnishes are used for the courses, none of their components should be repeated.

(e) Cooking Methods In a multi-course meal each course should ideally be prepared by a different method of cookery – this will give greater variety and prevent taste fatigue, as well as ensuring continued interest and expectation.

Accompanying vegetables and potatoes of a dish as well as the component parts of its garnish can be prepared differently with success, but gastronomic good sense if not logic usually demands some sort of compatibility between them and the main item of food. Boiled chicken does not eat well with sauté potatoes, neither is fried fish best eaten with mashed potato although a plain boiled vegetable in addition to a fried potato would be quite in order. Good judgement rather than a rigid exclusion of all repetition should be the guide in this case.

(f) Ingredients As a general rule there should be no repetition of fish, meat, poultry, game or vegetables in the same menu even though prepared and presented in different ways, neither should the ingredients of garnishes be duplicated in a single garnish; nor should they be repeated where more than one garnish is served. The only exceptions to this perhaps are the use of truffles, mushrooms and potatoes which may be used more than once in a meal although excessive use should be avoided.

The use of an ingredient in the preparation of more than one dish is permissible providing that it is not dominant in flavour or can be identified as a particular ingredient. For example, to serve an onion soup and a Sauce Soubise, which are both composed largely of onions, in the same menu would be absolutely wrong, whereas onion used in the making of two or three dishes for the same menu can be of no consequence.

Fruit as a garnish for meats and poultry and even fish is becoming more popular but it poses problems in relation to the Hors-d'Oeuvre and Sweet courses for which fruit is traditionally a popular choice. If the meal is less than four courses it should only figure once, but with a larger meal fruit can with care

76

be used in one other course in addition to the sweet – but not if it is a dressed salad, of which fruit is the major component.

4. *The Capabilities of Staff*

The level of skill and experience of staff employed in a catering operation should be determined by the particular type of catering business – different levels of skill and experience are needed for the successful operation of a fast food restaurant and for a de luxe hotel restaurant. Nevertheless, the range of staff skills should not be narrowly contained within any one type of business. Scope for staff to improve their expertise and qualifications must be available, and in the long run this can only lead to an improvement in standards.

However, the person compiling the menu needs to know the range and limitations of staff skills available as it has a marked effect upon the type of dishes that can be put on the menu.

It is no good selecting very complicated dishes if the cooks would find them over difficult to produce and customers then finding them less than perfect to eat. The chef's previous experience will enable him to produce meals up to a certain level; knowledge of this and of his qualifications, such as the holding of a City and Guilds certificate, indicate the level to which a caterer may write his menus. It is a principle that the menu must be thought out, first to satisfy every customer's possible likes and then to provide a challenge to the kitchen staff which will help to develop their potential; this means that the menu must be well researched and varied and never allowed to become stereotyped.

The competence of the serving staff is, likewise, a big factor in the writing of the menu; if there is a well-trained waiting brigade in a first-class establishment there need be no limit to the level of presentation. There would be no use featuring well-garnished dishes if the waiter is not going to present and serve them to customers correctly. Taking them to the sideboard and plating them there instead would be a waste of the kitchen's effort.

Similarly, the needs of a counter service would be taken into account if the menu in a fast food operation were to maintain its competitiveness. It would be quite inappropriate to place new items on the menu, or alter the degree of skill required for their production and service, if no account were taken of the staff's competence to do so.

5. *The Availability of Equipment*

When writing his menus a caterer will need to know what equipment he has in the kitchen and what its performance is, any lack of a piece of equipment which prevented the business from meeting the demands and needs of its clientele would have to be acquired. The same holds good for the equipment found in the dining room and all other items of small equipment. Even so, presuming that the business is equipped in keeping with the type of operation for which it was originally planned, there can still be needless constraints and determinants on

77

the range of dishes which can be offered unless this available equipment is versatile in terms of capacity and capability. In other words the equipment should not in itself prevent any desirable modification or adaptation of the menu taking place.

There may be sufficient scope and flexibility within the bounds of the particular operation and the compiler of menus should be well aware of this. But to place an item on the menu needing equipment which is not available, can mean compromise leading to poor production and finally customer dissatisfaction.

6. *The Seasons of the Year*

Air travel has made the world seem smaller and fresh produce is now air-lifted thousands of miles to appear on menus completely out of season. So it is not now as important to bear this factor in mind when writing menus for high-class restaurants. Yet seasonal home-grown foods ought to be featured because they become available in larger quantities, are then cheaper and add interest to the menu. Caterers should clearly recall the beginning and end of seasons for foodstuffs otherwise they can find themselves having to plead with suppliers to scour the market for a product that is no longer in season locally and has to be obtained from farther away at a much higher price.

Other aspects of this factor concern the weather and the time of the year. A cycle of menus should cover a season of the year, either winter, spring, summer or autumn, because the weather changes with the seasons and customers expect dishes to take some account of this. For example, salads should be available in warm weather and more substantial warming dishes in winter. The caterer will attempt to add interest to his menu by remembering that by tradition certain special occasions warrant a dish associated with them – fish on Fridays is one instance and is still adhered to even though the requirement for it was removed years ago. Special occasions such as Burn's Night, Royal Weddings or Election nights as well as the set holidays of Christmas, Easter and New Year are other times where specially prepared menus are expected.

7. *Availability of Resources*

A catering establishment located in a city or large town seldom experiences difficulty in obtaining a supply of practically any and every item it requires to fulfil its menu; it usually has a choice of several suppliers all ready to give prompt delivery. This is not generally the case for caterers in remote spots far from major sources of supply, who may well find that their choice of some commodities is restricted and can be reflected in the menu. The compiler will be aware of this drawback but feel compensated by being located in a region where there are sources of supply of local commodities that are fresher and cheaper than in town. The menu compiler must not be tempted to include items which may cause a problem of supplies because of transport difficulties, strikes, bad weather or unfulfilled promises of delivery. Even in town there may be a diffi-

78

culty in obtaining an extra large supply of a particular item for a banquet and it is advisable to give long notice of requirement.

Some establishments are required, or feel it desirable, to hold emergency stock of certain foodstuffs in non-perishable form that can be brought into use when cut off from normal deliveries.

8. *Nutritional Aspects*

In welfare catering a sound knowledge of nutrition and dietetics is essential; the caterer in this sector, having a captive clientele, must possess a very good knowledge of food values and of the nutritional requirements of his customers. He must know their needs in terms of necessary calorie intakes and ensure a balance of protein, fat and carbohydrate as well as vitamins and minerals. With this knowledge, allied to his professional abilities, he should be able to write menus which satisfy his customer's requirements. The dietetic part of his job entails the writing of menus for people placed on a special diet by their doctor; or having to meet the needs of ethnic or other groups who have to take notice of dietary constraints of a religious or cultural nature, like Jews, Muslims, Hindus and vegetarians.

In commerical catering there is no real requirement to adhere to rigid nutritional and dietetic principles. Nevertheless, the good compiler of menus will ensure that within any of his set menus there is a well-balanced selection which will satisfy the normal customer's nutritional requirements. The customer selecting his meal from an à la Carte menu is largely responsible for his own nutritional intake but the menu as a whole should still reflect a good nutritional balance.

THE WINE LIST

The aim of each licensed catering operation should be to persuade every customer to have something to drink with his meal, for not only does it tend to make the meal something more of an occasion but assists the firm financially, since the profit margins on alcoholic drink can be better than that from food sales. In order to promote the sale of drink some thought must be given to the planning of the wine list which in turn will influence the bar tariff and, where applicable, the banqueting wine list – this being usually an abridged version of the full wine list. The wine list like the menu can thus be seen as a tool of marketing.

THE PLANNING AND COMPILATION OF THE WINE LIST

The planning of the wine list should ideally be done in conjunction with that of the menu, the manager of the dining room, or head waiter, taking a leading role in consultation. Normally the menu would determine the kind of wines to be offered, although there are those restaurants where a superb wine list would to some extent dictate the style of the menu, and the reputation of it would stem from the professional expertise and capabilities of the buyer. As with the planning of the menu, the wine list must abide by the policy of the firm as regards sales of alcoholic drink. The demands of the customer will decide if magnums, half and quarter bottles be stocked, whether wine be served by the glass or carafe, how many sections there will be on the list and the number in each of them. The customer's spending power will decide whether fine wines or ordinary table wines are listed and what the tariff is. The location of the bar, staffing and service procedures will affect the inclusion of aperitifs on the wine list or whether these go on the bar tariff. The importance of these in promoting appetite and sales, especially if the profitable cocktails are featured, should not be overlooked.

When it comes to the actual compilation of the list a sound knowledge of wines is vital for selecting the items to be included, and a reputable supplier who carries all the important ones and can maintain supplies should be chosen. Some large establishements and groups maintain their own central depots and cellars and much of the buying is done directly through shippers and vineyards. If possible, a proper tasting should be held of each one to be included on the list. The following are the main points of compilation.

1. *The Wine, the Consumer and the Occasion*

It is of the utmost importance that the wine list matches the type of operation and that it meets with the consumer's expectations. The opening hours of business will have some bearing on the range and extent of the list even though the class of business may be the same; for example, a restaurant that is open only for lunch and another such as a hotel where lunch, dinner and special functions are catered for. In the first case the range of fine wines would not be so extensive and the accent would be on those excellent wines more suited to the time of day and the demands of more hurried meals. In the hotel a wider range of the finer wines would be expected to cater for the needs of those occasions such as dinner and the special function.

2. *The Selection and Range of Wines*

This must be sufficiently varied and large enough to suit all the possible tastes of its clientele and means being able to offer as wide a choice as would be correct for the particular type of business. For instance, ethnic restaurants would be expected to offer only or mainly wines from its own country. A small bistro would be expected to offer good wine at reasonable prices, either bottled of in carafe but with limited choice, and the de luxe restaurant would be expected to offer a multi-choice list of good to fine wines and liqueurs. Within these ranges,

80

though, certain basic tasts and likings should be taken care of – these are the personal preferences for wines which are still, sparkling or fortified; red, white or rosé; dry, semi-sweet or sweet; light, medium or robust; ordinary to better; reasonable in price to more expensive.

3. *The Sequences of the Wine List*

The sequence of wines on the wine list is not as clearly defined as that of dishes on the menu. The customer expects to find dishes in a certain sequence and is accustomed to eat them in that sequence with one or two minor exceptions such as cheese before or after the sweet. With wine, however, the choice is usually left to the customer as to what he will drink and in what order, although this last is usually regulated by gastronomic good sense. Nevertheless, he will still expect the quality wine list to follow a well established sequence. There can be minor differences in order, accent and range but the pattern is usually the same. The essential information required for each listed wine, and reading from left to right on the list should be:

The Number A number is usually given to all still, fortified and sparkling wines by the compiler of the list and this corresponds to its bin number in the cellar. Spirits, liqueurs, beers, ciders, etc. have different storage arrangements, as proprietary brands they are in continuous production and can always be held in stock. Numbering makes it easy for the customer to order, even to the extent of saving some embarrassment if having to read a long title in an unfamiliar language, it is easier for ordering by the waiter – the number reinforced by its name acts as a check; and it is an easier and more reliable method of using the number and name for requisitioning from the cellar.

The Name of the Wine This should be in full and in the case of fine wines should include its particular growth and region or area of origin, e.g. Château Calon-Ségur 3ème Cru, Pauillac. The name of the shipper can be given for other wines.

Date/Vintage Either may be used as a heading for the actual year of the wine's vintage where given. Of the Champagnes only vintage Champagne is dated.

Bottles and Measures The range of bottles offered is determined largely by demand – it being usual though to offer bottles, half bottles and magnums of the better red Bordeaux and Burgundies; bottles, half bottles, magnums and sometimes double magnums of Champagne; bottles and half bottles of most French and German white wines and also of some sparkling wines; most other wines are offered in bottles only. The measure for spirits such as Brandy and Whisky must be stated by law – the standard measure being one-sixth of a gill. Other drinks such as sherry are priced by the glass.

Price This should be given next to the column relating to bottle size or measure; the listing of each section should start with the cheapest and then in ascending order to the most expensive.

The following is the more commonly accepted sequence of wines, spirits and liqueurs, etc. as would be found on a first-class wine list, together with some notes where applicable.

BORDEAUX, Red

May have a sub-division for château-bottled wines.

BORDEAUX, White

May have a sub-division for château-bottled wines.

BURGUNDIES, Red

May have a sub-division for estate or domaine-bottled wines.

BURGUNDIES, White

May have a sub-division for estate or domaine-bottled wines.

LOIRE WINES

RHONE WINES

ALSATIAN WINES

Sometimes these wines are listed after the Rhines and Moselles.

RHINE WINES

MOSELLE WINES

ITALIAN WINES

ROSÉ WINES

ENGLISH WINES

AUSTRALIAN WINES

SOUTH AFRICAN WINES

AMERICAN WINES

HUNGARIAN WINES

The last six categories should be added if comprehensiveness is felt to be a desirable feature of the list.

CHAMPAGNES

The particular types, qualities and/or vintages should be listed under the producer's house name. Champagnes are sometimes listed at the beginning of the wine list and sometimes after the full range of French wines.

SPARKLING WINES

It is not necessary to list these under their country of origin. The name usually provides sufficient information.

SHERRIES

These are always priced per glass, and prices per bottle can be included. They are sometimes preceded by the Ports.

MADEIRAS

Should be added for comprehensiveness.

PORTS

Should be priced by glass and bottle. Information on vintage, bottling dates and type should be given where applicable.

LIQUEURS

The better known spirits such as Marc, Strega, Kirsch, etc. should be included here.

BRANDIES

These should be well and truthfully described.

WHISKIES

This section can be sub-divided into Scotch Whiskies and Malts, Liqueur Whiskies, Irish Whiskies and Imported Whiskies.

GINS, VODKAS, RUMS

Proprietary brands should be listed.

APERITIFS

These should only be included if there is no separate tariff.

COCKTAILS

These should only be included if there is no separate tariff. Sub-divisions can include items like Cobblers, Coolers, Fixes, Fizzes, Flips, etc.

MINERAL WATERS

This will include still and carbonated spa waters and flavoured items.

FRUIT JUICES

Fresh juices should be included.

BEERS

CIDERS

CIGARS

These are best listed under their country of origin. They are seldom seen on the wine list being more usually presented separately.

Observations

To fill out the foregoing sequence with an appropriate range of types and qualities and in sufficient numbers to justify so many sections would need a large and bulky list running to many pages. Only in the largest hotels and de luxe restaurants would this be a commercial proposition. Smaller lists would thus require some grouping together of sections, perhaps removing some sections altogether such as beers, ciders and cocktails. It is for each business concerned to make its own interpretation of what will meet with the expectations of its clientele.

As noted, it is possible to alter the sequence of fortified wines, e.g. Sherry and Port, without offending anyone. Likewise it is permissible to start the list with the Champagnes but the general rule should be to begin with the wines of the highest repute. This means that the Bordeaux and Burgundy wines should have pride of place followed by the wines of other French districts of repute.

Wines of other countries like Spain, Portugal, Chile, Austria and Romania, etc. could be added to the list after Hungarian wines, if thought appropriate and if sufficient demand was evident.

The selection of wines for listing on a banquet or special party menu is normally from the establishment's wine list although sometimes a customer will bring in his own wines – in this case he would be charged a nominal sum for its service and use of facilities. Where selected from the wine list the choice is usually made by consultation between the manager or head waiter and the customer, and is made with reference to the menu and an attempt made to balance the quality and special characteristics of the food with the wine and vice versa. The individual customer is obviously quite entitled to drink what he wants in any order and at any temperature he so desires, but for a number of people sitting together and eating the same food it is essential that all be satisfied with the type, quality and order of wines served. It is here that a knowledge of certain well-tried gastronomic considerations is more than useful. Among the most important are the following:

(a) The progression of wines served in a menu should be in an ascending order from the more ordinary to the finest, from the lightest to the more full bodied, and from the youngest to the older. In short this means serving wines in ascending order of quality.

(b) White wines are best served before red wines except sweet ones which can be served after them with the sweet dish. Dry white wines are best served with fish and shellfish and white meats such as poultry, pork and veal.

(c) Champagne may be served all throughout a meal though the dry are best with all courses before the sweet course, when a semi-sweet or sweet Champagne would be more suitable.

(d) Red wines are best served with dark meats; the more robust Burgundies being ideally suited to rich, highly flavoured beef and game dishes.

(e) Sweet white wines such as Sauternes, Barsac, Tokay, Beerenauslese and Piccolit are best served with the sweet course.

(f) Port is an excellent wine for serving with cheese and dessert.

(g) If a savoury is served instead of a sweet then the red wine served with the preceding course will be suitable.

(h) Rosé wines, as a compromise, can be served with any course of the menu but would be inappropriate for a fine, well-chosen menu of gastronomic excellence.

(i) It is not wise to serve wine with any Hors-d'Oeuvre or salad which has been dressed with vinegar and oil. The vinegar has a deleterious effect on wines and turns it acid.

(j) Asparagus and eggs do not take kindly to wine and create a taste which destroys the quality and flavour of both the food and the wine.

(k) It is quite acceptable for wines from more than one country to be served with a meal providing, of course, that there is an affinity between their quality and that they have a compatibility and sympathy for the food with which they are served. Differences in the style of wines can always add interest to the proceedings.

4. *Staff*

The skill and expertise of staff responsible for the storage and service of alcoholic and non-alcoholic drink must be consistent with the needs of the particular wine list being used. At all levels this requires a knowledge of the qualities and characteristics of all the items featured, together with the ability and skill to store them in optimum condition, to keep them ready for service and to serve them in their correct manner and at the right temperature. In short the quality of staff must match that of the list.

All staff concerned with this area of catering should continually keep abreast of new developments in viticulture and vinification. This means not only personal endeavour on the part of the individual but also that management gives time and opportunity for staff to attend educational courses concerned with the subject.

5. Cellaring and Storage

This must be considered to a large extent with the problems of continuity of supplies. If thought to be cheaper to buy in cask and to bottle on the premises then this requires the right staff and equipment together with sufficient working space in addition to storage space. In the case of fine wines in bottle, how large a stock should be carried and how much capital can the firm afford to have tied up in this kind of stock are some of the questions to be asked.

Smaller cellar space is required for medium quality wines bought in on a regular supply basis and where the major stock is held by the supplier, but very often this can result in fluctuating prices unless this has been agreed on a contract basis.

6. Continuity of Supplies

This poses no problems as far as branded spirits, liqueurs, beer and mineral waters and the like are concerned. They are always available and good ordering procedures will ensure that adequate stocks are carried. With wines, however, there can be certain problems because the same wine of different years or different vineyards in the same area can vary greatly, and more importantly there is only a limited amount of any one vintage available. This can mean alterations to prices, or deletions and additions to the list if precautions are not taken to ensure an adequate level of stocks. Buying procedures have to be delicately balanced to the fluctuations of supply and demand if the listed wines are to be on offer for a reasonable time. Customers like to find the wines they like still available for some time; frequent chopping and changing of the listed wines can be confusing and irritating.

7. Pricing

A policy of marking up wine by a very high percentage could make it possible to have the gross profit on food sales at a reasonable rate providing, of course, that the sales of wine could be kept at a high enough level. A careful balance must exist between the turnover of sales and the percentage of mark up, bearing in mind always that the customer expects value for his money. In any case it well behoves any catering business to consider a sliding scale for marking up the cheaper wines as compared with the more expensive. A 300 per cent mark up for a bottle of wine costing £2 wholesale would look reasonable whereas the same mark up on a bottle costing £10 may appear unreasonable. Where adequate storage and service facilities are available, volume of turnover should be the determinant and the policy of mark up should be related to this.

86

8. Descriptions

For some establishments it can be helpful to include a description of the area from where each wine comes together with short descriptive notes on taste. For others, recommending certain wines for certain foods, and perhaps offering a wine of the day, can be an acceptable way of helping their clientele. In first-class establishments these points are always the responsibility of the wine waiter; one of his prime functions is to be able to advise the customer truthfully and from knowledge.

THE DESIGN AND PRESENTATION OF THE MENU AND WINE LIST

In the full compilation of the menu or wine list certain information has to be added before printing. For Table d'Hôte menus this usually means the insertion of the name of the establishment, plus the name of the particular meal, i.e. Breakfast, Luncheon or Dinner, etc. and the date. The pricing and any other special information must be precise and unambiguous. For à la Carte menus the information needed is less precise. It always needs the name of the establishment and the word 'menu' or a similar descriptive word but the date is very seldom added. In high-class catering, where both types of menu are used concurrently, it would be necessary to distinguish the à la Carte menu by the inclusion of these selfsame words either on the cover or at its head. Other information apart from its sequencing would include prices and details of times needed for the preparation of certain items. Special Function menus would need to be well prepared in a mock-up form to show its proposed format and should include all relevant information. The wine list would need the same information as the à la Carte menu and for the particular establishment there should be an identifiable similarity between them in size and presentation.

The high cost of printing menus indicates that where possible à la Carte menus should be made to last as long as possible before having to be scrapped because of being out of date, or because of rising prices, seasonal goods, or because they are no longer clean. There will always be the restaurants that can afford to print a fresh Table d'Hôte menu for every meal but in most cases menus are designed to last for as long as possible. At the other end of the market there is not the same need for the printed menu card or wine list.

It is in keeping with a bistro to write the menu and wines on a blackboard or even on the shop window. A fast food firm can have its short menu displayed above the serving counter for all to see and have no need for table menus since customers go straight to the counter to get their meal. A factory canteen or college refectory, or other similar establishment, has no need to spend money on menu production since a copy of the cyclical menu in a strategic place, such as a notice-board outside the room listing the day's offerings, brief notes of the dishes displayed on notice-boards throughout the establishment, or a copy of the week's menus sent to all departments, will provide the necessary information.

The menu is the form of communication between management and customer and its job is to inform and sell. The reputation of a catering establishment stems largely from its menu, what it features and how it is marketed, so it must give its message in writing in the most suitable way. Management may not be the sole decision maker when it comes to the final presentation of the menu; in large companies this could be a corporate decision at a high level, but the management of each establishment would in any case be consulted in identifying the most suitable form of presentation which would derive from criteria formulated in the policy decisions of the company. Decisions would be needed over such things as the format and size; whether folded or single; the number of sheets if necessary; the thickness of paper and card and its quality and colour; the size of type and mixing of various types; the colour of the printing, and whether laminated covers would be necessary. Decisions will have already been taken on the language to be used, whether French, with English sub-titles, written entirely in English; in flowery prose; in literary style; if prices will be printed on or inked in later, and so on. And after all this the designer and or printer will need to be called in.

A commercial artist can be commissioned to create a menu suitable for the particular business, his job being to produce sample designs for the cover and any suitable illustrations to add interest to the inside. If the establishment already has its own distinctive logo or crest this, together with a printed artist's surround, may suffice and the designer's services will not be required.

Some printing firms which specialise in menus offer a complete design service and have the experience to advise on designing, writing and printing of both everyday and special menus. A restaurant will quite often use a small firm of printers because they will be interested in doing a short run at quick notice and at a reasonable price; samples of card, paper, type faces, ink colours, borders and surrounds would be always available for choice. Large organisations with many outlets would have the work prepared centrally even if this involved differences in presentation for each of their outlets.

Printed menus for special functions are a once only production for use on a particular occasion and can be as plain or fancy as the organiser of the function wishes, since he will have to pay for it. Full rein can be given to the artistry of these menus when cost is no object, and in many cases the full programme and seating plan is printed in. A degree of compatibility between function and menu is possible as, for example, a silver wedding dinner could have the menu printed in silver, a gala dinner on New Year's Eve could be topically illustrated, a menu for Burn's Night could be tied with tartan ribbon.

It is also very important that the lettering of the menu is clear and large enough to be read with ease in a dimly lit restaurant, or by the vain person who does not wish to use glasses.

Most of the foregoing points concerning the menu apply also to the wine list which, because of the profit to be derived from it, should be equally as attractive as the menu. Generally the wine list is printed as a separate card or book with hard covers. Some establishments are guided by their wine merchant who may not only help with the composition of the list but print it free of charge; this, however, has the effect of tying them to the supplier.

Whatever the type of printed menu card or wine list, it is of paramount importance to see that there are no spelling mistakes, no bad grammar and no errors in pricing, dates or names; the most careful reading and correction of printer's proofs is essential. Once printing is completed it is too late and anything wrong with presentation can only harm the reputation of the establishment.

PRICE DISPLAY OF MENUS AND WINE LISTS

The Price Marking (Food and Drink on Premises) Order 1979 makes it an offence for a restaurant not to display prices to its prospective customers so that before entering they may know what they are going to be charged. In a self-service restaurant or cafe they must have the opportunity to find out how much it is going to cost.

If VAT is paid, the prices must include it; if there is a service or cover charge this must be stated as an amount or added percentage. If there is a minimum charge this must be shown.

If there is a menu of less than thirty items (other than wine), all prices must be on display. If there are more than thirty items, at least thirty must be shown. Where the dishes are divided into courses, either all when there are less than five, or at least five must be shown for each course.

The price of the Table d'Hôte menu must be shown as well as any optional extras; in addition a de luxe restaurant must show the prices of at least thirty items of food and drink, and at least six wines. In a licenced restaurant, if there are only six wines available, all prices per bottle must be displayed; prices for at least six of a longer list must be displayed. If there are two or more of white, rosé and red wines the price of at least two must be on display.

The menu displayed should be clear and easy to read by the intending customer.

6 CONVERGENCE OF FACILITIES I – PLANNING THE AREAS

General Points of Planning - The Planning Team - The Sequence of Planning - Planning Methods - Allocation of Space for the Dining Room, Customer Amenity Areas, Kitchen Areas, Staff Facilities and Offices - Planning the Dining Room, Visual, Thermal and Auditory - Types of Dining Rooms - Planning of Customer Amenities, Bars and Cloakrooms - Planning the Dispense Bar and Cellar, Staff Facilities and Offices - Planning the Kitchen - Detailed Planning of the Kitchen Areas.

Unless planning allows for flexibility and duality of purpose catering departments may become inefficient and out of date very quickly. Planning therefore needs to be in accordance with a long-term strategy with probable changes during the life of equipment. In addition, the possibility of success leading to the need for expansion has to be allowed for – by redevelopment or redeployment rather than extension. Thus any measurements given in this chapter are approximate.

90

GENERAL POINTS OF PLANNING

The following points are applicable to the planning of all areas when viewing the layout from an overall approach. Ideally, the kitchen, dining room, bars and ancillary areas should be located on the same floor so that the communications are easy to follow; if possible, all these departments should be on the ground floor to obviate movement of goods and personnel upwards or downwards.

The overall plan should aim at putting the dining room next to the kitchen on the same level so as to avoid the need to install lifts for getting the food from the kitchen to the restaurant. Even a secondary servery between kitchen and dining room should be avoided as it means having to employ staff to operate it and is not conducive to serving food in its best condition. Bars should be adjacent to the dining room so that drinks required by customers do not have to be brought any distance. It is obvious then from the above that a clear identification of the sequence of operation must be made before plans are actually drawn up. The physical layout must emanate from, and should reflect (i) the needs and demands of the customer, (ii) the policy of the firm, (iii) the menu and its range of products, and (iv) the organisation of the establishment.

The Needs and Demands of the Consumer

A clear identification of the consumer's requirements is vitally important for establishing (a) his socio-economic status, (b) his purpose for visiting the establishment, whether for business or pleasure, and (c) the changing nature of his needs at different times, such as a business lunch requiring an atmosphere which will help to retain mental alertness, or dinner where his expectations could be for a relaxed atmosphere.

It is clear then that environment and atmosphere are a part of the planning of facilities and that decor and layout must be flexible enough to cope with changing demands. Other factors are the number of customers expected to be accommodated and the time they can spend eating as this has to be reflected in the prices they can be charged. The higher the prices charged the better the facilities have to be; how the level of facilities is achieved is part of the organisation's policy.

The Policy of the Firm

This should indicate how the consumer's needs are to be met in terms of satisfaction and the expected return on investment and entrepreneurial risk. Thus the organisation will lay both guide-lines and a structured framework within which consumer needs are to be met, utilising the findings of a feasibility study to establish the parameters within which the whole operation takes place. These will include specific points that affect the planning of both the food production and the food service areas. Also within these parameters will be certain other guide-lines which influence planning, these are (a) the overall image of the organisation which is generally featured in external and internal decoration, (b) the expected number of customers as it affects requirements of space and interior layout and decor, (c) specific budgets for the various departments of the operation for purchase of equipment and furniture, and for small equipment on an annual basis, (d) staffing policy as it could refer to uniforms which would go well with the overall effect of the decor, and (e) the method of food service and presentation as this has a bearing on circulation space and equipment requirements.

The Menu and its Range of Products

This establishes the framework for the methods of production to be followed and from this the range of products and the techniques of service and presentation. The more traditional the operation and greater the space requirements are for both kitchen and dining room and the larger the amount of equipment required. Thus in taking the decision whether to offer a specialised à la Carte menu as against a standard Table d'Hôte one with plate service means that a decision is also being taking in terms of space and equipment requirements for all departments. It is obvious that the full à la Carte menu that is cooked to order requires silver service and possibly some Guéridon service.

So the menu should act as the centre point of the planning function rather than, as often happens, this being made in ignorance of the kind of menu envisaged. When an à la Carte menu is planned this has to be further evaluated as to the proportions of raw and convenience foods that will be purchased; this in turn will have a bearing on the number of staff needed to produce the menu.

The Organisation of the Establishment

The planning of a department is further influenced by the envisaged organisation of the whole operation and this naturally relates to the level of occupancy and hours of opening. The longer the opening hours and the greater the take up of the facility, the more flexible must be the planning so as to cope with fluctuations in demand; for example, most restaurants close immediately after lunch and stay empty until the evening, but there may be a limited demand for a full meal service through the afternoon that one establishment should be willing to cater for. Each establishment has an image of its own be it a snack bar or ethnic restaurant, and the service offered by each is associated with a control system which covers the purchase of materials to a pattern of standardisation that governs the storage space requirements. In a large-scale kitchen the head chef can supervise the work more effecitvely if it is open plan, rather than can his

92

counterpart in a conventional set-up where responsibility is more delegated to the chefs de partie.

These four factors then reflect the planning needs and are the main points that have to be taken into consideration when management compiles its brief for the other specialists on the planning team.

THE PLANNING TEAM

Planning the production and service areas of an establishment is a complex task. Its successful outcome is dependent on a coalition of skills capable of evaluating the overall plan from its inception to its completion in the form of its output performance. The specialists required are normally drawn from the following three areas: (i) the management team possibly comprised of either the general manager, food and beverage manager or catering manager, the head chef, and the restaurant manager or headwaiter; (ii) the architect with the interior designer; and (iii) the catering planning adviser who will be an expert on equipment requirements and workflow.

The role of the management team is to interpret for the others on the team their understanding of the catering function as it applies to consumer requirements and operational characteristics. They also need an understanding of the principles of planning so as to be able to intervene when misunderstanding of their objectives is apparent.

The information that comes from these joint discussions is the basis for the drawing up of the plan by the planning adviser.

THE SEQUENCE OF PLANNING

The decision as to where in the sequence of operations the whole undertaking starts moving is a matter for each individual establishment, the main thing being that those doing the planning be aware of the logical sequence of activities that constitute the operation of a catering department. They should view it from a perspective that shows how each activity interlocks into a single co-ordinated functional operation. This sequence is common to all types of catering businesses and flows in the following manner: (i) the receipt of goods from suppliers, (ii) the correct storage and control of goods; (iii) the issue of these goods to (iv) the preparation areas where a certain amount of processing is done before they proceed to (v) the production area which is the kitchen; (vi) the distribution of prepared dishes to the servery and dining rooms; and (vii) the washing up areas where restaurant and kitchen utensils are cleansed before going back to (viii) the stowing away or custodian areas where utensils are kept in readiness for further

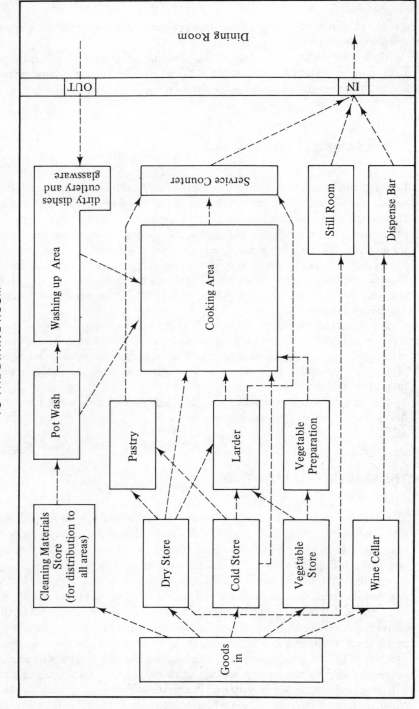

Figure 3

THE FUNCTIONAL FLOW OF GOODS FROM THE GOODS IN AREA
TO THE DINING ROOM

use. The final link in the sequence is (ix) the disposal area for rubbish and waste food.

Not all the numbered sequences have to be followed implicitly as they would not all apply to a fast food operation where most goods would be bought in prepared form on a daily basis. They certainly apply to a traditional operation where all preparation is done on site. Fig. 3 shows the functional flow of goods and work in such an establishment.

PLANNING METHODS

In planning an establishment it is often advisable to work backwards, starting not at the goods delivery bay but at the customer's entrance and the dining room. This is the first place the customer sees and as it is also the main revenue-producing department it is, therefore, the most important one. However, the planning of the dining room cannot be done in isolation from other areas, and the first essential is to know the total area available for the catering function and the approximate amount of space that is to be allocated to each component part of the whole including bars, kitchen, still room, stores and the other ancillary areas, in addition to the dining room.

The allocation of a total area allowed for a catering operation, which will be a part of a hotel or large business complex, can be worked out mathematically by reference to the expected type of business, volume of customers, hours of opening, and number of staff to be employed.

Where the operation is to be a self-contained, purpose built one and the total amount of space has been decided, or where a reorganisation of an existing operation is to be contained within its original boundaries, reference has to be made in the first instance to the expected or emerging type of business and its opening hours. This becomes the sole determinant of the volume of business and the number of staff needed to operate it. An explanation of these factors will show how important they are in the planning process.

1. The type of business can range from an individually owned, seasonal afternoon tea shop to a large hotel having many different eating and drinking outlets, several kitchens, banqueting facilities for perhaps several thousand guests and a catering staff running into many hundreds.

2. The volume and turnover of business is calculated on the number of seating places in the dining room, the average occupancy of them, the number of times each seat will be used during a meal period, and the total receipts from the sale of food and drink.

3. The hours of business when a dining room is open to customers show which meals will be served but staff will be on duty both before and after these times. This has a bearing on the number of staff required and whether they work split duties or alternate early and late shifts.

4. The number of staff employed has a bearing on the planning in so far as it affects the number required in a given department, as staff cannot work efficiently in a congested area. It also has an affect on the amount of space to be devoted to staff changing and amenity rooms. The specialist designer can provide the figures to be used in deciding the ratios of space by reference to publications of such bodies as government departments, the Gas Council, the Electricity Council, the British Standards Institute and equipment manufacturers' planning departments.

ALLOCATION OF SPACE

The following details show how space allocations can be made for a particular type of operation envisaged. These details show how they can provide a framework within which to start planning although it may ultimately require modifying when determining final allocations.

ALLOCATION OF SPACE FOR THE DINING ROOM

A dining room should be planned to accommodate the number of customers that can be catered for by the kitchen and vice versa, based on one to two sittings according to the type of clientele expected and the menu. The more the area can be filled with customers the more profitable will the operation be, provided that comfort and enjoyment are not sacrificed by so doing. Within a given area the manager must be able to draw plans showing various ways of furnishing it to seat various numbers, leaving sufficient circulatory space. Flexibility is sometimes an asset in that it allows the room to be used for different functions according to need. Capacity is determined by usage and it is sometimes desirable to be able to shut off some of the room if demand is slack.

Different styles or forms of service dictate optimum space allocation in dining rooms as shown in Fig. 4.

Figure 4
ALLOCATION OF SPACE FOR VARIOUS STYLES OF SERVICE

Style of Service	Allocation per Customer
Guéridon (individual service from trolley or table)	1.8 m^2
Silver (served from silver dishes to customer's plate)	1.5 m^2
Plate (ready plated for service)	1.2 m^2
Banquet, communal seating	1.0 m^2
Banquet, separate tables	1.5 m^2
Cafeteria (excluding service area)	0.8 m^2

With the exception of cafeteria service the allowances include space required for sideboards and, of course, all these figures cover circulatory space, though

96

gangways should be kept to the safe minimum to gain full use of space. The decision regarding what mixture of tables to use is one to be arrived at in the light of the customer's requirements, but a balance of tables for two, four and six is better than all two's; all tables for six will increase the capacity but may mean strangers sharing.

In the allocation of space for the dining room an allowance must be made for storage and holding areas for furniture and equipment in intermittent use, and for that held in reserve. Obviously this has to be in keeping with that of the seating capacity of the dining room.

Also related to the dining room are the dispense bar and cellar which supply the drink to be served. The dispense bar is the place where waiting staff order drinks for serving to customers in the lounge if there is no bar, and in the dining room. As such it need only be a functional area whether sited actually in the dining room or, as is more usual, behind the scenes but close to the dining room. It will carry all the stock as dictated by the tariff or wine list and the equipment necessary to keep stock in good condition for service. The counter and circulatory space need only be sufficient for the number of persons working there and for a reasonable number of serving staff on the other side of the counter.

The space allocated to the dispense bar could be part of that apportioned to the dining room and this would be determined by the type and volume of business done. As such it would be difficult to give an exact figure as a guideline for the amount of space required.

It is also not possible to provide exact figures for the allocation of space for the cellar. Whatever form the cellar may take the space allocation is governed by the extent of the wine list or bar-tariff, the size of the establishment, and the volume of business. Space is also governed by the policy as regards purchasing; for example, whether drink is held in bulk storage, whether wine is bottled on the premises, or if kegs or casks of beer are kept in stock. On the other hand, there could be frequent deliveries of easily obtainable supplies. The percentage of space allocated therefore can vary considerably and is more usually taken from the overall area devoted to the food and beverage operation, although quite often it can be part of the storage area.

By using the par system of stocking a bar from the cellar it is possible to ascertain fairly exactly what amount of stock will be carried and from it the amount of space required to store it in. The amount of stock never varies because at the end of each day all the empty bottles, kegs, etc. are returned to the cellar and a requisition is made up for each replacement item issued so as to bring the bar stock back to par, thus standardising the allocation of space.

ALLOCATION OF SPACE FOR CUSTOMER AMENITIES

A good class restaurant should offer facilities other than the room where meals are taken; an entrance hall and reception area, cloakrooms for men and women, a lounge bar, or other kind of bar, all assist in giving patrons a good impression of an establishment as soon as they arrive in it.

Reception and Bars

The reception area and/or lounge should be designed to accommodate customers wishing to have a drink before the meal and others who have not booked a table and will have to wait for one to become vacant. The furnishings and furniture need to be relaxing and comfortable and in keeping with the general decor of the dining room. A lounge bar may also act as a place of rendezvous for members of the public - whether or not they are taking a meal - who like this kind of atmosphere as compared with that of a public house. A lounge bar will provide comfortable seating arrangements around the room rather than concentrating it around the actual bar counter, and as it is not the sort of place where customers come to spend an evening the allocation could be as low as 2.5 m^2 per person, which would include the bar itself.

There are other kinds of bars such as cocktail bars in which there would probably be more contact with the bar-tender as he prepares the drinks, so that a long counter with stools and less comfortable seating around it would be appropriate. A public bar would obviously have a wider range of drinks than in a cocktail bar but its more functional nature means that an allowance of 1.5 m^2 per person is adequate.

Cloakrooms

Under Section 89 of the Public Health Act 1936 local authorities are empowered to require the provision of sanitary conveniences in such numbers as are considered necessary for persons using the premises. Licensing magistrates want to know if these needs are satisfied before they will grant a licence for the sale of liquor. The BSI issued a Code of Practice for the guidance of restaurateurs in satisfying these requirements.

Closets

Male   1 per 100 up to 400 persons.   400 and over – 1 per 250
Female 2 per 100 up to 200 persons.   200 and over – 1 per 100 or part.

Wash Basins

1 for 1 to 15 persons, 2 for 16–35, 3 for 36–65 and 4 for 66–100.
Persons – this applies to male and female toilets.

An allocation of 3 m^2 per water closet is necessary; a wash-hand-basin requires 1.5 m^2 and a urinal 1.3 m^2.

Cloakroom facilities for the use of customers require up to $0.08\,m^2$ per person where there is an attendant and $0.10\,m^2$ where customers hang up their own apparel.

ALLOCATION OF SPACE FOR THE KITCHEN AREAS

The overall space available for setting up a kitchen will vary greatly from one establishment to another and each must be planned individually. It has to be borne in mind when deciding on how much space to devote to the building of a kitchen that the revenue-producing departments of the establishment have first priority as regards available space. These are the dining room and, in a licensed restaurant, the bar; in the industrial sector they are the canteen with the vending machines or tea trolleys. The kitchen is not a revenue-producing area although obviously the dining room could not function without it. But it means that the allocation of space for this department must only be that necessary for it to carry out its function efficiently and safely.

There are no hard and fast rules about how large a kitchen should be to cater for a given number of meals. It is now accepted that it requires only about half the space of that assigned to the dining room. This rule of thumb measurement gives rise to the often quoted figure of approximately $0.5\,m^2$ of kitchen floor area for each chair in the dining room which gives a ratio of $1:2$, although this normally only applies to industrial situations where the figure of $1\,m^2$ of eating space per person is acceptable. In a conventional restaurant with waiter service the allowances are different and Fig. 5 shows how typical measurements for areas decrease in size as the scale of numbers increases. This cannot, of course, apply to the dining room where, obviously, a customer will still require the same amount of space whether the capacity is 100 or 600 and whether it is full up or not. The only variation to this is in an establishment that fills the seats more than once during a service period or during the hours of opening. Here the means of establishing the size of the dining room is by knowing or estimating the volume of business to expect at the peak periods of the day and to allocate space to cope with this. The rate of turnover, or length of time a customer is estimated to take to consume his meal, has a bearing as it is accepted that at busy times of the day a queue may form to get into the dining room, or customers are expected to go to the lounge bar until told their table is ready.

The most marked decreases in scale are seen in the storage areas and in the other departments of catering such as bar and lounge.

Figures for large-scale kitchen installations are given by various bodies such as the BSI who recommend in one of their Codes of Practice an allowance of $0.7\,m^2$ per 100 meals, $0.50\,m^2$ for 250, and $0.46\,m^2$ for a kitchen producing meals for 500 people; these allowances are per person thus the kitchen for 100 should be $70\,m^2$. Figures for school meals kitchens vary according to individual education authorities who suggest areas varying from $42\,m^2$ to $51\,m^2$ for 150 meals, and from $144\,m^2$ to $160\,m^2$ for 600 meals per day.

In arriving at any allocation of space it is necessary to know what the area actually includes; for example, one kitchen may have all its ancillary sections in close proximity to it, another will have its servery counter on a different level and away from the production area, while yet another may have large preparation areas sited as part of the stores.

Stores

In allocating space for the stores it is necessary to know the probable range of goods to be used, the rate of turnover of these, and the frequency of ordering fresh supplies. These factors apply mainly to non-perishables as the perishable commodities are usually ordered on a daily basis and require only overnight storage space. By measuring the packages of items in general use it is possible to arrive at the total amount of space required to house basic stocks and plan storage space accordingly.

Stillroom

A knowledge of the function of the stillroom and of the volume of business being done will provide information regarding the amount of space required for this department. The limited range of services offered by the stillroom shows the items of equipment that have to be housed, and work study will show where these should be sited so as to avoid any wasted space.

Platewash and Potwash

These two ancillary departments should not be very demanding of space since the range of activities taking place in them are fairly restricted, it being the anticipated volume of work and equipment holding areas that will dictate the size of each department.

The total number of staff likely to be working in these ancillary areas at any one time should be one of the factors taken into consideration when deciding on the allowances of space. Figures are given later in this chapter on the possible proportions of the total available area to be allocated to each, and on the area allowance for sample size establishments (see Fig. 5).

ALLOCATION OF SPACE FOR STAFF FACILITIES

By law certain facilities have to be provided for staff and as decided by various Acts of Parliament. The figures for male and female toilets are the same, being 1 closet per 15 employees, 2 for up to 30, and 5 closets where the number of staff is from 76 to 100 persons; separate facilities for males and females must be provided. According to the size of lockers supplied for staff to hang their outdoor clothes or uniform in, the amount of space required would vary from $0.08\,m^2$ to $0.12\,m^2$ per member of staff so that changing rooms would need to be large enough to hold all those arriving at the start of one of the shifts. The number of wash-hand-basins would be the same as for closets but only one shower per 50 staff need be installed.

A rest room should be provided where staff may relax when off duty for a short time, or between shifts. This may be supervised by the personnel department or by a social committee of members of staff, who will decide on the amenities needed. Apart from the furniture and fittings, pastimes in the form of a television set, video game, juke-box, newspapers and journals may be offered in the name of good staff amenities. The amount of space provided could be based on a minimum of $0.5\,m^2$ per person on the staff payroll. The staff dining room is an important part of this general area because in many cases meals are an emolument of the job. It is now more usual to provide a central dining room for all grades and kinds of staff where meals are served on cafeteria lines to coincide with meal breaks. There may be a separate staff kitchen with a cook in charge who comes under the control of the personnel manager, or if the amount of business warrants it a staff catering contractor would come in to run this amenity which is a charge on the payroll, not the kitchen percentage. The amount of room to allocate for this is approximately $0.75\,m^2$ per person taking this total area from the number of staff expected to attend at the peak period, or staggering mealtimes if space is at a premium. In addition there must be room for the service counter and storage space for food and equipment.

ALLOCATION OF SPACE FOR OFFICES

In large establishments the person in charge of the catering operation and also those persons in charge of the main departments require a room in which to carry out their organisation. Sometimes a clerk or secretary is necessary to do this work for the department or person which can be the head chef, the restaurant manager, the head cellarman or head storeman. Apart from these offices, which are an integral part of the practical areas of the food and beverage operation, there has also to be central offices where the work related to accounts, personnel and other business activities is carried out. The allocation of space for the departmental offices is usually accepted as being included in the total area assigned to these departments, whereas the business offices employing staff to carry out administrative activities must conform to government legislation as far as they relate to these.

In general these requirements are for a minimum of $3.7\ m^2$ per person engaged in the office; if the ceiling is lower than 3 m there must be 11 m^3 of room space per employee. These figures are taken as an aggregate having regard to the size of the room which is to be measured, but without regard to the space occupied by furniture, fittings and machinery. These obstructions have to be considered in relation to the amount of space left to move in.

The following tables show the average allocation of space between the sections of conventional catering establishments of various sizes operating a Table d'Hôte waitress or waiter service.

Figure 5
AVERAGE ALLOCATIONS OF SPACE

PRODUCTION AREA Number of seats	50	100	200	300	400	% of Total Production Area
Kitchen: including all preparation, cooking and food service areas.	25 m^2	40 m^2	50 m^2	65 m^2	80 m^2	50%
Ancillary Areas: Stillroom	6 m^2	10 m^2	14 m^2	16 m^2	18 m^2	12.5%
Pot wash	3 m^2	5 m^2	6 m^2	8 m^2	12 m^2	6.5%
Plate wash	6 m^2	10 m^2	15 m^2	16 m^2	20 m^2	13.5%
Goods Area: Goods receiving and storage.	10 m^2	10 m^2	16 m^2	25 m^2	30 m^2	17.5%
Total Production Area	50 m^2	75 m^2	100 m^2	130 m^2	160 m^2	
Area per meal produced	1 m^2	0.75 m^2	0.5 m^2	0.4 m^2	0.4 m^2	

DISTRIBUTION AREA Number of seats	50	100	200	300	400
Dining Room	80 m^2	150 m^2	260 m^2	350 m^2	440 m^2
Customer Amenities- reception, bars and lounge	20 m^2	25 m^2	45 m^2	70 m^2	80 m^2
Total Distribution Area	100 m^2	175 m^2	305 m^2	420 m^2	520 m^2
Area per meal served	2 m^2	1.75 m^2	1.5 m^2	1.4 m^2	1.3 m^2

STAFF FACILITIES					
Number of seats	50	100	200	300	400
Changing Rooms, Rest Room, Toilets and Dining Room.	14 m^2	22 m^2	36 m^2	47 m^2	60 m^2
% of total catering area	7.3	7	7	7	12

OTHER AREAS					
Offices	6 m^2	7 m^2	11 m^2	16 m^2	20 m^2
Customers' Cloak-rooms and Toilets.	20 m^2	27 m^2	50 m^2	62 m^2	80 m^2
Total	26 m^2	34 m^2	61 m^2	78 m^2	100 m^2

Total Area of Catering					
Department	190 m^2	306 m^2	502 m^2	675 m^2	840 m^2
Area Per Customer	3.8 m^2	3 m^2	2.5 m^2	2.25 m^2	2.1 m^2

PLANNING THE AREAS

Once the total area of the catering operation has been decided and space has been allocated to the various main departments and their supportive and ancillary areas, the next stage is to plan the way in which they will be furnished, fitted and equipped to meet the practicalities of production and service and at the same time meet the customer's needs and expectations as identified.

PLANNING THE DINING ROOM

The eating area or dining room is the place where the customer usually first comes into contact with the establishment, so it is important that the initial impact be one of harmony and aesthetic sympathy with the intended outcome. Basically what dictates the layout and the atmosphere resulting from it is the type of service offered in relation to the customer's needs. Taking two extremes as examples, that of a self-service cafeteria and a very conventional restaurant, in both it is important that the atmosphere is correct for each type of customer, since it will have an effect on his behaviour and colour his pleasure despite the fact that in the first he will be in and out quickly whereas in the other he will have longer to absorb his surroundings.

The atmosphere created in a dining room is an important part of its planning as customers often choose where to eat because of a congenial atmosphere that suits them, yet atmosphere is a very difficult thing to define. It could be attributed to a relaxed, intimate feeling equally as to a lively, noisy experience of hustle and bustle, but in fact the effect that the environment has on the senses is not consciously noted. Thus not only smell, hearing, looks, touch and taste but also temperature, pressure, balance and kinaesthetics play a part and these senses convey meanings to the brain where they are processed in the psychological activity of perception.

The feeling of atmosphere in a room is further moderated for the customer's physical and mental state by the ongoing activities within the area to which he is exposed on entering, and by his previous association with the restaurant. So it must be planned to provide an atmosphere which will attract the market segment as identified at the outset. To sum up, atmosphere comprises the following environmental aspects:

Visual – consisting of colour, form, texture, illumination, and the interaction of all these with the external environment;

Thermal – consisting of temperature, relative humidity, and air movement; and,

Auditory – consisting of acoustics, music, and other types of sound.

Atmosphere can be planned and it must be done to produce the particular result that will prove attractive to customers; it may be achieved by providing the premises with an identity that becomes familar to the clientele and gives them a feeling of belonging. This identity and the feeling of security that goes with it can be thrust home by reassuring a customer and his latent territorial instincts by means of breaks in any empty space including the use of walls and pillars, different floor elevations, seating arrangements, colour effect, and a sense of order.

Visual Environment

Colour   This is one of the most important factors in planning the atmosphere and it is a well-known fact that different colours elicit certain emotional responses from individuals, ascending in order from a state of relaxation in the cold spectrum of blues and greens to a state of excitement or even exhilaration in the warm range running from yellow to red, then returning to the state of relaxation as colours become more diffused in the deep reds leading towards brown. This topic is such a complex one that it merits study in its own right; it is also complicated by the fact that primary colours, as interpreted by an artist when painting a picture, are dissimilar from the psychological primaries obtained through mixtures of light. An artist's primary colours are red, yellow and blue, from them he creates secondary colours of green, orange and violet, and further intermediate colours. Colour can thus be used in many ways; light, warm colours with little contrast provide an atmosphere that will induce customers to move on quickly in a fast food restaurant. Deep, warm colours used in a bar in conjunction with diffused lighting can attract customers, put them at ease and induce them to stay and drink, leading to an increase in appetite. Deep, cold colours that are neutral and include some gold are suitable for a traditional restaurant. Warm colours can put emphasis on, and improve the appearance of food.

The use of colour can have the effect of making people look their best and certainly at a cocktail party deep colours on walls and diffused lighting do create a feeling of well-being in the customer, whereas a pale colour like green will make guests look pale and look and feel older than they are. Contrasts of colours allow fixed objects to be picked out and featured and the use of dark colours help to bring features closer while light colours give a feeling of distance and spaciousness. Care in the use of primary colours will avoid creating a feeling of restlessness and the overall harmony of a place can only be achieved by a careful blending of all the colours used, on walls, for carpets, furnishings, staff uniform, even the tableware and certainly the lighting.

Lighting As with colour, the lighting of a dining room plays a considerable part in creating atmosphere and if looked at from a marketing point of view it should appear inviting and tempting, causing customers to want to come in and once in to make them look their best. Natural light must be used, where available, to its full advantage so as to reduce costs and where only artificial lighting can be used the level must be adequate for safety, for ability to read the menu, and to create the desired atmosphere. The output of a lamp is measured in lumens and is used in conjunction with area to describe levels of illuminations as lumens per square metre (1 m/m^2, or lux); lux is the level of illumination over that area. Recommended lighting levels for various areas are: bar 150 lux, dining room 100 lux, cellar 150 lux, kitchen 500 lux which is about 30 watts per m^2 of floor area. To make a dining room look inviting and comfortable many combinations are possible, such as indirect lighting above dados and behind drapes, a chandelier projecting light onto the ceiling, wall lights, lamps on dining tables, spotlights to throw features into relief and rise-and-fall units. There is a difference between the lighting requirements for lunch, which should have some glitter or sparkle, and that for the evening meal where reduced levels are necessary; the change can be made by dimmer switches or by putting candles on tables to add further atmosphere. A third requirement is that of normal lighting to be used by waiters and cleaners when getting the room ready for use. Tungsten filament lamps give a bright appearance and add to the temperature of the room but need frequent replacement because of their shorter life as compared with other forms of lighting. Fluorescent lamps usually need to be integrated or concealed behind pelmets, cornices or suspended ceilings. Incandescent lamps give a warm effect and restful environment.

Emergency lighting to provide light when the normal lighting fails is obligatory under the 1971 Fire Precautions Act, though the standard of lighting specified varies between individual enforcing authorities. Customers must be able to leave the unfamiliar area of a restaurant quickly and without panic.

Thermal Environment

It is necessary to maintain a fairly even temperature in the restaurant all the year despite the weather outside and a constant 15°-18°C is generally acceptable except during a heatwave. Relative humidity should be 50-55 per cent and two to three air changes per hour prevent stuffiness, help to disperse odours and maintain comfortable conditions. Ventilation or air conditioning provide the answer and it is necessary to assess if normal ventilation is sufficient and seek the advice of an architect.

In a fast food restaurant the temperature can be kept at a slightly lower level than in a luxury restaurant because it can often result in a quicker turnover of seats.

Auditory Environment

Noise is a cause of stress and can make customers irritable, yet it does provide atmosphere in a restaurant if only caused by the sound of waiters serving and customers talking. A completely silent restaurant is not desirable so sound proofing need not be installed. But there should not be too much reverberation, no more than sufficient to prevent customers at adjacent tables overhearing what is said. Carpets and curtains are themselves sound absorbers and some kinds of ceilings act in this way. If background music on tape is featured it should be maintained at a constant level of 40-50 decibels at which it does not become too prominent a part of the environment. Live music by a group or a pianist playing during dinner time is more in keeping with a good class of place and is acceptable up to 60-70 decibels, always provided the music is chosen to suit the type of clientele. Waiting staff should be instructed to carry out their duties as quietly as possible and the noise of kitchen activities must not disturb even those customers nearest the service entrance.

The staff employed can also influence the environment. A fast food operation will prefer to employ young people who can serve at a rapid pace which gives a feeling of urgency and warmth that reacts on customers and makes them eat quickly and leave. In the traditional de luxe operation staff are taught to move at measured tread and never appear to be in a hurry or in any way hot and
106

flustered; even their dress matches their bearing which is usually cool, calm and collected.

To develop atmosphere to its fullest extent the three foregoing environmental aspects must be brought together and take form and shape in the structure, decor and furnishings of the dining room. This may best be done by an interior designer who may be given a brief to work from, which stems from the firm's policy as it concerns the theme or style, the type of customer, the menu, whether meals will be served in formal splendour or in an easy-going ambience, and the amount of money available to complete the project. A dining room should be a place for social contact and entertainment but with the focus on the table and the food; but if the decor is so dramatic that it causes gasps of surprise this is fine providing it does not continue to distract. All the decorations should be chosen to create a mood rather than to overwhelm the whole effect. This is not to say that everything must either match or contrast but the overall effect of the whole room should completely satisfy the customers who will frequent it.

There are many different kinds of dining rooms but in general they can all be separated into three categories. These are, (i) the conventional type of restaurant, (ii) the steak bar type using cafeteria methods, and (iii) the self-service type such as a refectory or canteen.

The Conventional Type of Dining Room

The location of this type is normally at ground level although if advantage can be taken of the outlook from the windows it may be on a higher floor, with access by lift. The entrance is usually via the reception area or through a lounge and bar. The shape of the room is often round or oval and with a part of it elevated. Very often the arrangement is towards a focal point which may be the dance floor in the centre, a buffet display, or an architectural feature, any of which in conjunction with the furnishings and fittings helps to create a particular atmosphere.

The space allocation has to allow for a mixture of sizes of tables to seat two, four or six persons, these being divided into stations of 16–20 chairs centred on a sideboard which will require a certain amount of circulatory space around it. A dining room which could seat 100 customers at 3 tables of six, 16 of four and 9 of two can be accommodated in a total area of 150–175 m² which will allow a central gangway and one at each side, of at least one metre width. If, however, more tables for two were required the seating capacity would be diminished because greater circulation space is needed. The decision as to the shape of tables to be used depends on the type of dining room. Round tables are more intimate than square ones; square tables can be placed against the wall thus saving space, but the answer is to have table tops that fit onto bases which can be altered as required thus giving flexibility of purpose.

The table will most likely be covered by a tablecloth which with cutlery,

107

crockery and glassware in keeping with the standard of service and type of operation, will give the correct effect. Table lamps or candelabra help to add atmosphere and floral arrangements using fresh flowers show that management is concerned that customers gain the best possible impression of the operation. The higher the prices charged the more luxurious must the environment be.

The Steak Bar Type of Dining Room

This is an extension of the traditional grillroom, one of its main features being that it is virtually self-contained. A counter is required for preparation and service behind which the staff work; this area requires up to 20 per cent of the total and will obviously require ventilation to prevent cooking smells reaching the customers. The theme of this type of dining room is often provided by the way it is divided into booths of fixed table and a number of chairs or forms which are made of solid and imitation wood in fairly sturdy form. The accoutrements of tableware are in keeping with the theme. Circulation space is minimal as no trolleys are used and waiting staff ratios are lower than in the more sophisticated type of room.

The Self-Service Type of Dining Room

This operation is designed to cater for the greatest possible number of customers in the most limited area of space and in the minimum amount of time. There can be a length of counter, or number of counters, arranged on the echelon system, necessary to serve the number of alternative dishes on the menu and this servery area must be given circulatory space where the queue can form without disrupting the flow of service. This area requires some 25 per cent of the total.

The counters should be self-contained so as to provide a customer's total meal and there will then be only a move to pay at the cash desk before entering the eating area.

Economic use of available space can be achieved by using standard size tables that seat six to eight people. Methods of clearing vary but circulatory space wide enough for a trolley is usually required.

Furniture may be utilitarian rather than comfortable and the decoration simple. Plain cutlery and crockery is the general rule and the floor covering must be hard-wearing. Nevertheless, this should not be an excuse for creating a dull, drab atmosphere.

Entrances and Exits

The entry to a dining room is better when it is via an entrance hall or lounge; if it is direct from the street some form of lobby is necessary to prevent any draught blowing in. The cloakrooms are best sited near the entrance.

Entry and exit from the kitchen service counter is usually by means of double doors that prevent any noise or smell reaching the dining room; negative air pressure from the air conditioning plant can be created so that the current of air flows from the room to the kitchen rather than the opposite way.

It must be borne in mind that disabled people will be using the dining room and that additional facilities are needed for them.

Fire exits must be indicated and be kept clear in case of an emergency.

Ancillary Areas of the Dining Room

The organisation of the dining room does not require many supportive service areas. As stated, the stillroom and wash up areas are usually regarded as being dependencies of the kitchen which leaves only linen and reserve stores to be accommodated.

Dining room linen may be collected daily from a main linen room or be kept in a dry, well ventilated room adjacent. Shelves or cupboards for clean and baskets for dirty linen are all that is required.

A store room for extra tables and chairs is necessary if flexible use is to be made of the dining room, for example, when holding a dance or cabaret it may be necessary to store the carpet or bring out a central parquet floor overlay. The vacuum cleaner and cleaning materials may be stored here plus the reserve stock of cutlery, crockery and glassware.

PLANNING OF CUSTOMER AMENITIES

Bars

As previously mentioned the size of a bar must be related to the extent of the bar tariff or wine list and the volume of business. The kind of drink being sold has some bearing on the planning; for example, if draught beer is on the tariff will the casks or kegs be stored in the cellar with lines connecting it to the pumps on the bar counter, or will it be keg beer, in which case space for these must be allowed in the bar itself. Another factor that has a bearing on the space allowance and planning depends on whether the washing up of glasses is done in the bar by an assistant barman, or whether they can be transported out through the back to the main wash up.

In deciding upon the position of the bar in the room it has to be rememberd that as well as presenting a good front to the customer, it is necessary to stock it from the cellar and possibly for the barman to leave it to take drinks to the table; these accesses must be suitably planned to avoid supplies having to be wheeled across the room.

The decor and the furnishings and fittings must be in keeping with the other service departments; it may be that the name given to the bar governs the theme of decoration, or that the name stems from the way the place is decorated. The lighting must be such as to add to the atmosphere already created by the decor; the heating and ventilation must keep the room at the right temperature whether it is full of customers or with only a few.

Music assists in creating an atmosphere and whether it is live or taped it must be suited to the kind of image that the bar is meant to present, which in turn is reflected by the class of customer who patronises the place.

Cloakrooms

As stated earlier in this chapter, a local authority has power to see that these facilities are adequately provided for. Unlike some continental countries, separate cloakrooms are required for female and male customers. Many customers judge an establishment by the quality of this facility as by the decor of the dining room. Whilst being purely functional in providing for guest's needs, there is a desire on their part for a certain ambience to make them feel good, rather like in a hairdressers. The best possible facilities kept in hygienic condition, consisting of water closets, urinals, wash basins, hot air hand dryers, as well as vending machines and wash and brush up facilities, together with discreet lighting that is good enough to enable ladies to re-do their make-up, and a perfumed atmosphere, will ensure that customers do not have cause to complain about this area.

In a small establishment hats and coats can be hung on hooks at the entrance or at points around the room; only on a rainy day is there likely to be any problem of custody. The large establishment will require a proper cloakroom, either manned or un-manned, probably adjacent to the entrance and to the toilet facilities. Security matters have to be given consideration.

PLANNING THE DISPENSE BAR AND CELLAR

These two are dealt with together because of their close association, the former being one of the selling points of the latter. This means they should be related in the sense that they are next to one another in the sequence of operations, and also that they should ideally be sited adjacently though not necessarily on the same floor, so that there is not too great a distance to carry goods from cellar to bar. If draught beer is sold and the casks are kept in the cellar, the supply line to the pumps must not be overlong. Location of both these departments is important as temperature in both is crucial; the cellar requires to be located in an area where the temperature stays roughly the same all year around, the ideal being from 10 °C to 12 °C. Then the red wines, especially those laid down to mature, will stay in good condition. Should one part of the cellar be slightly cooler, this or near the floor is where the white and rosé ought to be kept. It is not considered advisable to install heating or air cooling plant except where the existing cellar temperature is not suitable. The main thing is to avoid sudden changes of temperature as this can spoil the wine; it is not necessary to keep the cellar damp. Lighting should be dim so as not to cause any alteration in the colour of wines that remain in stock for any length of time.

To almost the same extent as in the cellar, there are restraints on location, temperature and facilities in the dispense bar. Here wines have to be kept at the condition in which they are to be served which means approximately 15 °C for red and 8 °C for white wines, but for less stock than is held in the cellar. It is important that all drink is served in prime condition which means proper storage and handling. Refrigeration is required here to ensure that serving temperature is always correct; a supply of ice for putting into drinks, and for ice buckets is essential. The question of where dirty glasses are to be washed has to be decided as this may mean the installation of a washing machine in the bar. The number of staff needed to man the bar has some bearing on the layout of storage areas. Security has to be considered so that entry from the outside is made difficult.

PLANNING THE STAFF FACILITIES

Several, possibly widely separated areas have to be considered here as the provisions for staff covers their changing rooms, toilets and showers for both female and male staff, the dining room, and a rest room. An establishment of any magnitude will require a separate staff entrance where they can clock on and off, and pass any security check considered necessary. The changing room should be fairly adjacent; this is a functional room equipped with lockers and benches, wash basins and mirrors and, of course, showers where these are not housed separately with the toilet facilities. A locker can take several forms according to the amount of space available and the number of staff who require one. They can be full length or half length or as hanging cages, each taking up a varying amount of space. Security, to deter petty pilfering, is very important. The staff dining room which may also have its own kitchen should be sited where all staff can have ready access to it. In a small establishment staff will collect their meal from the kitchen and take it to eat in what could also be the rest room. However, where there are a large number of employees a proper dining room with sufficient accommodation to seat all those expected at any one time, a serving counter and clearing area is necessary, and all these have to be provided for in addition to space where staff can relax in comfort whilst off duty.

111

OFFICES

These areas are at the heart of the operation. At one end of the scale it might be a room with a desk, a chair and a telephone from which the proprietor does all the work of running the establishment. At the other end, offices may be required to accommodate a number of staff dealing with such aspects as accountancy to produce the profit or loss account, to pay all accounts, to produce the day-to-day kitchen percentage figures, to do the stocktaking, to pay wages and deal with other matters of personnel, deal with customer complaints and many other matters. According to the number of staff required to cover all these, so the number of desks, chairs, filing cabinets, computer terminals, etc. can be decided.

This is solely a functional area, as are all back of the house departments and apart from providing sufficient space and amenable working conditions no special requirements are called for, except perhaps for an entrepreneur who takes a close interest in his business and will need a well-furnished office of his own.

PLANNING THE KITCHEN

Planning a kitchen from scratch is a daunting task that demands hours of concentrated effort just to get the work flow right. Then it entails visiting similar places to look at the good and bad points of their kitchens and discussions with the users about the problems they have encountered. It will be necessary to look at equipment in action and ask if it really meets all demands and is still working well after several years. It is worthwhile paying a visit to a catering exhibition if several manufacturers have stands there, so that comparisons between items can be made. The kitchen still has to be modern ten years after building so there must not be any white elephants amongst the chosen pieces of equipment; any item that gets less use than one hour a day can sometimes be regarded as being in this cateogry. It is no use leaving the planning to the architect on his own, far better to have a team of the people who will be closely connected with its operation to sit with the architect and catering planning specialist. The Electricity and Gas Boards offer a free planning service as do many equipment manufacturers, in the hope that the work done will result in a contract for them. The Boards recognise that the success or failure of a kitchen is decided at the planning stage and use a standard planning questionnaire form to obtain the necessary information as follows: type of installation, capacity, menu, food, building to include dimensions and obstructions, drainage, services, staff facilities, and so on.

But first management must determine the exact requirements of the operation as they alone know, (a) what kind of product the projected consumer will want, (b) the level of demand, (c) the pricing policy, (d) the method of presentation and service, (e) the customer's probable time limit, and (f) the need to respond to his demands within a specific time.

The location is of importance as ideally the kitchen should be sited on the north-east side of the building because there the walls will be cooler and natural light is an asset to work under. The unloading bay and stores area must be adjacent to the kitchen preparation areas.

As previously stated, the dining room should be next to the kitchen and as a separate department it should be divided from the dining room by two doors with a small lobby between them to act as a noise trap. In and out doors are necessary to prevent serving staff knocking into one another which means a one-way system must be instituted with doors that open only in the direction of traffic. Doors should be easy to open by a touch of the foot or shoulder, or they should operate automatically.

Once the location has been settled then the area or space to be provided must be decided. Space can be very expensive and must be used carefully to cover immediate and possible future needs, but without wasting any of it. Various guide-lines exist on ideal allowances, as previously given, but they are only approximations and the exact size, any more than the ideal kitchen, is seldom attained.

Any changes such as those brought about by the introduction of a new menu, different production procedures and purchasing arrangements can all have an effect upon space utilisation in the kitchen by bringing different equipment into use or altering the methods of service. Figures are available that demonstrate how requirements of different methods of service affect the area required. A full à la Carte kitchen service would require $0.9\,m^2$ of space per customer as against the average of approximately $0.5\,m^2$ for the conventional forms of service.

As a guide to the division of the available space the following figures are given: goods receiving area 5 per cent, stores 10 per cent, stillroom 8 per cent, washing up areas 10 per cent, staff facilities 5-6 per cent, and the kitchen proper 64-65 per cent. A breakdown of the kitchen area into the various sections will ensure that each one has the space and equipment it requires to fulfill its contribution to the menu. The number of sections varies between different establishments as does the extent of the menu; for example, a high-class kitchen may find it desirable to employ a full brigade of chefs divided into the traditional seven sections because of the extent of its menu. Another kind of kitchen can run on a smaller number of parties because the menu is not so extensive or the dishes not so recherché.

This part of the planning operation can be determined by looking at the tasks undertaken by each section, and doing this by an analysis of the menu and dishes to show (i) the ingredients and methods of each menu item, (ii) that each stage of production is a necessary part of the whole, (iii) the equipment required to carry out the task, and (iv) whether any changes or reductions to the tasks could be introduced that would improve efficiency whilst maintaining quality.

As an example of this need to analyse established practices, the following shows how fried chip potatoes are prepared from the raw potato – (i) storage, (ii) peeling, (iii) washing, (iv) cutting up, (v) blanching, (vi) holding, (vii) frying to order. If ready-peeled potatoes are purchased the first three stages are omitted; if ready-cut raw chips are purchased the first four stages are omitted; and if frozen chips are used only the last two stages are performed, but a deep freeze cabinet will have to be bought.

In the preparation of Vols-au-vent of Chicken the complete cycle using rough-plucked hens, unsalted butter and strong flour can be followed, or convenience Vol-au-vent and instant Chicken Suprême can be put together more quickly. It is in this light that each menu item must be analysed to determine what is intended, and to equip and staff to that end.

Having determined the equipment required to operate the kitchen it then becomes necessary to decide the optimum capacity or size required for each in terms of output. Using rolled sirloin of beef for 200 persons, the calculations for determining the size of oven needed for this amount can be arrived at as in the following example.

Define the raw weight to give a 90 g cooked portion	120g
Convert the raw portion size into total raw weight i.e. 200×120 g	= 24 kg
Convert the total raw weight into cubic capacity if 4 kg = 0.027 m^3 this gives $24 \div 4 \times 0.027$ m^3	= 0.162 m^3
Plus an allowance for air circulation (approx. 50%) which give a total minimum capacity needed for the oven of	0.243 m^3

Having arrived at the ideal capacity of the piece of equipment it may be thought that it is now only necessary to find the ideal location for it, but before that consideration must be given to aspects of work flow.

Sequencing

By examining the way that the various items pass through different stages of manufacture it is possible to plot the ideal work flow, which then helps to decide where each piece of equipment should be sited within a specified sequence. There may be a number of separate sequences but each must have a clearly defined work flow without them criss-crossing each other.

When the sequences have been defined on the plan the grouping of activities must be done by determining the number of central preparation and processing points that exist. For example, if the larder carries out most of the functions normally associated with this section and supplies all the parties with their requirements of raw food, then the grouping would be under larder – in this way all the kitchen's activities can be sectionalised and numbered, as in Fig. 6.

Grouping and itemising of activities ensure a logical sequence of events in a proper progression and prevents crossing over against the flow which can be time wasting. It shows the equipment groups to be formed and obviates the need for

114

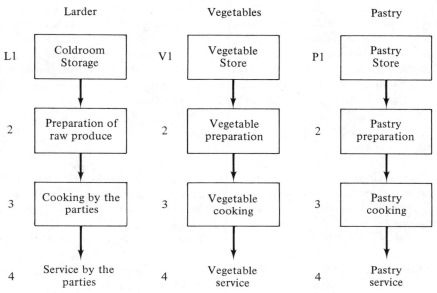

Figure 6
GROUPING OF ACTIVITIES

Larder	Vegetables	Pastry
L1 — Coldroom Storage	V1 — Vegetable Store	P1 — Pastry Store
2 — Preparation of raw produce	2 — Vegetable preparation	2 — Pastry preparation
3 — Cooking by the parties	3 — Vegetable cooking	3 — Pastry cooking
4 — Service by the parties	4 — Vegetable service	4 — Pastry service

much unnecessary fetching and carrying. Ancillary services of pot wash and small equipment shelves can be combined with the groups that use them.

Working space

The necessary amount of working space for each section must be assessed to take account of such aspects as the requirements under the Factories Act 1962 rev. 1970, as for example, the gangway space of at least one metre wide, doors to stores, cupboards, etc. which can be opened without causing obstruction. Having chosen the equipment the next thing is to put it into its allocated place according to the following guide-lines.

1. Place it at the most accessible point for the person who will be using it, not where the service supply point happens to be which is often on the wall.
2. Ensure it is made accessible for every person who will be using it; planners used to keep dry cooking equipment separate from wet because they need then run only one service supply to each area, usually gas only to one side and electricity and water to the other. This is no longer restricted and fryers can be sited next to steamers.
3. Site it in such a way that it is easy to get at to clean, maintain and repair. Perusal of the legal requirements contained in the Factories Act and Office Shop and Railway Premises Act 1963, as applicable to kitchens is necessary

in order to comply with them and with those of the Health and Safety at Work Act 1974.

It would be useful to make a study of the principles of ergonomics to ensure that working conditions do not cause unnecessary effort on the part of staff.

The information on each section having been gathered it is now possible to draw a plan to scale of say 10 mm per 1 metre starting at the stores and putting in all the necessary equipment, then going through the sequence of operations to finish with a plan in simplified form like Fig. 3.

Kitchen Fittings

The environmental health officer will have a big say in the internal decorations of any kitchens and can demand the correct hygienic wall and floor finishes, recommend the positioning of equipment so that it can be cleaned behind, and the closing in of shelves and the choice of working surfaces.

The floor must be non-slip and with a gentle slope of 1 in 100 towards a drain to facilitate cleaning; quarry tiles suit this requirement though when wet can be slightly slippery, but they do not stain and can support heavy equipment. Concrete floors are suitable for stores ares. The walls too must be easy to clean and should reflect the light thus assisting with the level of illumination. Glazed tiles to a height of $1\frac{1}{2}$-2 metres and white enamel paint above is the most suitable and the wall should be rounded where it meets the floor.

Noise is a source of distress and as a kitchen tends to be a noisy area there must be some means of acoustic absorbtion, preferably in ceilings which should be of porous absorbent material which will also help to prevent condensation. Needless to say the ceiling should be fire-resistant and washable. The height of the ceiling should be not less than four metres so as to accommodate extraction ducts and give good facilities for lighting and air circulation. Natural light is conducive to a high state of alertness and windows assist with this and in maintaining air changes and preventing condensation; but they must be covered to keep out insects by using fine wire gauze which must be kept clean.

Kitchen lighting

The importance of natural lighting lies in being able to see exactly how prepared dishes look; when a kitchen is operating over a long period each day the type and level of illumination provided by artificial light must be as good as the natural light, so that it is still easy to examine that finished dishes are correct in their appearance. The best type of artificial light is fluorescent lamps and the warmer tones of the better colour-rendering type are most suitable and give equal emphasis to all colours, whereas some lamps make green seem yellow. Open fittings with plastic reflectors provide the simplest installation that is effective and allows some light to the upper part of the room; they are easy to

116

take down and clean. The enclosed diffusing type is safer and gives a better appearance but must be properly sealed or it will become clogged with greasy dirt. It is possible to have recessed fittings, designed with supply air ducts in a false ceiling which incorporates the function of lighting and ventilation in one unit.

About 30 watts of lighting per m^2 of floor area is recommended using fluorescent lamps and for filament lamp lighting an allowance of 80 W/m^2 is necessary, so it can be seen that fluorescent lamps give from three to six times as much light for the same consumption of electricity, and their life is at least six times as long as filament lamps.

Light fittings under canopies must be able to withstand the steamy atmosphere and bulkhead type filament light fittings that are sealed with gaskets and are non-rusting provide the answer. High gloss finished surfaces that reflect the light can cause glare which can injure vision, cause fatigue and so contribute to accidents.

It is important that the lighting in the kitchen and dining room is of the same colour otherwise dishes that look all right in the kitchen will not appear so appetising in the dining room, or vice versa.

Heating and Ventilation

A constant temperature of 16 °C should be aimed at for efficient and congenial working conditions even though when working over the stoves it will be hotter. Cooling can be attained by continuous air changes at a frequency of two minute intervals and the correct relative humidity level for maximum confortable conditions will also help to reduce condensation; a system to supply sufficient air changes is important and the Health and Safety at Work Act 1974 insist on proper working conditions. The following methods are also used – one involves balancing the air velocity of the extraction system over the main cooking equipment, the other is to allow a specific volume of air extraction over each item of equipment. To prevent cooking odours from getting into the restaurant a negative air pressure must be maintained in the kitchen, meaning that air must flow in to replace the air vacuum in the kitchen from the restaurant.

Canopies and air ducts are frequent causes of fires and must be cleaned regularly; grease on the filters will clog and lower their efficiency so they must be taken down to wash. As not all contaminants are removed by air filters the outlets to the system must be approved by the environmental health officer.

DETAILED PLANNING OF THE KITCHEN AREAS

As explained in the section on the sequence of planning there are nine main activities which make up the production cycle. These cover the chronological

117

sequence of events from goods received to washing up and putting away, but each of these events may have to be subdivided into separate specialised functions according to the stage and state of preparation of the type of goods going through the system. For example, using fresh vegetables involves peeling and washing whereas frozen vegetables require only deep freeze storage; the components of other similar policy decisions on production must be assessed. It is of interest to follow the various routes taken by basic ingredients such as flour, onions or carrots, as they have a bearing on means of production. It might be equally rewarding to chart the route taken by supplies for the bar even although there is little processing to be done to these items on the way through to the customer. What this investigation might do is to see that each area where goods stop at on the production line has the right equipment and amount of room to do the job properly rather than one having too much at the expense of another. It can start at the point where the work flow begins as follows.

1. Goods Receiving Area

The size of this area does, of course, depend largely on the type of operation it is serving, the nature of goods being handled, the volume and frequency of deliveries, and the distance to storage and preparation areas. A secure area of storage of returnable containers and empties is necessary. The width of doors and corridors in this area is important.

It the size of the establishment warranted a separate staff entrance it would be here and this would mean having to appoint someone for the duties of time-keeper responsible for security of entry and exit of staff and goods.

2. Storage Area

The amount of space to be allocated to this area is based on the same set of operational factors as the goods received area together with those of stock levels, and budgeting allowance. If an establishment turns to the purchase of ready prepared goods this has an effect upon the storage area and stores requirements, more particularly in the sections for vegetables, meat, fish, and probably sweets. Prepared joints and portion control cuts of meat require much less storage space than carcasses; no allocations of preparations space is necessary, and there will be no need to pay a weekly wage for a member of staff to do the butchery.

The atmosphere of the dry store must be one that keeps goods in excellent condition and steps must be taken to keep it at approximately 50 per cent humidity and a temperature between 15–18 °C. Water pipes that run through the stores area must be lagged and the floor be made non-porous.

118

The Vegetable Store It is really only root vegetables that need storage space as the policy should be to have all green vegetables delivered fresh daily, and if they cannot be had early enough for use that same day then to hold them for not more than twenty-four hours. It pays to examine sacks of root vegetables on delivery to see that they are of good quality as it may be several days before they are actually used, by which time it is too late to send them back as unsound. Onions that have had a long sea voyage may have started to deteriorate and carrots and turnips of even Class 1 quality do not stay firm for long. Green vegetables may be packed in green coloured nets that give an impression of freshness which can be deceiving; it is foolish to spoil quality because of overlong storage.

Salad vegetables quickly lose crispness in store, so although the storeman may want to get in a week's supply at once because it cuts down his workload; this must be resisted.

Cold Storage Few establishments have sufficient refrigerated space and there seems to be a Parkinsonian law that the more an establishment has, the more refrigerators it needs. General coldrooms have their uses but are very costly because of being built on site to fit a particular area. Ready-made, free-standing refrigerators are more flexible especially if they have removable shelves so that carcass meat may be hung. They can be sited at any given point so that each partie can have its own units exactly suited to their particular use. Some are self-defrosting and require hardly any maintenance. Storage of all sorts of commodities including cooked and raw meat, fish, cheese, etc. in the same coldroom is not acceptable and is asking for trouble. These various commodities should ideally be kept at their appropriate temperature; fresh meat at $7\,^{\circ}$C, poultry at $4\,^{\circ}$C and fresh fish at $0\,^{\circ}$C.

Deep Freeze Storage There are many establishments that make the proud boast that no frozen foods are ever served to their customers; there are others that serve gourmet meals nearly all of which are purchased deep frozen, but they do not tell their customers who usually stay none the wiser. There are those, not necessarily in the welfare sector, that serve only frozen foods and are proud of it whether it is produced by themselves or bought in.

Frozen foods are normally very compact and do not take up much space and it is possible to pack 607 kg into a cubic metre, so a full frozen food operation that caters for 500 main courses each day and holding a week's supply will need freezer capacity as follows – the main meal will weight 250 g and a week's supply will be $500 \times 7 \times 250\,g = 875\,kg$ and $875 \div 607 = 1.44\,m^3$. If the meals are supplied in multi-portion packs it is necessary to add on 40 per cent for packaging and if entirely in individual portion packs 60 per cent giving total requirements of $2.0\,m^3$ and $2.3\,m^3$ respectively. In addition there will be a need for shelf space and as this is hardly likely to be filled 100 per cent, an additional allowance of 40 per cent must be made thus giving a total of $3.22\,m^3$ for individual packs. Expressed in terms of measurement it is necessary to provide a freezer that is approximately $1\frac{1}{2}$ m wide × $1\frac{1}{2}$ m deep × $1\frac{1}{2}$ m high. It is usual to allow space for additional stocks to cover such eventualities as late delivery or additional customers.

3. *Issuing Area*

This is the point where goods are weighed up for issue to departments and checked against the relevant requisition notes. Obviously it should be part of the main stores, set aside but large enough and fully equipped to handle all eventualities.

4. *Preparation Areas*

Traditionally there have always been separate areas for the different forms of preparation carried out in a kitchen with specialist staff in each. The EEC regulations go further than this and state that meat, poultry and fish must each be handled separately. This goes against a move by some planners to cut down on preparation space by having it all done together, an idea that has much to recommend itself especially for prime-location establishments.

Vegetable Preparation Area Unless a policy decision is taken and adhered to, and notified to staff, a lot of unnecessary expenditure can be incurred in the planning and equipping of this room. The planning expert and equipment supplier will probably include space for an electrically operated chip machine, a vegetable cutting machine, a mixer and peeler, none of which may be necessary if the decision is taken to purchase ready prepared vegetables; the consequence is that these machines lie idle to collect dust and dirt. If salads are prepared in the vegetable preparation area the purchase of a lettuce washing and draining machine may be considered but it would have to be a very large output to justify going to this expense. It may be necessary to have a salad refrigerator that has containers for the compound salads which are made in bulk.

The Larder This is the place where most of the preparation of raw foods in readiness for cooking by kitchen parties is done. In addition it does all the cold buffet work, makes sandwiches and canapés, prepares the hors-d'oeuvre and salads and sometimes the fruit, and it produces every savoury item on the menu that is served cold. Its importance is that it is a focal point of kitchen activity as it plays a part in so many of the sections. Although separate from other parties much of the efficient operation of the entire kitchen depends on a well run larder department.

The size of a larder depends on the establishment's menu but it is usually furnished with machines that include a mixer, slicer, bowl chopper, blender or liquidiser, as well as refrigerators for each of the items it prepares. It should be remembered that the larder supplies many items to order directly to waiters

120

so there must be either access to it from the dining room, or to the cold part of the service counter.

The question of waste disposal arises in the larder and vegetable areas and a decision has to be taken on the question of swill and whether to have it collected by a pig farmer or disposed of through a waste-disposal unit. The installation of a waste unit is sometimes a temptation to dispose of reusable commodities, and serviceable by-products or foods that have been badly made or burnt, since it can cover all traces.

The Pastry The size, indeed the very presence of the pastry department is a question that exercises the minds of many head chefs. The problem lies in the very specialist nature of pastry work and the difficulty of recruiting good crafts-men to do it. Whereas it is possible to move cooks from one partie to another in the main kitchen when one of them is short staffed, this cannot be done in the pastry with the result that many head chefs no longer have a pastry partie but buy in everything required and employ unskilled staff to serve it. If the head chef does not want to close his pastry section he may permit the purchase of ready-made pastry, cooked genoise, ice cream and so on to cut down on some of the basic work, using a few skilled staff to do the finishing touches.

All these factors have a bearing not only on the number of staff to be employed but also on the kind of machinery and equipment required and the area necessary to house it, without having any wasted space. The traditional pastry required its own very specialised equipment that no one else uses, such as rolling machines, dividers, enrobers, provers, steam injection ovens as well as high-speed mixers, boiling pans, steamers, stoves and refrigerators. When siting the pastry it must be remembered that it is traditionally a self-contained unit that carries out its own service direct to the serving staff and not usually through the kitchen service counter. Some establishments send a trolley of cold sweets into the restaurant which together with a selection of ice cream constitutes the sweet course.

5. *The Main Kitchen*

This is the central cooking area where the equipment for all the parties is located and where the staff actually cook. There are various ways of planning this section but it is not the most complicated part to install because it is at the end of the production line with only one further step to be taken in distributing the finished foods to the customer. Once a decision as to the number of parties to be operated has been taken, then it is known how many staff will be engaged in working in this area, and what pieces of equipment they require. It is a straightforward matter to link this area with its supply lines and its ancillary departments of pot and plate wash rooms to the service counter.

By putting all of the required equipment in one central area under a canopy and linking to services of electricity, gas and hot and cold water supplies there is a saving in space as well as in maintenance costs. Some kitchen designers favour putting cooking equipment against walls because it is easy to connect it to the various services; others like an I, L, T or E-shaped layout, but the view of most professionals is that the island site is best as the work benches can be directly in line with the equipment and there is less walking about to do.

There is no reason why kitchen floors should be constantly wet and slippery if there is a gulley against such wet cooking equipment as boilers and steamers. It is up to staff to exercise care in using these items to see they do not flood over.

Some items of equipment are for everyone's use. For example, all parties use a salamander but there is no call for installing several when one will do, provided a central point is found for it. Other equipment that is in general use includes the mixer, steamer, bratt pan, boiling pans and large ovens but each partie will require a stove or stoves for its own particular work.

6. *The Service Area*

The food service area varies considerably according to the type of establishment; some places use the indirect method of service which is where a server takes food to the customer at his table, and others use the direct method where the customer collects the food himself from a cafeteria counter.

The indirect method requires a solid top hot service counter with racks above it for silver dish lids and doors both sides of the hot cupboard for ease of access. The length must be such that the expected number of waiting staff can get to it to pick up their orders; approximately 50 cm of counter run per waiter is the suggested figure to work on. Calculating for a restaurant that seats 200 persons at one sitting and assuming that all the customers arrive together, that each course is served within one minute of asking for it in the kitchen, and that each customer is served one course in the space of thirty minutes, then the commis will call at the counter every six minutes, i.e. five times in every half hour. This means that there will always be four waiters collecting food at any one time, so the ideal length of hotplate should be two metres; if the waiting time at the hot-plate increased to two minutes then the length of hotplate would have to be doubled to four metres. This is for the hot section only; sometimes there is a length of unheated hotplate for cold dishes from the larder and pastry where there is no service direct from these departments.

Cafeteria counters and help-yourself hotplates often have to double as display counters to show customers what is on offer as well as being the source of service of the actual food. It is necessary to keep both the display and the bulk food in the best possible condition during service. The arrangement for these counters varies with the nature of the operation and the actual meal being served, where food is displayed on plates there is the need for infra-red lamps to make it look attractive and keep it hot.

A conventional long counter that customers have to follow to its end, because they cannot bypass any items they do not require, can serve from eight to ten persons per minute. This is restricting when perhaps 300 people all arrive for their meal break together and it takes half an hour to get them all served. The echelon system of short counters set at a slight angle within the same area, with each counter serving a different meal, cuts the length of queues considerably because customers can go to the chosen counter to collect that meal then to a central cash till, perhaps collecting ancillary items such as beverages from a general snack counter or vending machine. This free-flow system cuts the waiting time according to the number of echelons, so if there were five serving the same 300 people the waiting time should be only two minutes – provided all counters were equally popular. This is an isolated example of the way that planning works and illustrates the need for keeping up to date with new ideas in planning strategy and the equipment that is associated with it.

The Stillroom The stillroom can be considered as a division of the distribution area for the service of hot and cold beverages and toasted goods. In some establishments it may serve breakfasts and afternoon teas, fruit baskets and cheese boards. The main requirement is for a service counter to pass over the goods ordered, the equipment to be at hand to produce the required beverages and foods, and the serving utensils such as cups, saucers, jugs at the service point. This means that the circulatory space be kept minimal.

7. The Pot Wash

To achieve good results chefs require a supply of clean pans, whether fixed items for large-scale work or small ones for stove work. A good kitchen porter or pot-man can be an asset in this respect and his work is essential to the efficient operation of the kitchen.

With the advent of modern machinery this section is no longer a wet and dirty place to work, a pot washing machine takes all the drudgery and dirtiness out of the job and allows the operator to keep dry and clean. The normal model takes pots, preferably of the same height, and subjects them to high-powered jets of hot water that dislodge burnt-on food then rinses and sterilises on a five-minute cycle. Alternatively an electrically operated pot scrubber can make manual pot washing light work. It is safe and simple to work and has a variety of brushes for different uses which can be attached to the end of a rotating flexible hose. It can be mounted on the wall by the sink and has sufficient length to reach across the washing area and inside the largest size stock pot. The heads are of nylon or stainless steel bristles, as well as flat discs for polishing. This item of equipment can also be useful in the plateroom for cleaning the inside of coffee and teapots; it can also be fitted to a mobile sink to be taken around to other sites and as a trolley-mounted item to clean out fixed equipment such as bratt pans and boiling pans. It is also used for getting rid of carbon deposits on stove tops and griddle plates. Cleaned pots should be returned to racks adjacent to the cooking area, or even over the stove so that chefs have a constant supply of them to hand.

123

Dish-Washing Area The obvious location for this section of the operation is where the dirty dishes come from which is just outside the restaurant. It has to return the cleaned dishes to the points of service. The arrangement is to sort the various items and put like with like, to get rid of plate waste, soak soiled equipment, put it through the dish-washing machine and back into circulation hygienically clean and as quickly as possible. The size of the receiving area for dirty dishes must be able to cope with everything delivered to it whether it be from one waiter at a time, a trolley load from the restaurant, or the dirties from one course of a banquet for 500 persons. The layout should centre around this receiving point and the actual dish-washer; the policy decision is what equipment goes through the area. The same machine will clean crockery, cutlery, silver flatware, earthenware dishes, hollow ware and glassware, all one after the other, delivering them sparkling clean, dry, sterile, and smear-free. Yet the silver room is often divided from the plateroom, each having its own staff, machinery and space; moreover glassware is often dealt with by the dispense bar staff.

It should be remembered that these areas can be wet and often the staff have to work in a humid atmosphere. By installing a heat exchange system in the dish-washer much of the heat loss in the form of steam can be avoided and staff given a better working environment.

Other equipment that can be accommodated here are spring-loaded crockery dispensers – heated and unheated, a waste disposal unit, and trolleys for transporting clean equipment to the several service points. In general the equipment dealt with has to make a U turn to get back to its source of supply but this should not mean crossing over or getting dirty and clean mixed together.

8. Equipment Storage Areas

This is for items of equipment that have been used then washed up and put away in accordance with a routine. This way each item is returned to its correct place and stowed tidily so that when required it will be found in its customary abode.

A reserve equipment store from which replacements are issued for worn out or broken items should be kept; it will also house specialised items that are used only rarely and very expensive items that could get lost if not locked up after use.

9. Waste Disposal Area

There must be an area, preferably outside the premises, for the storage of waste bins. It has to be paved and drained so that it can be hosed down. The approval of the local authority is required for the type of refuse storage to be used and access has to be provided for vehicles to collect waste matter. It is usual to pay the local authority a rental charge for the number of special bins (Paladins) required according to the frequency of cleaning.

Only an approved swill collector may remove food debris for pig feed and he has to be a local farmer. If it is decided to dispose of food debris through a disposal unit to the public sewer the permission of the local authority has to be sought.

For use inside premises, plastic sacks in holders should be allocated to areas and when filled, sealed and put in the paladin. Cardboard should be folded flat for collection by a salvage firm or local authority for recycling.

In this area there may be a need for a compacting machine to reduce the bulk of refuse into more manageable size, either into waste sacks or if cardboard and paper, into blocks. This machine is useful to large-scale caterers who use a lot of A10 tins as it will crush them flat. A bottle crusher will break up non-returnable bottles so they take up less room. Care of returnable containers on which a deposit is charged means that someone has to be detailed to keep them under control and to maintain this area in good order and in a satisfactory state of hygiene.

7 CONVERGENCE OF FACILITIES II — EQUIPMENT, FUELS AND SERVICES

General Introduction – Needs Analysis – Cost and Budget Influences – Construction and Manufacture – Performance and Usefulness – Ordering of the Equipment – Kitchen Equipment – Heavy Duty Equipment – Kitchen Machinery – Stillroom Equipment – Holding and Service Equipment – Refrigeration – Small Kitchen Equipment – Modular Equipment – Care and Maintenance of Kitchen Equipment – Furnishings and Equipment for the Dining Room – Furniture – Equipment – Crockery – Glassware – Cutlery – Serving Dishes – Linen – Floor Coverings – Equipment for Bars and Customer Amenity Areas – Equipping of Other Areas – Fuels – Types of Fuel – Control and Economy of Fuels – Fuel Costs – Services.

When setting up a new catering operation a large part of the initial outlay will be spent on equipment which includes both fixed and mobile items, kitchen machines, small items such as crockery, glassware, cutlery and cooking utensils, as well as linen, furniture and furnishings. It must also be remembered that in addition to the capital outlay there needs to be an annual allowance for the purchase of new additional items and a further sum for maintenance contracts to keep the production equipment and machinery in running order.

Before buying any heavy duty equipment for the kitchen it is first of all necessary to decide which fuel is going to be used, and for the dining room it is important to have decided the policy as regards style of service, atmosphere and the amount of space being made available for the number of customers.

The total budget available has first to be divided amongst the main departments and although it is obvious that the kitchen with all its necessary equipment will cost more to equip than the dining room, this must not be at the expense of the latter. In fact the dining room and public areas should have priority in the matter of funds.

To a certain extent this advice would apply to the other reasons for putting new capital into a catering operation. The first is where it becomes necessary to replace several major items of equipment because they have all come to the end of their useful life or are outdated at about the same time, and the second where an emerging demand means major alterations to an existing operation involving structural changes, re-siting of equipment and redecoration – all in accordance with a new policy.

This chapter then will deal with the three closely related subjects of equipment, fuels and services in the sequence of (i) kitchen equipment, (ii) dining room furnishings and equipment, (iii) equipment for the bars and customer amenity areas, (iv) equipment for stores and other areas, (v) fuels, and (vi) services. It deals with these topics in a descriptive fashion in order to provide a fairly close acquaintanceship with most of the items and facilities available. But first it is necessary to look at the factors connected with selection and purchase.

NEEDS ANALYSIS

An analysis of each item of equipment should be carried out in order to ascertain if its purchase can be justified. This has to be done in relation to the menu and the service by following the movement of items of food through the various stages from their delivery to final distribution in the form of a meal and their consumption in the dining room. The production volume of the business has to be known so that the maximum number of portions envisaged equate with the capacities of the items of equipment. This in turn hinges on the policy of portion size and the form of purchasing, bearing in mind the difference between food in

127

its raw volume and that of the prepared volume; this also has an affect on the size and equipment of storage. Such an exercise will help to ensure that only essential items are considered for purchase and those that appear to receive less frequent usage be given lower priority. If it is possible to eliminate these items of lower priority from the list by minor adjustments to the menu it should be done, and different but more useful and versatile items could then be considered.

An exercise in calculating the normal daily usage of each item of equipment and machinery as a percentage of the working day can also assist in reaching the decision whether to purchase. It is well known by the nature of things that many processes take place at one and the same time and this exercise might reveal that these could equally well be done at different times, thus permitting better use of equipment and manpower and obviating the need to duplicate items. As certain activities must always precede others, placing them in chronological order will assist in equipment choice and also show up possible bottle-necks.

The optimum use of kitchen equipment and machinery has a bearing on fuel bills, for with energy becoming increasingly expensive and doubts about how long fossil fuels will last, staff must make every effort to conserve it. Even such a commonsense practice as adjusting the flame to the size of the pan should not be overlooked, while the old idea of turning on equipment first thing in the morning and not switching it off until the end of the dinner service is no longer valid.

The difference between operating a large-scale catering operation and a commercial firm is that traditionally the former works to a fairly restricted menu which means bulk cooking for the numbers, whereas the latter must offer a fairly wide choice of dishes and therefore works with small-scale equipment and runs on an à la Carte system of good advanced preparation and quick cooking methods, so restricting the range of equipment required.

As the type of menu and service and the volume of business will influence the decision as to the type and amount of equipment required in the kitchen, so these factors apply to the dining room. There can be additional requirements for a high-class establishment where there may be the additional need for trolleys and lamps, for a buffet display at lunch, or a daily roast joint which is carved in the room either from a trolley or from a service point. If the place is licensed then the form that the bar and lounge will take will decide the furniture needed to identify it with the particular type of establishment. This may be taken further with reference to the storage areas where justification for purchase of major items, deemed necessary, must still be made, and with the staff amenity rooms where the emphasis may be on comfort and robustness rather than elegance. Every item of equipment should be evaluated for performance and use as to how it meets operational needs, provides efficient output, and saves labour or conserves fuel. It must be judged on quality and not on price; poor quality furniture, furnishings and linen will soon need replacing.

Over-provision of capacity will lead to higher operational costs whilst under-provision usually leads to bottle-necks causing inefficient production.

128

COST AND BUDGET INFLUENCES

There are two approaches to this topic depending on the type of operation. In the first, the budget allowance is broken down to the actual cost of each item of equipment required then, if the sum exceeds that made available, it will be necessary to look for some suitable alternatives at lower prices, hopefully of the same quality. In the second, the total cost of all items is requested to be put in the budget. It is also possible to put the whole project out to tender; the firm that bids successfully doing everything from drawing up the plans, putting it all together and handing it over as a going concern. Then again it is possible to lease the equipment without any capital outlay at all.

The purchase decision will be that of management with the advice of the planning team and they will obviously try to choose standard production items, knowing that specially constructed ones to suit their particular need are going to cost much more. Considerations must be given to the cost and its relation to size, durability, usefulness or performance, design and finish – the more expensive item not necessarily being the best or more desirable. Desirability is often a deciding factor in purchasing and the buyer looks at the gauge of the metal and the possibility of obtaining spare parts, but it should be recognised that advances in technology assist manufacturers to improve performance and put new improved models on the market. It is therefore necessary to obtain the most up-to-date machinery which gives good performance in relation to its cost.

The cost of delivery and installation of heavy duty equipment must be included in the budget, bearing in mind that in some instances the floor may have to be strengthened or insulated.

It is important to calculate the operating costs of each item of equipment basing this on its likely use and loading. The high cost of fuel demands economical use and thermostats and sensory devices must be kept in good working order.

Upkeep costs may include a maintenance contract with a firm of kitchen engineers to service all equipment in all departments; it may include emergency call-out to do a vital repair job to keep the department in operation. The design of equipment has a bearing on ease of maintenance as the more straightforward it is the cheaper it is to keep it working, since manpower is the most expensive part of this contract. A planned programme of maintenance will help to keep all items of equipment and machinery in good working order.

Replacement of expendable equipment such as linen, furnishings and utensils that are worn out has to be budgeted for.

CONSTRUCTION AND MANUFACTURE

This involves the materials used and the design and finish of items of equipment. They should be sufficiently solid to stand up to hard use and also to look and handle well. The materials should be strong, non-absorbent and non-corrosive, thermal conductivity applies to some items whilst lightness in weight and smoothness of finish apply to others. When purchasing, the ease of cleaning so as to give complete hygiene in use should be borne in mind. Furniture should combine elegance and practicality so that it suits the particular requirements of the establishments yet be robust to give long service. The decisions whether to have chairs with arms, if they should be stackable, what material for the seats, how high from the floor, how wide the seat, all need careful consideration. It should not often be necessary to take down curtains to clean them and they should stay attractive without palling.

The ergonomics of equipment should be studied so that their design suits the people who use them and assists in making the working environment efficient, according to their capabilities. This includes a working height of approximately 100 cm for most jobs, or 90 cm for heavy work, a dining table should be 70 cms high and the seat of the chair 43 cms in height. Ergonomics help by reducing unnecessary stress and increasing the effectiveness of the staff employed. Work study is a part of the planning process and sets out to obtain the best use of manpower and resources by cutting out unnecessary movements and motion in carrying out any task. Making the best use of the equipment installed is a part of work study.

PERFORMANCE AND USEFULNESS

Equipment, whether it be a stove, an ice-making machine or a mixer, is evaluated by its performance which includes ease of operation. By performance is meant its output or what amount can be produced by its use in a given time. Manufacturers are able to give figures for output of certain foods in their items of equipment, basing them on production under ideal conditions which are not always easy to reproduce in ordinary practice. In large-scale or fast food catering, performance is of great importance as it bears on the length of time a customer may have to wait for his food. Durability and reliability are a part of this and recognition of it is not only by the cost but of design and construction.

The furniture chosen for the dining room and customer amenity areas must be chosen with the following criteria in mind – its suitability, ease of movement, comfort, strength, design, and materials used. The crockery, cutlery and glassware must be chosen to relate to the standard of the dining room and also for its durability, ease of replacement, functionality, weight and material used.

ORDERING OF THE EQUIPMENT

The techniques of ordering are shown in Chapter 9 and the details given there hold good for the purchase of equipment. Great detail is required to obtain exactly the right goods at the right price, by giving precise specifications so that the goods purchased fulfil all requirements. When the decision to purchase equipment is taken lightly and without a full assessment problems may arise which were not envisaged, such as difficulty in accommodating it, extra installation costs, lack of ventilation, unsuitability for its purpose, or poor operating performance.

An understanding of the materials used to manufacture items of equipment, especially the new man-made materials, is necessary. In the past heavy-duty equipment meant not only that it had to perform heavy duties but that it was solidly made of heavy gauge cast iron or steel; much modern equipment utilises lighter weight and gauge materials such as aluminium, duraluminium and stainless steel.

KITCHEN EQUIPMENT

The following details given an outline description of various important items of equipment installed in the kitchen and its servery. It is not meant to be exhaustive and neither are all the items necessary in every type of kitchen.

FIXED OR HEAVY DUTY EQUIPMENT

The Kitchen Range

In most kitchens this is the most used piece of equipment mainly because of its versatility; it is a composite unit that is designed to cope with a number of tasks by using the top and oven at the same time. The traditional solid top has the advantage that if it is fully loaded with pans some can be boiling, others simmering and others just keeping warm. It can be said to be uneconomical because whether operated by gas or electricity it has to be kept on full all the time, whereas a number of separate rings can be adjusted to suit the actual needs of the service, so cutting down on fuel costs. It is possible to have a half solid top with some individual rings. The oven can be thermostatically controlled with the heat source at the base with the heated air passing through the lining thus giving convected heat; there is a tendency to have different heat zones in various parts of the oven but the cook gets used to this. A disadvantage of the range is that it is ergonomically bad to have to bend down to manipulate the progress of food cooking in the oven; if the drop door is used when tending the food it means stooping to the task. The range certainly makes full use of floor space and is enhanced by the overhead rack which is used to hold cooked foods and serving dishes; the practice of siting a grill or salamander above the stove has advantages but also some disadvantages – it eliminates a potential bottle-neck at the point of distribution but can deplete the section of a supply of service dishes to hand.

An electrically operated range will take approximately thirty minues to reach an operating temperature of 180°C, but because of good insulation will maintain a good heat for up to half an hour after being switched off.

General Purpose Oven

This is a free-standing oven in which it is possible to load and attend without bending or stretching, so is ergonomically better for staff. It may be operated by radiant heat where the visible flame in the base gives a gradient of heat from bottom to top and is very good for roasting. Convected heat from semi-external burners which are housed below the bottom of the oven and enters the chamber through vents is good for baking as the heat is even.

Pastry Oven

This kind of oven is more usually electrically heated because of its good heat retention and evenness of operation. It is made in separate decks each operating independently and having a heavy bottom and a narrow opening of from 12.5 cm to 22.5 cm; the number of decks would be built according to the establishment's requirements. This oven is more suited to pastry and bread baking than to general use.

Reel, or Rotary Oven

This is usually required for bakery work but may be used for general baking and roasting. It has a wheeled mechanism carrying a number of racks on which the trays of food to be cooked are placed. The trays stay the right way up on a flexible axle and the wheels are driven by a powerful motor. This type of oven may be gas, electric, or oil fired and they are very economical in a large-scale operation and give a good even result. A version of this type of oven enables a loaded trolley to be wheeled inside and attached to a clasp at the top which suspends the trolley just clear of the bottom so that it rotates when the oven doors are closed.

Convection Oven

Convected heat is efficient and when generated in an oven and circulated as heated air it gives an evenness of result that no other oven can match. This type is sometimes called the forced-air oven because the electrically driven fan can blow the air at 80 km per hour reaching every part of the oven. As food cooks by the penetration of heat, vapour and moisture are released from the surface of the food and tend to slow down the penetration. With air being circulated at high speed the heat penetration is faster so speeding up the cooking process. This oven can be operated at a slightly lower temperature than an ordinary one and still give quicker results; shrinkage is lessened by the use of this oven. The oven operates better with a full load but there should be room at the side of the shelves for the forced air to circulate.

A convection oven does everything a normal oven does except perhaps the baking of bread, but roasting, braising and ordinary baking and the reheating of bulk packs of frozen food are accomplished efficiently. Ergonomically they are good since they are usually free-standing or bench-mounted and some models are loaded by pushing the trolley full of food inside and closing the doors on it. The doors are side opening and with heat-reflective glass panels; when opened the door should operate a fan cut-out switch to prevent hot air blowing onto the face of the cook. A timer that rings and shuts off the heat at the end of the cooking period is installed; an interior lamp shows how the cooking is progressing. Aerodynamic perforated oven linings give even temperature and high capacity low pressure fans assist in this. A humidifier is incorporated to prevent shrinkage, improve texture, and allows different dishes to be cooked in the same oven without transfer of flavours. These are available for gas or electricity and in various sizes having from eight to forty shelves.

Combined Forced-Air and Infra-Red Oven

This is a version of the convection oven with cold air being circulated around whilst infra-red tubes give off radiation that is pulse-powered to come on and go off. The large model also works as a refrigerator to hold frozen food until required, then it is thawed, regenerated and held hot until served. It is known as the Recon-plus oven and is for large-scale feeding operations such as on a big jet plane.

Grilling Equipment

The true grill enables food to be put on an adjustable grill bar above the fire – it uses either charcoal or coke to give an intense heat without smoke or flame but rather a glowing bed that lasts without refuelling for a long period. **Gas operated**

133

grills with lava heaped on top give the glowing effect but not the same taste, yet they are clean and efficient and may be installed in the dining room where grills are a speciality. A **salamander** is sometimes referred to as an over-fired grill as its source of heat comes from the top so that it will gratinate and glaze as well as grill. The heat is quite intense and when meat is grilled on the bars of a salamander, its juices tend to be extruded onto the tray beneath. By placing the meat on a tray to grill, the juices will not be lost and it will thus prevent much of the dryness found when grilling directly on the bars.

Grilling is also carried out on a **griddle plate** which is a solid slab of cast iron or steel heated by gas from beneath or by electric elements; some are ridged but a flat surface allows all kinds of foods to be dry fried, including eggs. The heat is conducted and it is necessary to have a film of fat to prevent food sticking; a lot of fumes and vapour are given off so ventilation is important and the grease filters need regular cleaning. The capacity of a griddle as for a grill can be calculated by its dimensions and by how long a particular item takes.

Microwave Oven

Microwaves are electromagnetic radiation waves contained in the narrow band of radio wavelengths and were originally developed for use in radar communications. Microwave cookery differs considerably from other forms of cookery but is not a principle of cooking in the same way that baking and boiling are, and few users obtain fully efficient use from it mainly because they do not understand its role in the kitchen.

The food placed to cook in a microwave oven is bombarded by the electromagnetic waves given off by the magnetron and absorbs this form of energy which causes the molecules in the food to oscillate at a very high rate. These vibrations cause intermolecular friction and create kinetic energy which is apparent from the vapour released from the food; the high frequency radio waves cook the food from within, and the effective penetration appears to be 2.5 cm from every direction. This means that the thicker the food the slower the rate of penetration but the moisture content and state of solidity also cause different rates of cooking, thus frozen foods are usually regenerated by pulse power in which the oven switches itself on and off for seconds at a time so as to defrost all parts evenly before cooking.

The oven will not seal or colour foods and the sinew or collagen in meat is not converted into tender, juicy, gelatinous matter as happens when roasted or grilled. A special browning plate is available that gives a nice appearance particularly to steaks if cooked in this way and some ovens are fitted with a turntable so that foods are cooked more evenly and quickly.

Cooking in a microwave oven is approximately seven times faster than in an ordinary oven; poaching and shallow frying can be done satisfactorily and regeneration and defrosting of cooked dishes is very good. As such it is frequently used at the point of service to ensure the food is very hot when distributed to waiting staff. It is not possible to use metal dishes in a microwave oven as it

134

causes arcing – even a gold band on a dinner plate causes this and the microwaves will gradually destroy the metal together with the glaze.

Ceramic and glass dishes are used to cook food in and these stay fairly cool during the cooking operation. The size of oven for a catering establishment is according to the use to be made of it and the amount of food to be put to cook. There is a range of models rated from 800 watts to 1,300 watts; some are capable of operating on half or full power, the former being useful for quick defrosting of frozen foods. It is possible to have automatically opening doors that operate when the timer expires; it is impossible to open the door whilst the oven is operating and BS 5175 specifies the safety requirements of microwave cookers. If the oven is not cleaned regularly food splashes on the door seal can affect it so causing leakage of the microwaves which are very dangerous to the operator; a small calibrated radiation reader can be used to check on this.

Combined Microwave and Convection Oven

The advantages of microwave and forced-air convection cookery have been combined to produce the Mealstream oven and metal dishes may be used in it. The two energy sources can work at one and the same time, the microwave bringing food to the cooking temperature and the convected heat carrying through the process and providing flavour and tenderness to roasts that the microwave alone cannot give.

Micro-processor Oven

Another new type of oven is a fully automatic micro-processor oven that has a heat probe to tell when meat is cooked. The oven is surrounded with a low density thermal cable to give uniform distribution of radiant heat that obviates the possibility of hot spots. It is not a forced-air oven. It works at an ambient temperature of 105–120 °C and switches itself off when the internal temperature of the meat reaches the required level. It then stops cooking but holds the joints at 66 °C. The oven holds 53 kg meat which takes six hours to cook at 2,600 watts. The cooking loss is claimed to be approximately 7–8 per cent but in practice is about 13 per cent.

Fryer

Deep fat frying is the fastest method of cookery because it operates at 150 °C–196 °C, but at these high temperatures it is not easy to control so unless a purpose-built item of equipment is used, the result can be costly in the use of oil as well as in unsatisfactory results. The two main types of fryers are, (i) where the fat is contained in a V-shape pan and the heat is directed to each side leaving

135

a cool zone at the bottom, and (ii) where the electric element is in the pan of fat so heating the oil above but leaving a cool zone below, its purpose being to receive particles of food that would otherwise get burnt so spoiling the oil. The smaller the opening the less exposure there is at the top and consequently less chance of oxidisation of the oil.

Oil is an expensive commodity and should be made to last as long as possible, this means minimal absorption by the food and avoidance of breakdown caused by an excessively high temperature. The amount of oil necessary to fill the fryer is important because if it is possible to reduce the amount by putting in less food at a time, then it is possible to cook at a slightly lower temperature thus decreasing the amount of fuel used but not allowing absorption. It is calculated that $2\frac{1}{2}$ litres of oil is required per 500 g of food to be immersed at one time.

Control is essential for this item as there are obvious hazards in its use; a gas operated fryer may have the snap-action form of thermostat adjustable up to 190 °C with a second overheat cut-off fitted to operate at 215 °C in case of thermostat failure. A cooking timer also acts as an automatic cut-off. An electric fryer has the second thermostat bonded to the heating element which becomes operational if the main thermostat fails.

The capacity of a fryer is expressed in output of food, usually kilograms of chip potatoes per hour, taking them from the raw state.

Pressure Fryer

Deep frying carried out in a pressure sealed frying kettle keeps the natural juices and flavour inside foods and this item of equipment is suitable for frying raw chicken portions. The oil is heated to 190 °C–250 °C and the food is immersed and is immediately sealed and coloured; the lid is sealed down and cooking takes place under pressure at 120 °C at which temperature no further colouration takes place. The cycle is timed to switch off and exhaust before the lid can be opened; a pressure gauge indicates the pressure in the fryer and shows when it is exhausted. Foods must be coated before being submerged and although it is possible to blanch chipped potatoes this item will not fry them.

Bratt Pan

This item of equipment is capable of fulfilling a number of tasks; it can be used for boiling, braising, stewing, shallow frying, and as a bain-marie. Claims are made for its use as a deep fryer but as it lacks a thermostat control and a cool zone it is not really suitable.

The bottom of the pan is of cast-iron or stainless steel heated by gas or electricity and it has a tilting mechanism which must be good otherwise spilling can happen. This is a labour-saving item as it is easy to control by means of the switch or tap and is very easy to clean. The normal size pan is 76 cm × 61 cm ×

136

180 cm with a capacity of 32 litres or approximately 200 portions and it can cope with 25–30 kg of shallow fried meats per hour. The stainless steel base may cause food to burn in certain spots and it is best to thicken a stew when nearly ready rather than at the halfway stage.

Boiling Pan

There are three main types of boiling pans – the direct heated type, the double pan, and the steam type; the direct heat one is good for boiling vegetables, making stock and thin soup. A steam boiling pan, or kettle, as the small size one is called, has steam under pressure circulating through the two walls of the pan and differs from the double pan which is actually the direct type with some water in the cavity, and does not work as fast as the pressure type. All have stainless steel linings and the smaller sizes can be tilted rather than having to run off the liquid through a tap. The steam kettle cooks viscous liquids such as soup and gravy very well. Baskets that fit perfectly are used for batch cooking green vegetables and it is possible to have a quick chill type in which cold water circulates through the jacket to cool a sauce or stew prior to chilling or freezing. A power mixer attachment will purée the contents of the kettle.

The sealed jacket contains water, rust inhibitor and anti-freeze and electric elements to produce the steam – the 22 litre and 45 litre models can be used over and over again during a busy service period and as these do not need a lid because they work so quickly, it is easy to keep glancing at how the contents are cooking. Models with a capacity up to 545 litres are also made but with such a capacity it is obviously an advantage to bring the hot and cold water supplies close by. Some boiling pans have a rectangular casing to give an orderly look to the battery of kitchen equipment.

Steamer

There are several types of steamer to choose from; there is the atmospheric steaming oven, the pressure steamer, the dynamic pressureless steamer, and the flash steamer. In a steamer there is no water to weigh down upon the food and thus possibly causing distortion; only steam comes into contact with it and consequently there is no cooking liquid, since foods must be cooked in perforated trays to allow the steam to cook from all sides.

The **atmospheric steamer** produces its own steam from the container of water at the bottom which is heated by gas or electricity; the water is fed in as required and controlled by a ball valve. When the water reaches 100 °C it gives off steam which is trapped in the chamber so cooking the food and the door is sealed to prevent escape. Five or six trays of foods may be placed in to cook at the same time. To install this type, only fuel, indirect water supply and drainage is required.

A **pressure steamer** allows cooking at a higher temperature than 100 °C to take place thus shortening the cooking time as well as retaining more nutritional value, natural colour and flavour. Some models need water poured onto the base of the oven to produce steam, others generate steam by means of water jets onto the bottom of the steamer compartment. The **jet steamer** has a boiler sited under it which generates the steam which is piped into the cabinet under pressure. For steamed puddings, the atmospheric steaming oven is best but for batch cooking of potatoes and green vegetables, both fresh and frozen, the pressure steamer gives a better result. It does, however, require great care as the slightest extra cooking time can spoil the colour of the food. The timing device will control the cooking and there is often an audio as well as a visual signal to signify the end of the cycle but the door will not open until all pressure has been vented; there is a danger of scalding water gushing out if an attempt is made to force the door open. Solid trays are available for steaming meat and chicken without loosing all the juices; only minutes are needed to cook vegetables but larger items need nearly as long as in the atmospheric steamer.

Ovens that operate with steam in them but without pressure are used for cooking meats and are successful in keeping cooking losses very low. There is no build-up of pressure so the oven does not have to be sealed though some models are dual purpose and may be operated as a pressure cooker.

The newer type of **pressureless convection steam cooker** is smaller than the atmospheric type and it allows the door to be opened at any time without stopping the cooking process it operates off a 5 kW electric supply. The steam generator is self-contained and operates at zero pressure yet will cook trays of frozen peas in two minutes, and beef at ten minutes per 450 g. Some foods such as rice need water in the pan and, where needed, juices can be retained when cooking meat by using a solid tray.

KITCHEN MACHINERY

Machines used in the kitchen are powered by electricity although there are some that are hand operated and work well, but the need for machines is to lighten the burden of work and for this reason they are often referred to as being labour-saving. It is doubtful if the purchase of any one of the twenty or more machines available actually leads to making a member of staff redundant.

Mixing Machine

This is probably the most used machine because it can do a wide range of jobs very efficiently with just the bowl and the three mixing attachments of whisk, paddle and dough hook. There are different sizes of mixers for different uses, small and medium table models and several sizes of floor mounted ones; the size used to be stated in US quarts of 16 fluid ounces but are now given in litres. With some models, different sizes of bowls may be used by attaching a small collar to take the smaller bowl, but this also means having two sets of mixing tools. Mixers have three-speed gears for various uses which assist in obtaining speedy aeration and smooth liquid mixes, and also for dense or elastic mixes such as fruit cake, hamburg mix and bread dough. Large models have a power lift to bring up the bowl to operating level and a timer that allows staff to get on with something else while the mixer is working; a trolley to take the larger bowls reduces manhandling.

So many operations are carried out so much more efficiently than by hand that is is difficult to visualise a kitchen without one, indeed so many people use it daily that the pastry, larder and kitchen usually each need their own model. The versatility of a mixer in operating such attachments as a mincer, vegetable cutter, and hamburg moulder can lead to a bottle-neck where only one mixer is available and all sections need to use it.

A very **high-speed mixer** which takes up a small amount of room and produces much better bread than by using the normal mixing machine is useful if the policy is to serve bread and rolls made on the premises. An ordinary mixer will make a good yeast dough but it will not make a perfect one and this type uses a system called the Chorleywood process, also known as the no-time dough, in which all the ingredients including cold water and an improver are mixed and developed at very high speed in a few minutes. The dough is then ready for moulding.

Another form of mixer is the **air whip** which is useful where a large quantity of whipped cream is used in pastry work; this machine doubles the cream in volume and does not overmix.

A mixer for placing into a boiling pan to mash the contents, and known as a **mobile turbo-mixer**, saves having to remove food from the pan to the mixer and lessens the chance of it getting cold; a revolving knife unit is surrounded by an interchangeable sieve for fine or course mixes and is lowered from its stand into the boiling pan to produce, for example, mashed potato, vegetable purées, or soup.

Vertical Bowl Chopper

This is a form of mixing machine that uses cutting blades to produce various mixtures. The ingredients for a pâté or Hamburg steaks can be put in, the meat being in large pieces, and within a short space of time results in a very fine mixture. The bowl does not rotate but can be moved on its pivot to empty out the contents. It can chop cabbage, make pastry, prepare breadcrumbs, emulsify sauces and is available in several sizes for various operations.

139

Bowl Chopper

This is a useful type of machine which works similarly to a vertical bowl chopper but does not have its speed or range of uses. The bowl with the food in it rotates fairly slowly whilst a set of knives rotate at a very fast rate under a safety cover. It will produce quenelle or mousseline mixtures but care has to be taken with the timing or it will produce a rubbery result; breadcrumbs, minces and pâtés can also be made successfully.

Heavy Duty Blender

This is a widely used piece of machinery which saves the need to pass soups and and purées through a sieve, although it may still be necessary to use a fine strainer afterwards to obtain the best results. It can process raw and cooked foods and is also useful for making emulsified sauces such as mayonnaise and salad cream.

Other Machines

In the pastry a **roller** and a **moulder** are useful machines where the volume of production justify them. The pastry roller will roll out any kind of paste to the desired thickness and length and, once the operator is experienced, will do it quicker than with a rolling pin. It is fully automatic and the operator simply has to stand and operate the switches and occasionally dust with flour.

The moulding of round rolls by machine is only justifiable when it runs into several hundred each day. The weighed piece of dough is pinned out to the required diameter, placed into the machine which first divides it into perhaps thirty pieces, then rotates so as to mould them perfectly round in shape. The size and weight will be according to the weight of dough put onto the moulding plate.

Not many ordinary catering establishments can justify the purchase of a pie-moulding machine which will line various shapes of moulds by hand pressure, but where pies are featured this is a fairly inexpensive machine. After filling the pies the die can be changed to lid them ready for baking.

Another form of moulder is used for Hamburg steaks and other similar mixtures where the raw meat mixture is fed into a mincer which extrudes it into square or round-shaped pieces of even weight and size.

A **mincing machine** can be either an attachment to the hub of a mixer, or as a complete machine on its own with an optional sausage extruder. It is possible to render second quality slices of meat into frying and grilling steaks by putting them through a **tenderising machine**. This consists of a large number of pointed blades or needles that pierce the meat without shredding but which cuts through connective tissue and sinew. Some machines can amalgamate pieces of meat and textured vegetable protein into pieces which resemble thin steaks.

140

There are several machines for the vegetable cook's use including the **potato peeler**, the **chipping machine**, and the **cutting machine**. The decision to purchase any of these is linked to operational policy as it is possible to purchase potatoes ready peeled, ready to fry frozen chips, and other vegetables in prepared form ready for cooking. The use of these items can thus obviate the need for these machines.

Peelers rub and wash off the skins of potatoes, carrots, turnips and swedes but care must be taken that only the outer skin is removed otherwise there will be a high loss. Management needs to calculate the peeling and eyeing losses and the time it takes someone to produce the prepared result against the cost of buying ready peeled vegetables.

Where bacon is purchased by the side, or cooked meat is served to large numbers either hot or cold, a **slicing machine** will prove useful as it does the job of carving much quicker and more evenly than by hand, it is a good tool of portion control. A slicer can be fully automatic with the operator taking the slices as they are cut, but as he is already standing at the machine he can operate it manually so regulating production. The thickness is adjustable for different kinds of meat and on some machines the speed of slicing can be adjusted. Bread, cucumbers and tomatoes may be sliced by this machine. In normal use all the requisite safeguards are present. Careful cleaning is essential for reasons of hygiene but care is needed when dismantling and reassembling the blade.

An important item of equipment for use in establishments preparing large numbers of plated cold meals, or where frozen or chilled meals are packed for delivery, is a **food wrapping and sealing machine**. This holds a roll of transparent polythene in which food is wrapped and sealed mechanically.

An **ice-making machine** is used by many departments so must be sited where all can have ease of access to it; the size and shape of the ice it produces must be ideal for all users. Different machines produce different sizes and shapes such as cubes, ovals, rounds, tablets, flakes, and crushed ice. Octagonal cubes are ideal for drinks as they cool the liquid to the right drinking temperature in the space of a minute and a half without diluting it. Flaked ice is best for cocktails and crushed ice for kitchen use. The ice is made by running a measured quantity of water over a freezing plate until it solidifies and is then defrosted so that it slides onto a net of hot wires which cuts it into pieces; or water is pressure sprayed into small moulds; or refrigerated paddles turn in a container of water until they ice up and when defrosted fall off into the ice container. A sensor cuts off production when the container is full. Production must equal peak period demand bearing in mind that an ice bucket for wine will use as much as 1 kg of ice. The cubes do not stick together once produced.

There are many other machines purpose-made for use in particular kitchen operations; some, like an **electric can opener** or a potato peeler which use knives instead of carborundum, are adaptations of existing machines; others such as a French fried **potato dispenser** are an aid to portion control whilst others are designed for use only in very large-scale operations.

To assist in the disposal of waste there are a number of different machines –

the ordinary **waste disposal unit**, either free standing or as part of a sink, a **compactor** which is good for dealing with disposables, and a **crusher** which breaks up bottles thus reducing the content of the paladin.

For general use in the catering department there is a **hand drying machine**, which is more hygienic than roller or paper towels although some operate in conjunction with a paper towel; and an **insect killer** which attracts flying insects by rays emitted from an ultra-violet tube electrocuting them instantly and which has a collecting tray for them to fall into. There is also a wall mounted **lamp unit** using fragrant oils and insect repellant which will break down and overcome odours and eliminate flying insects; some of the fragrances claim to alleviate asthma and other bronchial complaints.

STILLROOM EQUIPMENT

In the stillroom an **electric egg boiler** that has two, three or four buckets that will each hold up to six eggs will automatically cook eggs for any time up to $6\frac{1}{2}$ minutes then withdraw them from the water. In addition to the various kinds of **toast makers** which should be judged on output as models vary from 200 to 1,000 slices per hour, there are several kinds of toasted sandwich-makers made with non-stick toasting plates which seal in the filling and do the job in seventy seconds. A toaster can be either the pop-up or rotary type, or the toast may be made under a salamander. Waiting staff can use the ordinary toaster themselves, doing it to order so that customers get it hot; the rotary toasting machine is for very large-scale establishments.

A **water boiler** for making beverages may be heated by gas or electricity and provide a constant supply of water at 98 °C. It may be allied to a **coffee-maker** where the heated water is run into the coffee filter at one side and maintained at the right serving temperature and milk kept in a separate urn also at the right temperature. Boiling water is constantly available for making tea in pots and urns. Several different coffee machines are in existence for use in stillroom, dining room and cafeteria serveries; they are good because they make coffee quickly to order with minimum supervision. These work by means of a filter with water at 98 °C poured over the ground coffee and filtering into the service pot; in another system the water is put to boil on the machine and it goes up into the top container and funnels down through the ground coffee through a filter paper. A machine to dispense the right amount of concentrated liquid coffee and hot water by the cup or jug full is operated by a press button. For counter service a machine will grind coffee beans and dispense a cup at the touch of a button, and will not cause bottle-necks in the queue. Espresso coffee is made by boiling water being sprayed under pressure over finely ground well-roasted coffee.

A **dispensing machine** for serving chilled milk, fruit juices and carbonated drinks allows for self-service by waiting staff or customers by delivering a measured amount or a glassful, some having a paddle to ensure the concentrate is evenly distributed through the total liquid. Others draw water through a chilled faucet which is then carbonated and dispensed onto a small amount of concentrate. A chilled drinking water font fills a need and may be so sited that customers may serve themselves or jugsful be drawn off by waiting staff.

HOLDING AND SERVICE EQUIPMENT

The ideal way of serving food so as to give maximum customer satisfaction is by the à la Carte system where food is cooked to order and served immediately. Under the Table d'Hôte system, however, it is usually necessary to cook much of the food in advance of serving and retaining it in a heated zone until the customer arrives. It is during this holding period that rapid deterioration can occur unless food is held in the best possible condition so that it is safe and hot enough for customers to enjoy.

Hot Cupboard or Hotplate

This item is used to keep cooked foods in good condition and also to keep plates and dishes warm; the optimum temperature setting for keeping food hot is $76\,^{\circ}C$–$88\,^{\circ}C$ giving an internal temperature of $65\,^{\circ}C$ – the recommendation is to keep it above $62.8\,^{\circ}C$. The temperature for keeping plates warm is $65\,^{\circ}C$ at which they are just right for handling and the glaze is not damaged. So ideally crockery and silverware should be heated in a separate hotplate away from the food, but an electrically heated plate-warming unit is the best way of maintaining the supply of hot plates and other items of crockery.

A hot cupboard can be sited in the kitchen area at the end of the production line and the cooked foods kept in it; for this purpose a cabinet hot cupboard which has an upper and a lower compartment is useful. The hotplate or counter service hot cupboard is the point to which prepared dishes are brought for distribution and it has a plain top and sliding or rollaway doors both sides of the cupboard part. It is heated by gas or electricity and sometimes from a live steam supply.

Service Counter

A service counter for cafeteria and self-service operations would have a **bain-marie** top into which fit the containers of various components of the meal, with dry heat or hot water at the bottom to keep it hot during the service period.

143

Reserves of food may be kept inside the hot cupboard and the operating temperature must ensure that the food both on top and inside is maintained at approximately 82 °C so that it does not dry out or get cold. Service counters are usually made of stainless steel on the outside, possibly with enamel doors and mild steel interiors. It is helpful to have a water supply and drainage for the bain-maries.

The kitchen sections or parties need a bain-marie for keeping prepared foods in, either a large one for general use or one for each section of the kitchen. Sauces and soups are placed in the bain-marie in special tall pots that take up little space, and are served from here. A stew, or prepared vegetables, will also keep hot in a bain-marie for Table d'Hôte service.

REFRIGERATION

Refrigerators in one form or another are essential in a food production area to maintain food in good condition; low temperature storage renders most spoilage organisms inactive or slows their rate of activity and most foods with a high water content require to be refrigerated. A refrigerator is an insulated chamber with a compressor attached that keeps it at a lower temperature than that outside. By pumping a refrigerant through a system of pipes and coils it absorbs the heat of the food as the refrigerant is changed from a liquid to a vapour. The vapour is compressed and forced into the condenser which, being cooled by a fan, causes the vapour to return to its liquid state; the cycle is repeated and the absorbed heat is released into the air. The lower the temperature at which the particular refrigerant boils, the more efficient it is at removing the heat from the food.

Thermostatic control of a refrigerator is vital because different foods have different storage requirements; not only the fresh quality of foods but also their rate of evaporation is affected by the temperature and the relative humidity of storage in the refrigerator. The thermostat must maintain operation at the selected level.

Some of the points that need to be considered in the purchase of a refrigerator are, (i) how the size fits in with the overall kitchen plan, and the capacity with the probable amount to be stored, (ii) if it has an automatic defrosting device that works efficiently, (iii) the length of guarantee of the motor, (iv) the cost of a maintenance agreement, and (v) whether there are half doors on an upright freezer cabinet to lessen cold air loss on opening.

A walk-in coldroom should be well lit and have an alarm fitted in case anyone should get shut in. It is inadvisable to put very hot food directly into a refrigerator as it will raise the temperature of other food inside; nor should it be overloaded or its efficiency will be diminished.

144

SMALL KITCHEN EQUIPMENT

The following gives an idea of the wide range of small kitchen equipment and utensils in everyday use.

Pans and Moulds – these include stewpans, braising pans, sauté pans, sauteuses, sugar boiling pans, bain-maries, frying pans, and omelette pans, dariole, charlotte, savarin, jelly and all types of pastry moulds as well as sponge tins, cake hoops, flan rings, etc.

Cutting Instruments – these include slicers, graters, peelers, knives, zesters, corers, column and aspic cutters, spoon cutters, secateurs, cleavers, choppers, saws, and the like.

Thermometers – sugar boiling, brix hydrometer, dough, brine, relative humidity.

Strainers – colanders, conical strainers, skimmers, salad basket, sieves, muslin and tammy cloths, and soup machine.

Kitchen utensils made of wood – mushroom, triangle, chopping boards, sieves, salt box, spoons, spatules. Substitutes for wooden chopping boards and butchers blocks are based on rubber and do not cause splinters or harbour germs.

Other utensils – whisks, fish grills, frying baskets, scoops, brushes, spoons, ladles, serving tongs, etc.

But one of the most difficult decisions to take when purchasing small equipment is that of deciding what kind of pans to buy, so a knowledge of what is available and the advantages and disadvantages of each should be helpful. Cooking pans are made of copper, aluminium, stainless steel, or enamel, and some combinations are available.

Copper Pans

By tradition this is the choice of the professional chef who will claim that only with them can he achieve perfect results of the highest quality. It has a high melting point, is heavy, malleable and possesses high thermal conductivity, it resists corrosion. When copper is exposed to carbon dioxide and acids it tends to form verdigris which is poisonous, therefore the insides of nearly all copper pans are lined with tin to prevent contamination. This means that care must be taken in their use as the tin used in lining melts at about 232°C. When a copper pan is used for shallow frying the oil will be at approximately 200°C which softens the tin and it may melt. An unlined copper pan must be used for sugar boiling as it goes to a high temperature. Handles are usually of bronze or brass

145

as these are not such good conductors of heat; the outside can be kept burnished with steel wool or a mixture of silversand and vinegar made into a paste with flour. It is important to have copper pans retinned if the lining has been destroyed by improper use such as using a metal scourer to clean it, or stirring with a spoon that has a sharp edge.

The retinning of saucepans has been not only expensive but unsatisfactory, partly because the items were wiped by hand and also because the use of hydrogen peroxide failed to eliminate grey areas. A water-soluble concentrate of tin oxide gives a uniform matt finish and with the use of controlled current density anodes there is no roughness or bending anywhere and no beading.

Aluminium Pans

These are made from an alloy which hardens the metal so that they keep their shape under the heavy work of a kitchen. Spun or cast aluminium with a ground base will withstand heavy duty and give good conductivity especially on solid top electric stoves. Aluminium pans are much cheaper than copper or stainless steel and even the big ones are fairly light so that female cooks can move them about. They tend to discolour after some use and it is difficult to get them shining again. Making white sauce or soup is difficult as the action of a whisk or metal spoon against the soft metal gives a dark colour. Aluminium pits easily which means that pans require careful cleaning to get rid of minute particles of food; soda must not be used in washing up, only detergent and a scourer.

Stainless Steel Pans

These look good and feel heavy but are expensive to buy. Being an alloy of nickel, chromium and iron they tend to have hot spots which can cause foods to burn in them even when care is being taken and they also tend to distort if made of thin gauge steel. The disadvantage of hot spots may be overcome by fitting pans with a copper base which spreads the heat evenly. Pans made for professional use are available in all the shapes as made from copper; there are many qualities but if 18–8 is selected this means there is 18 per cent chromium content and they will keep their good appearance.

Stainless steel is the best metal for bain-marie containers as there is no discolouration of foods and no corrosion or contamination. It is easy to keep these pans clean but unless properly rinsed and wiped they will look smeary.

Enamelled Pans

These are not very suitable for professional use because they need very careful handling to prevent chipping. Enamel is made of powdered glass mixed with clay and water which is sprayed as a thin cream onto iron or steel utensils, these are then baked at 800 °C so that the glass fuses with the metal. Pans, skillets and casseroles made like this are very colourful and attractive enough to cook and serve in but are heavy to carry and expensive to purchase.

Cast Iron and Wrought Iron Equipment

Cast and wrought iron are frequently used for frying pans, roasting trays and baking sheets; the heavy gauge metals used will withstand high temperatures without buckling. They should not go rusty unless put away wet and as they are often used in conjunction with fat there is usually a coating left which prevents food sticking to them and then being spoilt by corrosion.

Tinned Steel

This is tinplate with a very thin coating of tin on both sides and many kitchen utensils are made of this material such as baking tins, patty pans, flan rings, serving spoons and most wire items, such as conical strainers, frying baskets, spiders and cake racks. The covering of tin has good resistance to air and water corrosion but after long use may wear off and the steel underneath will rust if not dried after use. It is not usual to have these items retinned as it is cheaper to purchase replacements. Moulds are sometimes made of tinned steel but are now mainly of aluminium rather than copper because of price.

Glassware

Fireproof glass cooking and serving dishes are attractive and often well decorated but the drawback of using glass in the professional kitchen is the danger of breaking, with the possibility of splinters of glass getting into food undiscerned. Its use should be confined to the dining room although it is often necessary to use glass dishes for cold sweets from the pastry and salads from the larder.

Earthenware

The use of earthenware serving dishes enhances the standing of the establishment; they are placed onto silver flats for presentation with a silver cover to keep the food hot. The food may have been cooked in the dish or merely served into it; some dishes are eaten from the earthenware dish. Some of these dishes are fireproof and withstand high oven temperature whilst others are only for serving cold items such as an hors-d'oeuvre selection.

Porcelain Ware

This is a very white china that is excellent for cooking in as it withstands a very high temperature. Apart from the shallow round, oval and oblong dishes other items are casseroles, egg cocottes, marmites, soufflé moulds and oeufs sur le plat dishes.

Plastic Ware

These man-made materials are so versatile in their use that they are continually being developed as replacements for traditional materials. Nylon is used for pot scourers, brushes and string and many machines have nylon gears. Vinyl is used as a flexible film for covering and packing foods to give hygienic display. Polythene is a rigid plastic used for making storage containers, mixing bowls, buckets, measures, and dustbins; it is also produced as a film for food packaging and as refuse sacks. Polystyrene is another thermoplastic, made into transparent and translucent trays and dishes suitable for larder work. Phenolics are dark coloured plastics used for heat resistant saucepan handles. Urea plastics are used to make switches and handles for stoves and refrigerators. Melamine is a very hard plastic that is used for items of crockery and as basins. Polypropylene is of the same family as polythene and is formed into crates as used in dish-washing machines, and also to make pudding basins.

Very lightweight trays and crockery as used for in-flight catering are made of methylpentine polymer.

MODULAR EQUIPMENT

Modular equipment is a great asset in the kitchen as it ensures that full use can be made of all available space in every major item of equipment. It makes sense to have baking dishes and all other containers made of a size that fits ovens, steamers, refrigerators, service counters, etc., particularly when the containers hold a given amount of food and therefore a definite number of portions.

The Gastronorm system of modular equipment is widely used because it is very flexible and saves space; the module is 527 mm × 324 mm for the full-size container with halves, quarters, thirds, sixths, and even ninths, all with lids and to several depths for various uses. They are made in stainless steel and in aluminium so can be used in the oven; for steaming they are perforated.

This standardised system also applies to fixed and mobile equipment including ovens, hotplates, refrigerators and trolleys which are made in a size to hold a given number of standard modular containers, or fractions of that size. This ensures that it is possible to utilise fully every centimetre of space whether cooking joints in an oven or storing cooked foods in a deep freezer.

148

THE CARE AND MAINTENANCE OF KITCHEN EQUIPMENT

If equipment is cared for in a proper manner it is more likely to give good service and to last for a longer time than if routine care and maintenance is not carried out. This applies not only to fixed and mobile equipment but also to small utensils. It is necessary to instruct staff in the correct way of cleaning and looking after equipment and to draw up a planned programme which will ensure that every item is taken care of over a period of time and that nothing gets neglected.

There are three levels of maintenance of large equipment: the first is when the item is cleaned after being used – to ensure it is kept in a satisfactory state of hygiene, the second level is when the item is given a routine examination to see that there is nothing wrong with it, such as no screws missing or to make sure that it has been oiled. The third level of maintenance is usually done under contract by a firm of kitchen engineers who will attend at regular contracted intervals to overhaul and clean every item thoroughly, test it and confirm that it is in perfect working order.

Some of the metals used in the manufacture of equipment require special cleaning methods as follows:

Cast Iron and Mild Steel – this is cleaned with an abrasive such as wire wool or emery cloth.

Stainless Steel – this should be cleaned with detergent diluted in hot water and a cloth or nylon pad. If not properly rinsed stainless steel items look smeary but it is possible to finish them with a special finishing polish that gives a bright shine.

Aluminium – this should be washed with hot water and detergent but no washing soda because this will pit and tarnish it. The alloys of aluminium are harder than the natural metal but can be scratched by using any harsh abrasive.

Stove Enamel – equipment made or finished with stove enamelled fittings should be washed with detergent well diluted in hot water, then rinsed and dried. Only nylon scouring pads should be used to rub off stains.

FURNISHINGS AND EQUIPMENT FOR THE DINING ROOM

When consumers eat and drink anywhere except at home they take part in what has come to be termed as 'the meal experience' – an expression that at its most basic interpretation means the impact or impression created by the mixture of food, drink, service and atmosphere offered in an establishment. The first two are tangibles and the skills to prepare them can be taught, the third one is intangible as it depends very largely not just on knowledge and skills but on the social skills of the employee doing the service and his pleasant, courteous manner. The fourth of these is in many ways the most important because it is that which the consumer meets first on entering the place. This is the atmosphere in which he finds himself, the ambience or milieu which may be quite striking and makes an immediate impression, or it may be something more intrinsically insubstantial that is nothing more than a background or setting to the excellence of the food and service. Certainly the furnishings and fittings play a large part in the creation of atmosphere in a dining room whether it be in a canteen or an exclusive membership-only restaurant; it must all be chosen from the view of the consumer in making him like it and feel at home and comfortable.

Every single item of furnishing and equipment must be chosen with care and must be in keeping with the particular type of operation as envisaged and related to the customer's expectations.

FURNITURE

Dining room furniture is available in so many variations of finish and colour that only the most relevant factors can be dealt with here.

Tables are purchased in standard sizes and with a supply of extensions and various sizes of table tops; square ones can be made long or round as required for the bookings as taken. Obviously the chairs and sideboards should be in keeping with the theme of the decor but it is not so important for the tables as they are nearly always covered by tablecloths and thus remain unseen.

The **chairs** must be comfortable no matter what kind of room they are to be used in and they should combine elegance and formality. They should be solidly made and without protuberances that customers might bump against and very smoothly finished so as not to ladder stockings. A space to put away chairs not actually in use is vital as spare chairs stacked in the corner look bad; chairs that do stack need not remind people of the church hall as they can also be elegant.

Finishes to furniture are intended to keep them looking good throughout their life. Plastic is used in many ways in the dining room without necessarily making things look cheap. Designers use plastics to give shapes that wood cannot achieve and in so doing offer greater variety, more toughness and easier maintenance.

Plastic paint is easy to apply, plastic flooring needs no maintenance or polishing, and plastic wall coverings are washable and available in all colours.

Chromium-plated steel tube, epoxy resin and stove-enamel finishes to steel, plastic-coated steel mesh and anodised aluminium finishes are all used in furniture manufacture. Wood is laminated with clear plastic melamine to give a tough finish and over-printed teak or rosewood patterns from photographs are sealed in, making it difficult to tell from the genuine article. Furniture is available in pine, beech, teak, oak, mahogany, rosewood, and walnut but mostly veneered.

150

Modern veneers are usually coated with synthetic lacquer and can look authentic.

Sideboards made especially for a restaurant will cost more than ready-made ones, but unless they are to be a feature of the room are best kept in the background as being utilitarian items of furniture that hold the equipment needed to facilitate the service.

DINING ROOM EQUIPMENT

Trolleys

These play a large part in food service and thus it is necessary to ensure that gangways in the dining room are wide enough for them to move along without encumbrance; the wheels are very important as they often cause trouble in use and some types do not run smoothly on carpet – swivel castors are essential. If the dining room is on two levels then there may have to be different trolleys for each level to save lifting them up and down. For the restaurant that features a joint each day and likes to show it to customers at their table it is an asset to have a heated carving trolley made of carved wood and/or silver plate.

There is also the service trolley for Guéridon work incorporating a spirit or gas cylinder lamp to cook food; even if the restaurant does not feature flambé work there could possibly be a special request for some crêpes Suzette.

A sweet trolley, hors-d'oeuvre trolley, cheese trolley, iced salad trolley, cold buffet trolley, liqueur and cigar trolley may all have a part to play in some classes of restaurant. A general purpose trolley for brining in equipment or stock for laying up needs to be more utilitarian than elegant since it will not be seen by customers. A truck to move stacks of chairs and table tops is also useful. Clearing trolleys operated by staff of a refectory should be narrow enough to get through the gangways and look good even when loaded with dirties. For a self-clearing operation high trolleys that will accept trays of dirty dishes are necessary.

Heaters

Heaters for keeping food and crockery hot are considered as part of the waiter's sideboard and may be built-in or free standing. They are usually electrically operated and made of stainless steel or plate glass, some are preheated on a stove and brought in and some are slotted into a heated cabinet for removal as required. Others have candles or methylated spirit burners and for some dishes a table hotplate heated by a candle is enough to keep dishes warm.

151

Table Lamps

The decision whether to have table lamps has to be taken in conjunction with the size of the table, but as some types can act as emergency lighting should the supply fail there is something to be said in their favour. It is not advisable to have a pendant light over each table as the room arrangement may sometimes have to be changed around. Table lamps can operate by batteries or candles; candles used in candelabra should be non-drip.

CROCKERY

Bone China

The advantages of equipping the restaurant with bone china are that it looks much better than any other kind of pottery and it is strong, very white, and translucent; it is also vitreous and non-porous. Its strength makes bone china a good long-term investment because it is fired at a very high temperature and the decoration, being fired at a much lower temperature, allows for a wide range of colours.

Earthenware

Earthenware crockery is usually much thicker than bone china; it is not as white and is completely opaque; it weighs more than bone china but is much cheaper to purchase. It is porous under the glaze and is made in many colours.

Porcelain

This is made from 50 per cent china clay, 25 per cent quartz, and 25 per cent feldspar and is vitreous and translucent, though compared to bone china it has a blue or grey tinge. Much of what is used is made in France and used as oven-to-table ware.

English Translucent China

This crockery is of better quality than earthenware and is very strong but cheaper to buy than bone china.

Stoneware

This crockery is hard, tough and vitreous and is fired at a high temperature, it is available in deep colours and is very suitable for a thematic restaurant where such crockery is better suited to it than the white.

Oven-to-Table Ware

No ovenproof dish can be put on the stove or in the oven without something in it and it is unwise to subject it to rapid changes of temperature as the glaze may craze or the dish may crack. If a dish is marked flame-proof it means it is possible to cook in it on top of the stove. The various kinds are: *Glass* - either opaque or transparent, very hygienic and with good thermal shock resistance; *Cast-iron* - rough finish and very heavy, with a tendency to rust if not kept oiled; *Enamelled Cast-Iron* - very strong and heavy, and very expensive; available in many colours and with decorations. The enamel can splinter if not used carefully. *Earthenware* - good heat retention but porous and may craze if subjected to a high temperature; not all are ovenproof. *Enamelled Steel* - much lighter and cheaper than enamelled cast-iron but the lightweight ones develop hot spots; plain colours and stencilled decorations are available. *Porcelain* - withstands a high temperature, very strong and high thermal shock resistant which means it can go straight into the deep freezer from the oven without cracking; available in all white, brown exterior and also in gold and silver for use particularly in cold dishes. *Terracotta* - very rough and cheap but ideal for presentation of peasant-type foods; porous and unglazed and cracks easily.

Decoration of Crockery

Underglaze decoration is where the pattern is applied to crockery before it is glazed so it is protected and does not come off with repeated washing. On-glaze decoration is put on after the crockery has been glazed and the items are then fired for a third time but this kind is more likely to wear off. Banding is where a simple band of colour is applied to the rim; it may be in gold in which case it could be Best Gold which is real gold with other precious metals, fired onto the glaze. Liquid or Bright Gold has a metallic appearance and is not so durable as Best Gold; Acid Gold is not so widely used because it is the most expensive form of gold banding.

The Purchase of Crockery

When purchasing crockery the size and shape of all items should be chosen with a view to limiting the number of different pieces by selecting those that will

153

serve several purposes. An elegant yet functional shape that will withstand being washed up several times each day and that stacks firmly so as to take up little storage space is of importance. Handles of cups, rimless plates, saucers that keep the cup in the centre, ease of cleaning coffee pot spouts, a shape of teapot that sits level when inverted for machine washing, are all things to be considered.

If crockery is to be badged with the name or motif of the establishment it will mean placing a large initial order and having to pay extra each time more is ordered. If the order is for several thousand pieces it can be placed directly with a pottery but if a stock pattern is decided upon, and some stay in production for many years, it will be better to buy from a wholesaler or even a retailer who will be able to supply even a small number of replacement items from stock. It takes a long time for a potter to put a particular order into production and the order has to be given at least six months in advance.

GLASSWARE

Soda-lime, or soda glass is the ordinary type of glass used for making everyday drinking glasses. It can be made into tough glasses suitable for general use in a restaurant or thicker for public house use, or into beautifully shaped designs for high-class establishments. For a more elegant and more expensive range of glassware an establishment could possibly decide to buy full lead crystal glass. Adding lead when making glass results in a softer glass that gives a high light refraction and makes it easier to cut giving a brilliant effect. The pattern on cut glass is done with abrasive stone wheels which cut in fairly deep. Moulded cut glass cannot be mistaken for real cut glass because it does not have its brilliance and it is usually possible to see a line running down the side showing it was machine pressed in a mould.

It is possible to have the establishment's name or motif sandblasted onto glasses where jets of abrasive sand and compressed air are directed through a stencil which eats away at the glass leaving the pattern on it. The only coloured glasses used in catering are those for serving German wines which have the traditional colours of green for Moselle and brown for Hock incorporated into the stems.

Each kind of drink seems to require a different shape of glass and although it is not possible to have just two or three general purpose glasses there is no need to have too many different ones, especially if cut full lead crystal is chosen as being representative of the standard of the restaurant. For example, the old shape champagne glass has been virtually dropped in favour of a tall flute which allows the bubbles to keep rising and which could also double as a glass for white wine on the table. It is necessary to have brandy glasses, one kind of glass for port and another for sherry, one for liqueurs, and goblets – often referred to as Paris goblets – which come in several capacities and are good enough for most wines and short drinks such as gin and tonic water.

154

Toughened glass withstands a lot of hard wear but shatters into thousands of pieces rather than into splinters when dropped too heavily; they are virtually shockproof and usually available as tumblers.

Disposable plastic glasses are available in half pint and one pint sizes for beer, and in many other sizes for all kinds of drinks.

CUTLERY

When choosing the cutlery for a dining room it is not just a matter of deciding whether to select stainless steel as against plated silverware, it is a matter of choosing from the very many designs available in both metals ensuring that they are comfortable to use and easy to keep clean. Silver plated cutlery is usually made in the traditional designs and although it stains easily a long-term silver polish makes it possible to keep it clean for a considerable time. It is best when of A1 quality. This relates to the thickness of the deposit of silver plating on each item; if it is not A1 and is thin or badly used the plating will wear off quickly. To keep a high shine and to remove stains it is advisable to put cutlery through a burnishing machine in which thousands of small ball-bearings, in conjunction with a measured amount of detergent, gently clean and polish without removing the silver plating. Silver holloware can also be cleaned in this machine. Plate powder is used to polish items required for special occasions as it gives a brilliant look to silverware but takes a long time to do. A chemical dip is ideal for removing a bad stain, such as egg, from individual items; it acts immediately and effectively but tends to remove the plating if used regularly. The Polivit method of cleaning cutlery is very efficient and is kind to silverware. A sheet of Polivit is placed in a sink of water, the stained silver is immersed and after a short while the stains transfer to the Polivit leaving the silverware shining. Most E.P.N.S. knives have a stainless steel blade which is soldered into the silver handle; a poor quality one will soon discolour at the joint, go black and be almost impossible to remove.

Stainless steel cutlery of average quality is cheap but tough, and is labour saving as compared with silver. The two best qualities are those marked 18/8 which indicates the use of 18 per cent chromium and 8 per cent nickel, and 12/12 which is 12 per cent each of chromium and nickel. The better qualities have a good finish, are comfortable to use and look elegant; the cheaper imported types are very light and not very well designed even though they may look attractive when first purchased. Unless it is washed off quickly and well rinsed, stainless steel soon becomes dull in use because it tends to get stained to some extent by acids such as lemon or vinegar; it will not rust but it is difficult to keep it looking like new. It is available in matt or shiny finish and is often made

155

with handles of bronze, wood, horn, ivory and celluloid, some made with tangs and others with rivets to keep handles in place. Each can look good in its own particular setting but not all of them will stand up to the harshness of the dishwashing machine and the high temperatures of the water used.

Chrome or nickel plated cutlery is still made and has the advantage of cheapness and toughness, but they are largely being replaced by cheap stainless steel items.

There are a wide range of items from asparagus tongs to ice cream spades and the menu of an establishment will decide what needs to be purchased. Thus, for example, an establishment that specialises in grilled steaks may decide it is advisable to purchase all knives with serrated blades for ease of cutting the steaks.

SERVING DISHES

Serving dishes are made of E.P.N.S. or stainless steel in a wide range of shapes and sizes for particular purposes, from soup tureens to timbales. The shapes are the traditional oval and round but also oblong for modern style dishes. The gauge of stainless steel used has a bearing on the price and also whether finished with trimmed or wrapped edges and whether satin or shiny finish.

Some serving dishes are made in copper usually with a polished 18/10 stainless steel or nickel interior and brass handles. This kind of finish will not require re-tinning as it is resistant to heat and acids; some are made so that the copper does not tarnish and they are excellent for kitchen-to-table use. Aluminium service dishes are also made but as these soon become dull looking they are more suitable as underdishes when used with earthenware. The lids for serving dishes can be aluminium as they are usually removed before presenting the dish to the customer.

Aluminium foil flats are made in many sizes for cold buffet use where foods are to be arranged neatly for display; they are not suitable for serving hot foods at table.

Restaurant silverware should be kept in good condition. It is often thought that the cost of resilvering condiment sets or pieces of cutlery costs more than buying new but this is not necessarily true, especially as it is the practice to send away items for repair. Dents can be repaired, scratches obliterated, prongs straightened and spouts and handles made as new but it is as well to have these replated to give a renewed lease of life. Obviously an ornate pattern on the cutlery will require more work than a plain pattern but given a twenty-year replating means that upkeep costs will outweigh the purchase of new items, although the current price of silver will always have a bearing.

156

LINEN

Linen is the general term given to all the different kinds of tablecloths and table napkins, and the choice is governed by the standard of the establishment and by the frequency of laundering.

Linen is undoubtedly the best material as its snowy white double damask appearance is unequalled even by the blends of linen and other fibres. Stains are easy to remove. Cotton is also good and is available in a much wider range of colours than linen; it is also much easier to launder. Linen and cotton in a 50/50 blend can be further improved by the application of non-iron and stain-resistant processes. Man-made fibres are not very good as table napkins because they are not very absorbent but these materials may be used as tablecloths.

Tablecloths and **table napkins** are made in standard sizes to suit different requirements – tablecloths for long, square and round tables and napkins in sizes of up to 60 cm. It is possible to have a full size cloth on a table with a runner over it to take the stains, as this helps to cut laundry costs and it is usual to have a felt cover under the tablecloth tied to the legs which helps to prevent the cloth from slipping. Some fabrics are plastic-coated which allows the tablecloth to be wiped clean.

A **teacloth** is an important item of linen because of its wide range of uses by many different members of staff. Its main use is for drying equipment after washing where this is not done by the action of the dish washer. A teacloth must be absorbent so that a large number of items may be dried before it gets too wet to be effective. This means that the materials used to make them must be linen, cotton or rayon, or a combination which has been fully bleached and is lint free so that it leaves no fluff on glasses for example, after being polished. Teacloths are used in the bar and dining room for the specific use of polishing cutlery, crockery and glassware; they are issued to kitchen staff for the purpose of drying their knives after washing or for wiping pans and dishes before use. In practice they serve many other purposes such as removing pans from the oven.

Table mats have their use mainly on formica top tables where they can add colour, and on a good wooden table which a hot dish would mark. Rush or cork table mats are essential on a table that does not have a heat-resistant finish as linen will not protect it; plastic mats on a slippery surface tend to slide off.

When purchasing table coverings and napkins, waiter's cloths, teacloths and tray cloths the probable cost of laundering all these items has to be considered and as some of them need to be starched and folded in a special way, the choice of a good laundry which can do this work at reasonable cost and give a good return service will not always be easy to find.

Other Items of Dining Room Equipment

These include flower cases, table numbers, bread baskets, cruets, finger bowls, ash trays and many specialised types of serving tools such as asparagus tongs, snail tongs, lobster picks, and so on. The choice of materials in which these items are made must be in accordance with the main type of equipment used.

If skilled staff are employed there should be no need for waiter's trays in the restaurant except for when clearing away at the end of the service. If trays are to be issued, other than silver salvers such as used for handling around trays of drinks at a reception, they should be of a size that can go easily through swing doors and of a material in keeping with the class of establishment. It should not sag when fully loaded and not have a moulded edge where food debris can lodge unseen.

FLOOR COVERINGS

The choice and selection of floor coverings will be decided in accordance with the kind of dining room and the amount of money available. It is recognised that the covering selected will play a large part in creating the desired atmosphere. A traditional dining room run on formal lines will need to offer a relaxed atmosphere so that a dark coloured covering of good quality is desirable. In contrast, a popular restaurant will want to create a more lively atmosphere that is always fresh looking, lively and bright. Ease of cleaning, wearing properties, the possibility of replacing worn areas, resistance to stains from spillage and marks from furniture, and resistance to dirt, are factors to be taken into account.

The following are amongst those coverings suitable for use in dining rooms:

(i) **Tiles** – ceramic or quarry, are available in a wide range of patterns and colours and help to create a cool environment; they are inclined to be noisy in use but need not be slippery; (ii) **vinyl** – usually foam backed to give a soft tread, available in rolls and as tiles in many patterns and colours often representing tiles and other materials by being embossed or textured; it is inexpensive when compared with other floor coverings; (iii) **carpeting** – this can be comparatively very expensive. It is available by the roll or as squares and there are many different qualities and different mixtures of fibres that give a wide range of choice. The wearing quality varies and even all wool carpets can wear differently. The thickness, backing, colour fastness, need for underlay, plain or patterned, colour, and relationship with the rest of the decor, must all be considered before deciding on what to use; and (iv) **wood floors** – there are many kinds to choose from including hardwood strips and blocks for laying in various patterns; parquet flooring available as short strips or glued in panels; wood mosaic squares made of fingers of wood arranged in basket pattern. This form of covering is good-looking, warm and hard-wearing but expensive and excessive heat may cause shrinkage. Other kinds of floor covering for use in dining rooms to give a particular effect include mosaic made of glass silica, bricks of various sizes and colours, terrazzo which uses marble chippings, natural marble, stone of various kinds and colours, cork tiles, linoleum and rubber.

158

EQUIPMENT FOR BARS AND CUSTOMER AMENITY AREAS

There are many different kinds of bar each having its own particular characteristics; some attempt to serve every possible type of drink whilst others may
sell wine only. Some have a long counter to encourage customers to sit or stand
and drink at the bar whereas others have comfortable seating and waiters to
take the order and serve. There is another type known as the dispense bar which
is usually hidden behind the scenes and supplies drinks to serving staff for
customers; there are also mobile bars which can be set up anywhere they are
required for a special function. The customer amenity areas of a high-class
catering establishment can include a foyer or reception and lounge area where
people can await their friends or for their table to be ready and can have a
drink; the cloakroom for leaving hats and coats; and the toilets.

Bars

The main point to observe about equipping a bar is that it should keep the
stock in perfect condition and that whatever a customer requests is immediately
available and ready to serve. This means that if draught beer is served either the
cellar must be adjacent or there is sufficient space under the counter for the
range of casks and kegs. If from the cellar there may be a need for hydraulic
air compressors, suction engines and impeller pumps in order to facilitate the
service and deliver the beer in good condition. It is necessary to keep wines in
readiness for immediate service so there must be a refrigerator to hold white
and rosé wines and a place of normal room temperature for red wine. A refrigerator shelf for bottles of beer, mineral waters, cyder, etc. saves having to open
the door of the refrigerator each time one is ordered.

In some places all washing is done centrally so that waiting staff would take
all used glasses there; in others they are washed up in the bar either by an
electric machine that will wash, rinse and dry a tray load in under two minutes,
or by a water pressure machine that washes them whilst they are held over it. An
ice-making machine should be sited in or near the bar, and a cash register if
money is handled, complete the large items of equipment.

The following lists indicate the general range of utensils needed to operate a
bar efficiently. An experienced bar-tender will seek to satisfy every customer
requirement by providing every drink on the bar list, as well as any others that
may be requested, and this will mean carrying a full range of equipment where
possible.

For the Making of Cocktails and Mixed Drinks – Shakers, Hawthorn strainer,
mixing glass and spoon, bar glass, squeezer, drinking straws, swizzle stick, cocktail sticks, spirit measures, cutting board and knife, ice crusher, small ice bucket
or bowl and tongs, soda syphon, jugs, ice pick, crown cork opener, corkscrew,
bitters bottles, sugar sifter, nutmeg grater.

For Wine Sales – Ice buckets and stands, corkscrew, champagne cork remover, carafes, strainer and funnel, salvers, wine knife.

For Cigars and Cigarettes – Humidor, cigar cutter, matches.

Foyer and/or Reception

Where there is a foyer or reception area generally only chairs and small tables, either fixed or free standing are required. The reception head waiter's desk may be sited here or just inside the dining room; telephones for external and internal calls can be here or at the cashier's desk.

Cloakroom and Toilet

The provision of toilet facilities is decided by local government regulations which state the number and type of facilities to be provided according to the possible number of persons on the premises at any one time. This naturally decides the total area to be allocated for these services. Toilets and wash-basins can be selected in accordance with the standards to which the establishment is geared, and this applies to the ladies room with its furnishings of chairs, mirrors and dispensers for special needs. Hand-drying equipment can be roller towels, individual towels, paper towel dispensers or warm air hand-dryers. Instead of providing soap, soap dispensers are useful accessories to the general washing and tidying facilities for customers. Provision for the storage or holding of hats, coats, umbrellas and other carried items is dependent on the class of establishment. At one end of the market the provision of hat and coat stands in the dining room is sufficient whereas for a high-class establishment an area, usually adjacent to the toilets, is called for. This requires some sort of staffing, plus shelving and counters for the efficient holding of personal effects plus a well organised security system.

EQUIPPING OF OTHER AREAS

These areas relate to those at the very beginning and end of the catering operations, being the receiving, storing and issuing departments and the waste disposal area. The equipment and machinery used here is usually fixed but in fact space allocation for them is not over-demanding as noted in Chapter 6.

160

Goods Receiving Area

There should be adequate space to receive the expected size and amount of any one delivery, with the possibility of having two suppliers arriving at the same time. In order to inspect goods properly it is necessary to have a table or bench; to check the weights a platform scale or set of scales is necessary, and to transport goods from the area into the stores a trolley and a truck are required.

Storage and Stores Issuing

There can be several kinds of stores for different sorts of commodites but in general all that is required is shelving fitments that make the best use of available space. They are best if adjustable and with the possibility of adaptation for all types of goods and re-siting if necessary. Ready-made systems have this advantage over fixed built-in shelving. Bins for storage of dry goods make better use of space if they are square rather than round. If root vegetables are stored the decision whether to keep them in the original sacks or to turn out will determine what kind of bins to install.

Refrigeration is needed for perishable commodities such as dairy produce, vegetables and salads, meat, poultry, and fish.

Scales and measures for the issuing of commodites to the various departments are necessary and some office equipment can be required for the keeping of records, such as typewriter, calculator, desk, chairs, filing cabinet and shelving for the holding of books and boxed or filed items.

Stores Office

There is a need for an office with the usual office equipment of telephone, desk, chairs, filing cabinets and so on, for the use of the person responsible for running the stores area. It should be adjacent to the receiving area.

Cellar

Racks for laying wines horizontally so as to keep them in good condition, lockable cages for spirits and liqueurs, mobile baskets for empty bottles, trucks and special trolleys for the transfer of goods from cellar to bars are the requirements for the wine and spirits store. If bottling were to be carried out in the cellar then specialised equipment such as bottling and labelling machines, trestles and funnels would be necessary.

Waste Disposal

The equipment in this area may consist only of the firm's bins or the council's paladins; if there is a very large amount of waste a skip may be necessary. All sorts of waste, including cardboard and cans may be compressed into manageable proportions by means of a compressor which crushes everything into a plastic sack that is sealed when full. A baling machine for cardboard, a crushing machine for empty bottles and possibly a refrigerator for keeping swill bins in are other possible items of equipment needed for this area.

FUELS

The fuels used in the running of a catering establishment constitute a large item of expenditure. The general use of electricity for lighting needs care taken in the selection of the type of lighting and its equipment, but the question of choice of a fuel for lighting does not really exist. However, when it comes to the choice of fuel for cooking many factors have to be taken into consideration before a decision is made, bearing in mind that other than for lighting or heating premises the consumption of fuel for cooking is the largest in almost any catering enterprise. It is for this reason that the following information is related to the kitchen.

TYPES OF FUEL

Electricity and gas are the two main fuels used in the cooking of foods, though in some remote places, where supplies of either are very costly or difficult to connect, other fuels such as calor gas in returnable containers, solid fuel for slow-burning stoves such as the Aga and Esse, and of course fuel oil are still widely used.

Oil-fired equipment is mainly gas-fired appliances converted to use oil which was at one time the most economical of all sources of energy; it is clean and efficient but has, of course, to be stored on or near the premises. In large-scale catering the central boiler plant may be oil-fired and the steamer in the kitchen could be run from it, provided the steam is clean and non-smelling.

Coal-fired stoves are still to be found in use and in some restaurants where old traditions die hard and the proprietor makes the claim that his food tastes the better for being cooked by it. Cooking by solid fuel is more demanding in terms of expertise in knowing just when to stoke up in the middle of a busy service period to keep things cooking; the heat it gives off is intense. Coal has to be kept in a cellar near to the kitchen, a porter has to be paid to lay, light and keep the fires going and it is inevitable that there will be a certain amount of dust and ashes which will have to be contended with in the kitchen; but generally speaking the use of solid fuel, except for firing grills with coke is largely outmoded.

Electricity

Electricity is generated by steam-driven turbines the steam being raised by coal, oil, natural gas or nuclear energy; in the UK it is usually transformed to 240 volts AC for use in equipment and is almost 100 per cent efficient, provided the equipment is operated wisely. It is a clean fuel and there is little or no dust or contamination, and no fumes; although trunking is required in the kitchen it is only for ventilation and dispersal of cooking fumes and odours. All items of kitchen machinery work off it including mixers, bowl choppers, dish-washers, pot washing machines, waste disposal units, refrigerators, ventilators and air conditioning. Some equipment can only be electrically operated such as micro-wave ovens, the Recon-plus and Mealstream ovens but after these the caterer can choose between electricity or gas.

It has long been the practice to have some equipment operated by each fuel on the grounds that if there should be disruption in the supply of one, customers could still be fed on food cooked in equipment fired by the alternative fuel. In practice it should not be necessary as these two vital forms of energy are seldom subjected to cuts caused by shortage, industrial disputes or causes other than the weather. It is a fact that electrically operated equipment is more expensive to purchase than gas-fired items and that if they were the same cost per unit, gas would be the cheaper fuel.

Gas

Because it is a visual heat gas is easier to control than electricity and it can usually be adjusted to give the desired degree of heat. It is combusted in conjunction with air to give the correct mixture as denoted by the colour of the flame, and is maintained at constant even pressure by means of a gas governor in the pipe-line to each item thus giving consistency of performance.

Nothing can really go wrong with gas equipment as the parts are simple; blow-backs, caused by the gas becoming unknowingly extinguished, do happen but a flame failure device which cuts off the supply should the pilot fail, guards against it. If a leak in the supply is detected the user is responsible for turning off the supply at the mains and notifying the local gas board.

Many items of gas equipment have electrical devices such as automatic ignition, electric motors to drive fans in convection ovens, lights inside ovens, drives for rotary spits, or warning lights on the outside to indicate if ovens are working. Some items have electrically operated steam injection incorporated, especially for bakery work and for cutting cooking losses by roasting in a humid atmosphere.

163

Liquefied Petroleum Gas

This fuel is particularly suitable for outdoor catering where the cooking is done away from base and, as mentioned, for sites where gas and three-phase electricity are not supplied. They are propane and butane and are sold in cylinders under trade names; they require a different kind of burner from that on a natural gas stove. Stoves, ovens, boilers made for gas can be converted to burn liquid petroleum gas and each item can be connected to a cylinder by a rubber tube to be instantly operational anywhere.

Assessment of Fuels

What the caterer, opening a new business or re-equipping an existing one, wants to know about fuel is how one fuel compares with another and in relation to the equipment.

For assessing a fuel the following points have to be considered,
1. which is the most economical,
2. which is the most efficient,
3. which is the cleanest,
4. which will require the least maintenance, and
5. which is the most reliable as regards supplies.

CONTROL AND ECONOMY OF FUELS

Both electricity and gas are constantly on tap and require only switching on for almost immediate use; a solid top stove, whether fired by electricity or gas, takes time to reach full temperature and since it is designed to hold the heat, it maintains heat after being turned off. So although this is usually the ideal top from the cook's viewpoint, because pans are protected from direct heat and do not burn, it is wasteful to heat; the thinking is that small open rings use fuel more efficiently and give immediate use. Once a solid top stove is turned on it is usually left on whether being fully used or not, partly because the flame cannot be seen and because, as mentioned, it has to be heated well in advance.

Normal ovens have to be turned on beforehand to heat up before putting food in to cook, but with a convection oven it is possible to put in the food almost immediately it is lit as the fan drives the heated air around the oven giving much improved heat transference. Many items of equipment now available are designed to use fuel economically with more accurate thermostats, timing devices and humidity controls; electronic control systems can monitor the temperature in an oven by means of a probe which sends information to the control centre which then adjusts it according to a pre-set programme, and will

164

switch it off when the food is cooked to the desired degree. Ovens are available with a keyboard onto which are fed the weight of each joint, the total quantity of meat loaded in, cooking temperature and required degree of cooking, and it then calculates the programme and gets on with it, thus eliminating all human error but ensuring exact use of fuel and perfectly cooked meat.

With the need to save energy so as to cut their costs, caterers must investigate all possible ways of reducing consumption. Heat recovery from a dish-washing machine is an example. When a dish-washer is in operation much of the energy is lost in the form of steam which is why the atmosphere in the plateroom is always so humid and extra ventilation or air conditioning often has to be installed to make it endurable by staff. A heat recovery pump will cut up to 75 per cent of this lost energy and save 50 per cent in energy costs by drawing the heat from the hot air and water vapour in and around the machine, condensing it and recycling the heat back into the machine. It can supply and maintain the entire heating requirement of the wash water tanks and boost the temperature of the rinse water.

A heat exchange system can be more economical than a heat recovery pump. Here energy is saved through the exchange of heat between the condensation installation and the boiler for rinsing plates with fresh water.

It is obvious that consumption of fuel is affected by the way in which kitchen staff use it; although it must be said that a conscientious cook will use it economically. If, as is sometimes the case, the kitchen is over-equipped, consumption is bound to be higher than if it were just adequately equipped. Old equipment although in good working order may be less efficient than new items which have improved heat-transfer or insulation built in.

Menu planning can reduce the number of items of equipment used or needed. The greater the variety of dishes on the menu the greater will be the cost of fuel, but some methods of cooking can be more economical than others, for example, boiling as against roasting. The size of the portion served, the number of courses per meal and of course the total amount of food cooked can affect the consumption of fuel.

Some firms operate a service to industry which guarantees a saving in the cost of using energy. This is done by indicating the cheaper and most efficient use of energy and showing possible savings by comparison of past and current bills. The charge is 4 per cent of the total annual energy bill or a single sum plus 50 per cent of any energy savings.

FUEL COSTS

The cost of fuel to run a kitchen must be closely controlled and if possible be metered separately from the rest of the establishment, so that the percentage of turnover charged to it can be ascertained and kept as a target not to be exceeded.

165

At present fuels are still measured in non-metric units with electricity being sold by the unit which is at the rate of one kilowatt for one hour. This means that a 10 kW item of equipment will consume 10,000 watts or 10 kW of electricity in one hour. One kilowatt hour is equal to 3.6 MJ (Megajoules) as used under the continental International System of Units (SI); a watt is one joule per second.

Gas is still supplied by the BTU or British Thermal Unit and is sold by the therm which is 100,000 BTU's its heat content is 1042 BTU's per cubic foot which is equal to 1 MJ.

Comparative Costs

When comparing the cost of using the two main fuels it is necessary to calculate that 20 units of electricity = 1 therm of gas. Consumption as registered on the gas meter is shown in cubic feet and to change it into therms the calculation is CV (Calorific Value) × hundreds of cubic feet consumed ÷ 1000. The CV of natural gas is 1042. This will give the number of therms consumed and be shown on the account at the non-domestic tariff per therm. The electricity account will show consumption in units (KWh) and for comparison with gas the cost has to be divided by 20. Both accounts will bear standing charges and meter charges. The problem though is that there will possibly be figures for efficient usage to confound the comparison.

The energy charges for both electricity and gas, since both are used by most establishments, have to be reflected in the prices charged to customers and may make tariffs uncompetitive if there is careless use of fuels.

SERVICES

By services is meant the supplies of gas, electricity and water needed to run an establishment; stemming from these are drainage, ventilation, central heating and air conditioning. The planning team that is designing a new catering department or drastically altering an existing one requires to know what the service needs will be. This is a part of the building information required before the layout is planned and before any equipment is put into place.

A fully detailed plan of the necessary service runs and points for gas, electricity, water and drainage must be prepared and the people doing the installation will work from these plans. For example, as the total electricity demand builds up, according to the various items of equipment and machinery required, it becomes necessary for an electrical engineer to balance the phases of the supply, which will mean a particular specification of single and three phase supply requirements according to the loading of the items of equipment. These technicians must complete their work before the wall and floor surfaces are put in

166

and their work must be carried out in accordance with the Institute of Electrical Engineers regulations, and the various codes of practices. It is the responsibility of the services engineer to ensure that installation work complies with the regulations of the Water Board, the Local Authority and the Boards for Electricity and Gas.

It is usual to run supplies to within one metre of appliances; the exposed pipework should be minimal and be clear of walls and there should be no corrosion from water pipes. Water supplies to equipment on central sites should be both hot and cold and the problem of drainage must be solved so that there is no danger from wet and slippery floors. It should be remembered that a dish washer must have a water softener if the hardness of the water is above 8° Clark and that a calorifier is also necessary.

Greasetraps can be fed with a biological dissolvent that obviates the need to keep taking them up for emptying. The water supply to fire hydrants is often built in as a part of the service supply, or a sprinkler system may be installed. Central heating and air conditioning systems may also be built in rather than being added at a later stage.

A knockoff button to act as a safeguard in cutting off all power to electrical equipment is now frequently installed.

The hot water supply must be adequate to produce the volume of water per hour and at the right temperature to cope with the envisaged amount of business.

All the services installed should allow for spare capacity to cope with any increase in demand and there should be standby equipment for emergency use.

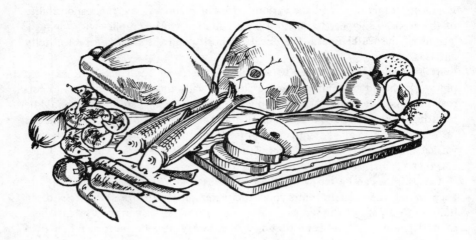

8 PROVISIONING I – COMMODITIES

Food Commodities - Alcoholic and Non-Alcoholic Drinks - Cigars - Cleaning Materials - Stationery and Paperware.

This chapter deals with the commodities both food, liquid and non-food which are in daily use in the catering industry. All the main goods required are described with a view to providing a broad understanding of their value and importance to catering. The information given is not exhaustive but given in a form sufficient to act as a guide only to the various items in each of the main groups of commodities. Not only food but also alcoholic and non-alcoholic drinks are dealt with, the cleaning materials required to keep premises clean and hygienic, and those important items of stationery and paperware that play an ever increasing role in the operation.

The importance of this subject may be recognised by the amount of money being spent on the purchase of commodities which now vies with that of the cost of staff as the major form of expenditure in a catering establishment. With so much money being involved it is vitally important that every penny is spent wisely and that the person responsible for buying obtains the best quality and value for money of every single item of merchandise.

FOOD COMMODITIES

The traditional style of catering demands a wide variety of foodstuffs to produce the requisite dishes and an average stores will hold a stock of as many as two hundred or more different commodities. The more complex the menu the greater the number of goods required and the more the menu is changed so does the extent of the stock. This is in sharp contrast to a fast food operation where the menu seldom changes and is very limited so restricting the number of commodities required to a minimum requirement level.

Food commodities may be divided into two broad categories which are known as perishable and non-perishable foods. The first refers to those fresh foods with a short storage life and the latter to those provisions that can be stored for a considerable length of time. The full list can be divided into approximately a dozen categories. The commodities are given here in the generally accepted order beginning with meat because it is deemed to be the most important item on the normal menu.

Each group is dealt with from the following aspects – recognition of quality, sources of supply and availability, ordering units for optimum usage, the various forms in which goods are available, and the best means of storage for keeping the particular commodity fresh and in its best condition.

MEAT

Meat is the word used to describe the flesh of animals which is prepared for human consumption and includes the offals or interior organs. There are four main types of meat in general use: beef, veal, pork, lamb and mutton. Meat is not a seasonal commodity and in all its forms it is possible to include it on menus throughout the year. It is true that new season's lamb, either home-killed or frozen New Zealand, has its season and may be featured as such when it first appears each spring. At one time pork was considered to be a seasonal commodity; this is no longer the case.

Meat is composed of muscle, connective tissue, fat and bone in various amounts according to type, age, sex, and breed. The muscle part is the actual lean flesh and is composed of bundles of muscle cells which are held in place by the connective tissue. The connective tissue is mainly collagen which softens during cooking; this should not be confused with the tough sinew which does not become tender and should be removed from the joint. The fat of meat varies in colour from the hard white fat of lamb to the deep yellow of old cow beef and the amount of bone and its hardness is an indication of the age of the animal.

The tenderness of meat is determined by the age, breed and part of the animal according to the degree of activity a particular joint in the anatomy undergoes. It is usual to hang meat for a varying length of time to allow it to develop tenderness and flavour – beef for up to fourteen days, lamb for not quite so long and neither veal nor pork really need any hanging.

In most catering establishments the amount of money spent on the purchase of meat outweighs that of all other commodities put together, it being estimated that more than 30p of each £1.00 of expenditure in the kitchen goes on meat in its various forms. This is because on most menus meat is the main item and, except for vegetarians, it plays a part of everyone's diet each day. Its importance also derives from its nutritional value as the most valuable source of protein – the substance in the diet which provides growth and repair of the body tissues.

The race and creed of people have a bearing on the kind of meat a particular person and even a nation, or religious sect, will consume. To some people beef is obnoxious whilst to others pork is absolutely forbidden because of religious laws and a caterer needs to know the rules governing the eating habits of such groups so as to avoid serving unsuitable meat.

BEEF

Beef is the name given to meat obtained from domestic cattle and is the most widely used kind of meat. The best breed for beef is reckoned to be the Aberdeen Angus which is a small, stocky animal; other breeds are the Herefords and Shorthorns and crosses of these. Charolais cattle have been brought over from France to cross-breed with some British stock to improve the quality.

Quality

The following is a generally accepted classification of grades of home-killed (T.K.) beef.

1. **Prime** Meat from young, well-fed heifers and steers which is thick, blocky and compact in form; the fat brittle, firm, waxy, white, and smooth; the lean surface silky to the touch; the bones soft and porous with red blood showing through them.
2. **Choice** Meat from young, well-fed heifers and steers and also from young cows; the fat firm and white; the cut surface red to slightly dark red in colour; bones soft red, ending in pearly white.
3. **Good** Grass-fed heifers and steers; fat yellow, soft and slightly oily; the lean, red to dark red and maybe soft and watery.
4. **Standard** Young heifers, steers and cows, rangy, angular, thinly fleshed and with poor conformation; fat soft; cut surface red to dark red in colour.

There is also a commercial quality which is suitable only for manufacturing purposes. Scotch beef is noted for good quality and usually costs more than English or other beef.

170

Sources of Supply

Most supplies are home produced with additional sources from the EEC countries, also a limited amount from Kenya, Botswana, New Zealand.

Beef is available all the year round and there is no season when it is thought to be at its best.

It may be obtained in the form of carcass beef either as a forequarter or a hindquarter, in wholesale cuts either on the bone or boneless and as boneless wholesale cuts in Cryovac packs which being airtight keep the meat in very good condition; it is available in fresh, chilled, and frozen forms.

Ordering Units for Optimum Usage

A whole side of beef is divided into two quarters between the tenth and eleventh ribs which gives a hindquarter with three rib bones and a forequarter with ten rib bones in it. Each quarter will weigh from 60 kg to 80 kg from a heifer or up to 90 kg from an older animal.

There are a number of terms used in the meat trade for the various ordering units the following being those most commonly used:

Hdqtr X (Hindquarter X)	A hindquarter minus the thin flank.
Hdqtr XX (Hindquarter double X)	A hindquarter minus the thin flank and kidney.
Baron	A pair of sirloins in one piece.
Rump and Loin	A rump and sirloin in one piece.
Loin	A sirloin.
Thick	Abbreviation for thick flank.
Strip Loin	A boned sirloin.
Top bit	The topside, silverside and thick flank in one piece.
Crop	The chuck rib, middle rib and fore rib in one piece.
Pony	The chuck rib and middle rib in one piece together.
Coast	The plate and brisket in one piece.

A hindquarter of beef has most of the best quality cooking joints and is mostly used in high-class catering establishments.

The illustration, Fig. 7, shows a hindquarter of beef viewed from the inside and the more usual joints into which it is dissected for catering.

171

Figure 7
HINDQUARTER OF BEEF

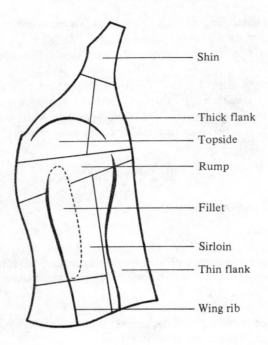

- Shin
- Thick flank
- Topside
- Rump
- Fillet
- Sirloin
- Thin flank
- Wing rib

The following table lists the joints that can be cut from a hindquarter of approximately 70 kg, their approximate weights and the optimum uses of each.

Name of joint	Approx. weight	Optimum uses
Shin	7 kg	Consommé, stewing
Topside	8 kg	Roasting, braising, stewing
Silverside	10 kg	Pickling for boiling, stewing
Thick flank	10 kg	Roasting, braising, stewing steaks
Rump	9 kg	Steaks for grilling
Sirloin	10 kg	Roasting, poêling, steaks for grilling and shallow frying
Fillet	3 kg	Roasting, poêling, steaks for grilling and shallow frying
Wing rib	4 kg	Roasting
Thin flank	8 kg	Boiling, stewing

In addition there is a kidney and a quantity of suet.

172

Many small cuts of beef are prepared from some of these joints, which may be cut on the premises or purchased in the form of portion controlled meats; they are:

Name of cut	Description	Average portion weight
Sirloin steak	Steak cut from a boned sirloin.	180–200 g
Double sirloin	Double thickness steak cut from a sirloin.	350–400 g
Minute steak	Thin sirloin steak flattened.	150 g
Porterhouse steak	Steak cut through a whole sirloin with the bone and fillet.	550–650 g
Chateaubriand	Thick steak for minimum of 2 people cut from the head of the fillet	250 g
Fillet steak	Steak approx. 3 cm thick cut from the upper part of the fillet.	180–200 g
Tournedos	Round steak cut 3 cm thick from the centre of the fillet.	120–150 g
Filet mignon	Small steaks cut from the tail end of the fillet.	2 x 75 g
Rump steak	2 cm thick slice of the rump.	150–200 g
Point steak	Steak cut from the triangular corner of the rump.	150–200 g

A forequarter of beef provides only one good quality roasting joint – the fore rib – the remainder of the carcass being more suitable for braising in joints or cut into cubes for stewing. This suggests that the forequarter is generally tougher than the hindquarter and has a slightly higher bone and fat content.

When cutting beef for stewing it is preferable to use meat all from one cut rather than to have it mixed from more than one joint. The meat from, for example, the clod and sticking piece is tougher than other joints.

Figure 8
FOREQUARTER OF BEEF

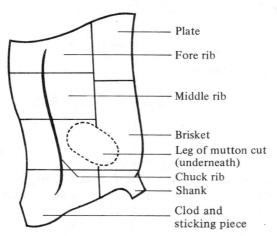

Plate

Fore rib

Middle rib

Brisket

Leg of mutton cut (underneath)

Chuck rib

Shank

Clod and sticking piece

173

The illustration, Fig. 8, shows a forequarter of beef viewed from the inside and the more usual joints into which it is dissected for catering.

The following table lists the joints that can be cut from a forequarter of beef of approx. 70 kg together with their approximate weights and the optimum uses of each.

Name of joint	Approx. weight	Optimum uses
Shank	5 kg	For consommé, stewing
Leg of mutton cut	8 kg	Braising, stewing
Plate	8 kg	Boiling, stewing
Brisket	12 kg	Pickling for boiling, stewing
Clod and Sticking piece	10 kg	Stewing
Chuck rib	13 kg	Braising, stewing
Middle rib	8 kg	Roasting, braising
Fore rib	6 kg	Roasting

No small cuts are prepared from this part of the carcass except for perhaps a large steak cut on the rib-bone.

Storage

Fresh beef should be held at $2\,^{\circ}$C and allowed to improve and thus become more tender by hanging in an atmosphere where the relative humidity is 80–90 per cent. Cuts of beef should be laid on trays in the refrigerator and covered to prevent drying out with consequent loss of weight. Vacuum packs of beef should be stored similarly although the relative humidity is not important as the meat is protected.

Chilled beef should be held at $-2\,^{\circ}$C so that it stays hard on the outside but is soft within.

Frozen beef should be stored at $-18\,^{\circ}$C or below.

VEAL

Veal is the word used to denote the flesh of young calves which have been specially fed for the table; the method used to rear them aims at producing a high-class carcass of approximately 100 kg at three months of age.

Quality

The flesh should be pale pink in colour, firm in texture and the cut surface dry; a thin covering of fat which should be firm and also light pink in colour
174

except over the kidney which should be well covered with fat; bones heavy in proportion to the size of the carcass and pinkish white in colour. As produced by the intensive farming method, veal is very tender and of prime quality but expensive. Stewing veal is often the meat from bobby calves which are the unwanted animals from dairy herds that are slaughtered at a very young age; they are wasteful because of the high bone content and generally are of poor quality.

Sources of Supply and Availability

Supplies are available from the United Kingdom, Holland and France. Frozen boneless stewing veal is imported from New Zealand and Australia and fresh veal which is available all the year round is usually handled only by catering butchers.

Ordering Units for Optimum Usage

Veal is available in the following joints – hindquarter; leg with rump; loin and rump; saddle; shoulder; and best end. It is also possible to purchase by the carcass and the price will be less than for the best cuts but there will be some stewing meat to be utilised.

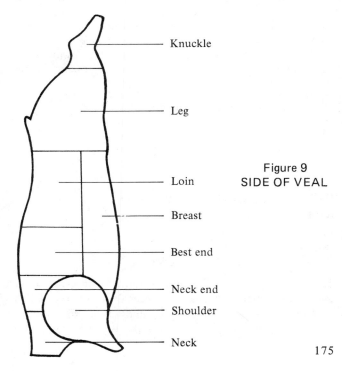

Knuckle

Leg

Loin

Breast

Best end

Neck end

Shoulder

Neck

Figure 9
SIDE OF VEAL

175

Fig. 9 shows a carcass of veal viewed from the side and the usual joints into which it is dissected.

The following table lists the joints that can be cut from a side of veal of approximately 50 kg together with their approximate weights and the optimum uses for each; it also shows the small cuts obtainable.

Name of joint	Approx. weight.	Optimum uses and small cuts
Leg	12 kg	Roasting, poêling, braising
Knuckle	2½ kg	Stewing; cut into thick sections on the bone (Osso Buco)
Cushion	2½ kg	Roasting, poêling, braising; cut into escalopes, grenadins
Under-cushion	2½ kg	Roasting, poêling, braising; cut into escalopes, grenadins
Thick flank	3 kg	Roasting, poêling, braising; cut into escalopes, grenadins
Rump	2 kg	Roasting, poêling, braising
Saddle	8 kg	Roasting, poêling,
Loin	4 kg	Roasting, poêling; cut into chops for grilling and shallow frying
Best end	3 kg	Roasting; poêling; cut into cutlets for grilling and shallow frying
Neck end	2 kg	Stewing
Neck	3 kg	Stewing
Breast	2½ kg	Roasting, stewing, braising
Shoulder	7 kg	Roasting, poêling, braising, stewing

Cushion, Under-cushion, Thick flank and Rump are *Cut from the leg*.

In addition there is a kidney attached to the loin.
The bones from the leg weigh approximately 2 kg.

Storage

Veal is usually bought fresh and ready for use so needs only to be held in the refrigerator at 2°-4°C.

LAMB

Lamb is the young sheep and is normally classified as such up to one year of age; frozen imported lambs are animals up to six months of age which is why home-killed lamb is usually larger and heavier than the New Zealand imported.
   Some lambs are described on the menu as being Pre-salé which indicates

176

they are from a flock that grazed in the salt marshes by the sea; this grass is supposed to give the meat a distinctive flavour.

Baby lamb, or House lamb is reared particularly well in France and is excellent, being very small and naturally very tender and of a fine flavour.

Quality

Conformation of carcass is particularly important in lamb; it means a compact shape that will yield the maximum amount of usable meat without excessive waste and bone loss. The eye of lean in the best end and loin is an indication of this and it should be large in relation to the surrounding fat. The colour of the lean should be dull red, the fat clean white and bones small.

Sources of Supply and Availability

The main supplies of lamb are from the United Kingdom and New Zealand, the latter being in deep frozen form and cheaper than home killed which is almost always sold fresh. Both are available all through the year but new season's lamb from both countries may be featured on menus in the spring. Welsh and Scottish lamb both enjoy high reputations as quality meats.

Ordering Units for Optimum Usage

Lamb may be bought by the whole carcass, as halves cut between the saddle and best end or as individual joints. If only roast lamb is featured on the menu it would be unwise to purchase by the carcass as there will be a quantity of stewing meat to dispose of.

Storage

English lamb should be held in cold storage at $2°-4°C$; it does not normally require ageing to make it tender. Frozen New Zealand lamb should be stored at $-18°C$ until required then allowed to defrost at $4°-7°C$ in 80-90 per cent relative humidity in a refrigerator.

The following table lists the joints with their approximate weights as cut from a PM grade lamb; it also shows their optimum uses and small cuts obtainable.

Name of joint	Approx. weight	Optimum uses and small cuts
Shoulder	2 × 1½ kg	Roasting, stewing
Leg	2 × 2 kg	Roasting, boiling
Breast	2 × ¾ kg	Roasting, stewing
Middle neck	1 kg	Stewing
Scrag end	¾ kg	Stewing
Best end	2 × 1¼ kg	Roasting; cut into cutlets for grilling
Saddle or	4 kg	Roasting, poêling
2 Loins		Roasting, poêling; cut into chops for grilling or into noisettes or rosettes for shallow frying

MUTTON

The exact age when lamb becomes mutton is not laid down in strict terms but is usually taken to be when the animal is over twelve months old. Where the qualities of tenderness and flavour are concerned it is better that the animal is not over fifteen months old, and is for preference a hoggett, i.e. a castrated male or maiden ewe showing not more than two permanent incisor teeth at slaughter. In general its flavour can be excellent but stronger than that of lamb. The colour of the flesh is darker and the bone flinty and more heavy in proportion. The equivalent joints are 20–25 per cent heavier than those of lamb.

The sources of supply, ordering units and uses, and storage are as for lamb.

New Zealand lamb and mutton are closely graded into a number of categories; the following are the prime grades offering the best quality for catering, i.e. well fleshed in the loins, legs and forequarters with an adequate but not excessive fat cover.

Lamb		Mutton (Hoggetts)	
Grade	Average weight	Grade	Average weight
PL	8–12½ kg	HL	up to 22 kg
PM	13–16 kg	HM	22½–26 kg
PH	16½–19½ kg		
PHH	20–25½ kg		

Figs. 10 and 11 show two views of a carcass of lamb or mutton and the more usual joints into which it is dissected for catering.

178

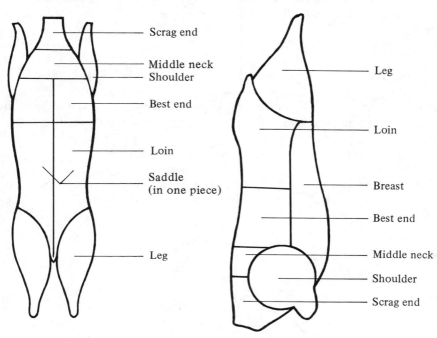

Figure 10
CARCASS OF LAMB OR MUTTON
(viewed from above)

- Scrag end
- Middle neck
- Shoulder
- Best end
- Loin
- Saddle (in one piece)
- Leg

Figure 11
CARCASS OF LAMB OR MUTTON
(viewed from side)

- Leg
- Loin
- Breast
- Best end
- Middle neck
- Shoulder
- Scrag end

PORK

Pork is the name given to the flesh of the pig; good quality pork comes from animals of up to twelve months of age and there is little difference between one carcass and another because of the methods of rearing.

Quality

The flesh should be light pink to greyish-pink in colour, firm in texture and finely marbled; the fat covering firm and milky white and not brittle; bones should be small and pinkish in colour and with a very small proportion of bone in relation to the weight of the carcass; the outer rind thin, smooth, golden and with no hairs left on it.

Sucking pigs are specially reared for the table and are up to six weeks of age; the smaller and plumper they are the better.

Sources of Supply and Availability

Pork is in season all the time and available fresh or frozen. Most of that consumed in the United Kingdom is home killed although some frozen imported pork is available.

Ordering Units for Optimum Usage

Pork is sold by the side, in joints, and in portion controlled cuts. It is the usual practice to sell the spare rib and loin as one long joint for either roasting or cutting into chops; it is also available as short loins. It is usual to sell pork with the skin on but it is available with the skin and some of the fat removed.

The following illustration, Fig. 12, shows a carcass of pork viewed from the side and the more usual joints into which it is dissected for catering.

Figure 12
SIDE OF PORK

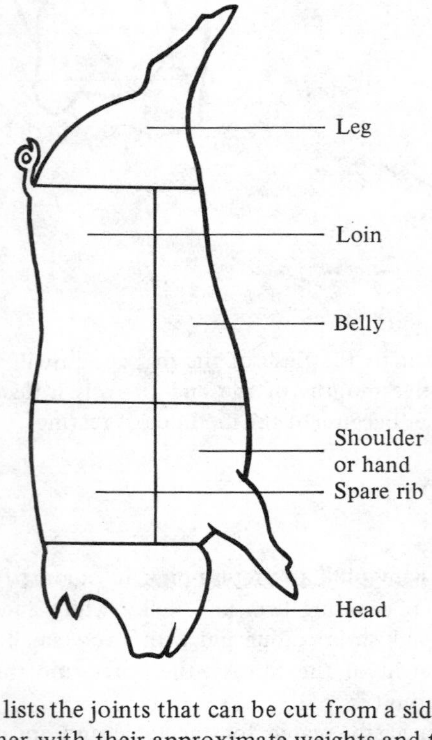

The following table lists the joints that can be cut from a side of pork of approximately 23 kg together with their approximate weights and the optimum uses for each; it also shows the small cuts obtainable.

180

Name of joint	Approx. weight	Optimum uses and small cuts
Leg	$5\frac{1}{2}$ kg	Roasting, boiling
Loin	6 kg	Roasting; cut into chops for grilling and shallow frying, escalopes
Spare rib	$3\frac{1}{2}$ kg	Roasting; cut into chops for grilling; shallow frying and braising
Shoulder or hand	$3\frac{1}{2}$ kg	Roasting, stewing, pies, forcemeats
Belly	3 kg	Boiling, pies, pâtés, stuffings, forcemeat
Head ($\frac{1}{2}$)	2 kg	Boiling for brawn

Storage

Pork can be used as soon as delivered as it does not improve to any extent by hanging. It should be used as soon as possible as it deteriorates quicker than other meats. Storage is in a refrigerator at 2 °C.

BACON

Bacon is the cured flesh of pigs specially bred for processing as bacon. The whole sides are cured by dry salting or by immersing in a brine. It can then be sold as green or unsmoked bacon, or undergo further curing by smoking until it develops additional flavour. Smoking of bacon was originally employed so as to enhance the preservative action of curing but is now used because many people prefer it and are prepared to pay more for this kind.

Quality

The preference is for lean bacon with a low salt content and a good bright colour. The side of bacon should be dry with no sign of stickiness or smell of taint; there should be no excess of fat as compared with the lean; the fat should be smooth and white and the lean firm and a pale pink or dark pink in colour.

Sources of Supply and Availability

Much of the bacon sold in this country comes from Denmark with smaller supplies from Holland and Poland and also some excellent home produced bacon. It is available all the year round.

Ordering Units for Optimum Usage

There are only five joints in a side of bacon which are the gammon, back, streaky, collar and hock; it can be purchased in any of these joints or by the whole side; as a Middle which is the back and streaky only in one piece; as a Spencer which is the whole side minus the gammon; or as a Fore-end which is the collar and hock in one piece.

Fig. 13 shows a side of bacon and the more usual joints into which it is dissected for catering.

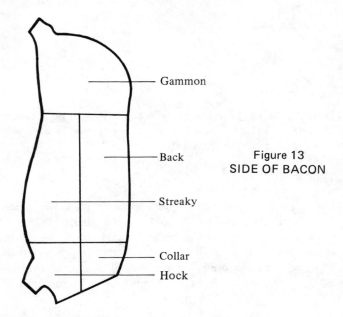

Figure 13
SIDE OF BACON

The following table lists the joints that can be cut from a side of bacon of approximately 23 kg with their approximate weights and their optimum uses; it also lists the small cuts obtainable.

Name of joint	Approx. weight	Optimum uses and small cuts
Hock	$3\frac{1}{2}$ kg	Boiling; pies
Collar	3 kg	Boiling; pies
Back	$7\frac{1}{2}$ kg	Cutting into bacon chops; slicing into rashers for shallow frying and grilling
Streaky	$3\frac{1}{2}$ kg	Cutting into rashers for shallow frying and grilling
Gammon	$5\frac{1}{2}$ kg	Boiling; braising; cutting into gammon steaks for shallow frying and grilling

Storage

If purchased by the side, bacon should be hung in a cool, well ventilated place at no more than 10 °C; it is not necessary or advisable to store under refrigeration. Bacon in joints and as rashers are available in vacuum packs and may be stored in an ordinary refrigerator or in a deep freeze but once opened should be used quickly.

OFFALS

This word refers to certain internal organs and other parts of domesticated animals slaughtered for consumption. The ones most used are: from the beef – tongue, kidney, heart, liver, sweetbreads, tripe and tail; from the calf – head, brain, liver, kidney, heart and sweetbreads; from the sheep – heart, liver, kidney and sweetbreads; from the pig – head, kidney and liver.

Quality

This is judged by its nice fresh colour, firmness and weight; any untoward smell and stickiness means it is stale and not fit to be used.

Sources of Supply and Availability

Offals are available in fresh form and available all through the year, and together with frozen supplies is obtainable from most butchers. Some items such as a calf's head may require time to obtain.

Ordering Units for Optimum Usage

The unit is per single item for such items as heads and by weight for all others. It is possible to purchase sets of lamb's plucks consisting of the liver, heart and lungs attached to the windpipe; in addition there are other less popular offals such as chitterlings, bone marrow, spinal cord, calf's feet, pig's trotters, pig's tails and pig's and lamb's caul. Brawn, haggis and black pudding are examples of available foods produced from offals in prepared form.

When ordering offal it is important to specify the exact requirements, as, for example, calf's liver which is of much better quality and thus more expensive than ox liver, and veal sweetbreads which are better than lamb's sweetbreads; again the round or heart sweetbreads are of better quality than the long or throat ones.

183

Storage

This is the same as for all other fresh or frozen meats although if anything, offals deteriorate quicker than fresh meat. Storage should be on trays at 2°C.

POULTRY

The word poultry denotes all domesticated birds reared for the table; it includes the various kinds of chickens, turkeys, ducks, and geese as well as guinea fowl and pigeon.

Figure 14 lists the general range of poultry available together with descriptions, seasons, weights and cooking methods.

Quality

Poultry should have plump, well-fleshed breasts and legs, and the colour of the skin and flesh should be natural and not discoloured – chicken and turkey have white flesh, ducks and guinea fowl are darker and pigeons have quite dark flesh. Poultry should be cleanly plucked and neatly prepared and the smell very fresh; the pliability of the end of the breastbone and the small size of the wing tips are signs of a young and tender bird.

Chickens are often graded into three qualities – Grade A is the best being excellent birds all within a small weight range, Grade B chickens will have a few minor blemishes and Grade C some deformities and blemishes and be unequal in size.

Sources of Supply and Availability

It is normally possible to obtain every item of poultry throughout the year although, as indicated on the list, there are certain times of the year when they are at their best. Poultry is available whole in fresh, chilled and frozen form in a range of weights as shown; it is usual to purchase them plucked and cleaned and ready to cook. The price is at so much per kilogram and as modern production methods on factory lines produce birds of a uniform quality and weight, portion and price control is made easy and more exact.

It is also possible to purchase poultry, especially chickens, as portion controlled items in such forms as suprêmes, escalopes, and drumsticks. Turkey is available as rolled joints for roasting and as frozen cooked rolls for slicing.

184

Ordering Units for Optimum Usage

Ordering is by number of birds of an approximate weight.

Storage

Fresh birds should be kept at 5°C and frozen ones at not higher than −18°C then removed to a normal refrigerator and allowed to defrost for up to thirty-six hours.

Frozen turkeys may require forty-eight hours or more to thaw out depending upon the weight and it is very important that frozen birds are allowed to defrost completely and the bags of giblets removed, before placing them to cook. Many cases of food poisoning are caused by incomplete thawing and cooking of frozen poultry, particularly the very large birds.

GAME

There are two main kinds of game – feathered game and furred or ground game. In general it can be said that game birds differ from poultry in being stronger in flavour and the same can be said for the meat from game animals as compared with beef. In most cases game should be hung for a length of time for it to acquire a more pronounced flavour and to become tender.

FEATHERED GAME

Quality

Feathered game is usually purchased rough plucked and the skin should be unbroken and the limbs undamaged by shot. There should be no bruises and the breast should be plump; the size and hardness of the spurs and the softness of the end of the breastbone are guides to tenderness. Except for pheasant cock birds are usually better eating than hen birds.

Source of Supply and Availability

Game birds are protected and are available only as shown in the accompanying list; frozen birds may be used out of season. Game is purchased from either a specialist dealer, from a poulterer who also deals in game and also from some fishmongers who hold a licence to deal in game.

185

Figure 14
POULTRY

Name	Description	Best season	Best average weight	Suitable cooking methods
Capon	A castrated cockerel which grows large and plump; tender moist white flesh and delicate flavour.	Winter	$2\frac{1}{2}$–$3\frac{1}{2}$ kg	Roasting, poêling
Chicken	A well-fleshed medium size bird, good colour and excellent flavour.	All year	$1\frac{1}{4}$–$1\frac{3}{4}$ kg	Roasting, grilling, shallow frying, poêling
Fowl, fattened	Not quite as large as the capon but well fleshed, excellent white colour, flavour and texture.	All year	2–$2\frac{1}{2}$ kg	Poaching, poêling
Fowl, boiling	An old hen; needs prolonged cooking.	All year	2–3 kg	Boiling
Poussin	A very small milk-fed chicken.	Spring	Single: 350 g Double: 600 g	Roasting, grilling
Turkey	Large bird with excellent flesh to bone ratio; flavour stronger than chicken but still very good; texture can be pronounced and dry if overcooked.	Autumn and Winter	5–12 kg	Roasting, boiling
Duck and Duckling	Loses a lot of weight in cooking because of high fat content; dark tender flesh of excellent flavour; texture can be pronounced and dry if overcooked.	Summer and Autumn	2–3 kg	Braising, roasting, poêling

	Description	Season	Weight	Cooking methods
Goose	Similar to duck but much larger and flavour more pronounced; high fat content; the older bird can be tough and needs braising. Very good flavour.	Sept–Feb	5–7 kg	Roasting, braising
Guinea fowl	Slightly smaller and thinner than a chicken with yellow skin and darkish flesh; very good slightly gamey flavour. Can be dry and stringy if overcooked.	Summer	$1\frac{1}{2}$ kg	Roasting, poêling, shallow frying
Pigeon	Dark flesh which can be decidedly tough and stringy in an older bird; strong almost gamey flavour.	Spring	500 g	Braising, roasting; poêling; grilling

Ordering Units for Optimum Usage

Game birds are sold by number and not by weight; pheasants are normally sold by the brace which is a cock and a hen bird. As shown in the list the most popular method of cooking is by roasting so it is important to check for tenderness before committing them to the oven. Older birds are larger in size and are usually reckoned to be suitable only for braising or using in pies and terrines.

Storage

Unplucked and rough-plucked birds should be hung in a cool, dry place for several days in order to develop flavour and tenderness; they should then be cleaned and trussed and stored in the refrigerator at 5 °C until required.

Figure 15 lists the main kinds of feathered game, their season, number of portions, methods of cooking, together with a brief description of each.

FURRED GAME

Under this heading is included the several different types of deer, hares and rabbits. For the United Kingdom these are the only furred game generally available although it is still possible to obtain wild boar and some other game animals from the Continent although with marked difficulty. Meat from the deers is known collectively as venison.

Quality

Venison – the colour should be a clean, deep reddish brown with a little flecking of fat in the flesh and preferably with a slight covering of fat on parts of the carcass. The flesh of the doe (female) is usually better for tenderness and flavour than that of the buck (male) and a young beast up to four years old being in both cases more tender. The flesh of older animals is invariably stringy, tough and very dry.

The animal should be skinned and eviscerated as soon as it has been killed and should then be hung for two to three weeks in a refrigerator with a good circulation of air and not too high humidity, to mature and develop its flavour. Always check for excessive shot and mangled bones – the minimum is always more desirable.

Hare – the young animal is to be preferred for its tender and less stringy flesh. The ears of the young animal tear easily and the claws are generally short. The skin should be removed and it should then be hung downwards in a refrigerator for up to a week before being processed. If bought already hung and with its entrails removed, care should be taken to check that the diaphragm is intact thus containing the blood and offals which are essential for preparing jugged hare.

Rabbit – the young animal is to be preferred for its more tender delicate flesh. The animal should not be hung for too long as this can develop a strong unpleasant flavour. The flesh should be plump, white and free from any pronounced smell. The ears of the young animal tear easily and the bones of the underjaw break easily under pressure.

Sources of Supply and Availability

Venison is deemed to be in season from July to March and is generally only available from specialist dealers in game although some is available throughout the year in frozen form. Hare and rabbit is available fresh from August to March. Frozen rabbit is available all the year with most of it imported from Australia. Hares are usually obtainable from specialist dealers but rabbit is usually to be had from most butchers.

Ordering units

Venison is obtainable in carcass form usually the forequarter and hindquarter which is more commonly called the haunch. Joints such as the whole saddle, loins, shoulder or leg can be provided but it should always be borne in mind that ordering should be for specific requirements. Customer demand is not very high and there can easily be excessive waste. Good steaks can be cut from the leg and the loins can supply excellent chops.

Hare are obtainable and ordered by number either whole and unskinned or skinned and paunched (eviscerated). Rabbit can be provided unskinned but eviscerated or skinned and eviscerated. Frozen rabbit is also obtainable whole or in boned form. They are usually ordered by number and where applicable weight.

Storage

Venison should be stored in a hanging position in the refrigerator at a temperature of approximately 4°C. Sprinkling with pepper and flour and hanging in a cool, well aired place is now an outmoded practice although some country areas still adhere to the practice. Small cuts and joints are best kept on trays in the refrigerator.

Figure 16 gives some brief details concerning the three main kinds of furred game obtainable in the United Kingdom.

189

Figure 15
FEATHERED GAME

Name	Description	Season	Av. number of portions per bird	Ordering unit	Suitable cooking methods
Capercaillie	Like a very large size grouse, slightly dark flesh; tender and very good flavour.	Aug–Dec	10–12	By number	Roasting, pies, terrines, escalopes
Grouse	Grey plumage with grey furry legs; very tender when young up to 18 months; perhaps the best of all game birds; excellent and distinctive flavour.	12th Aug– 15th Dec	1–2	By number	Roasting. Old birds – pies, puddings, terrines
Partridge	Smaller than the grouse; when young and plump, very tender; the grey-legged partridge is better quality than the red-legged; excellent delicate flavour.	Oct–Feb	1	By number	Roasting. Old birds – braising
Pheasant	A largish bird; the cock bird is very beautiful but the hen is usually much plumper and more tender; the flesh is whitish but inclined to be dry and needs to be larded and well basted when roasted; needs to be hung for some time to develop its gamey yet excellent and delicate flavour.	Oct–Feb	2–4	By number	Roasting, poêling. Old birds – braising
Plover	Small plump bird, the best for eating being the golden, grey and green plovers. They are now mostly protected species in the UK and thus rarely available; excellent, delicate and distinctive flavour.	Oct–Feb	1	By number	Roasting
Quail	Small, plump and very fatty bird mostly reared commercially on quail farms; should be eaten very soon after being killed; good texture, tender and very good delicate flavour.	All year	2 per portion	By number	Roasting

			2 per portion		
Snipe	A small marsh feeding bird with long legs and bill; dark flesh, good texture and excellent flavour.	Aug–Mar	2 per portion	By number	Roasting
Teal	Small species of wild duck; pronounced flavour which is sometimes fishy; needs to be young and if roasted not overcooked.	Aug–Mar	1	By number	Roasting, braising
Wild duck	In the UK this refers to the Mallard; very dark flesh which can be lean and tough if not young and carefully selected; strong pronounced flavour which can sometimes be fishy.	Aug–Mar	2	By number	Roasting
Woodcock	Similar in appearance to the snipe but larger; enjoys a high reputation for gastronomic excellence.	Oct–Feb	1	By number	Roasting, pies, terrines

Figure 16
FURRED GAME

Name	Description	Season	Average number of portions	Ordering unit	Suitable cooking methods
Venison	Includes red deer, fallow deer and roebuck; dark flesh with little fat; excellent if slightly strong flavour; often needs larding and marinating for many preparations; the flesh of older animals can be very tough and stringy.	July–March	depends on size and weight	by weight or joint	Roasting, stewing, braising, grilling
Hare	Dark flesh with a pronounced gamey flavour; can be tough with a coarse texture in older animals; needs marinating for many preparations; be careful of splintered bones and shot.	Aug–March	6–8	by number	Stewing, roasting
Rabbit	Whitish flesh with a delicate almost chicken-like flavour when fresh; tender and of good texture; do not hang for too long as the flesh quickly develops taint; beware of splintered bones and pellets in those that have been shot.	all year	4–6	by number	Stewing, roasting, pies

FISH AND SHELLFISH

Fish contributes a great deal of interest to the menu and is second only in importance to meat for the provision of protein in the diet.

There are many different kinds of fish used world-wide in catering and in this country everyday supplies enable as many as twenty varieties to be featured on the menu; in the following section only the most commonly used in catering are dealt with.

There is a big difference in price between the cheapest and dearest kinds of fish brought about by supply and demand, in which the weather sometimes plays a big part; but fish is still quite an expensive commodity and as such deserves to be handled with care. It is also a highly nutritious, delicate and very perishable commodity which merits proper attention in storage and cooking.

The Fishmonger's Company is a City livery company which employs inspectors to inspect fish coming into markets in the City of London and elsewhere, and has certain statutory powers under various Acts of Parliament. The Department of Agriculture, Fisheries and Food and the White Fish Authority also have certain controls over the sale of fish.

Fish can be classified under many different headings such as salt water and fresh water fish and these again can be divided into white and oily fish. There are also the shellfish which can be subdivided into crustaceans and molluscs. Available as well are those fish and shellfish which have been processed, such as the salted, cured and smoked ones known collectively as dry fish in contradistinction to fresh fish which are known collectively as wet fish; in addition to these are frozen, tinned and pickled fish products which play a very useful part in cookery, adding much in the way of variety to menus.

SALT WATER FISH

This heading includes those fish caught in the oceans which are available in commercial quantities either in fresh or frozen form, whether fished by a British trawler in the seas around this country or from as far away as the Arctic Ocean, or those landed here from a foreign boat.

In this section they will be classed under the heading of white fish and oily fish and will include the round bodied ones which feed near the surface and the flat ones which in general inhabit the depths of the oceans.

FRESH WATER FISH

Fish from the rivers and lakes are not generally available commercially excepting for salmon and trout; apart from these, freshwater fish do not often appear on menus in this country. In this section only those fish that are featured to some extent will be dealt with and as with salt water fish they are classed under the headings of white fish and oily fish.

The following information relates to both salt and fresh water fish.   193

Quality

The quality of fresh fish is ascertained by checking for the following points: eyes – prominent and bright; gills – deep red colour; smell – very clean and fresh; skin – undamaged, moist and covered with its natural glaze; scales – these should be abundant on fish which have them; flesh – fairly firm and elastic to touch. If fish is ordered filleted the fillets should be clean cut, smell fresh and not be sticky.

If frozen and ordered defrosted the foregoing points are mostly applicable especially a fresh, clean smell and the firmness of the flesh. If ordered to be delivered frozen for storage then the fish should be frozen hard and delivered from a refrigerated van. There should be no sign of dryness or dehydration and all surfaces should be covered with a coating of frozen moisture.

Sources of Supply and Availability

There are now very few wholesale fish markets in this country so it is necessary to purchase this commodity from a local wholesale fish merchant who will obtain his supplies from one of the fishing ports. He will most probably deal in both fresh and frozen fish and be able to obtain every kind required. Most salt water fish are in season all the year but there are certain times when they are at their best as shown in the following lists; storms at sea sometimes cause shortages. The supply of the popular fresh water fish is governed by the fishing season, for example salmon is in season between February and August but differs by a few days between England and Scotland; frozen fish is always available.

Much fish is imported from other countries and many types are now being bred in fish farms. To make up for the high cost and short supply of several fish such as cod and haddock, some varieties previously ignored are being marketed as suitable cheaper substitutes; these include pollack, red snapper and monk fish.

Ordering Units for Optimum Usage

In markets fresh fish is usually quoted by the stone (6 kg) but any weight or number may be ordered from the fishmonger. Many fish, including fillets of fish, are graded into weights plus or minus 15–20 g and portion control cuts are available either fresh or frozen. Fillets can be cross-cut which is two fillets of a flat fish held together by the skin, or individually cut; large size ones are cut into portion size pieces. Whole fish such as cod can be obtained without the head. It is advisable that fish should be ordered fresh for the actual day of use.

194

Storage

All fresh fish is highly perishable and requires careful storage to ensure its freshness and quality. Ideally a separate fish refrigerator with good humidity should be used but if it has to be stored in a refrigerator with other foods it should be covered with crushed ice and kept at approximately 2°C. Frozen fish should be stored at −18°C until required then transferred to a normal refrigerator to defrost for up to twenty-four hours.

Figs. 17, 18 and 19 list those salt water and fresh water fish in common use together with descriptive quality points, best seasons and average sizes or weights and some of their most suitable cooking methods.

SHELLFISH

These can be placed in two groups – the crustaceans such as lobsters which have an external articulated shell and jointed limbs, and the molluscs which are complete soft bodied animals provided with a shell such as the mussel and oyster. This group also includes the squid and cuttle-fish.

Most of these shellfish tend to be expensive with the lobster, crayfish and oysters being in the de luxe class. The lobster has become progressively scarce through over-fishing and by law only those over a certain length are now allowed to be landed.

Care has to be taken that shellfish such as oysters and mussels are not taken from contaminated waters and all shellfish should be cooked or processed as soon as possible. Likewise there should be the minimum of storage for them once cooked as the slightest signs of taint can render them dangerous to eat.

The contribution to the menu of shellfish lies in their versatility. They are useful for hors-d'oeuvre, soups, canapés, innumerable garnishes and many classical hot and cold dishes.

Quality

All shellfish for cooking on the premises should be bought live. Lobster, crabs, crawfish and crayfish should not be sluggish and there should be no cracked shells or missing claws. They should feel heavy in relation to their size. Oysters, mussels and other bivalves should be closed tight with unbroken shells.

If bought cooked, items such as lobsters and crab should be heavy in relation to their size, should have a clean fresh smell and have no signs of stickiness on the shell. Other cooked shellfish should always be checked, a fresh clean smell being the best guide.

195

Figure 17
SALT WATER FISH
White Fish

Name	Description	Best season	Ordering unit	Best av. size or weight	Suitable cooking methods
Brill	Large flat fish with red-brown skin on one side and very small scales; close fairly firm texture; good flavour but not quite as good as turbot neither is the flesh as white.	April–Aug.	whole; by number and weight. fillets: by weight	whole and for cutting on the bone: 3–4 kg	braising; poaching; shallow frying
Cod	Fairly large round fish, grey-green skin with dark spots and silvery belly; good firm texture with clearly defined flakes; very good flavour. Small fish are known as codling.	Oct–Feb	whole: by number and weight. fillets: by weight	for cutting on the bone or for filleting: 3–4 kg	boiling; poaching; grilling; shallow frying; deep frying
Coley	Medium size round fish similar to cod, having greyish-pink flesh; fairly firm texture; fair to good taste. Cheaper than many other fish. Also known as coalfish.	June–Dec	fillets: by weight	for filleting: 3–4 kg	poaching; shallow frying; deep frying
Dab	Small flat fish with light brown skin and rough scales; fairly firm opaque texture; fair to good flavour. Usually served whole with the head removed.	Feb–April	whole: by number and weight	300–400 g each	grilling; shallow frying; deep frying
Haddock	Medium size round fish similar to cod but with a dark patch on the shoulder and pronounced scales; good flaky texture; very good delicate flavour.	Nov–Feb	whole: by number and weight. fillets: by weight	whole: 1–1½ kg for filleting: 1–2½ kg	baking; poaching; shallow frying; deep frying

	Season	Purchasing	Weight	Cooking methods
Hake	Medium-large round fish of the cod family but longer and narrower in proportion; slate coloured skin; fairly firm flaky texture; very good flavour that compares favourably with haddock.	June–Jan	whole: by number and weight. fillets: by weight	for cutting on the bone or for filleting: 3–4 kg	baking; grilling; poaching; shallow frying; deep frying
Halibut	Very large flat fish with smooth dark olive coloured skin and marbled white underside; good firm texture that is flaky but inclined to be dry; very good flavour.	all year excepting May and June	whole: by number and weight. fillets: by weight	for cutting on the bone: 4–5 kg for filleting: $2\frac{1}{2}$–$4\frac{1}{2}$ kg	braising; grilling; poaching; shallow frying; deep frying
John Dory	Oval body which is flat-sided with large spiny head and fins; olive brown skin with metallic sheen; firm texture; excellent flavour that rivals that of Dover sole or turbot.	Sept–Jan	fillets: by weight	for fillets 150–200 g each	braising; poaching; shallow frying; deep frying
Plaice	Flat diamond shape fish, brown skin with red spots; soft texture that breaks easily; good to very good flavour that sometimes has a slightly 'muddy' taste.	Apr–Sept	whole: by number and weight. fillets: by weight	whole: 450–500 g. for filleting: $1\frac{1}{2}$–$1\frac{3}{4}$ kg	grilling; poaching; shallow frying; deep frying
Sea Bream	Round fish with large head and broad back fin, orange-red to brown skin; fairly firm, flaky texture; fair to good flavour; slightly off-white colour when cooked.	Feb–Nov	whole: by number and weight. fillets: by weight	whole: 1–$1\frac{1}{2}$ kg. for filleting: $1\frac{1}{2}$–$2\frac{1}{2}$ kg	baking; braising; grilling; poaching; shallow frying; deep frying
Sole, Dover	Flat fish, elongated oval shape, brown to dark grey upper skin, white underneath; close, firm texture that detaches easily from the bone when cooked; excellent flavour	Sept–Mar	whole; by number and weight. fillets: by number and weight	whole for table d'hôte: 250 g. whole for à la carte: 350–360 g. for filleting: 600–700 g	grilling; poaching; shallow frying; deep frying

Name	Description	Best season	Ordering unit	Best av. size or weight	Suitable cooking methods
Sole, Lemon	Broad flat fish with brownish-yellow upper skin, white underneath; softer texture and much less flavour than Dover sole.	July–Feb	whole: by weight and number. fillets: by number and weight	for filleting: 800 g–1 kg	grilling; poaching; shallow frying; deep frying
Skate	Flat fish of the ray family, only the two triangular side pieces known as wings are used; fairly soft ribbed texture; excellent flavour. Skate is always skinned but never filleted.	Oct–Apr	by weight	wings: 750–800 g each	poaching; shallow frying; deep frying
Turbot	Large flat fish, brown to dark slate grey skin with tubercules on upper side, no scales; firm texture with pronounced flakes; excellent flavour. Small ones are called chicken turbot.	May–July	whole: by number and weight. fillets: by weight	whole: 2½–5 kg. for cutting on the bone: 4–5 kg. for filleting: 4–5 kg.	braising; grilling; poaching; shallow frying
Whiting	Medium size round fish, long compact body, grey to olive brown on back and silver below; fairly firm and flaky texture; very good delicate flavour.	Dec–Feb	whole: by number and weight. fillets: by weight	whole: 300–400 g. for filleting: 400–500 g	baking; poaching; shallow frying; deep frying

Oily Fish

Name	Description	Best season	Ordering unit	Best av. size or weight	Suitable cooking methods
Herring	Medium size round fish, bluish-silver skin, large easily removed scales; fairly compact soft texture; excellent identifiable flavour. Herring lends itself to processing by salting and curing.	Jan–June	whole: by number and weight	whole, or for further preparation: 200–350 g	baking; grilling; poaching; shallow frying

198

Fish	Description	Season	Purchasing	Size	Cooking methods
Mackerel	Medium size round fish of the tunny family, dark green silvery skin marked with black wavy bands; fairly flaky, softish texture; excellent distinctive flavour. Mackerel must be used as fresh as possible.	Spring and Summer	whole: by number and weight	whole, or for further preparation: 300–450 g	baking; grilling; poaching; shallow frying
Mullet, Red	Smallish round fish with red back and silvery pink belly and big broad scales; firm, flaky texture; excellent distinctive flavour. Red mullet must be used very fresh as it quickly deteriorates.	Summer	whole: by number and weight	whole: 200–450 g	baking; grilling; shallow frying
Sardine	Very small round fish of pilchard family with silvery skin; compact lightly flaky texture; excellent pronounced flavour. Sardines are most usually sold in canned form.	Aug–Mar	by weight	12–15 cm in length	grilling; shallow frying
Sprat	Small fish of herring family, similar to sardine but with flat sides; firm texture with light opaque flakes; excellent flavour.	Aug–Mar	by weight	10–12 cm in length	grilling; shallow frying
Whitebait	Tiny round silvery fish thought to be the fry of herring, pilchard and sprat; eaten whole after deep frying giving crisp, crunchy texture; excellent distinctive flavour.	Apr–Sept	by weight	not more than 5–6 cm in length	deep frying

Figure 18
FRESH WATER FISH
(a) *White Fish*

Name	Description	Best season	Ordering unit	Best av. size or weight	Suitable cooking methods
Carp	Plump round fish with olive golden-brown skin and yellowish belly; firm flaky texture; good flavour which is sometimes muddy if not correctly farmed.	Oct–Apr	by number and weight	whole or for further preparation $1\frac{1}{2}$–$2\frac{1}{2}$ kg	baking; braising; poaching; deep frying
Pike	Elongated round fish with dusky olive brown skin; yellow sides and silvery belly; coarse dry texture; very good flavour.	Winter	by number and weight	whole: 2–$3\frac{1}{2}$ kg. for further preparation $1\frac{1}{2}$–5 kg.	baking; poaching; stewing
Sparling or Smelt	Long small round fish with silvery skin; delicate smell of cucumber; opaque, firm yet friable texture; excellent pronounced flavour.	Sept–Mar	by weight	15–20 cm in length	baking; grilling; shallow frying; deep frying

FRESH WATER FISH
(b) Oily Fish

Name	Description	Best season	Ordering unit	Best av. size or weight	Suitable cooking methods
Eel	Elongated snake-like fish with brown, grey or green coloured skin; close, coarse oily texture; good distinctive flavour	All year excepting May	by weight	55–70 cm in length	braising; poaching; stewing; deep frying
Salmon	Large round fish with steely blue skin and silvery belly; firm, well-flaked texture; excellent flavour; pink to red coloured flesh.	Feb–Aug	by number and weight	whole or for further preparation: $3-5\frac{1}{2}$ kg	braising; grilling; poaching; shallow frying
Salmon-trout	Round fish similar in appearance to salmon but smaller and darker skinned; firm, well-flaked texture; excellent flavour; pink to red coloured flesh that is more delicate than that of salmon. Also known as sea trout.	Mar–Aug	by number and weight	whole or for further preparation: 1–4 kg	braising; grilling; poaching; shallow frying
Trout	Small round fish of several different species; brownish black to silvery in colour or with rainbow effect; firm finely flaked texture; excellent flavour; light creamy-brown to light pink coloured flesh.	Feb–Sept All year from trout farms	by number and weight	whole: 200–300 g	braising; grilling; poaching; shallow frying

Figure 19
SHELLFISH
Crustaceans

Name	Description	Best season	Ordering unit	Best av. size or weight	Suitable cooking methods
Crab	Oval shell with 2 claws and 8 legs, reddish-brown colour which deepens after boiling; long thickish fibrous flesh from the claws that is firm and slightly chewy, dark meat from the body is soft and moist; very good distinctive flavour.	May–Dec	by number and weight	$1\frac{1}{2}$–$2\frac{1}{2}$ kg each	boiling; and for further processing
Crawfish	A large lobster-like shellfish, light reddish-brown colour that stays after boiling, no claws; fairly coarse texture; good flavour not so pronounced as lobster. Also known as rock lobster or spiny lobster.	Summer	by number and weight	1–3 kg each	stewing; boiling; and for further processing
Crayfish	A miniature lobster-like shellfish from streams and rivers; dark blue that changes colour to bright red when cooked; smooth, firm fibrous texture; excellent flavour.	Winter	by number and weight	for soup: 30–40 g. for garnish: 50–60 g. for dishes; 80–100 g	boiling; stewing
Lobster	Smooth blue-shelled with claws of unequal shape and length; changes colour to bright red when cooked; firm white flesh; excellent distinctive flavour.	Summer	by number and weight	450–700 g	boiling; grilling; stewing

Prawns	Bright grey when fresh turning pink after cooking; firm slightly chewy texture; excellent flavour. King prawns from warm seas are much larger than British prawns.	Feb–Oct	by weight or by the litre	in the shell: 8–10 cm in length	boiling, and for further processing
Scampi (Dublin Bay prawn)	Shellfish similar to the lobster but smaller and with more elongated claws; orange pink colour and whitish legs that do not change after cooking; softish texture that is slightly chewy; excellent distinctive flavour.	all year	by weight	in the shell: 15–25 cm in length	boiling; poaching; stewing; shallow frying; deep frying
Shrimps	Similar to the prawn but smaller, grey-brown to pink in colour; firm slightly chewy texture; excellent flavour.	all year	by weight or by litre	in the shell: 6–8 cm in length	boiling, and for further processing

Molluscs

Name	Description	Best season	Ordering unit	Best av. size or weight	Suitable cooking methods
Cockle	Small bivalve with ribbed shells; chewy, rubbery texture; fair to good flavour.	Summer	by weight or by the litre	in the shell: $3\frac{1}{2}$–5 cm across	boiling; steaming
Mussel	Long narrow bivalve, greeny-blue to black shells; partly soft and partly chewy texture; good flavour. Care must be taken that mussels are from uncontaminated waters.	Sept–Mar	by weight or by the litre	in the shell: 5–8 cm in length	boiling, and for further processing
Oyster	Round, flat bivalve having ridged shells; soft texture; excellent flavour. Oysters are cultivated commercially.	Sept–Apr	by the one hundred, or individual count	graded by size of shell	usually eaten raw, poaching; deep frying
Scallop	Bivalve with radial ribs on shells – one flat the other convex; white flesh and orange colour roe; fibrous, chewy texture; excellent flavour.	Jan–Feb	by number	in the shells: 11–13 cm across	poaching; stewing; shallow frying; deep frying
Squid (Calamare)	Elongated body with tentacles that have suckers at the end, contains a bag of dark liquid and a cuttle shell; rubbery texture that is easy to chew; good flavour.	all year	by weight	16–20 cm in length	poaching; stewing; deep frying

204

Sources of Supply and Availability

Most shellfish can be obtained from fish wholesale but live lobsters, crabs and oysters are best obtained from specialist dealers. Much of the supply is determined by season and weather and for lobsters as an example the price tends to fluctuate widely.

Frozen prawns, shrimps, scampi, scollops, mussels and crawfish tails are obtainable all the year round together with frozen raw or cooked lobster. Much of these are imported from Norway, South Africa and the Far East.

Ordering Units for Optimum Usage

Lobsters, crawfish, crayfish and crabs are ordered by weight and number; oysters are ordered by the dozen or by the hundred – they are graded numerically according to size into 1's, 2's or 3's with 1's being selected as the largest and best. Prices of course are related to the grades. Raw mussels and cockles are sold usually by capacity, i.e. the quart, gallon or litre whichever would be applicable. Scallops are ordered by number, prawns and shrimps by weight or capacity and squid by weight.

Storage

Live shellfish should not be stored for any length of time although live lobsters, crabs, crayfish and crawfish can be kept successfully for some hours if covered with wet sacking in a box and held in the refrigerator. The normal refrigerator temperatures for cooked shellfish are suitable but prolonged storage is to be avoided at all costs because of the danger of incipient spoilage and consequent severe food poisoning if eaten.

Frozen shellfish should be held at a temperature of at least $-18\,^\circ$C.

Fig. 19 lists those shellfish in common use together with descriptive quality points, best season and average sizes or weights and some of their most suitable cooking methods.

PICKLED, CURED AND SMOKED FISH

Several of the fish described in the previous section, particularly those of the oily type, lend themselves to curing either by being salted or pickled, or by taking the process a stage further from salting and being smoked. These processes change the natural flavour of the fish by giving it a more concentrated flavour.

The fish are processed raw, the result being that they become preserved and will keep in good condition for a considerable time; in many cases they can be eaten as they are.

205

The fish are either pickled in vinegar or wine, or dry or wet salted with a colouring matter and then hung to dry. Smoked fish is first salted then subjected to either cold or hot smoking so as to dry and flavour the flesh but without actually cooking it. Provided it is kept dry and in a cool dry atmosphere it will then keep for some time with little risk of deterioration.

Quality

The quality of fish preserved in vinegar, acetic acid or wine is determined mainly by its appearance as the colour and smell will be that of the liquid and condiments used rather than that of the fish; it should look plump and have a good colour. The quality of cured and smoked fish is denoted by its dryness, its good colour and pleasant smell. Cured fish such as finnon haddock and kippers are usually only lightly cold-smoked and coloured artificially to give the appearance of fully smoked fish; if they are sticky to the touch then they are likely to be stale.

Sources of Supply and Availability

Pickled fish in sealed jars are often sold as a general grocery line; cured fish are sold by ordinary fishmongers who may not handle the more expensive smoked fish which are usually obtained from the same firm that does the actual smoking. All these items are available throughout the year and the price does not fluctuate very much. It is usual to purchase only sufficient to cover a given period of time.

In addition to their being available in fresh processed form most smoked fish are sold in vacuum sealed packs in which they will keep, or in deep frozen form. They are available whole, opened out flat, or as fillets. In the case of smoked salmon it is available in sides, and sliced ready to use in weighed packs. When purchasing smoked mackerel either whole or as fillets it should be ascertained if they have been hot-smoked so being ready to serve, or are intended to be cooked prior to serving.

Ordering Units for Optimum Usage

Many of these items will have been selected on size and quality before being processed and are sold graded as to weight which gives a correct portion control either per whole fish or per fillet; larger fish need to be cut into portions before serving. All these items being in preserved form keep well under correct conditions and can safely be purchased in wholesale size units which are the 4.5 litre jar, the box, and the side or whole fish.

206

Storage

Pickled fish can be stored on the shelf in the stores but will be better for keeping under refrigeration at approximately 8 °C. Cured fish must be treated as for fresh fish by being kept in the fish refrigerator at 2 °C and used fairly quickly. Smoked fish not vacuum packed should be kept under refrigeration. If deep frozen, storage should be at −18 °C until required then transferred to normal refrigeration temperature to defrost. Canned fish are kept in the store at its normal holding temperature; if canned in oil the shelf life is for several years but if in say tomato sauce it should be used within a year of purchase.

The following list gives a brief description of the pickled, cured and smoked fish in general use:

Arbroath Smokie – a small size, whole smoked haddock named after the Scottish town where it is produced.

Bismarck Herring – a whole herring opened out flat, the bone removed; pickled in vinegar.

Bloater – a whole herring first cured by salting then very lightly smoked; usually served grilled as a breakfast dish.

Buckling Herring – a whole herring that has been fully smoked; can be eaten as it is purchased or further cooked.

Smoked Eel – the whole eel, fully smoked; served cut into sections free from skin and bone.

Finnan Haddock – a medium size haddock boned out and opened flat with the head removed; slightly salted and lightly smoked to give a yellow colour. Served poached as a breakfast, high tea or supper dish.

Kipper – a herring opened out and the centre bone and head removed; lightly salted and fully smoked having a deep brown colour. Grilled and served as a breakfast dish.

Maatjes Herring – the Dutch version of the Bismarck herring; is spiced during curing.

Mackerel – available as the whole fish or fillet smoked to a golden brown, sometimes flavoured for example with crushed peppercorns; served as an hors-d'oeuvre.

Roll-mop – the whole boned herring or a fillet of herring, rolled up with a few slices of onion and pickled in vinegar with aromats. Served as a hors-d'oeuvre.

Smoked Salmon – the whole side salted, then smoked until the outside is dry but the interior still moist; served cut into very thin slices.

Salt Cod – the opened and boned cod, dry salted until it becomes very hard; it will keep indefinitely. For use it needs long soaking before being cooked.

Smoked Sprats – these are cured and smoked whole for serving as an hors-d'oeuvre.

Smoked Sturgeon – this is usually imported; whole smoked fillets prepared in the same way as smoked salmon.

207

Smoked Trout – whole cleaned trout of 200–300 g smoked for use as an hors-d'oeuvre.

FISH OFFALS

The roes and livers of certain fish are available in various forms and can be used in certain dishes including hors-d'oeuvre and savouries, the main ones in general use are:

Cod roe – available in fresh form usually ready boiled for further use. It is also available as smoked cod roe which is served as an hors-d'oeuvre.

Herring roe – the soft herring roe from the male fish is esteemed as a gourmet dish being used as a garnish with other fish or poached and served on toast as a savoury. The hard roe from the female of the species may also be used but is not so acceptable. Soft herring roe is also obtainable in frozen and canned form.

Liver – fish liver is rich in Vitamins A and D and those of cod and halibut are usually converted into oils for medicinal purpose.

VEGETABLES

Vegetables play an important part in the normal person's diet because they are nearly always served as an integral part of a main meal; certain ones are served as a course on their own and they also make admirable garnishes.

Given the right care vegetables could assume an even more important position in our diet both from the point of economy as well as that of nutritional value as they contain certain important vitamins and mineral salts.

In this section only the more commonly used vegetables are described and they are classified into root and green categories which are then subdivided into roots, tubers, and bulbs, leaves, flower heads, legumes, stems and fruits. Reference is made to frozen vegetables but the pulse vegetables are dealt with in a separate section. As is customary, edible fungi are also listed.

Quality

Quality grading by the grower is done in accordance with EEC regulations and a general guide to the quality of all vegetables cannot be really precise because of their widely differing characteristics. The following broad observations can however be useful. Green leaf vegetables including salad stuffs should be crisp to firm, of a good colour and heavy in relation to size. Flower heads such as cauliflower, stems such as celery and legumes such as French beans should be firm and crisp and have a good colour where applicable – they should not be limp and tired looking. Fruits such as the tomato should be firm and have a good colour

208

without specking or wrinkling of the outside. Roots, tubers and bulbs should also be firm and dry without signs of decay or moisture.

More detailed quality descriptions will be found in the following lists.

Sources of Supply and Availability

Many vegetables, particularly root ones, are available all the year round, some have a definite season with none being imported to make up supplies, but certainly the more expensive vegetables can be obtained from some country or another in the world at any time. Bad weather can affect crops and subsequent marketing with fluctuating prices.

Many vegetables are available peeled, cleaned or cut ready for use as well as a wide variety of frozen ones.

Ordering Units

Vegetables are packed in many different ways and prices vary according to whether the particular item is quoted per unit such as for globe artichokes, the bundle for asparagus, the bunch for parsley, the sack of 25 kg for many root vegetables, the head for celery, the bag of $12\frac{1}{2}$ kg for Brussels sprouts, the boat of 11 kg for tomatoes, the crate of two dozen for lettuce, and so on. More details are given in the following lists.

Storage

Leaf vegetables, legumes and flower heads are best ordered daily for use on the same day. They can be stored for a short time in a cool room with good ventilation but prolonged storage results in rapid deterioration. Salad vegetables are best kept in a refrigerator. Root vegetables can be stored for longer but require a dark store with protection from frost and dampness and with good ventilation. The question of whether to empty root vegetables from the bags into hoppers is one that depends on usage, but care should always be taken to see that they are used in rotation.

Frozen vegetables like all other frozen food should be held at a temperature of $-18\,^{\circ}$C or lower.

Figs 20 and 21 list those vegetables in common use given under the accepted categories together with descriptive quality points, best seasons, ordering units and some of their most suitable uses.

Figure 20
ROOT AND GREEN VEGETABLES

(a) Roots

Name	Description and quality points	Best season	Ordering unit	Suitable uses
Beetroot	Round or elongated in shape with reddish-purple flesh; best when firm and round, not sprouting, and not too large; available raw or ready cooked.	all year	by weight	for salads; as a vegetable when young and small
Carrot, new	New season carrots should be used immediately; should be of a reasonable size for preparation and of good colour.	May–June	by weight or bunch	for garnishing; as a vegetable
Carrot, old	Should be firm, of good shape and stubby rather than over-elongated, unblemished especially during winter months, of a good colour and not split or broken.	all year	by weight or bag	for salads; as a vegetable; for garnishing
Celeriac	Variety of celery; the thick turnip-like root only is used; should be firm and heavy in relation to size, not damaged or rotting; discolours quickly whilst being prepared.	Autumn–Winter	by weight	for hors-d'oeuvre; for salads
Parsnip	Long white to yellow tapering root; best when medium size; should be fresh looking, without blemish or soft brown patches; the flavour is improved after having been touched by frost before being pulled.	Autumn–Winter	by weight or bag	as a vegetable
Radish	Pungent small root of many varieties, some round, oval or long and tapering. Select when young, not too large and firm; should have a good colour with fresh green leaves and should not be split.	Spring–Autumn	bunch	for hors-d'oeuvre and salads
Salsify	Long white root which should be firm and not be too thin nor too thick; also known as the oyster plant; Scorzonera is a larger variety with black skin.	Autumn and Winter	by weight	as a vegetable; for garnishing

210

	Description	Season	Sold	Use
Swede	Large turnip-shaped root with yellow flesh; should be firm and without blemish, not too dirty and heavy in relation to size. The smaller ones have the better flavour.	all year except Jul–Sept	by weight or bag	as a vegetable
Turnip	Swollen root with white flesh, either round or elongated; should be firm and unblemished; should not be spongy or wormholed; the small early season ones are crisper and better flavoured.	May–Feb	by weight or bag	for garnishing and salads; as a vegetable

(b) Tubers

	Description	Season	Sold	Use
Artichoke, Jerusalem	A very knobbly tuber with white watery flesh; best when not too small or too misshapen; should not be wrinkled or flabby but firm and crisp.	Dec–Feb	by weight	as a vegetable
Potatoes	Should be firm, well shaped, free from blemishes, not tinged with green, clean and without too much soil attached. Good varieties – Main crop: Desirée, King Edward, Maris Piper. Early: Home Guard, Maris Peer, Arran Comet.	all year	by weight or by bag	as a vegetable; for garnishing and salads
Potatoes, Sweet	Similar in shape to the potato with very soft sweetish flavour somewhat perfumed; usually served as a vegetable rather than as a potato; should be firm, heavy and even coloured.	all year	by weight	as a vegetable; for garnishing

(c) Bulbs

	Description	Season	Sold	Use
Chives	Small thin member of the onion family with very delicate flavour; should be bright green and freshly cut with no discoloured stems or flowers.	Spring–Summer	bunch	for flavouring
Garlic	Round white bulb divided into many segments called cloves; strong pronounced smell and flavour; should be dry and firm to pressure with unbroken outer skin and no signs of sprouting.	all year	by weight	for flavouring
Leek	A member of the onion family; best with long white stems shading to pale then to dark green at the top; should be plump, clean, unblemished and no signs of wilting or yellowness.	all year except May	bundle or by weight	as a vegetable; for flavouring

211

Figure 20

ROOT AND GREEN VEGETABLES

Name	Description and quality points	Best season	Ordering unit	Suitable uses
Onion	Perhaps the most widely used flavouring for cooking. Should be firm, dry, compact in shape, even in size and have no signs of sprouting; moistness and softness to pressure is a sign of decay. There are many varieties, the large Spanish onion being the mildest in flavour. If stored properly will keep well for some months.	all year	by weight or bag	for flavouring and garnishing; as a vegetable
Onion, Button	These are the first onions to be cropped just after they have formed a nice round bulb; should be of even graded size, small and with no signs of sponginess or sprouting.	Summer	by weight or bag	for garnishing; for pickling; as a vegetable
Onion, Spring	These are the thinnings of the onion bed; should not be too bulbous at the root and should have a good colour ranging from white to dark green with no signs of wilting or discolouration.	Spring–Summer	bunch	for salads
Shallot	Member of the onion family with many varieties; usually small, compact shape but a tendency to grow into separate cloves. Colour of the flesh ranges from light green to pale violet. Should be firm without any sprouting; any softness or sponginess is usually a sign of decay.	all year	by weight	for flavouring for pickling

(a) *Leaves*

Name	Description and quality points	Best season	Ordering unit	Suitable uses
Brussels Sprouts	Variety of cabbage which produces small round growths called sprouts on the axils of its leaves all along the central stem; should be small, tight and compact and of a good bright green colour.	Sept–Nov	by weight	as a vegetable
Cabbage, green	Member of the brassica family of which there are many varieties, some smooth-leaved and others curly leaved such as the Savoy cabbage; select those which have a good colour with unblemished leaves.	all year except April and May	by weight bag or crate	as a vegetable; for salad

Name	Description	Season	Sold	Use
Cabbage, spring	Early season cabbage which have not yet developed much in the way of heart; very tender and of a very good colour when not overcooked; should be fresh and crisp without blemished leaves.	Jan–Mar	by weight bag or crate	as a vegetable
Cabbage, red	Should be firm, compact of a good reddish purple colour; reject if there is too much opening of the leaves and any sign of limpness or dehydration.	Aug–Feb	by weight or bag	as a vegetable; for pickling
Cabbage, white	Very heavy in relation to size, very firm and close texture, and pale green to white in colour. Also called Dutch cabbage.	all year	by weight or bag	for salad and making into sauerkraut
Cabbage, Chinese	Also known as Chinese leaves, looks like a cross between a large cos lettuce and a celery but larger and heavier; long white leaves that are very crisp; reject if limp and wilted.	all year	by weight and number	as a vegetable; for salad
Chard	This is the name given to the leaves of a beet grown mainly as a leafy vegetable; dark green in colour with whitish mid-ribs. Best when young and fresh; when old can be very stringy. The mid-ribs can be stripped and cooked separately like sea-kale.	Autumn–Winter	by weight	as a vegetable
Chicory	Has longish thin stalks, white at the base to a green frizzy top; should look fresh and be crisp without any blemishes. The long thin root is roasted and blended with coffee.	Summer	by number	as a vegetable; for salad
Corn salad	Small deep green leaves on a small stem; should be fresh without wilted or blemished leaves.	Spring	by weight	for salad
Endive, Belgian	Variety of cultivated chicory; has closely packed, long blanched leaves which are just yellowy green at the top. Should be selected when very firm and unopened and with no signs of brown on the outside leaves.	all year	by weight	as a vegetable; for salad
Kale, curly	Dark green, curly leaves without any heart; select when crisp, unblemished and not too many stalks.	Jan–Mar	by weight	as a vegetable
Lettuce, cabbage	Similar in shape to a small cabbage; should be crisp with a good firm heart; check for rotting leaves or browning in the centre of the heart.	Apr–Sept	by number or crate of 24	for salads or garnishing; as a vegetable

Figure 20

ROOT AND GREEN VEGETABLES

Name	Description and quality points	Best season	Ordering unit	Suitable uses
Lettuce, cos	Elongated shape, deep green in colour with close packed leaves; should be crisp and unblemished with no signs of brown rust disease.	Summer	by number	salad
Sorrel	Broad green leaves that look similar to dock leaves; should be fresh looking and crisp with no discoloration; used as a garnish rather than as a vegetable.	Spring	by weight	for garnishing and flavouring
Spinach	Fresh looking green leaves; best without too much hard stalk; should not be sandy or dirty.	Aug–Nov	by weight	as a vegetable
Watercress	Best when packed in named grower's bunch; should be bright green with short stalks and no discoloured leaves.	all year	bunch or chip	for salad; for garnishing

(b) Flowers

Name	Description and quality points	Best season	Ordering unit	Suitable uses
Artichoke, globe	A member of the thistle family of which the unopened flower head only is used; should be tight and close packed. Large ones provide the artichoke bottom which is the flat part out of which the flower grows. Small varieties when young can be eaten whole.	June–Sept	by number	for hors-d'oeuvre and salad; for garnishing; as a vegetable
Broccoli	There are many varieties of this vegetable which is similar to cauliflower though having a smaller head and of different colours – white, dark green and purple. Select well shaped and close packed flower heads with no wilting green leaves on the outside. There are early sprouting varieties.	Feb–Sept	by weight	as a vegetable

Cauliflower	A variety of cabbage used for its unopened flower head which is referred to as the 'curd'. This should be well formed, tightly packed, of a good white to light yellow colour and with no signs of spotting. Reject any where the flower is opening and loose.	all year except April	by number	as a vegetable; for garnishing

(c) Fruits and Seeds

Aubergine	Elongated pear-shape, dark purple in colour with yellowy flesh; should be plump firm and glossy with no signs of wrinkling or other blemishes.	June–Oct	by weight	as a vegetable
Courgette	Small baby marrow; best when not too large. Should be crisp and firm with no signs of blemish on the skin.	May–Aug	by weight	as a vegetable; for garnishing
Cucumber	Many varieties of which the most common used is hothouse cultivated. The small variety is known as the gherkin. The best quality salad cucumbers should be selected fresh and crisp with no signs of flabbiness, preferably as straight as possible, approx. 25 cm in length and not too thick.	all year	by number	for salad and garnishing; as a vegetable
Marrow	Should be young and firm though the skin must not be hard but a good dark green colour; best size is approx. 30 cm long.	June–Sept	by weight or number	as a vegetable
Pimento	Hollow pod with a few seeds, crisp shiny outside with short stem; available as green, red and yellow varieties; also called peppers or capsicums. Should feel firm and crisp and have no signs of wrinkling or flabbiness.	Aug–Dec	by weight	for salad and garnishing; as a vegetable
Sweetcorn	The seed of the Indian corn or maize plant, frequently served on the head (cob); these should be young, well filled, and covered with fresh green leaves; the grains should be milky looking in colour and soft; they should not be hard and yellow.	Jul–Sept	by number	as a vegetable
Tomato	Many varieties of a branching plant, which bears a bright red fruit; should be firm, of even shape and a good colour.	all year	by weight or box	for salad and garnishing; as a vegetable

Figure 20
ROOT AND GREEN VEGETABLES

Name	Description and quality points	Best season	Ordering unit	Suitable uses
(d) Legumes				
Beans, broad	A large, broad pod which should not be flabby or going dark; best when young and well filled with small beans which do not require skinning when cooked.	June–Aug	by weight	as a vegetable
Beans, French	A green pod which is eaten whole or cut, when the beans inside are barely formed; should be stringless, crisp, straight, flat and not showing the shape of the beans through the pod.	June–Dec	by weight	as a vegetable; for garnishing and salad
Beans, runner	Another green pod eaten usually sliced; best when young and small; should snap crisply; reject if too large, flabby, dry, yellowish in colour or the shape of the beans showing through the pod.	Jul–Sept	by weight	as a vegetable
Mangetout	A flat green pea pod cooked and eaten whole; should be crisp, very green in colour and not too large or broad.	Summer	by weight	as a vegetable
Peas	A green pod of which the peas only are eaten; should be plump and crisp without being over full or too tight and of a good green colour. Usually purchased ready shelled.	May–Sept	by weight	as a vegetable; for garnishing and salad
(e) Stems and Stalks				
Asparagus	A plant of the lily family of which the young shoots are used as a vegetable; select when straight with tight unopened heads; wrinkling and browning at the stalk ends is a sign of staleness; good varieties: Lauris, Evesham, Argenteuil, Malines, Genoa. The thinnings are sold in bundles under the name of sprue.	May–July	bundle	for garnishing and salad; as a vegetable

Celery	A plant cultivated for its long leaf stalk; best when white and crisp with a good firm heart; check for discolouration and insect damage to the interior.	all year	by number	for flavouring; as a vegetable; for salad
Fennel	A plant of which the swollen base of the leaf stalks form a very tight bulbous shape; should be white with little green showing; check for splitting or brown discolouration.	June–Oct	by number	as a flavouring; as a vegetable; for garnishing
Kohlrabi	The swollen base-stem of a member of the Brassica family: looks very similar in some respects to the turnip; should be not too large but firm and heavy in relation to size; if too large and old kohlrabi are inclined to be woody.	Apr–July	by weight	as a vegetable
Seakale	A plant cultivated for its leaf stalks which are usually blanched and forced; should be a good whitish colour without blemishes and be crisp and firm.	Dec–June	by weight	as a vegetable

217

Figure 21
EDIBLE FUNGI

Name	Description and quality points	Best season	Ordering unit	Suitable uses
Cep	Also known as the flap mushroom; very fleshy, wide and flat and brown in colour. Select as being young and fresh with minimal damage.	Autumn	by weight	for garnishing; as a vegetable
Chanterelle	Irregular funnel shape, bright egg yellow in colour, toughish texture, aroma of apricots and slight taste of pepper. Inclined to be fragile when raw, so select as undamaged as possible.	Summer and Autumn	by weight	for garnishing; as a vegetable
Morel	Has an irregularly pitted cap which is somewhat conical in shape, yellowish-brown in colour with a white short stalk. Select as being young and fresh.	Autumn	by weight	for garnishing; as a vegetable
Mushroom	The cultivated mushroom rather than the field mushroom is now more generally used in catering and is available in 3 grades: buttons which should be small, firm and white with no signs of opening; caps which are larger, partially opened but still white and firm; flats which are the fully opened mushroom darker in colour and much larger. All mushrooms should be selected as fresh, unbroken and unblemished.	cultivated all year; (field July–Oct)	by weight	for garnishing; as a vegetable
Truffle	Black with hard, rough skin, should be even in size, with very strong flavour and aroma; the best come from the Perigord region in France. White truffles have a more pronounced flavour and are mostly found in the Piedmont region in Italy.	Oct–Mar	by weight	for garnishing; as a vegetable

PULSES

Pulses are the edible seeds of leguminous plants that are removed from their pods and dried. They are available in this dried form and as ready cooked in cans. Pulses can be made into good class dishes both as a vegetable, a vegetable purée and as a garnish. They are all suitable for making into soups and some act as a meat analogue for vegetarians.

The following are the pulses in general use: Butter beans; Haricot beans: Lentils; Marrowfat peas; Green split peas; Yellow split peas; Flageolets; Red beans.

Quality

The shape and size should be even and without any broken pieces or foreign objects. The colour should be good and whilst being dry they ought not to be too thin which would indicate staleness. It is best to use these products within the year of production when they do not require soaking before use.

Sources of Supply and Availability

Most of these items are imported from the various countries where they are grown and processed; they are always available and seldom in short supply. The more unusual ones will be handled only by specialist grocers.

Ordering Units for Optimum Usage

The commercial pack is generally $2\frac{1}{2}$ kg and the transparent film bags enable the quality to be discerned without having to open them. They are also sold in 25 kg sacks.

Storage

These goods should be kept in the dry stores either in the original packaging or tipped out into bins. They are prone to contamination by weevils so should be kept covered and inspected regularly.

FRUIT

The use of fresh fruit adds much interest to the menu because of the many ways in which the various kinds can be featured as sweet dishes, garnishes for main courses and as the dessert course. Fruit may be classified as: hard fruits, citrus fruits, stone fruits and soft fruits; in addition there is a category of other fruits which do not fit into any of the above and also the more rare exotic fruits which are used only occasionally.

Quality

Hard fruits – apples and pears should be on the firm side, well shaped and coloured and of a good size; it is better to purchase under-ripe and allow them to develop in storage.
Citrus fruits – these should be firm, thin skinned, juicy, seedless or with few seeds and without blemishes.
Stone fruits – these should be firm and just ripe, well coloured and heavy in relation to size.
Soft fruits – these perish very quickly especially if picked damp; they should be clean, dry, well coloured, whole and sound with no contamination or bad ones.

Sources of Supply and Availability

Both dessert and cooking apples and pears are on the market all the year around. Citrus fruits are all imported and when the season ends in one country it is just starting in another, the main sources of supply being Israel, Spain, South Africa, Morocco, Cyprus, Italy, Brazil, USA.

Apples and pears are imported at different times of the year from New Zealand, Australia, South Africa, United States, Canada, Argentina, France and Italy. Bananas are available all the year around.

Ordering Units for Optimum Usage

Most fruits are bought by weight and are available in boxed form for hard and citrus fruits. Soft fruits are supplied in punnets of different weights ranging from $\frac{1}{2}$ lb to 2 or 3 lb.

Storage

Some fruits such as apples, continue to breathe in storage and should be allowed to do this in a cool, dark atmosphere with a relative humidity of 60 per cent.

220

They can be left in the boxes as delivered though if not in partitions it may be as well to look for one that may have gone bad as it soon contaminates the others. The smell of fruit in a closed store or in a refrigerator can be transferred to other commodities such as butter and eggs. Soft fruits and stone fruits are best under refrigeration until the moment of serving. Bananas will start to go black if stored below 13 °C.

The following tables, Figure 22, list the main fruits in each category, with descriptive quality points, best seasons and ordering units.

In addition to the foregoing fruits there are several others that can be classified as exotic fruits; they are not always available. They include the custard apple, guava, kiwi-fruit also known as Chinese gooseberry, kumquat and loquat, lime, lychee, mango, ortanique, passion fruit, paw-paw, persimmon, pomelo and physalis or Cape gooseberry.

DRIED, GLACÉ AND CRYSTALLISED FRUITS

There are several kinds of dried fruit in use – the very dry kind including currants, sultanas and raisins which are used mainly for cake making and are known as vine fruits; they are used either individually or as a mixture which may also include chopped candied orange and lemon peel. Glacé fruits such as cherries and pineapple are first candied then rolled in sugar syrup to give a good glaze; crystallised fruits such as cherries, plums, figs, pineapple, angelica and many others are the most expensive form. These should not be too dry, if so they are probably old stock.

The quality of these fruits should be plump in relation to size and have a certain moistness which indicates that they were fairly recently packed.

Dates are available in compressed blocks or sacks or arranged in glove boxes for dessert use. Dried figs are available in pressed form. Prunes are dried plums and are graded in sizes ranging from 14 to 80 per 500 g, the large ones being the most expensive.

Dried fruits such as apricots, peaches and pears are sun or vacuum dried and reconstitute well when cooked; sliced apples are also dried in this way and are subjected to sulphur dioxide gas fumes to preserve their colour and prevent damage by insects. In all these fruits there should still be some moistness and they should not be too hard, dry or shrivelled.

NUTS

Nuts are mainly used in the pastry department, occasionally in the kitchen as a garnish, and they form part of the dessert being served in a basket with a

Figure 22
FRUIT

Name	Description and Quality points	Best season	Ordering unit
	(a) Hard Fruits		
Apple, cooking	Many varieties the best known being the Bramley; should be even size, firm and unblemished. Best flavour when late picked and stored for some time.	Autumn to Spring	by weight or box
Apple, dessert	Many varieties including imports from several countries; should be of medium size, a pleasing colour, firm and have a good aroma; good eating varieties: Cox's Orange Pippin, Golden Delicious, Laxton, Granny Smith.	all year	by weight or box
Pear	Best known varieties are Williams, Comice, Beurre Hardy, Conference; should be medium size, even shape, firm and juicy, and not over-ripe	all year	by weight or box
	(b) Citrus Fruits		
Grapefruit	Imported from many countries all mainly of good quality. Choose large size fruit with smooth firm skin and even colour; should be heavy and juicy; some pink-fleshed ones are available.	all year	by number or box
Lemon	Used for flavouring and garnishing only; select even, oval shape, with good yellow skin which should be thin; essential to be juicy and with not too many pips.	all year	by number or box
Mandarin	The mandarin, tangerine, clementine, satsuma are all small varieties of the orange having slight differences of size and flavour, some have loose skins but most should feel firm.	Winter	by weight or box
Orange	There are two main varieties the Valencia and the Navel the latter being seedless; should be firm, ripe, of a good colour and juicy.	all year	by number or box

(c) Stone Fruits

Apricot	Pale to deep orange colour, nice aroma and flavour. Check for bruising.	Summer and Autumn	by weight
Cherry	Available as yellow, red, dark red and black varieties; also the Morello cherry for garnishing; check for ripeness and freedom for blemish.	Spring and Summer	by weight
Damson	Looks like a small plum, deep blue colour, used for cookery.	Sept	by weight
Greengage	A variety of plum, yellow to green in colour, used when of a good size and ripe as a dessert fruit. Mainly used however for cooking.	Aug–Oct	by weight
Nectarine	Very similar to a peach but with a smooth skin and not usually so large; care should be taken that they are ripe with the flesh firm but juicy; check for bruising.	Summer	by number or tray
Peach	A round stone fruit with velvety skin, golden yellow and red in colour with white or yellow-orange flesh and distinctive flavour; should be firm but juicy. Good quality fruit imported from Italy and France. English hothouse peaches are available during the winter but are expensive.	Summer	by number or tray
Plum	Oval stone fruit with smooth skin; there are many varieties with different colour skins ranging from yellow to dark purple. Some large varieties such as the Victoria plum make excellent dessert fruits when ripe and juicy. Check for bruising and insect damage.	Aug–Sept	by weight

(d) Soft Fruits

Blackberry	These grow wild but cultivated varieties have better flavour and are larger. Check carefully for insect damage and maggots.	Aug–Oct	by punnet
Cranberry	A small dark red berry with a very tart taste used mainly for a sauce. Select those of a good even red colour. Check for rotting berries and unwanted stalks.	all year	be weight
Currant, black, red and white	These should be bold in size, fresh, juicy and with not too much stalk. Used mostly for cooking.	July–Aug	by punnet

223

Figure 22
FRUIT

Name	Description and Quality points	Best season	Ordering unit
Gooseberry	The small green ones are used for cooking, the larger varieties when ripe may be served as a dessert fruit.	June–Aug	by weight
Loganberry	This resembles a raspberry but has a soft seedless flesh. Used mainly for cooking.	July–Aug	by punnet
Raspberry	These should be whole, large, fragrant and sweet; it is advisable to examine underneath the contents of punnets as mouldiness starts very quickly here; do not store for any length of time.	June and July	by punnet
Strawberry	Many varieties are grown, choose medium size of good red colour, sweet, well flavoured and clean and fresh.	June–Aug	by punnet
Wild Strawberry	Cultivated ones are available, should be small, multi-coloured, wonderful aroma and flavour.	Summer	by punnet

(e) Other Fruits

Name	Description and Quality points	Best season	Ordering unit
Avocado pear	Dark, shiny green to purple skin, smooth or rough skin, used mainly as a savoury fruit; imported from Israel, USA, southern Africa. Select when ripe with soft flesh but firm to the touch. Mottled brown skin can be a sign of being over-ripe.	all year	by number
Banana	These are picked whilst green and ripened for sale; should be yellow, firm and unbruised, and in bunches rather than loose.	all year	by weight
Fig	Fresh figs are green to deep purple in colour with a smooth skin and reddish pulp. Select when unblemished and fairly firm to the touch; should not be split or over-soft.	Autumn	by number

Grape	These are available as black or white; they should be plump and in neat bunches with their bloom unblemished and with no bad ones discernable. Belgian hothouse and Cape grapes are best for dessert.	all year	by weight
Melon	These should be firm, heavy and without blemishes; fragrant varieties include Cantaloup, Charentais, Honeydew, Musk and Ogen. A ripe melon will have a pronounced perfume and be soft to touch at the flower end.	all year	by number
Pineapple	These should be fairly firm, heavy, fragrant, have fresh looking leaves, browny-yellow skin, good shape and size; they should be stored in a humid atmosphere.	all year	by number
Rhubarb	Although strictly a vegetable stalk, rhubarb is classified as a fruit as far as catering is concerned. The stalks should be a good colour, firm and straight, with not too much leaf; forced rhubarb is pale pink and has thin stalks, outdoor is red and has thick stalks. Reject if limp and discoloured.	Apr–June	by weight

225

selection of fruit; they are also used in the bars and for cocktail parties. The nuts used in cookery need to be ready shelled as well as those for the bar but for dessert use they are best purchased in the shell.

Quality

Shelled nuts should be clean, fresh looking, large and even in size; if withered or very dry they tend to taste stale or even rancid. Unshelled nuts should feel heavy in relation to weight; check for old dry stock from the previous season.

Sources of Supply and Availability

Shelled nuts are always available whereas those for dessert are in much greater demand around Christmas time and are then plentiful. Most nuts are imported from abroad after having been kiln dried.

Storage

Both shelled and whole nuts should be kept in a cool dry store where they won't deteriorate, become desiccated or go mouldy; it is advisable to keep them in the vacuum pack container and unshelled nuts in an airtight container preferably in the refrigerator.

Fig. 23 lists the nuts in common use together with descriptive quality points, best seasons and ordering units.

DAIRY PRODUCE

This group of foods includes the ones that are connected with dairy farming, in other words all those based on milk. It therefore includes not only milk and cream but yoghurt, cheese and butter. Very often eggs are included under this heading but for the purpose of this book butter and eggs are dealt with separately.

MILK

Fresh milk is possibly the most complete food available and as such plays a big part in catering being used in many different drinks and dishes. Most milk is pasteurised to destory pathogenic organisms using the HTST (high temperature – short time) process which means it is heated to 71 °C for fifteen seconds then
226

Figure 23
NUTS

Name	Description and Quality points	Best season for dessert	Ordering unit
Almond	Oval in shape, very distinctive flavour, used for dessert and as shelled, split, nibbed, flaked, ground or shredded for pastry and kitchen use.	Autumn and Winter	by weight
Brazil	Slightly curved and elongated three-sided nut, used mainly for dessert.	Autumn and Winter	
Cashew	Small kidney-shaped nut usually served roasted and salted.	all year	
Chestnut	Shiny brown, round nut similar to a horse chestnut, used mainly in pastry work but also in the kitchen; sold candied as Marrons Glacés.	Winter	
Hazelnut	Small round nuts; used in pastry work and for dessert; also referred to as a filbert.	Autumn and Winter	
Peanut	Oval-shape, light brown and available in the shell, skinned and with skin on. Used salted in the bar and at receptions.	all year	
Pine kernel	Very small nut obtained from various species of pine cones, mainly in Italy. Used mainly for pastry work.	all year	
Pecan	Similar in shape and taste to the walnut but smoother and sweeter; used mainly for serving at cocktail parties.	all year	
Pistachio	Small soft, green fleshed nut covered with a purple-green skin, used mainly for cooking purposes.	all year	
Walnut	Has a light brown crenellated double shell; used for dessert, pastry work and in the kitchen	Autumn and Winter	

227

cooled rapidly. For the caterer who buys milk in bulk for a variety of uses pasteurised **homogenised milk** is most suitable as in this case the fat globules are broken by machine into very small droplets. These remain distributed throughout the whole and do not come to the top as with unhomogenised milk.

Sterilised milk – is homogenised milk heated in the bottle to 100°C for twenty to thirty minutes; it will keep for several weeks without refrigeration.

UHT milk – is homogenised milk heated to 132°C for one to two seconds then poured into containers and sealed, it will keep for several months; it is also called long-life milk and is available in sealed packets and individual portions.

Channel Island milk – is milk from Jersey or Guernsey breeds and has a higher butterfat content than ordinary milk.

Evaporated milk – is where the water content is distilled off to leave a concentrated form of the milk which is then homogenised and sealed into cans before sterilising.

Condensed milk – is where skim milk is mixed with sugar and boiled under pressure to remove the water. It is then sealed into cans.

Milk powder – is produced by evaporating the water from liquid fresh milk by heat to produce solids containing 5 per cent or less moisture. The fresh milk is homogenised, heat treated and usually pre-concentrated before drying.

There are several filled milk powders available for use in cooking; in this product the butterfat is removed and replaced by vegetable fat in the form of a refined, dehydrogenated hardened oil which enables a cheaper product to be marketed. As vegetable fats are more stable than milk fat the product has a longer shelf life. This product is not really suitable for making tea when reconstituted.

Quality

Whichever of the kinds of milk is used in a catering establishment, the quality is always sound and completely fit for human consumption because of rigid controls.

Sources of Supply and Availability

Fresh milk is usually delivered daily, usually in the early hours of the morning, from a responsible supplier. Being produced twice daily, the only possible breakdown in supplies would be one caused by transport probably due to adverse weather conditions. The price is regulated by central government.

228

Ordering Units for Optimum Usage

Milk is sold by the pint (568 ml) in crates holding thirty bottles, in churns and half churns, in plastic containers of 5 gals. (approx. 263 litres) for vending purposes, and in mini-jugs of 18 g for single portions.

Storage

Fresh milk should be kept under refrigeration at 5°C and withdrawn for use as required and not allowed to stand in a warm atmosphere. Other kinds of milk including long-life milk can be kept under normal storage conditions.

CREAM

Cream has a wide variety of uses in the kitchen, mainly as an ingredient for enriching and finishing a dish, as a garnish and for decoration purposes. It is important to know the difference between the various types available and to use the right kind for a particular job as in the following.

Single cream must have a minimum butterfat content of 18 per cent, this does not allow for it to be whipped so it is used for cooking, for pouring over sweet dishes and for serving with ordinary coffee.

Whipping cream must have a minimum butterfat content of 35 per cent but is usually sold at 40 per cent cream. It will have been pasteurised but as the name implies, it whips very well and can be piped successfully.

Double cream must have a minimum butterfat content of not less than 48 per cent; it can be used as it is, or whipped.

Clotted cream is whole cream that has been cooked to produce its characteristic flavour; the butterfat content is as high as 60 per cent. Usually sold by the kilogram rather than by the litre.

Miniature single cream portions of **UHT cream** for use in coffee, are available as well as **soured cream, canned cream** and **frozen cream**.

Quality

The quality of cream is seldom in doubt as dairies have to ensure it is of the stated quality and usually date stamp the product. This, of course, needs checking where applicable.

Sources of Supply and Availability

Fresh cream is always available and most dairies can supply adequate amounts of the desired quality.

Ordering Units for Optimum Usage

Cream is sold in 1 pt (568 ml) and 2 pt cartons, in 4.5 litre and 22 litre containers as well as in mini-jugs of 18 g for coffee.

Frozen cream is packed in plastic bags holding 1pt or 2pt, sometimes divided into small pieces for ease of defrosting.

Storage

Fresh cream can be kept refrigerated for up to three days in summer and four days in winter; it must be kept out of bright light and sunshine and away from foods that might transfer their flavour and smell to it. Sterilised cream and UHT (ultra high treated) cream when packed in sealed cartons can be stored for a long period under normal storage.

YOGHURT

Yoghurt originated in the Balkans and peasants living there thrived to a great age, ascribing this to the fact that yoghurt was a staple food in their diet. Yoghurt is now a familiar part of the diet of most Western nations as well as in Eastern Europe and the Near, Middle and Far East. It is milk which has been soured, usually with Lactobacillus Bulgaricus and Streptococcus Thermophilus, heated to 70–95 °C for between five minutes to one hour, then homogenised to help to bring out the creamy flavour and smooth velvet texture. Most of it is available in sealed cartons and should be stored at approximately 5 °C. Yoghurt should be eaten within a few days of manufacture.

CHEESE

Cheese is a commodity which can amply repay the giving of some thought and study on the part of the caterer, particularly where customer satisfaction is concerned. The make-up of a cheese board or trolley comprising a number of cheeses from several different countries demands careful selection if it is to please all tastes.

Quality

This is generally judged by the fresh appearance of a cheese even though it be one that has needed maturing over a period of time to develop its flavour.

Cheese can be classified as hard, firm, soft, cream and blue vein, and the person entrusted with the purchasing and selection of any of these categories needs to have a well-developed palate and experience of the particular qualities and tastes of them. Tasting becomes the best way of determining quality.

230

Sources of Supply and Availability

Cheese is best obtained from a reliable cheese merchant who carries a wide variety. Most cheeses are available all the year round either whole, cut to weight or in vacuum packs of varying sizes and weights.

Ordering Units for Optimum Usage

The list which follows shows the wholesale units of the well-known cheeses as supplied by cheese merchants, but it is always possible to purchase cut cheese at a slightly higher price. It is advisable to order in accordance with known demand.

Storage

If a cool, clean and dark cellar with slate shelves is available whole cheeses may be stored for a long time if desired; if not it is better to purchase at intervals according to demand. If stored in too warm a place cheese may start to ferment and will certainly sweat. If kept too cold it will lose flavour, if too dry it can go hard and mould can develop when the air is too moist. Each piece is best wrapped separately and kept at approximately 5-7 °C.

The following tables list the more commonly used cheeses under their categories together with the country of origin, descriptive notes, shapes, approximate weights, ordering units and best seasons.

EGGS

Hen's eggs are a very versatile commodity and have a myriad of uses in the kitchen being used as they are both cooked and raw, and to emulsify, enrichen, coat, bind, glaze and thicken foods. They can be used whole, or as yolks and whites separately.

Quality

To test if fresh it is useful to crack one open. The yolk should have a good curve to it and stay banked in the centre of the white which should be quite thick. As

231

Figure 24
CHEESE

Name	Country of origin	Description	Shape	Approx. weight	Ordering unit	Best season
		(a) Hard Cheese				
Parmesan	Italy	Made from cow's milk; delicate granular texture; straw colour, hard, brittle and crumbly, sharp fruity flavour; used mainly for cooking purposes.	cylinder	24-39 kg	by weight	all year
		(b) Firm Cheese				
Bel Paese	Italy	Made from cow's milk; smooth consistency; creamy colour; lactic smell and mild flavour.	thick disc	2 kg	by weight	all year
Caerphilly	UK	Made from cow's milk; sold fresh and young; has a wettish texture; mild slightly sour flavour; white in colour.	round flat	$3\frac{1}{2}$ kg	by weight	all year
Cheddar	UK	Made from cow's milk; firm texture; white to yellow colour; slightly nutty flavour; very good for cooking.	cylinder or box	18–27 kg	by weight	all year
Cheshire	UK	Made from cow's milk; crumbly texture; available as orange or white coloured; very salty and fatty, excellent flavour.	cylinder or box	22 kg	by weight	all year
Derby	UK	Made from cow's milk; resembles cheddar; good flavour and texture; can turn sour quickly.	rectangle	6 kg	by weight	all year
Edam	Holland	Made from cow's milk; smooth red or yellow rind, nice round shape; rubbery texture; pale yellow colour; slightly nutty taste.	ball	$1\frac{1}{2} - 1\frac{3}{4}$ kg	by weight	all year

232

Name	Country	Description	Shape	Weight	Sold	Availability
Emmenthal	Switzerland France	Made from cow's milk; smooth rind, yellow colour with large round holes; good aroma and flavour; firm texture.	cartwheel	80–98 kg	by weight	all year
Gloucester, Double	UK	Made from cow's milk; golden red or white colour; mild bland flavour; good texture.	cylinder	28 kg	by weight	all year
Gouda	Holland	Made from cow's milk; stiff, yellow wax rind; little smell, bland taste; smooth texture.	round flat	3 kg	by weight	all year
Gruyère	Switzerland France	Made from cow's milk; smooth skin, light yellow to amber in colour, small holes spaced far apart; firm texture; good smell; fruity flavour; very good for cooking.	large wheel	29–39 kg	by weight	Sept–Feb
Leicester	UK	Made from cow's milk; deep orange-red in colour; very mild flavour; melts quickly	cylinder	13–18 kg	by weight	all year
Mozzarella	Italy	Made from buffalo's milk; oval or round shape; very white, rubbery texture; strong lactic smell; mild flavour.	variable	$\frac{1}{2}$–1 kg	by weight	all year
Stracchino	Italy	Made from cow's milk; pink rind, yellow colour; strong smell and fruity flavour; soft supple texture.	square	1–2 kg	by weight	Autumn–Winter
Saint-Paulin	France	Made from cow's milk; smooth rind and velvet smooth texture; very mild flavour	disc	2 kg	by weight	all year
Wensleydale	UK	Made from cow's milk; white, slightly sour tasting cheese that is sometimes aged to develop as a blue veined cheese.	cylinder	$4\frac{1}{2}$– $5\frac{1}{2}$ kg	by weight	all year

Figure 24
CHEESE

Name	Country of origin	Description	Shape	Approx. weight	Ordering unit	Best season
(c) Soft Cheese						
Brie	France	Made from cow's milk; soft thin white rind, straw coloured; supple texture; nice smell and pronounced taste.	flat disc	1.8–3 kg	by number and weight	all year
Camembert	France	Made from cow's milk; white rind; ripe flavour but not over-ripe or too runny in texture; should be slightly firm when ready to serve.	small flat disc in round box	250 g	by number	all year
Carré de l'Est	France	Made from cow's milk; soft white rind; smells slightly of mushrooms; bland flavour.	small square	120–260 g	by number	all year
Munster	France	Made from cow's milk; smooth shiny red rind very strong smell and flavour.	disc	0.3–1.5 kg	by weight	all year
Pont-l'Eveque	France	Made from cow's milk; smooth golden rind; nice smell and pronounced flavour; soft, supple texture.	square	350 g	by number	Summer– Winter
(d) Cream Cheese						
Boursin	France	Enriched cow's milk cream cheese; very soft texture; can be flavoured with garlic, herbs, etc.	small square	100 g	by number	all year
Demi-sel	France	Salted cream cheese with mild flavour wrapped in foil.	small square	75–100 g	by number	all year

234

Name	Country	Description	Shape	Weight		Season
Petit-Suisse	France	Cylinders of very white unsalted cream cheese; must be eaten fresh.	small cylinder	30 g	by number	all year

(e) Blue vein Cheese

Name	Country	Description	Shape	Weight		Season
Bleu d'Auvergne	France	Similar to Roquefort but made from cow's milk; strong smell and sharp flavour.	flat cylinder or smaller packs of varying size	$2-2\frac{1}{2}$ kg	by weight	Summer–Autumn
Danish Blue	Denmark	A blue veined cheese of reasonable quality but in different class from Stilton and Gorgonzola; rather sharp taste.	thick disc	$2\frac{1}{2}-3$ kg	by weight	all year
Gorgonzola	Italy	Grey-red skin; soft runny texture and strong smell; white to yellow in colour with even veining.	cylinder	6-8 kg	by weight	all year
Mycella	Denmark	Similar to Gorgonzola; a better quality of Danish Blue.	cylinder	5-9 kg	by weight	all year
Roquefort	France	Made from sheep's milk; should have uniform veining, salty flavour, firm but smooth texture.	tall cylinder	$2\frac{1}{2}$ kg	by weight	Spring-Autumn
Stilton	UK	Crinkly grey rind; abundant blue veins; good strong aroma and flavour; firm smooth texture when properly matured.	tall cylinder	$4-4\frac{1}{2}$ kg	by weight	Autumn Winter, Spring

it becomes stale so the yolk loses its shape and the white spreads out in a watery layer. The colour of the shell has no bearing on the quality of food value of an egg neither does the depth of colour of the yolk.

Sources of Supply and Availability

Eggs are available all the year round though there are certain times, such as at Easter, when they are more plentiful and may be slightly cheaper for a while. It is best to obtain eggs from specialist dealers.

Ordering Units

Eggs are sold by the long hundred which is 120 and packed into cases of 360; half cases are also available and it is also possible to buy packs of six or twelve eggs. They are graded by size as follows,

Size	Weight
1	70 g or over
2	65–70 g
3	60–65 g
4	55–60 g
5	50–55 g
6	45–50 g

Frozen and dehydrated egg is also available for commercial users.

Storage

It is advisable to keep fresh eggs in the refrigerator at approximately 5 °C in their cases, but not together with any commodity that has a strong smell as eggs are porous and will soon absorb it.

In general only hen's eggs are used in catering; **duck's eggs** may be offered but should be viewed with suspicion in case of staleness and utilised only in dishes where they will be well cooked.

    Quail's eggs are available in fresh and canned form; the size is that of a cherry and the use is for hors-d'oeuvre and canapés.

    Plover's eggs were once a very popular item served hard-boiled as an hors-d'oeuvre but all species of plovers are now totally protected. For catering these eggs have been replaced by gull's eggs. They are in season during the spring and are usually bought already hard-boiled.

FATS

Fats and oils belong to a large group of naturally occurring substances called lipids; they are a mixed group of compounds having little in common except that they are soluble in organic solvents and insoluble in water.

Butter There are two types of butter, one is made from sweet fresh cream and is known as farm or dairy butter, the other is made from ripened cream and is known as creamery butter; most of the butter produced is creamery butter and much of it contains salt. Salt helps to keep the butter, improves the flavour and is approximately 2.3 per cent of the total weight; unsalted butter is more expensive than the salted kind.

Butter is about 85 per cent fat and 13 per cent water; by law it must contain a minimum of 80 per cent fat and a maximum of 16 per cent water.

The superiority of butter over all other kinds of fat is mainly due to the presence in it of fats of low melting point and Vitamins A and D. The volatile fats of which the chief one is butyrin give butter its pleasant taste and smell; the smell of rancid butter is largely due to butyric acid formed by decomposition of the butyrin. The unsaturated fatty acids, oleic and linoleic tend to become oxidised when exposed to air and light; this is why it is important to pack butter in light-resistant foil or greaseproof paper and to store it well covered in a cool place.

Margarine Table margarine is made from a blend of various vegetable oils and salt with flavouring agents and Vitamins A and D added.

Cake margarine This must be readily workable to a cream and have the body to absorb egg; the flavour and aroma derived from it must be good. Coconut or palm kernel oil having a low melting point is used with ripened milk and brine and the resultant fat is texturised.

Shortenings These are required to be a 100 per cent fat, suitable for use particularly in cake-making. It must be soft in texture with excellent creaming properties and resistant to rancidity; for this a mixture of liquid and semi-liquid oils are hydrogenated to produce a white aerated fat with air being forced into the solution.

Puff paste fat This must be a highly plastic yet tough fat that will stand up to the manufacture of pastry by commercial machines. It is made from a stable liquid oil, a hardened oil, soured milk, brine and salt in solution.

Lard This comes from the fatty tissues of pigs and is rendered at low temperature to produce a snow white fat that is firm to the touch yet plastic and without graininess. It does not have very much taste or aroma until it is melted; it has a lower smoke point than vegetable oils and is not much used for deep frying. Leaf lard is the highest quality and is made from the fat surrounding the kidney and abdomen.

Tallow This word is used to designate either beef or sheep fat, and edible tallow is called dripping in the kitchen. The two types are used in blended shortenings for bakery use.

Vegetable oil and fats Vegetables constitute the most important source of edible oils and fats; they are prepared and refined from oil-containing seeds such as peanuts, or from fruits such as the olive. Oils in use include soya bean oil, cotton seed oil, palm oil and olive oil which is obtained from the ripe black fruits and is used without purification. Most vegetable oils, however, contain a number of impurities such as moisture, free fatty acids, colouring matter, resins, gums and some have vitamins; these affect flavour, odour and clarity and are removed during refining.

Quality

The purchase of fats and oils from firms of repute is necessary to ensure satisfaction. Where several different kinds of fats are in general use it may be advisable to experiment with the products of different firms until the best results are found. Oil for deep frying is judged by its length of use and some of the cheaper brands may not last proportionally as long as those that cost more initially but are cheaper in use.

Sources of Supply and Availability

Shortenings for pastry use are usually ordered from the specialist supplier to the bakery industry; oil is available in liquid or solid form and can be purchased from the normal grocery supplier or from a supplier of oils who may also be a purchaser of waste oil.

Ordering Units

Most fats are sold in bulk packs holding $12\frac{1}{2}$ kg and this applies to butter as well though it is equally possible to buy it in portion control units of 8, 9 and 14 grams. Most fats are also packed in 250 g foil or greaseproof wrappings. Oil is put into 20-litre drums as being the cheapest wasy of packing although some companies still use 5-litre cans.

Storage

Fats are perishable and require storage under refrigeration and once issued and opened, the contents should be used fairly quickly, especially during warm weather. Fats will absorb the aroma of strong smelling commodities in the same coldroom unless they are in unopened cases.

238

CONDIMENTS, SEASONINGS, HERBS AND SPICES

These terms cover those ingredients that are in everyday use for adding flavour and aroma to food. Every kitchen has its salt box and its pepper box and it is usual to put a cruet of these together with the seasonings of mustard and vinegar onto every table in the dining room for consumers to add additional seasoning to their food and to their own particular taste.

Quality

The quality of these items is determined by the brand name or that of a firm which has a reputation for supplying good quality and unadulterated goods.

Sources of Supply and Availability

In this section it is the assumption that all the many items listed are in dried form and as such many will have been brought into this country by a company specialising in these products and which knows the best sources of supply.

Ordering Units for Optimum Usage

Apart from salt all the items in this section are mostly used in small quantities; this means that the smallest wholesale pack should be purchased rather than a large quantity which will remain in stock for such a long time that it deteriorates and loses its original aroma and flavour. The type of operation and menu will decide the extent and list of seasonings, herbs and spices to be kept in stock.

Storage

The point about using any of these items is that a very small amount will have the necessary effect upon the foodstuff to which it is added, and the only way to achieve this is to keep each one separately in a tightly closed pack, or preferably an airtight tin. Given this, normal storage conditions are adequate.

CONDIMENTS

Mustard Mustards are made from the seeds of certain plants which belong to the cabbage family. The pungency comes from an essential oil which is formed when these crushed seeds are moistened with a liquid causing its particular hot taste to emerge. English mustard is made from finely powdered black Nigra seed blended with some yellow Alba seed and a little wheat flour; sometimes tumeric is added to give colour.

French mustard is sold only ready mixed and it is not so hot or pungent as English mustard. It is light in colour, sharp and salty with a clean taste that does not mask the flavour of the food.

German mustard is darker than French mustard and has a sweet-sour taste that is well flavoured with herbs and spices.

The best known brand of English mustard is Colmans of Norwich. In France the best brand names are Amora, Grey-Poupon and Maille. Olida make mustards in Normandy and Lovit is a well known firm in Bordeaux.

Vinegar The word vinegar comes form the French *vin aigre*, or sour wine. Weak wine, cider and ale when left exposed to the atmosphere will go sour and change into acetic acid; it is this which gives the characteristic flavour of vinegar.

There are two main classes of vinegar – the fermented type which is brewed, and the non-brewed type which is made of diluted industrial acetic acid, coloured and flavoured to taste. In this country vinegar is brewed and derived from various grains such as barley and maize.

Non-brewed vinegar consists of acetic acid diluted with water, coloured with caramel and possibly, flavoured; it is harsh and pungent as compared with brewed vinegar. A more recent process of production from alcohol by acetone fermentation gives a less raw flavour; it can be purchased as a concentrate to which water must be added.

Vinegars vary from country to country, in France the basis is grapes, in the USA it is apples, in Scotland distilled vinegar is preferred. Vinegar may be flavoured with herbs, fruits and spices such as tarragon, shallot, garlic, chilli, raspberries and elder flowers. Wine vinegars are available as either red or white; verjuice is sometimes used in place of vinegar – it is made by pressing the juice from unripe grapes, crab apples or sorrel.

Pickles and Ketchups Products such as chutney, pickle and the various sauces known as ketchups have a part to play in catering, evidenced by the fact that there are many firms whose names are household words still producing a wide range of products to a very high quality.

Most establishments will keep a stock of these items, the range and type being in accordance with customer's tastes. These will be of well-known brands and consists of mustard or Branston, pickles, pickled red cabbage, mango chutney, tomato ketchup, Worcester sauce and other bottled relishes.

SEASONINGS

Salt In the UK table salt is derived mainly from natural brine made by rain percolating through stratas of rock salt formations in places such as Cheshire and Worcestershire. It forms underground lakes containing about 25 per cent salt in solution and from here is pumped up into reservoirs and then into iron or steel pans in which it is heated, and this evaporates the water. According to the degree of heat applied and the length of time of application, so it forms as coarse or fine salt. At $110\,^{\circ}$C, which is the boiling point of brine, it results in fine table salt, at 71-$75\,^{\circ}$C it forms cooking salt, and at $38\,^{\circ}$C it produces the coarse freezing salt. *Fine table salt* has a small percentage of magnesium carbonate added to ensure that it stays free-running; another name for coarse salt is bay salt and it is this kind that is put into salt mills for customers who prefer freshly ground salt on their food.

Seasoned salt has certain spices, onion, garlic and herbs added to it. *Garlic salt, celery salt* and *onion salt* have their use as special seasonings for certain dishes. *Sea salt* is available from health foods stores for people who consider this kind of salt as superior to the usual type.

MSG This is the abbreviation for Monosodium Glutamate, a seasoning made by hydrolising wheat or beet; its great asset is that it blends in with most savoury flavours and helps to enhance and stabilise the original taste. It is, therefore, widely used by manufacturers of soup and gravy powders, spreads, pies, sausages and canned meat and it also plays a large part in Chinese cookery. It is a white powder 99 per cent pure.

Pepper This condiment comes from several countries in the Far East, mainly India, Malaysia, Sumatra and Java where it grows as a climbing vine. It is picked in its unripe state and allowed to dry in the sun in the form of peppercorns. It is then exported, much of it finely ground. The idea that the black peppercorn is stronger than the white is a fallacy as they are one and the same thing, the white ones merely having had the black outer skin removed.

Cayenne pepper is made from small red chillies and is the strongest kind of pepper; consequently it must be used sparingly.

Seasoned peppers are available as for example, lemon flavoured pepper. *Paprika* pepper is made from the mild variety of pimento and is used mainly in Hungarian cookery.

Pickled green peppercorns which are unripe when bottled in vinegar are a recently introduced form of flavouring; they may be used in the same way as other peppercorns but are most suited to oriental dishes.

HERBS

Herbs are the leaves and stems of plants which are used for food, medicine, scent and flavour; they are important in cookery because they help to make food more appetising not by their bulk, but by the aroma and flavour. Some of the more common ones are in daily use in the kitchen whilst others are more exotic and have only specific uses in special dishes.

It is possible to purchase and use some herbs in fresh form but many are available only in dried or pickled form.

Balm – a lemon-scented leaf used mainly as a tisaine and in fruit punch.

Basil – has a very strong flavour that blends well in tomato dishes and in salads.

Bay leaves – can be used fresh or dried but the dry leaves are best; must be used sparingly.

Bergamot – has the pungency of sage plus the scent of rosemary.

Borage – these hairy leaves have the aroma and flavour of cucumber, used mainly in drinks; the five-pointed blue flowers are crystallised for use as cake decorations.

Chervil – a fern-like leaf spray with a fresh spicy taste of aniseed.

Chives – long grass-like shoots smelling sweetly of onion; nearly always used fresh.

Garlic – has a very strong smell when raw but the smell and flavour is not so pronounced after cooking.

Marjoram – greyish soft leaves similar to basil but more subtle; quite pungent in its dried form.

Mint – mainly used as an accompaniment with lamb and mutton in the form of mint sauce; there are many varieties.

Oregano – very like marjoram but more pungent and hot.

Parsley – this herb is indispensible in all good kitchens; is used mainly as a garnish either fresh or deep fried.

Rosemary – spiky leaves with a very aromatic smell and flavour but limited uses, mainly in Italian cooking.

Sage – grey-green hairy leaves used mainly in stuffings for pork and duck.

Savory – similar in appearance to thyme but has long, narrow leaves and a pungent, peppery aroma; useful as a flavouring in stuffings.

Tarragon – has long, thin, green leaves growing on a long stem and a distinct tart aromatic flavour; used in many sauces and stews.

Thyme – there are many varieties of this herb the most commonly used being garden thyme; very subtle flavour and excellent aroma.

SPICES

The word spice comes from the same source as species, meaning classes of an object, and refer to any dried aromatics. Most spices originate in the area from China south to Indonesia, South India and Sri Lanka.

Allspice – dark berries which combine the aroma and taste of cinnamon, cloves and nutmeg in themselves; used whole as pickling spice and ground as a part of mixed spice; sometimes called pimento or Jamaican pepper.

Cassia – the bark of an evergreen tree of the laurel family; rolled into quills it is like coarse cinnamon; in powder form it is a constituent of mixed spice.

Chilli Powder – usually a mixture of dried ground chilli peppers, aromatic seeds, spices and herbs; can be mild or fiercely hot to the taste.

Cinnamon – the inner bark of a species of laurel available in rolled sticks or powdered form.

Clove – the dried flower buds of a tree; available whole for flavouring and in ground form for spicing such items as buns, mincemeat and apple.

Ginger – this spice grows as a root in Asia, Africa and the West Indies, it is dried then either preserved in syrup, crystallised, or ground to a powder.

Mace – this is a scarlet coloured lacy network found inside the shells of nutmeg and has a slightly more pungent flavour than the actual nutmeg; available as blade mace or ground.

Nutmeg – has a pleasant crisp aroma that makes it blend with most items made with milk; available as the whole seed or in ground form.

Saffron – this is the dried orange coloured stigmas of the mauve flowering crocus; it has a warm bitter aroma, an exquisite flavour and golden colour; is used in a very small quantity to produce the desired result. Available as the original stigmas and in ground powder oform. Very expensive.

Tumeric – a member of the ginger family, its brilliant yellow colour is useful in the manufacture of pickles, chutneys and mustard blends; the flavour is not very pronounced but adds to the total spiciness of curry powder.

Curry Powder – available commercially in many different formulas, with no one single recipe for its composition. Basically it is a blend of mild and hot spices including cinnamon, coriander, cloves, allspice, ginger, nutmeg, mustard, cayenne and black pepper, and tumeric. Depending on the type of curry dish required, some of these spices may be omitted and others added.

Curry Paste – this is the mixed curry spices in an oily base which eliminates the raw curry taste because the ingredients have been cooked together.

AROMATIC SEEDS

These seeds comprise both herbs and spices and are used to add flavour to certain dishes where the use of the powdered article would be inappropriate.

Aniseed – small oval seeds with the smell and taste of liquorice and are used for their digestive properties.

Caraway – elongated seeds with the taste and smell of aniseed and are useful as a digestive; used in rye bread, seed cake and in pickles.

Celery – small brown seeds with a strong flavour and smell of the vegetable.

Coriander – small, slightly oval ripe seeds used in several sweet dishes and also in ground form for curry powder.

Cumin – these have a similar flavour to caraway seeds and are used for pickling and in Near Eastern foods; in ground form they are included in curry powder and chili powder.

Dill – these are used to sprinkle on rolls, in cooking sauerkraut, in pickling cucumbers and for making dill water for babies.

Fennel – these seeds have an aniseed aroma and flavour and are used in pickles and for cooking certain fish and meat dishes.

Juniper – small dark berries used when cooking sauerkraut; they blend well in game dishes.

Mustard – dark brown and orange seeds mixed together, mainly for grinding for making mustard but also whole in salads, chutneys and some cheese dishes.

Poppy – these slate blue seeds are used mainly in Eastern cookery but also on bread rolls and strudels.

FLAVOURINGS, ESSENCES AND COLOURINGS

These items are used largely for pastry work where their judicial use will enhance much of what is produced in this important department of the kitchen. Many of the flavourings used are in fact spirits or liqueurs.

FLAVOURINGS

Kirsch A colourless spirit made from dark coloured wild cherries which are fermented together with the kernels from their stones. It is used mainly in pastry work and is often added to fruits and fruit salad. Produced in Germany, France and Switzerland.

Maraschino A colourless liqueur similar in taste to Kirsch except that it is very sweet. It is made from a sour black cherry originating in Dalmatia in Yugoslavia. Its uses are the same as for Kirsch.

Others in general use include **Curaçao**, **Chartreuse**, **Grand Marnier**, **Crème de Menthe**, **Brandy** and **Rum**.

ESSENCES

These are concentrated flavourings of which only a few drops are needed to produce the desired result. As used today they are mainly synthetic preparations which replace the more expensive volatile oils of the original ingredient; they are considered acceptable since they are usually incorporated into a mixture before being cooked. For example, genuine vanilla essence is distilled from the vanilla pods whereas that popularly used is based on a coal tar derivative and is much cheaper to buy.

The essences in general use are: almond, banana, caramel, coffee, coconut, chocolate, cherry, lemon, orange, peppermint, raspberry, rum, strawberry and vanilla; for some flavours it is possible to purchase a combined essence and colour.

COLOURINGS

More care is necessary in using these than for the flavourings and essences; a colour must only be added to restore a dish to its natural appearance after it has unavoidably been lost in the process of preparation. Only natural food colours should be used.

BEVERAGES

TEA

Tea is derived from an evergreen plant now grown in many countries, mainly India, Sri Lanka, Indonesia and countries such as Kenya in East Africa. The leaves are picked while they are still young, allowed to wither to reduce the amount of moisture in them, then crushed by rolling which frees the juices from the leaves. This causes a reaction in the oxydising process forming as moisture which dries on the leaves.

The dried tea is sorted into different grades – broken, fannings, and dust, the last two being sought after because of their quick-brewing qualities. The dust which is left when the fannings are sifted is popular as catering tea and in tea-bags because it infuses quickly and is quite strong. The tea dealers use letters to denote the various grades of tea and these can be seen stamped on tea chests. Pekoe is denoted by the letter P and indicates larger pieces; Orange is marked by O and indicate a good quality tea; F can indicate a flowery grade of good flavour. The tea companies blend various qualities, sizes and grade of teas to give a uniform product.

Some of the special kinds of tea are:

Earl Grey – perhaps the most famous; a blend of China and Indian teas and bergamot oil; light and delicately scented.

Assam – a strong recuperative tea.

Darjeeling – a wonderful tea with a flavour of muscatel; can be drunk with milk or lemon.

Green Gunpowder – a China tea with curled leaves which give it its name because they look like gunpowder.

Jasmine – this is a delicate China tea mixed with scented jasmin flowers; best drunk with a slice of lemon.

Lady Londonderry's Mixture – a special blend of China, Indian and Formosa teas, named after the great hostess.

Lapsang Souchong – a distinctive China tea with a tarry taste which is quite pungent.

Various teas having a herbal base and known as tisaines are also available; two of the very many varieties are camomile and jasmine.

245

COFFEE

Coffee is the berry of an evergreen shrub which is grown in tropical and subtropical climates at high altitudes. The beans are washed out, dried and skinned then shipped in the green state. Roasting develops the flavour of coffee beans, and the degree of roasting, from 195-300°C, determines the colour and strength of the brewed coffee; for example, the coffee for espresso use must be roasted at a high temperature and also be finely ground to give the desired result.

Coffee purchased as beans or ground is usually a blend made up in various ways to suit all possible needs at different prices. Basically there are two main qualities or varieties of coffee – the Arabica which is the quality bean, and the Robusta, grown mainly in Africa, which is not of the same high quality because it gives a strong, harsh and pungent coffee with only a neutral flavour.

The famous coffee from Brazil is the Santos bean, Columbian coffee is excellent, Jamaica is famous for its Blue Mountain coffee and Java and Puerto Rico both produce first-class beans.

French coffee is a mixture of dark roast coffee and chicory which gives it a more bitter flavour. Instant coffee is usually made with Robusta beans, the liquid coffee being dehydrated to a powder.

COCOA

Cocoa is grown mainly in Ghana and Nigeria and also in South America; when the pods are ripe they are cut open, emptied out and the beans allowed to ferment and oxidise which develops its particular flavour. They are then dried in readiness for export. At the factory the beans are cleaned, roasted, cracked to remove the nibs which are then ground to a smooth liquor containing about 55 per cent fat. This fat is then pressed out to leave about 22 per cent of the original and this resultant mass is ground into cocoa powder. Drinking chocolate is basically cocoa powder with the addition of sugar.

PATENT BEVERAGES

Bournvita – a mixture of malt, sugar, glucose, cocoa powder, dried milk, dried egg, salt and flavouring, blended together then cooked under vacuum until brittle; it is then carefully broken up.

Horlicks – a malted milk drink made from wheat flour, malted barley and milk.

Ovaltine – made from barley malt, milk, cocoa powder, soya flour, eggs and vitamins.

Milo – made from condensed milk and malt extract with cocoa powder, milk powder and added vitamins.

Quality of Beverages

As coffee and tea are the most popular beverages in this country it is important that they leave no room for criticism, this means knowing the various qualities available and buying those that best suit the particular consumer and obtaining it from a firm that specialises in these products. Experience in tasting them is useful when judging several blends before deciding which to purchase.

Ordering Units and Storage

Tea can be purchased in 45 kg chests for weighing loose but for most catering uses teabags in sizes to produce anything from a single pot to a bulk urn are best. Ready roasted coffee in ground form and as beans is purchased by weight either in catering size packets and tins or in the form of bags similar to tea bags for placing to brew in boiling water.

Instant coffee is available in tins and packets of various weights; there are several kinds of instant coffee – powder, granules and decaffeinated which is for customers wishing to avoid the stimulating effect of ordinary coffee. Decaffeinated coffee is also available in ground form.

Patent beverages are available in tins, jars and packets of various weights.

Beverage products need to be stored in well sealed containers and kept in a dry, cool atmosphere. Careful stock control is necessary to ensure items are used in correct rotation.

CANNED FOODS

The role of canned foods in catering establishments varies according to the type of operation – a large-scale unit may make full use of the wide range of goods packed in cans; a high-class restaurant will probably use small size cans of the more expensive ones such as truffles, foie gras, hearts of palm, artichoke bottoms and turtle meat.

Most foods can be successfully canned and the range of different sizes of can covers the requirements of all sectors of the industry; the brand name be it a national or international one is sufficient guarantee of quality.

Storage of canned goods is in a dry store away from warmth and dampness. The Canned Foods Advisory Bureau issues information concerning the shelf life of these products and indicates that some of them need to be used within a twelvemonth of purchase.

CEREALS

Cereals are grains produced from cultivated grasses used for food, and in one form or another are part of the everyday production of dishes. The following are the most widely used.

This important cereal is the source of production of both flour and semolina. Before milling the wheat is conditioned so as to faciliate the separation of the bran which is the outer skin.

Semolina   This is produced when cleaned wheat is passed through rollers which crack the grains open and release the inside; this is then put through a second set of rollers the result of which is semolina which can be produced in coarse or fine forms. It is sold for use as a pudding cereal and for making into various farinaceous dishes.

Flour   Instead of producing semolina, the product can go through a process of ever finer rollers to make the wheat into flour. Strong flour is made from hard wheat, a type not normally grown in the UK. It is a flour with a high gluten content and is used extensively in the baking of bread. Soft flour is produced from soft wheats such as those grown in the UK, it is more suitable for cake and biscuit making and is often referred to as high-ratio flour; being very finely milled it can absorb a high proportion of sugar and liquid.

Barley   This is usually used in catering in the form of pearl barley which is polished barley after the bran and germ have been removed. Barley flour which is sometimes used as a thickening agent, is ground pearl barley.

Maize   This is the seed of Indian corn; coarsely ground it is the main ingredient for polenta, finely ground it becomes cornflour and is used frequently as a thickening agent.

Oats   Oats are used mainly for making porridge and also biscuits; usually purchased in the form of oatmeal.

Rice   There are many varieties of rice but only a few are in everyday use; they are produced as a main commodity in the United States, Australia, South America and Italy. The two main types are the long grain Patna and the round (or short) grain Carolina, but these types no longer come solely from the places after which they were named. The many types of Italian rice are all bold, i.e. large grain and very hard.

Parboiled rice in dried form is widely used because it does not need to be washed and dried out after cooking. It is good quality rice processed by steam pressure to remove some of the starch and is sold under brand names.

Ground rice is the poor quality and broken grains, finely milled; it is used for milk puddings and for thickening certain soups.

Rice paper which is an edible paper used in the making of macaroons and nougat Montelimar, is not actually made from rice but from the pith of a tree.

The following although not strictly cereals are included here because of their customary association with these products.

Arrowroot   This is obtained from the manioc plant found in the West Indies; the root is pulped, dried out then finely milled into a white powder which is used for thickening soups and gravies.

Sago   This is obtained from the pith of a kind of palm tree which grows in

India and the Far East. After being washed, drained and dried it is roasted to produce a mass which is then milled into various grades of sago.

Tapioca This is produced from the juice expressed from the rhizomes of the cassava plant. After drying it is roasted then milled into either flakes or seeds.

FARINACEOUS PRODUCTS OR PASTAS

Products such as spaghetti, macaroni and noodles are included here under this title because their basis of production is mainly flour.

Commercial pasta is made from one of the three main groups of wheat known as Durum wheat; this is milled to the semolina stage only, so that less water is absorbed when making the paste and thus speeding up the drying process. The dough that forms is kneaded to a stiff plastic consistency, then forced through a plate of the desired shape; it is then dried. There are several hundred different shapes and types.

BREAKFAST CEREALS

All the breakfast cereals such as cornflakes come under the heading of cereals, even Muesli and Swiss-stype cereal containing as it does, oats together with nuts, sultanas, sugar, salt, and sometimes dried apple. These are available under brand names which are a guarantee of their quality.

All flour and cereal based items must be stored in a very dry place as they are quickly affected by damp and most of them are attractive to insects which will infest them if left in sacks or paper bags. Flour is usually purchased by the 32 kg bulk bag and kept stored and stacked on slats off the floor; once a sack is opened the contents should be tipped into a storage bin.

SWEETENING AGENTS

This section comprises the various kinds of sugar and other sweetening agents used in cookery.

Sugar This is made from the sugar cane and sugar beet and there is no difference between the two. A catering establishment will keep most of the following kinds of sugar in stock. See Fig. 25.

In addition there are coffee crystals available in one colour or a mixture of several.

Syrup After the various grades of brown sugar have been made, the syrup that remains is called molasses and this is used to produce treacle. Golden syrup is a mixture of refined molasses and glucose syrup.

Maple syrup is, as the name indicates, made from the sap of the maple tree;

Figure 25
WHITE SUGAR

Type	Uses
Granulated	General purpose.
Caster	Pastry work.
Cube	Beverages, pastry work.
Icing	Glazing, icing, decorative work.
Preserving	For making preserves such as jam and marmalade.
Sachets and wrapped cubes	Beverages; used by airlines, steamship companies, hotels and restaurants; often printed with their name.

BROWN SUGAR

Pieces	Christmas puddings and cakes.
Soft brown	Christmas and wedding cakes, puddings.
Demerara	Cakes, puddings, as coffee sugar.

it has its own peculiar flavour and is much used in Canada and the United States.

Honey This is made by bees from the nectar of flowers which the bees collect and store in their hive in the cells of a honeycomb. The honey is extracted by machine and packed in jars or tins as either a clear liquid or a viscous granular liquid. The aroma and flavour and colour of honeys differ according to the floral origins of the nectar taken by the bees, thus each region and country will yield a different kind.

Saccharin This is made by a series of reactions from the hydrocarbon iolene and is some 300 times as sweet as sugar. It is the only compound permitted by the Artificial Sweeteners in Food Regulations 1969; it is not permitted in ice cream and there is a legal maximum for the amounts which may be present in soft drinks.

Sorbitol This is a sugar that is used in diabetic sweets as it is absorbed from the digestive tract only and can be tolerated in limited amounts by diabetic sufferers. It is similar to dextrose, has 60 per cent of the sweetening power of sugar and is used in the manufacture of sweets, chocolates and preserves for use by diabetics.

CONFECTIONERY GOODS

Amongst the many commodites used in cooking are some which are peculiar to the pastry section, seldom being used in any other part of the kitchen. They are best obtained from specialist suppliers of confectionery goods. They include:

Angelica – the candied stem of a plant used for decoration purposes.

Dragees –small silver and golden sugar balls used for decorating iced cakes and fancies.

Fondant – a kind of cake icing made by boiling sugar and water to 115 °C then cooling and working it to a creamy mass, it is more usually bought ready made.

Gaufrettes and wafers – used for serving with ice cream and are available in various shapes and qualities.

Glucose – used for boiling sugar and is sometimes added to cake mixture to keep it moist. It is usually purchased as a viscous liquid but is also available in powdered form.

Marzipan – often purchased ready made for use in petits-fours and cakes. It is made from ground almonds, eggs and sugar.

Preserves – under this name are included the various flavoured jams, marmalade and curds used mainly for cakes.

Raising Agents – the items included here are baking powder and yeast; the first is a combination of two parts of cream of tartar and one of bicarbonate of soda and can be made up on the premises. It is used mainly for cakes. Yeast is best purchased from a bakery supply firm in fresh form although it is also available in dried form as flakes or granules. It is used in the production of bread, brioche and buns.

GELLING AGENTS

Gelatine – this is collagen produced mainly from sun-dried bone. It is purified and processed as granular, flakes or thin sheets of gelatine. It is also available as sweet jellies and aspic jellies.

Gum Tragacanth – comes from a shrub and is purchased in the form of a white powder; it forms a mucillage when added to water and with the addition of icing sugar it makes a paste used in the pastry section for modelling; It is also used for glazing dry petits-fours.

Gum Arabic – this comes from the acacia tree; it is dissolved in water but without allowing it to boil as this impairs its setting qualities; used to make jelly centres for sweets and chocolates and also for marshmallow.

Carrageen – this is extracted from the red seaweed known as Irish Moss and used as an emulsifier and stabiliser; it has little food value and is used in slimming products.

Alginates – there are very many different forms of this powder which is extracted from seaweeds and each form has a slightly different use. They are used as thickeners, stabilisers and binding agents in foods.

Agar-Agar – Used as a stabiliser and thickener and is a vegetable gelatine extracted from seaweed.

Pectin – a commercial product available in liquid or powder form for ensuring the good setting of jams and preserves, especially when made from watery fruits; it is made from apple peelings and cores.

DELICATESSEN AND SPECIALITY DE LUXE GOODS

This section covers some of the more expensive luxury items of food as well as other items which are infrequently used and thus stocked by specialist dealers.

FOIE GRAS

This is the enlarged liver of the goose and is available raw or cooked ready for use. It is produced mainly in the Strasbourg region of France but also in Hungary and Israel. The geese are kept in pens and deliberately over-fed which results in grossly enlarged livers which are then denerved and cooked according to their quality and ultimate use; the colour of good quality foie gras is pinky beige, the texture firm and the flavour excellent.

Most foie gras is cooked in the can or in earthenware or porcelain terrines of various sizes from which it can be served direct. It can be also bought as a cooked pâté – a tall pastry case in which a number of livers have been baked.

Foie gras is also available in block tunnel and long round tins, sometimes garnished with whole or chopped truffle. Some comes in the form of a purée with the addition of other kinds of liver; products made mainly of pig's liver are often sold as pâté of foie gras but should not be confused with the authentic product.

CAVIARE

Caviare is the prepared roe of the sturgeon and there are several different kinds each coming from a particular variety of the species. Caviare is probably the most expensive of all goods because of the big demand world-wide and the limited production. It is produced mainly in Russia and Iran from that part where both countries meet around the Caspian Sea.

The roes from the sturgeon are sieved to remove the surrounding membrane and immersed in brine so as to preserve it, the amount of salting being determined by the grade and quality, with up to 6 per cent in poor quality caviares. The best quality caviare which contains about 4 per cent salt is called Malossol. Other names used to denote a particular caviare are Beluga, Ocietrova and Sevruga; the colour and size of the grains can vary considerably. Sterlet is another name used and it indicates a small species of sturgeon from which only a small amount of fine grained caviare is obtained. The colour of caviares varies from black through dark grey and green to brown and even golden; Beluga is the largest grain of all.

Caviare is packed in tins of various weights; it must be kept cold but not frozen; at 0°C it will keep for several weeks. Being a perishable commodity some importers prolong its life by pasteurising it in sealed containers but once opened it must be consumed as soon as possible.

The roes of other fishes are processed and sold as caviare, the most common one being lumpfish roe from Denmark and Germany but its grains are small and hard and the taste is nothing like the genuine article. Salmon roes are treated as caviare and this bright red commodity is known as Keta caviare. The Italians give the name Botarga to the caviare they make from the tunny and red mullet.

TRUFFLES

Truffles are valued for culinary use because of their superb aroma and their natural black colour; they are a subterranean fungus of an irregular round shape but of many sizes. Truffles have not been cultivated and many years of investigation have failed to reveal the exact reasons why they grow where they do; what is known is that there are certain areas, mainly in France, that are apparently just right for their growth. The main area is in Perigord where the presence of iron in the soil and beech trees, together with a hot summer with thunderstorms and then light autumn frost can yield truffles ready for collecting from December to March.

Truffles can be obtained fresh in the season but are usually purchased in small tins containing 50 g, 100 g and 250 g of truffle in a little Madeira wine. These may be whole peeled or unpeeled, they are in great demand and the price is very high.

White truffles are found in the Piedmont area of northern Italy, they have a highly perfumed aroma and look something like a new potato.

Artificial truffle is known as garnishing paste and can be used for decorating cold buffet items. It is made of charcoal, beef and albumen and is packed in cans; it has none of the taste and aroma of real truffle but serves a useful purpose in some classes of catering.

SNAILS

Although it is possible to collect edible snails in the chalky areas in the south of England most snails consumed here are brought in from France, Germany, Switzerland, Hungary or Rumania. These are the 'gros Bourgogne' variety and are generally purchased ready cooked in cans, containing twenty-four graded snails and a packet of the shells to serve them in; they are graded as grand, extra large, large, good size, medium and small.

TURTLE MEAT

This is used mainly as a garnish in real turtle soup and is available in sun-dried form and in cans. Supplies are mainly from Australia and the Cayman Islands in the West Indies.

HAMS

A ham is the hind leg of a pig cut from the carcass, with a rounded end, and cured by a special process which varies according to the country or district of origin. The leg cut from an already cured side of bacon is called a gammon and is not, strictly speaking, a ham.

Hams of all kinds are available all the year round from specialist suppliers and are more widely available around Christmas time. Hams for cooking are always bought whole on the bone and weigh from 5 kg to 8 kg approximately. Smoked hams for eating raw are available whole on the bone, boned, or sliced in vacuum packs. The following are some of the best known hams listed under their country of origin.

England *York ham* – a large one of 6–7 kg with an elongated rounded end; it is dry-salted, lightly smoked and hung to mature for three to four months. *Bradenham ham* comes from Chippenham in Wiltshire, it is black on the outside and the flesh is bright red. The cure includes some treacle. *Suffolk sweet-cured ham* has a golden skin and is pickled with beer and sugar. *Cumberland ham* is flavoured with brown sugar during the dry-salting process.

France *Jambon de Bayonne* is a dry-salted ham from the town of Orthez. It is usually thinly sliced for eating raw as an hors-d'oeuvre. *Jambon de Toulouse* is salted and dried and can be used either raw or cooked.

USA *Virginia hams* are cured with salt, saltpetre, hickory ashes and molasses, they are smoked in green hickory sawdust then packed in pine ashes to mature.

Italy The best known Italian ham is *Parma ham*, very delicate flavoured and almost always eaten raw, thinly sliced to serve on its own or with melon, pears or fresh figs. In Italian it is called Proscuitta.

Germany The best known German ham is the *Westphalian* but excellent ones are also produced in Stuttgart, Mainz, Gotha and other towns. The Westphalian is cured with brine then smoked over resin-free beech or ash sawdust to which some juniper berries have been added.

Other foods which can be included in this section include: **Bird's Nests** which are imported from Malaysia in dried form for use in soup; **Frog's Legs** which are eaten as a fish dish – they comprise the hind legs which are obtainable as the dozen impaled on skewers; **Vesiga** which is the dried spinal column of the sturgeon and used mainly in dishes of Russian origin.

The speciality commodities used in ethnic restaurants in this country would come under this section but the majority are used mainly in their particular establishments. If needed, it would be wise to purchase items such as Bombay duck, poppadums, masala, ghee, bamboo shoots, bean sprouts and water chestnuts from specialist suppliers.

CHARCUTERIE

This is a French word used to describe in general the wide range of various items of pork butchery, although other meats can be included. The products are usually made-up items and can be classified under three headings.

254

1. Prepared meats and sausages of many types which are already cooked and need no further preparation. These include salami, mortadella, the various types of German and other continental sausages which are smoked or air-dried such as cervalat and teewurst, the various pâtés and terrines and items such as black pudding, brawn, liver sausage, garlic sausage, rillettes.
2. Sausages and other preparations which although cooked usually undergo further preparation such as poaching or grilling. Examples of these are Frankfurter and Vienna sausages, white puddings, fleischwurst.
3. Raw sausages which are usually fried and grilled. These include the popular British pork and beef sausages and some continental sausages such as Saucisson de Lyons.

Availability and Sources of Supply

There are many good UK manufacturers of this type of product although much is imported from the Continent mainly from France, Belgium, Germany, Italy and Poland. Supplies are always obtainable from specialist dealers.

Storage

Cured and dried products such as salami and cervalat are best hung in a cool dry store with a good circulation of air. Other items have a limited life and should be ordered frequently. They are best held under normal refrigeration temperatures.

CONVENIENCE FOODS

The definition of a food that comes into the category of convenience foods could be 'a food to which the degree of preparation has been taken to a fairly advanced stage by the manufacturer so as to have made it a labour-saving alternative to a less highly processed product'. This interpretation indicates that a convenience food is not one that is completely cooked needing only to be reheated ready for consumption, but is one where the ingredients have been taken to the stage when the minimum amount of preparation will make them ready for use. There are several ways of classifying these items, either by the stage to which preparation has been taken, or by the actual process used to render them convenient in use. The first is where foodstuffs are partly or fully prepared raw products or partly or fully prepared processed items ranging from, for example, poultry that has been cleaned and plucked or fish that has been filleted, to instant mixes and ready-made entrées and gateaux. The second is to look at the products of drying, canning, chilling, freezing, vacuum packing and irradiating. It is from this point of view that the following information is given.

Dehydrated foods The drying of foods is the most elementary form of processing and preserving and is very effective because micro-organisms that cause spoilage cannot survive without moisture. In its most primitive form it is the drying of food by laying it out in the sun exactly as currants and sultanas have been dried throughout the ages.

The modern method is to evaporate the moisture from the food by low pressure dehydration. Hot air drying, roller drying, spray drying, and freeze drying are all forms of dehydrating foods. No special storage is required for these products and the sealed tins or packages can be kept at up to $10\,^{\circ}$C without fear of deterioration.

Canned and bottled foods The process of preserving foods in sealed containers was discovered as long ago as 1809. It was perfected later in the century when Pasteur discovered that spoilage was caused by bacteria rather than contact with the air, and that the application of heat ensured complete safety. All foods can be canned and bottled though the latter are more expensive.

There is no problem with storage as even the softest foods such as canned plums and asparagus have a long shelf life.

Frozen foods The freezing of food retains nearly all the original colour, flavour, texture, nutritional value and appearance of the food, and makes seasonal commodities available all the year at a steady price. The list of frozen foods includes fish, meat, vegetables, snacks and sweets in both raw and cooked form and as ready dishes. Storage is in a deep freezer at down to $-40\,^{\circ}$C.

Chilled foods Many convenience foods are available in this form which is where the temperature of the food is held constant at $0\,^{\circ}$C. Raw meat in carcass and portion cut form, oven-ready poultry, fish such as whole salmon, fruits, and prepared dishes are examples of chilled foods. They have a short shelf life.

Vacuum packed foods By exhausting the air before sealing foods inside the bag, it is possible to keep them in good condition over a period of time under normal refrigeration temperature, and for a shorter time in a cool room. Boneless cuts of meat, bacon rashers and cheese are items commonly packed in this way.

Irradiation of foods This process is carried out extensively in the United States and gives food an unlimited shelf life in normally sealed packages and under ordinary storage conditions.

ALCOHOLIC AND NON-ALCOHOLIC DRINKS

The subject of drink is dealt with from the point of view of it being another commodity of which the buyer needs to be knowledgeable in exactly the same way that he does in food. A comprehensive knowledge of the subject of wines and spirits requires a depth of study beyond the compass of this book which however, offers a guide to the varieties, purchase, storage, handling and sale of these commodities.

A wine list, where required, should be drawn up to complement the menu and its extent and scope will be governed by the consumer's spending power, the amount of capital the business is prepared to tie up in laying down stocks, and the amount of cellar space required to store these items. The expected turnover of stock is also a contributory factor.

The sale of wines and spirits can be a profitable part of the food and beverage operation as it bears fewer overheads, but although it is much easier to control than food this control should be as foolproof as possible.

Much of the space on the wine list is usually devoted to bottles of wine to accompany the food but there are a number of other entries that are also important. These are mineral waters, beers, fortified wines, spirits, liqueurs, all of which require a similar knowledge to that of wine and pose similar decisions of storage and control.

Allocation of space for cellar and dispense bar where these commodities are stored must be adequate for the envisaged amount of stock, be situated in the correct position to give ideal storage conditions, ease of distribution and be capable of offering strict security. The decision on space is also tied to that of whether certain of the better wines will be laid down to mature over a long number of years or if these usually more expensive wines will be purchased as required. These factors require qualified advice by an expert who may be a wine buyer capable of taking decisions on what and where to buy and how much capital should be invested in stocks of wine. Such a person would obviously command the sort of salary which only a large organisation could afford, the more modest establishment will have to rely on the good judgement of the person responsible for purchasing and the wine merchant he chooses to deal with. Together they should be capable of drawing up a list of all the products to be included on the lists of the various outlets where alcoholic and non-alcoholic drink is to be sold. In doing this they will be aware of the consumer's expectations as regards range of selection and price, and the probable turnover of stock.

WINE

Wine is produced in this country but only in small quantities each year because the climate is not exactly right for it. British wines can be included in the wine list but the main section will be of wines imported from France followed by a selection from several other countries including probably Italy, Germany, Spain, Portugal and the United States.

257

Wine is the naturally fermented juice of the grape, the sugar in the grape being converted into alcohol. The alcohol content of wines such as claret, burgundy, hock and similar wines which are known as table wines is about 7 to 14 per cent which is low when compared with most spirits which are on average 40 per cent alcohol. The various kinds of wine fall into three categories – still, sparkling and fortified, and they are made as white, pink and red, the red colour coming from the grapes used. The juice of any colour of grape is white or very pale yellow which means that white wine can be made equally from black grapes as from white. The colouring of pink and red wines develops as the skins and pips of black grapes are left in contact with the must or grape juice, so colouring it.

The variety of grapes used in making a wine give it its characteristics; there are many different varieties of wine grape and finest of them being the Cabernet Sauvignon, the Pinot Noir, and the Riesling. Great wine is produced often from a single variety, other wines are freqeuntly produced from several varieties of grapes.

The soil on which the grapes are grown, the way the vines are cultivated, the climate in which they grow, the climatic conditions whilst growing, all have an effect upon the wine produced. For example, grapes grown in the northern zone of production have less sugar, are lighter and have less alcohol than those grown in the more southerly parts, but they are higher in acid and so keep longer.

Wine making and selling is a huge international business employing many people in many countries in some of which it acts as a major source of income. The caterer needs a professional knowledge of drink and must constantly seek to improve his knowledge of this wide and fascinating study. In the practical sense he should be able to judge not only the great wines of Bordeaux and Burgundy but also respectable wines for everyday drinking that can be put on the wine list without detracting from its distinction; it is the search for and appraisal of these lesser known wines that demonstrate the ability of the buyer.

White, rosé and red house wine can be kept for sale by the bottle, carafe or glass and at a reasonable price that makes it attractive to drink with the Table d'Hôte menu. But house wine does not have to be a cheap one of no distinction whatsoever; the brand decided upon should be that which will satisfy the wishes of the clientele as regards quality and price and it should be possible to continue to obtain a supply over a reasonably long period. There is a wide choice of bulk wine from the main wine producing countries and it is available in 5 and 10 litre collapsible plastic packs, 2 litre bottles and even in nip size bottles. White wine can be kept in a refrigerated container which dispenses it at the desired temperature into $\frac{1}{4}$, $\frac{1}{2}$ or 1 litre carafes and by the glass; it is kept in perfect condition without fear of deterioration.

A standard bottle of wine of 75 or 70 cl capacity will yield five $1\frac{1}{2}$ dl portions in standard 8 fl oz goblets or six in $6\frac{2}{3}$ fl oz size. A 2 litre bottle will give fifteen good glasses for receptions. Sherry, port and vermouth are usually sold in $\frac{2}{6}$ out measures which yields sixteen measures per 70 cl bottle. Spirits are sold by the 6 out which yields thirty-two portions to a bottle containing 75 cl or $26\frac{2}{3}$ fl oz.

258

Storage

Wine is usually bought by the bottle but can be had in bulk for bottling on the premises. The standard bottle used to be 75 cl or $26\frac{2}{3}$ fl oz but 68 cl and 70 cl bottles are also sold nowadays. Half bottles, magnum bottles and 1 litre and 2 litre bottles are also available and a lot of these are bottled in the country of origin and packed six or twelve to the case; different regions use different shapes of bottles. Wine must be stored horizontally so as to keep the end of the cork moist thus preventing it from drying and allowing the contents to leak and/or spoilage organisms to gain access to the contents. Each wine kept in stock should be given a bin number and be kept together in a particular section, white wines in the coolest part. The cellar must be kept dark and the storage temperature at 10–13 °C which is suitable for all kinds of wines until required for issue.

FRENCH WINES

There are six major wine growing regions in France each of which produces some remarkably good wines; they are Bordeaux, Burgundy, Champagne, Alsace, Loire and Côtes du Rhône. There are other regions which produce a large quantity of good quality but lesser known wine; among these are Savoy, Provence, Languedoc Roussillon, the Jura, and the Dordogne, and they are usually featured as French regional wines. The wine growers of France are governed by the Ministry of Agriculture's classifying system of guaranteed authenticity which protects the buyer from being sold wines of dubious origin and doubtful character. There are two terms used on French wine labels to denote the authenticity of the contents: AOC which means Appellation d'Origine Contrôlée indicates that it is a fine wine that has been made in accordance with the local practice of the place named on the label; VDQS which means Vins Délimités de Qualité Supérieure and indicates a more simple wine that comes from an area other than the main designated AOC areas. The conditions for entitlement are laid down by a body called the Institute National des Appellations d'Origines des Vins et Eaux-de-Vie which is abbreviated to INAO. Many wines bear on the label further proof of authenticity by placing the name of the district in the title as, for example, Appellation Beaune Contrôlée, which means that this wine will have come from any vineyard in the Côte de Beaune. Even a first growth wine such as Château Rieussec will have Appellation Sauternes Contrôlée included on its label.

The main shippers of French wines are all firms of great standing and may be relied upon to supply wines of the required quality in wholesale lots. The names of some of the most well known ones are: Bouchard Aîné, Bouchard Père et Fils, Calvet, Deinhard, Dopff, Geisweiler, Harvey, Hugel, Jaboulet-Vercherre, Latour, Lebegue, Patriarch, Jules Regnier, Thorins.

Bordeaux When a connoisseur of wine thinks about the subject dearest to his heart his thoughts automatically turn to France and more specifically to the region known as Bordeaux from whence come more fine red and white wines

259

than anywhere else in the world. The red wine that comes from this region is known in the United Kingdom as claret.

The best wines of this region were classified into an order of quality as long ago as 1855 being graded into 1st, 2nd, 3rd and 4th or 5th growths together with Bourgeois, Artisan and Peasant growths. The list was revised in 1966 under different headings and as well as being given numbered growths they were graded into Outstanding, Exceptional, Superior and Good growths, but in general the 1855 grading is used. All the different districts and communes of Bordeaux are listed, there being nearly 150 very well-known wines that give great distinction to any wine list. They are of course wines that are in great demand and therefore command high prices, but besides the classified wines there is a vast production of mainly good to excellent table wines whose quality is guaranteed by the name of the broker or shipper appearing on the label.

There are eleven districts of Bordeaux producing both red and white wines and each district is divided into communes or parishes. The following paragraphs give a general description of the wines of the main districts and the names of their most notable communes. This is followed by tables showing the names and qualities and some of their better wines, R or W denote whether red or white wine. See Figure 26.

Médoc is the largest district of Bordeaux and the one where most of the great red wines are produced. They are all different in character but in general are astringent when young developing into elegant wines of subtle yet fragrant bouquets with a robust body. There are five notable communes each embracing many famous vineyards; these are Saint-Estèphe, Pauillac, Saint-Julien, Margaux and Cantenac. The whole district is sometimes subdivided into Haut-Médoc and Bas-Médoc, the Bas not often being used thus making the division of little value.

Graves is the next large district and is noted for its gravelly soil; it is the only place in Bordeaux that produces both red and white wines of considerable note, there being three times as much white to red.

The white wines of Graves are dry, fruity and very individualistic with good acidity so they keep well. The red wines are full bodied and very robust and although Château Haut-Brion was the only one from Graves to be included in the 1855 classification list there are now many more well-known names and the lesser known ones are also very good. The communes of Graves are Pessac, Léognan and Martillac.

Saint-Emilion is a district of Bordeaux that produces many remarkable wines that are almost up to the standard of Médoc being very rich and high in alcohol. The list of great growths contains many well-known names and there are a number of communes within the district including Lussac-St Emilion, Parsac-St Emilion and St Georges-St Emilion.

Pomerol is the district next to Saint-Emilion and the smallest of them all. The wines produced here are all red ones and are rich and full bodied with a deep colour and perhaps a little more breeding than the wines of Saint-Emilion. The communes of Pomerol are Lalande de Pomerol and Néac.

Fronsac is a small district close to Pomerol with six small communes producing red wines that are deep in colour, soft to the palate but robust and rather like the Pomerols, but with perhaps slightly less breeding.

Sauternes and *Barsac* are two main parts of the same small district of Sauternes and give their names to two of the greatest sweet white wines of the world. Barsac is in fact a wine from Sauternes but has its own appellation and prefers to keep its slight distinction. The sweetness of these wines comes from allowing the grapes to shrivel and dry and then to develop the so-called Noble Rot which increases the concentration of sugar and thus its high alcoholic content. These wines are highly perfumed, very rich to the taste and keep for a long time. The other districts of Bordeaux are Bourg, Blaye, Entre-Deux-Mers, Premières Côtes de Bordeaux, St Croix-du-Mont, Lupiac and Cérons; all produce both red and white wines in large quantities, the red ones being soft but rich and fruity. Many of the white wines from these districts are blended and include some that resemble Sauternes, being quite sweet.

Burgundy   This region produces wine second only to that of Bordeaux, its wines being more full bodied and heavier in contrast to the delicacy of claret. Both red and white wine is produced and many of them are great wines which can command very high prices. Most of the wine produced in Burgundy is red but the few whites produced are all very well known and include Chablis, Meursault and Pouilly-Fuissé.

The main districts of Burgundy are the Côte de Nuits, Côte de Beaune, Côte Challonaise, Mâconnais, Beaujolais and Chablis.

The Côte de Nuits district produces deep, fruity full-bodied red wines that keep well and become smoother and more round; the notable communes are Gevry-Chambertin, Chambolle-Musigny, Vosnès Romanée, Nuits St Georges, and Vougeot.

The Côte de Beaune district produces wine that is fruity and soft and matures more rapidly than that of the Côte de Nuits. The town of Beaune is the centre of the wine trade and more than sixty shippers have their head offices and caves there. The Hospice de Beaune is a charity that receives its support from the proceeds of the wine it grows in its own vineyards that have been left as legacies; the wine is sold at public auction every November and bottles bear details on the label that they have been purchased at this great charity sale and give the names of the donors. The seven notable communes of Côte de Beaune are Aloxe-Corton, Pommard, Beaune, Volnay, Meursault, Puligny-Montrachet, Chassagne-Montrachet, and Santenay.

The Côte Challonaise district lies just south of the Côte de Beaune; two communes Mercury and Givry produce mainly red wine and another two Rully and Montagny produce mainly white. Rully also produces a large quantity of sparkling wine, made by the Méthode Champenoise. These sparkling Burgundies may be white, pink or red and as a general rule are sweeter and more full-bodied than Champagne.

261

Figure 26
BORDEAUX WINES

(a) *Main District* – MÉDOC

Notable commune	General description	Examples of notable names	Classification
Saint-Estèphe	Produces mainly red wines, full bodied and rich but not so notable as those from other Médoc communes. A few classified growths; many good to excellent Bourgeois growths.	Ch. Montrose (R) Ch. Calon-Ségur (R) Ch. Rochet (R)	2nd growth 3rd growth 4th growth
Pauillac	Produces the largest quantity of wine of the Médoc, full bodied, great bouquet, generally distinguished. The list of fine wines is lengthy and there are many very good Bourgeois growths.	Ch. Latour (R) Ch. Mouton-Rothschild (R) Ch. Pontet-Canet (R)	1st growth 2nd growth 5th growth
Saint-Julien	Produces outstanding red wines that are even finer than those of Pauillac and fuller than the ones of Margaux.	Ch. Léoville-Poyferre (R) Ch. Gruaud-Larose (R) Ch. Beycheville (R) Ch. Talbot (R)	2nd growth 2nd growth 4th growth 4th growth
Margaux	Produces many remarkable clarets of great breeding and keeping qualities. Some dry white wine also produced.	Ch. Margaux (R) Ch. Rausan-Ségla (R) Ch. Palmer (R)	1st growth 2nd growth 3rd growth

Other Communes

Ludon – Produces many good Bourgeois clarets as well as a 3rd growth.
Cussac – Produces good red wines that resemble those of Saint-Julien.
Listrac – Produces many sturdy and inexpensive clarets, some good Bourgeois growths.
Moulis – Produces large quantities of very dependable and well balanced red wines.

(b) *Main District* – GRAVES

Pessac	Produces the finest of the red Graves; they keep well and remain sturdy.	Ch. Haut-Brion (R) 1st growth Ch. Pape Clément (R) Classified growth Ch. La Mission-Haut-Brion (R) Classified growth
Léognan	Produces very distinguished red and white wines.	Ch. Carbonnieux (W) Classified growth Ch. Haut-Bailly (R) Classified growth Ch. Olivier (R & W) Classified growth
Martillac	Produces red and white wines; the red are better on the whole and are sturdy and mature slowly.	Ch. Smith-Haut-Lafite (R) Classified growth Ch. La Tour-Martillac (R) Classified growth Ch. La Garde (R) Bourgeois growth
Talence	Produces a few good red wines and one of the finest white Graves.	Ch. La Ville-Haut-Brion (W) Classified growth Ch. La Tour-Haut-Brion (R) Classified growth

Other Communes

Beautiron, Cadaujac, Castres, Gradignan and Portets produce some principal red Bourgeois, Artisan and Peasant growths as well as some excellent unclassified red and white wines.

(c) *Main District* – SAINT-EMILION

Saint-Emilion	Robust full-bodied wines, of excellent colour and keeping qualities.	Ch. Ausone (R) 1st great growth Ch. Beauséjour (R) 1st great growth
Graves-St Emilion	Produces wines that are very similar to those of St Emilion.	Ch. Cheval-Blanc (R) 1st great growth Ch. Figéac (R) 1st great growth

263

Other Communes

Lussac-Saint-Emilion – Produces some very full inexpensive red wines and a large amount of white under the appellation of Bordeaux Blanc.

Montagne-Saint-Emilion – Produces full-bodied red wines of good quality, less expensive than St Emilion.
Puisseguin-Saint-Emilion – Produces strong full-bodied red wines of good value.

Parsac-Saint-Emilion – Produces poorer quality wines than from St Emilion, but full bodied.
Saint-Georges-Saint-Emilion – Produces some good quality red wine.
Sables-Saint-Emilion – Produces some acceptable fruity young red wines that are best drunk young.

(d) *Main District* – POMEROL

Notable commune	General description	Examples of notable names	Classification
Pomerol	Produces some fine as well as a large quantity of good average red wines. Most are short-lived.	Ch. Pétrus (R) Ch. Certan (R)	Exceptional growth Unclassified
Lalande de Pomerol	Produces red wines that are very similar to Pomerols but somewhat less fine.	Ch. Bel-Air (R) Ch. de la Commanderie (R)	Unclassified Unclassified
Néac	Produces some very good red wines; generally soft and smooth and usually inexpensive	Ch. Garraud (R) Clos du Castel (R)	Unclassified Unclassified

(e) *Main District* – SAUTERNES AND BARSAC

Notable commune	General description	Examples of notable names	Classification
Sauternes	Produces the most famous sweet white wines in the world; they are very smooth, have a remarkable bouquet and a high alcohol content. Those of good vintages are very long lived.	Ch. d'Yquem (W) Ch. La Tour-Blanche (W) Ch. Filhot (W)	1st great growth 1st growth 2nd growth
Bommes	Produces white wines which are similar in every way to those of Sauternes.	Ch. Lafaurie-Peyraguey (W) Ch. Sigalas-Rabaud (W)	1st growth 1st growth

264

District	Description	Château	Growth
Barsac	Produces excellent white wines similar to Sauternes though somewhat less sweet but of greater delicacy.	Ch. Climens (W) Ch. Coutet (W) Ch. Romer (W)	1st growth 1st growth 2nd growth
Preignac	Produces white wines similar in most respects to those of the communes of Sauternes.	Ch. Suduirait (W) Ch. de Malle (W)	1st growth 2nd growth
Fargues	Produces some very good sweet white wines of the usual Sauternes quality including one 1st growth.	Ch. Rieussec (W) Ch. de Fargues (W)	1st growth Classified growth

(f) OTHER DISTRICTS

BOURG AND BLAYE	Produces both red and white wines of medium quality though full bodied. Sold as Côtes de Bourg and Bourgeais and as Côtes de Blaye or Bordeaux Rouge.
PREMIERES COTES DE BORDEAUX	Produces mostly white wine that is mellow and soft to sweet and some sound inexpensive red wines.
FRONSAC AND COTES-DE-FRONSAC	Produces some good, robust red wines similar to the Pomerols, usually of good value.
ENTRE-DEUX-MERS	Produces vast quantities of ordinary and inexpensive white wines much of it sweet but increasing quantities of dry white wine are being produced. The red wines from this district are not very distinguished and are sold as Bordeaux Rouge or Bordeaux Superieur.
SAINTE-CROIX-DU-MONT	Produces very sweet and fruity white wines that are heavier than the Sauternes and of less elegance. Well-known names include Ch. de Tastes and Ch. Grand Peyrot.
LOUPIAC	Produces very sweet and heavy white wines, similar to Sauternes but nowhere near so elegant
CERONS	This district adjoins Sauternes and Barsac but is officially part of Graves. It produces very good sweet white wines, golden coloured with a high alcohol content and similar in many respects to those of Sauternes.

The Mâconnais district produces large quantities of fairly good red and white wine and is most famous for its Pouilly-Fuissé, a quality white wine; much of the lesser white wines are sold as Mâcon Blanc. The red wine from this district is named simply Mâcon.

The Beaujolais district produces a vast quantity of red wine sold under the labels of Beaujolais-Villages, Beaujolais-Supérieur, and just plain Beaujolais. All are made from wines from various parts of this large district, the best ones bearing the name of the commune where they are grown. These are Brouilly, Chénas, Chiroubles, Côte de Brouilly, Fleurie, Julienas, Morgon, Moulin-à-Vent, and Saint-Amour. Beaujolais is generally a lighter wine than other Burgundies and most should be drunk whilst young. Some from the better named vineyards, however, are better if kept for three to four years.

Between them, Beaujolais and Mâconnais produce more wine than all the other districts of Burgundy put together.

The Chablis district lies at the northern end of Burgundy and produces only the light, dry, white wines that are so well known as being the ideal accompaniment for fish dishes. As with Beaujolais, the demand far outstrips production. The wine is pale straw yellow in colour, very clean on the palate with a very delicate flavour that is almost flinty. The best Chablis is classified as Grand Cru and comes from several small vineyards next to each other, the bottle may bear the name of the particular vineyard. Chablis Premier Cru often has the name of its vineyard on the label and there are also some 1st growth wines from single vineyards. The name Chablis by itself on the label without a Cru number or named vineyard is of lesser quality, Petit Chablis is a very light blended wine suitable for carafe sales.

Fig. 27 shows the main districts and the names of the more notable vineyards together with the names and qualities of some of their better wines. R or W denotes whether red or white wine.

Champagne This is undoubtedly the most famous wine in the world being the only one that is entirely suitable to be drunk as a means of celebrating any great occasion. Champagne is the name of the area east of Paris around the city of Reims which is strictly defined as the only place where grapes may be grown to produce this wine. No other sparkling wine may be sold as Champagne even though it is made by the same method.

The grapes are sold by the growers to the Champagne firms who do the pressing, blending and bottling in their own cellars which are deep underground. The temperature is kept at 4°C all the year round. Apart from a little pink Champagne only white is produced and only certain years are declared as being vintages which makes them expensive. Non-vintage Champagnes are blends of wines of several years. Vintage Champagne has to be tested and approved by a panel of experts and cannot be sold until at least three years old.

The quality of a Champagne is denoted by the name of its shipper who may or may not own a vineyard. The finest Champagnes are made by the firms of Krug, Bollinger and Roederer. Other well-known shippers are Ayala, Heidsieck, Lanson, Mercier, Mumm, Perrier-Jouet, Piper Heidsieck, Pol Roger, Pommery et Greno, Moët et Chandon, Taittinger and Veuve Clicquot.

The degree of sweetness of Champagne is printed on the label: Brut – very dry; Extra-Sec – quite dry; Sec – slightly dry; Demi-sec – fairly sweet; and Doux – sweet. Champagne is available in bottles (75 cl); Magnums (1½ litres), Jeroboams (3 litres); Rehoboams (4½ litres); and Methuselas (5–6 litres).

Côtes du Rhône The wines from this valley of the Rhone lying between Avignon and Lyons are known as Rhône wines. They are big and heavy, dark red in colour and ideal for drinking with game dishes. Many of the names are well known – Châteauneuf-du-Pape, Hermitage, Crozes-Hermitage are some of those that appear on labels, the lesser ones being bottled under the Côtes du Rhône label. Tavel is the most famous rosé wine of France and it comes from this area; it has abundant flavour and bouquet and like all rosé wines, should be drunk young.

Alsace This important wine growing area is in northern France around the city of Strasbourg. It produces elegant white wines which are dry and fruity and with a very fragrant bouquet. The tall slender green bottles are labelled with the name of the type of grape, the name of the village or a brand name, and that of the grower. Riesling, Traminer, Gewurztraminer, are some of the names of these wines; the words Grand Vin, Grand Cru and Grande Réserve are used to describe superior wines of good alcohol content.

Loire The Loire Valley covers a large wine growing area producing many well-known wines. The wines are named after the districts where they are grown; they are mainly white and range from dry to slightly sweet. A few reasonable red and sparkling wines are also produced as well as the popular Anjou Rosé.

The districts of the Loire are Pouilly-sur-Loire, Pouilly-Fumé, Sancerre, Reuilly, Vouvray, Saumur, Chinon, Anjou, Côteaux du Layon, and Muscadet. The sparkling wines come from the Vouvray and Saumur districts and are labelled Crémant de Loire being made by the Méthode Champenoise. The red wines are light and should be drunk whilst young and are excellent when slightly chilled. Pouilly-Fumé is a delicate dry white wine with a slightly smoky perfume which comes from the particular grape used.

French Regional Wines The wines from the less notable districts of France may not enjoy the prestige of those from the great wine growing areas but are very presentable and merit their place on any good wine list. The following are the well-known districts with a few examples of the better named wines:

South West (Dordogne) Red – Bergerac; Côtes de Bergerac; Cahors; Gaillac. White – Montravel; Bergerac; Monbazillac. Rosé – Rosé de Béarn. Sparkling – Gaillac.

Figure 27
BURGUNDY WINES

Notable commune	General description	Examples of notable names	Classification
	(a) *Main District* – CÔTE DE BEAUNE		
Aloxe-Corton	Produces red wines similar to those of the Côte de Nuits including good keeping qualities and also some outstanding white wines. These are similar to the Chablis but are more full bodied.	Corton-Charlemagne (W) Corton Clos du Roi (R) Le Corton (R)	Great growth 1st growth Great growth
Pommard	Produces light, fruity well-rounded red wine. These wines are very popular and named vineyards on the label are sometimes the only guarantee of authenticity.	Clos de la Commaraine (R) Pézerolles (R) Les Poutures (R)	1st growth 1st growth 1st growth
Beaune	Produces very good quality red wines that mature quickly, as well as some white. The commune wines are often blended wines; wines with a village name followed by Côte de Beaune can be quite good.	Les Cent Vignes (R) Champs-Pimont (R) Clos-des-Mouches (W)	1st growth 1st growth 1st growth
Volnay	Produces some fine red wines of good colour and bouquet. Can be drunk fairly young but the best of the named vineyards keep well	Clos-des-Ducs (R) Clos-des-Chênes (R) Caillerets (R)	1st growth 1st growth 1st growth
Meursault	Produces some excellent white wines, very dry but with a certain softness. A certain amount of red wine is also produced most of it sold under the Volnay label.	Clos des Perrières (W) Genevrières (W) Charmes (W)	1st growth 1st growth 1st growth
Puligny-Montrachet	Produces perhaps the finest dry white wines; generally full bodied with a remarkable bouquet. Le Montrachet undoubtedly the greatest.	Le Montrachet (W) Chevalier-Montrachet (W) Batard-Montrachet (W)	Great growth Great growth Great growth
Chassagne-Montrachet	Produces some excellent white wines and almost an equal quantity of red wines of generally not quite such good quality, although there are a number of excellent 1st growths.	Ruchottes (W) Clos St-Jean (R) Morgeot (W)	1st growth 1st growth 1st growth

268

| Santenay | Produces some good dry white wines and some soft and full-bodied reds of which only three are classified as 1st growths. | Les Gravières (W) | 1st growth |

Other Communes
Savigny-les-Beaune, Monthélie and Auxey-Duresses all produce mainly fair to good red wines with a few respectable classified 1st growths.

(b) *Main District* – CÔTE DE NUITS

Gevrey-Chambertin	Produces big heady red wines of good colour, full bouquet and finesse. They keep well and develop smoothness.	Latricières-Chambertin (R)	Great growth
		Charmes-Chambertin (R)	Great growth
		Chapelle-Chambertin (R)	Great growth
		Chambertin-Clos de Bèze (R)	Great growth
Chambolle-Musigny	Produces fruity red wines of very good colour, good vinous flavour and smooth body that have great breeding, that is unequalled by any others. A little excellent dry white wine is also produced.	Musigny (R)	Great growth
		Les Amoureuses (R)	1st growth
		Les Combottes (R)	1st growth
Vosne-Romanée	Produces outstanding red wines of great breeding, elegance and keeping qualities. Production of the classified growths is small resulting in high prices.	Romanée-Conti (R)	Great growth
		Richebourg (R)	Great growth
		La Tache (R)	Great growth
		Les Petits-Monts (R)	1st growth
Nuits Saint-Georges	Produces very soft full red wines with good bouquet. They are inclined to be a little less dry than wines from the more northerly vineyards of Burgundy. Much sparkling Burgundy is also produced.	Les Pruliers (R)	1st growth
		Les Richemones (R)	1st growth
		Clos-des-Grandes-Vignes (R)	1st growth
		Clos de la Maréchale (R)	1st growth

Notable commune	General description	Examples of notable names	Classification
Vougeot	Clos de Vougeot the largest of the vineyards in the commune, produces red wine of great quality and excellent bouquet but perhaps not so full bodied as Chambertin. The remaining production of the commune except for a few small vineyards is sold under the Vougeot label. A very small amount of white wine is also produced.	Clos de Vougeot (R) Clos Blanc de Vougeot (W)	Great growth 1st growth
Fixin	Produces some excellent classified red wines. The commune wines are generally very good in quality and value.	Clos-de-la-Perrière (R) Clos-du-Chapître (R) Clos Napoléon (R)	1st growth 1st growth 1st growth
Morey-Saint-Denis	Produces some very good, full-bodied red wines which are slow maturing and keep well. The best growths compare favourably with those of Gevrey-Chambertin.	Clos de Tart (R) Bonnes Mares (R) Clos des Lambray (R)	Great growth Great growth 1st growth

Provence, including Var Red - Bandol; Domaine des Moulières, Ch. de Selle; Domaine des Mauvannes. White - Cassis, Blanc de Blancs.

Jura Red - Château-Chalon; Château d'Arlay. White - Poligny. Rosé - Rosé d'Arbois. Sparkling - Etoile.

Savoy Red - Frangy; Marestal; Monthoux; Ayse Arbin. White - Crépy; Seyssel Apremont; Marignan.

Languedoc Red - Corbières; Minervois; Costières; Fitou. White - Clairettes; Banyuls; Bellegarde; Muscat de Frontignan. Sparkling - Blanquette de Limoux.

Corsica Red - Sartene; Calenzana; Paviglia.

GERMAN WINES

The wine growing areas of Germany lie at the southern and western parts of the country alongside the banks of a number of streams that flow into the Rhine. There are two main types of white wine produced - Hocks and Moselles, Hock being a term used in the United Kingdom only to denote wine grown on or near the Rhine, while Moselle denotes wine from the River Moselle and its tributaries, the Saar and Ruwer. Some red wine is produced, but little is exported. The following details relate to white wine.

The vineyards are the most northerly ones in Europe and under such conditions and climate it is not easy to produce good quality wine yet some of the German wines are counted amongst the really great wines of the world.

Germany's wine law defines and controls the types of wine made and divides them into three main qualities - the ordinary table wine for everyday drinking, the quality wines from specific areas abbreviated to the letters QbA, and quality wines with Predicate shown as QmP both of these two being good quality wines as indicated by the titles. These table wines are divided into two groups; those made entirely of German wine are designated Deutscher Tafelwein (DTW), and those of German wine blended with wines of other countries in the European Economic Community can only be designated Tafelwein. The higher quality QbA and QmP wines must indicate which of the eleven districts they were produced in. The eleven districts are: (a) Ahr, (2) Hessiche Bergstrasse, (3) Mittelrhein, (4) Mosel - Saar - Ruwer, (5) Nahe, (6) Rheingau, (7) Rheinhessen, (8) Rheinpfalz, (9) Franconia, (10) Württemburg, (11) Baden; the Rheinpflaz is sometimes referred to as the Palatinate. These districts are subdivided into Bereichs (areas) and within these areas are the named vineyards; wines from a collection of vineyards in one of these small areas can be blended provided they all are of equivalent quality.

A German wine label will give the following information: (i) the area of production; (ii) the quality classification; (iii) the vintage year; (iv) the village or composite area; (v) the name and address of the shipper; (vi) the brand name, if any; (vii) the name of the grape from which the wine is made; (viii) if a Predicate wine, its name, e.g. Spätlese; (ix) the official control number; (x) the contents followed by the letter 'e' which shows it is a measure approved by the EEC.

The producer may put the year on the label if over 85 per cent of the contents are of that year and the wine has the characteristics of the year. Where two varieties of grapes are named they are given in descending order; if only one is named it will be at least 85 per cent content.

The following terms are used in conjunction with Predicate wines:
1. *Kabinett* – a quality wine just above that of QbA wine.
2. *Spätlese* – wine made from late gathered and very ripe grapes, producing a rich sweet wine.
3. *Auslese* – wine made from only the best quality grapes, any bad ones having been excluded.
4. *Beerenauslesen* – wine made from selected individual grapes when over-ripe and full of sugar.
5. *Trockenbeerenauslesen* –wine made from individual grapes left to rot and become semi-dried in the sun until like raisins – they are therefore very sweet and more concentrated.
6. *Eiswein* – wine made from grapes left on the vines until the cold weather freezes them. This gives a fine wine of concentrated flavour.
7. *Originalabfullung and Originalabzug* – this means that the wine was bottled by the producer.

Liebfraumilch as a name was originally given to many mildly agreeable Rhine wines but is now a quality designation for wines from Rheinhessen, Rheinpfalz, Rheingau and Nahe. Hock is the name given to Deutscher Tafelwein from the Rhine area and made from Riesling or Sylvaner grapes or their crossings.

Germany also produces a great quantity of sparkling wine made by the Méthode Champenoise and the Cuve Close method. Schaumwein is the name given to any basic sparkling wine; Sekt is sparkling wine of better quality with at least nine months of age.

Fig. 28 shows the wine growing districts together with a brief description of the wines they produce and some of the well-known names.

ITALIAN WINES

Italy produces so much wine that it is almost as cheap and arguably much healthier than the water supply. The vine grows profusely all over Italy and the result is that although the quantity of wine produced is vast the quality is not always as good as wine from other countries where the vines require greater care and attention. There is a tremendous variety of different kinds of wine and no less than thirteen main districts of production, some of them covering vast areas. Most of Italy's best red wines are produced in the Piedmont region.

Italy's wine law delimits the zones of production and controls production. A wine with the letters DOC (Denominazione d'Origine Controllata) on the label means that the controlled denomination of origin has been granted as having met certain stipulated standards as to type of grape, methods of planting, cultivating

Figure 28
GERMAN WINES

District	Description	Well-known Wine Names
Rheinhessen	Mellow, mild and soft wines; the fine ones are fruity and of great elegance.	Nierstein, Oppenheim, Nackenheim
Rheinpfalz	Mild, mellow wines that are rich and without acidity; some are very sweet.	Neustadt, Durkheim, Forst, Deidesheim
Rheingau	Delicate wines, excellent aroma, take some time to mature and become very elegant.	Erbach, Mittelheim, Winkel, Rudesheim, Hallgarten
Nahe	These wines combine the features of Hock and Moselle and are very attractive being steely and of fine aroma.	Bockelheim, Neiderhausen, Kreuznach
Franconia	Dry wines of good quality and character; full bodied.	Juliusspital, Wachenheimer, Ruppertsberger, Deidesheimer
Baden	Fresh wines with a flowery bouquet and delicate flavour.	Nonnenberg, Sonnenberg, Kirchberg, Altenberg
Württemberg	Produces mostly red wines; some good rosés.	Spätburgunder, Schillerwein
Ahr	More red than white is produced; it is very light in body and alcohol.	Sonnenberg, Pfaffenberg
Mosel-Saar-Ruwer	Very light, delicate wines tending towards sweetness; good elegant bouquet; low alcohol content, some are slightly effervescent.	Bernkastel, Piesporter, Bockstein Würzgarten, Sonnenuhr, Brauneberg, Zeltingen, Scharzhofberg
Mittelrhein	Delicate wines with good bouquet but very little body, much of it is made into sparkling wine.	Klosterberg, Furstenberg, St Martinsberg

273

and fertilisation, bottling, alcohol content and age. A higher standard of control is exerted over a wine bearing the letters DOCG (Denominazione d'Origine Controllata e Garantita) on the label; this means that the wine is not only controlled but has also a guaranteed denomination of origin. It will have the names of the grower and wine merchant on the label in addition to the information required for a DOC wine. The letters VQPRD are also used on labels to show the wine is one of quality produced in a determined area of the EEC.

There are a number of words used on labels to describe the contents, Riserva – has been aged in cask or bottle; Superiore – has a slightly higher alcohol content; Vendemmia – vintage year; Secco – dry; Abboccato – a sweet wine; Frizzante and Spumante – sparkling.

Both sweet and dry vermouth is produced in Italy mainly in or near Turin in Piedmont where most of the large firms have their headquarters. Vermouth is a fortified wine mostly made of white wine which means that some brandy has been added to give it extra strength and the addition of many different spices and herbs give it a distinctive smell and flavour. Dry vermouth has an astringent taste and light colour and is usually referred to as being French type vermouth; the sweet is known popularly as Italian vermouth; there are red, rosé and white varieties.

Marsala is a fortified wine from Palerno in Sicily; it has a very attractive bouquet, high alcoholic strength and is amber in colour, it is much used in cooking. Some bottles may be marked with the letters OP (Old Particular), LP (London Particular), SOM (Superior Old Marsala).

The following are the main wine producing regions with examples of some of their better known wines:

Calabria Red – Cirò; Savuto; Donnici.

Campania Red – Falerno; Ischia Rosso; Gragnano. White – Lacrima Christi; Falerno; Greco di Tufo.

Emilia-Romagna Red – Lambrusco; Gragnano; Sangiovese. White – Albana; Trebbiano.

Friuli White – Verduzzo; Riesling Renano; Picolit.

Latium White -- Frascati; Est! Est!! Est!!!; Montefiascone.

Lombardy Red – Valtellina; Sassella; Grumells; Valgella Sforzato; Frecciarossa; Botticina. White – Frecciarossa; Lugana; Riviera del Garda Rosato.

Marches Red – Rosso Piceno; Rosso Conero; Sangiovese. White – Verdicchio; Orvieto.

Piedmont Red – Barbaresco; Barbera Barola; Carema; Nebbiola; Grignolino; Dolcetto; Malvasia. White – Erbaluce; Caluso. Others – Asti Spumante, Moscato d'Asti; Vermouth.

Puglia Red – San Severo; Santo Stefano. White – Moscato di Salento; San Severo.

Sardinia Red – Vermentino; Vernaccia; Cannonau; Cirò di Cagliari. White – Nuragus; Moscato di Bosa.

Sicily Red – Corvo; Segesta. White – Corvo; Segesta; Zucco. Others – Marsala.

Trentino Red – Santa-Maddalena; Caldaro. White – Trentino-Riesling; Lagrein.

Tuscany Chianti; Elba Rosso; Brunello di Montalcino. White – Montecarlo
Bianco; Vernaccia di San Gimignano; Vino Santo.
Umbria Red – Torgiano; Sagrantino; Rubesco. White – Orvieto; Grechetto.
Veneto Red – Bardolino; Valpolicella; Recioto; Valpantena. White – Lugana;
Soave; Conegliano-Valdobiadene; Tokai.

SPANISH WINES

Spain is the third biggest wine producing country in the world having twenty-
seven controlled districts regulated by the Instituto Nacional de Dominaciones
de Origen or INDO, which can indicate that there is a large quantity of good
quality wine produced.

The best known districts are Rioja, Valdepeñas and Catalonia and of these
three the wines of Rioja are the finest, the best of these coming from Rioja
Alta and Rioja Alavesa and only wines from these will be labelled as such. Rioja
red wines improve with keeping both in cask and bottle and become mellow and
with much character; the word Reserva or Reserva Especial indicates mature
wines. Valdepeñas is on the other side of Spain, south of Madrid and produces
big, full-bodied red wines that are light in colour but high in alcohol, and also
white wines that are dry and full bodied. Both should be drunk whilst young and
fresh. Catalonia is the district around Valencia and produces some very good
white and rosé wines.

Spain also exports some very good sparkling wines made by the Méthode
Champenoise and also by the Cuve Close method. Spain, however, is far more
famous for its sherry than for its table wines. This wine takes its name from the
town of Jerez de la Frontera in Andalusia where many of the Bodegas (wine
storage sheds or cellars) are to be found. The vineyards producing the wine lie
to the north-west and south-west of Jerez; the main variety of the grape grown
is the Palomino although others such as the Bebo, Mollar and Mantuo are also
widely grown.

Sherry is made by what is known as the Solera system where wines which
have been fortified with brandy are put into oak casks stacked on top of each
other. The bottom layer contains sherry that is ready to draw off for sale and
as this is done those casks are refilled from the row above which is younger
sherry. That is now filled in turn from the row above and so on. Wines of the
different kinds and qualities are kept in different Soleras. This means that sherry
is a blend of blended wines of many different years, but it also means that each
firm can keep the particular quality of its brand names the same year after year.
There cannot of course, be a vintage sherry.

Sherry is thus a blend of wines fortified with brandy to give it a strength
according to type of between 15–18 per cent alcohol by volume; its use is
mainly as an aperitif and it is made in many varieties.

The main types of sherry are:
Manzanilla – very dry, very pale in colour, very light body.

275

Fino – very dry, pale in colour, medium body.

Amontillado – dry, pale golden colour, fairly full body.

Oloroso – sweet, full bodied, golden colour, nutty flavour.

Cream – sweet, smooth, deep golden colour.

Brown – very sweet, dark brown colour, nutty flavour.

The manufacturers recommend that all these types be served cool either by chilling the bottle or pouring the sherry over ice cubes, but this is a matter of taste and many prefer it served at room temperature.

Some other fortified wines are produced in Spain including Malaga and Tarragona; they are both very sweet and are served as an accompaniment with dessert and have the same alcoholic strength as sherry.

Montilla is a wine that is quite similar to sherry being made as dry, medium and cream, but because it is made outside the delimited zone cannot be classed as sherry even although it is made by the Solera system.

PORTUGUESE WINES

When we think of Portuguese wines the name of its second most famous one, **Mateus Rosé**, springs immediately to mind. Much of the wine exported from Portugal are rosés and like Mateus, when served chilled they are a good compromise and can be consumed with almost any food. The wines from Dão are good, being full bodied and rich in flavour and the red ones are considered the best in Portugal as they can be kept for a good length of time. Vinho Verde is the name given to young wines produced in the province of Entre-Douro-e-Minho; they can be white, rosé or red and they are very light and refreshing with a slight sparkle.

The most famous wine of Portugal is, of course, port, the fortified wine produced in the town of Oporto on the River Douro. **Port** can be served as an aperitif, particularly the white variety, but it is mainly served at the end of the meal when it should be passed and for drinking the toasts. It is the ideal accompaniment with cheese and especially with the nuts of the dessert course.

The varieties of port are as follows:

Vintage Port – this is deemed fit to be bottled whilst still young in the sure knowledge that it will keep for many years. It is bottled after about two years in cask and marked with the year, then left to mature and improve with the passage of time. A heavy sediment is thrown and vintage port has to be carefully decanted before being served, the white 'splash' on the bottle shows how the bottle was binned and indicates that the crust will be on the opposite side.

Vintage Character – this is good ruby port to which is added some older port to give body and flavour thus eliminating the long time it takes to produce authentic vintage port; it does improve in bottle.

Crusted Port – this is the port produced in a non-vintage year and is given the

276

same care as for vintage port; it can be made from a blend of wines of several different years. As the name implies it throws a sediment.

Ruby Port - this is a fairly young port that takes its name from the lovely rich ruby colour of new port before it is stored; it is fruity but rough.

Tawny Port - this is port that has been allowed to mature so losing its ruby colour and becoming a deep amber and growing in flavour to a mature nutty taste.

White Port - this is made from white grapes only but otherwise is the same except that it is usually chilled and served as an aperitif.

Madeira is an island in the South Atlantic which belongs to Portugal and which gives its own name to the very fine wine produced there. The island is actually a defunct volcano and the vines are grown on the slopes which are so steep that no mechanical means of cultivation can be used. The must from the crushed grapes is carried down the hill in goatskins. Fermentation of the wine is halted by the addition of brandy made from ordinary Madeiran wine and is then heated to up to 60 °C. Madeira is a blended and fortified wine with an alcoholic strength of about 20 per cent; it is made in several varieties as follows:

Sercial - very dry, delicate, pale to golden in colour.
Verdelho - medium sweet, golden colour.
Bual - medium sweet, golden colour, rich enough for a dessert wine.
Malmsey - very rich, very sweet, fragrant, dark colour, served as a dessert wine.

Madeira keeps very well and continues to improve for many years. It is frequently used in cooking.

OTHER WINE PRODUCING COUNTRIES

Austria Austrian wines are fairly light and fragrant, mostly white and similar in some ways to the wines of Germany although nowhere near so elegant and refined. They are mostly drunk whilst young and fresh; German wine terms are used on the label.

America More and more wine is being exported from the United States and such is its quality that it deserves a place on most wine lists. Most of the wine imported here comes from California, where there are nine wine producing districts most of them circling San Francisco. But much wine is also produced in the eastern region of the USA.

Red, rosé and white wines are produced as well as sparkling wines, brandies and fortified wines. Growers label their wines using three types of name. First are the Generics, mostly the older vineyards giving their wines European names such as Sauternes, Chablis and Sherry. Second are the wines named after the predominating grape used such as Pinot Noir, and lastly those wines with names created by the proprietor or winery itself.

Australia The climate in Australia is ideal for vine growing and every year can be a vintage one. All kinds of wine are made, most of them being given the well-known European names. The quality is excellent.

Bulgaria Blended wine is imported under shippers brand names, the whites being light and fruity and the reds ranging from light to dark full-bodied ones.

Chile Some very good quality wines are imported from Chile and despite the long voyage they are moderately priced and travel well. They usually bear the type names of their European counterparts.

Hungary The best known wines of this country are the Tokays and Bull's Blood but many other pleasant wines, especially whites, are produced. The Tokays are very distinctive white wines and are produced in different varieties as follows:

Tokay Furment – this is a traditionally produced full flavoured, fruity wine.

Tokay Szamarodni – this is produced from dry, late gathered grapes. It can be very sweet in a sunny year but is usually dry.

Tokay Aszu – this is produced from late gathered grapes which have reached the stage of Noble Rot; they are individually selected then crushed and the result added in varying proportions to wine produced in the same area. The labels are marked with the number of 'Puttonos' or measures of the special crushing added to each hogshead of wine. The more 'Puttonos', up to six, the more sweet the wine, and it will keep well for a long time.

Tokay Essence – this is a wine produced from over-ripe grapes or with Noble Rot and results in a very sweet liqueur-type dessert wine with remarkable keeping qualities.

Bulls Blood (Egri Bikaver) – is a very dark red wine inclined to be sometimes bitter but very full bodied and rich.

Israel Wines of many kinds and of good quality are imported from Israel and can be relied upon to give satisfaction not just to Jewish customers. Unlike many other countries it does not use European equivalent names for its wines.

Romania Although only a small country Romania is in fact the eighth largest wine producing country in the world. Red and white table wines and sweet dessert wine of very acceptable quality are exported, some of it being sold under well-known brand names.

South Africa A wide variety of wines are imported from South Africa, many of them bearing the Wine of Origin (WO) seal on the capsule which is a guarantee of authenticity. The white wines are pleasingly fresh and dry and the reds are quite distinguished. It is possible to obtain better quality wines under the Wines of Origin Superior seal.

Switzerland Because the Swiss drink more than they produce there is very little available for export. Names of the better quality wines include Dézaley, Dorin, Perlan, Salvagin, Fendant, Neuchatel, Cortaillod, Clevner and Dole which is accepted as Switzerland's best red wine.

Yugoslavia The part of this country where the best wines are produced used to belong to Austria so the wine tends to resemble that of Austria being full but without great refinement. Those most usually featured are the white wines of Ljutomer in Slovenia.

278

United Kingdom It is not easy to produce wine in this country mainly because the temperature over the growing period does not reach anywhere near the required degree on a sufficient number of days. Despite this the growers usually manage to produce a million bottles of wine each year in more than a hundred vineyards, most of it coming from very small vineyards as compared to those of southern France, the largest being about 10 hectares whilst many are only a seventh of a hectare in extent. The production is almost all white wine with a little rosé; as yet no good red wine has been produced. The most widely used variety of wine is the Muller-Thurgau which is derived from the Riesling Sylvaner giving a fairly acid wine with medium sugar content. It can take until early in November for grapes to ripen sufficiently. The industry is young and as the growers gain in knowledge and experience the quality will rise still higher. More vineyards are being planted and with ensured supplies there should be a place for British grown wines on every wine list. The quality of these dry white and rosé wines merit their inclusion in preference to some lesser quality imported ones.

SPIRITS

A spirit is made by distilling a fermented liquid so as to concentrate its essential flavour and which also results in a very high alcohol content. Substances as diverse as rice, potatoes, maize, corn and fruits are used, the most popular spirits being Brandy from grapes, Whisky from barley, Gin from grain, Rum from sugar and Vodka from potatoes or wheat. The French name for a spirit is Eau-de-Vie.

Spirits are really made for drinking on their own but are versatile in use and go well with carbonated waters and in cocktails. They should be stored upright in the bottles until required for service.

Brandy This spirit is made by distilling ordinary white wine which means that every wine-producing country can produce brandy. Although France produces the best brandies some good quality ones are also produced in Germany and Spain. Cognac is the name given to brandy produced in a strictly delimited district in what is known as the Champagne country of Charente in France. There are seven areas of this district and Cognac is a blend of brandies distilled in these areas. The wine is kept for five years before being distilled, but even so emerges as a fiery, raw liquid which needs to be matured in oak casks for it to become smooth and develop its distinctive bouquet. Some Cognacs have the words Fine Champagne on the label indicating that at least 50 per cent of it will be the brandy produced on the two major areas which are the Grande and Petite Champagne areas.

The label on a bottle of brandy is marked with stars or letters to denote quality as follows: one star not less than three years old; two stars not less than

279

four years old; three stars not less than five years old; VOP meaning Very Old Pale – from five to ten years old; VO meaning very old – from seven to twelve years old; VSO meaning Very Superior Old and VSOP meaning Very Superior Old Pale – over ten years old.

Once it has been bottled there is no further improvement; there is no such thing as vintage brandy. Liqueur brandy would be a blend of mature brandies the age having made them mellow but not sweet.

Armagnac This brandy is distilled from wine produced in the Armagnac district in France. It is not so well known as Cognac but the best produced is highly praised by connoisseurs who appreciate it for its pungency and body in contrast to the smoothness of Cognac. Three star Armagnac is five years old, VSOP is twenty years and XO forty years old.

Whisky There are several types of whisky, the most popular being Scotch. This is made from barley which is malted, dried over a peat fire, then crushed, mixed with water and fermented with yeast. This liquid is heated and the vapour condensed and is then immediately re-distilled. Wheat is used in the same way to make a grain whisky and the popular Scotch whiskies are a blend of these two. The difference between the various brand names lies in the different whiskies blended together to produce a particular flavour; none is less than three years old.

Irish whiskey is made in the same way as Scotch whisky except that the malt is kiln dried and the smoke from the peat fire does not come into contact with it. It has a different taste to Scotch being more fiery.

Bourbon, Corn and Rye Whiskeys are American types made respectively from grain (must be no less than 51 per cent maize), maize and rye.

Gin This spirit is distilled from grain, usually maize, in a patent still which delivers it as ethyl alcohol. This is re-distilled to give a pure and mellow spirit which is then diluted and flavoured with juniper berries, dried citrus peels, corianders and various other flavourings. It is ready for drinking after three to four weeks.

Genever gin is Dutch gin, which is distilled four times then allowed to mature in wooden casks. It has more aroma and flavour than English gin and can be drunk as an aperitif. It is sold in tall earthenware bottles of 72 cl and at 71° proof.

Vodka This spirit is made from potatoes or grain and is virtually tasteless and odourless. It is meant to be drunk neat and ice cold but can be used in cocktails. Zubrowka is a yellow coloured vodka flavoured and coloured by a grass grown in Poland. Some vodkas are imported from Poland, Russia and the Baltic countries.

Rum This spirit is distilled from the fermented juice of the sugar cane or by-products of the sugar factory made into molasses. The brown rums are full bodied and have a distinctive smell whilst white rums are light bodied with very little taste and odour.

Other spirits in common use include:
Calvados – an apple brandy produced in Normandy.

280

Grappa – distilled from the residue of grape crushings. Italy.
Kirsch – made from cherries and cherry stones, delicate flavour, white in colour. France, Germany, Switzerland.
Marc – distilled from the residue of grape crushings. France.
Tequila – a fiery spirit distilled from cactus. Mexico.

There is also a large range of colourless Eaux-de-Vie derived from fruits such as, damson plums – Slivovitz; mirabelle plums – Mirabelle; pears – Poire William; raspberries – Framboise; strawberries – Fraise; pineapple – Ananas, etc.

LIQUEURS

Liqueurs are sweetened and flavoured spirits normally used for serving at the end of a meal or as a flavour in foods. They differ owing to the type of alcohol used as a base such as brandy or whisky and also to the particular flavouring agents used. Some of them have digestive properties from the herbs and spices used in their manufacture. Most countries produce a liqueur that is based on the popular national spirit and there are many hundreds available some very old established, but only about twenty are in very popular demand.

The best known liqueurs are as shown in Fig. 29; they are usually sold in 24 ml measures and in the main they are made at between 37 and 43 per cent alcohol by volume.

APERITIFS

As the name implies, these are drinks designed to stimulate the appetite before a meal; they are served in measures of 1 dl – more than for a liqueur but less than a glass of wine. It is usual to serve them chilled or with ice in the glass. The flavour is derived mainly from herbs and spices and quinine is used in many of them. The liquid base is usually wine and most of them are sweet.

Figure 30 shows the most widely used aperitif drinks; in general they are made at between 16 and 25 per cent alcohol by volume.

BITTERS

Bitters are concentrated flavourings which add a subtle taste and aroma to many drinks and dishes; orange, lemon and lime bitters are used to give fragrant

Figure 29
LIQUEURS

Name	Country or origin	Flavour	Base
Advocaat	Holland	Egg yolks	Brandy
Apricot Brandy	UK Hungary	Fresh or dried apricots	Brandy
Atholl Brose	UK	Oatmeal, honey, cream	Whisky
Bénédictine	France	Herbs and roots	Brandy
Chartreuse (green and yellow)	France	Herbs. The green has a higher alcohol content	Brandy
Cherry brandy	UK, France, Germany, Holland	Cherries and cherry stones	Brandy
Cointreau	France	Orange	Brandy
Crèmes	France	Very sweet. Available as Crème d'Ananas (pineapple), de Bananes (banana), de Cacao (cocoa), de Café (coffee), de Cassis (blackcurrant), de Fraises (strawberry), de Framboises (raspberry), de Menthe (mint)	Brandy
Curaçao	Holland	Orange	Brandy or gin
Drambuie	UK	Honey	Whisky
Fiori d'Alpi	Italy	Flowers and herbs	Brandy
Grand Marnier	France	Orange	Brandy
Kümmel	Holland	Caraway and cumin	Grain spirit
Lindisfarne	UK	Honey	Whisky

Name	Country	Description	Base
Malibu	Holland	Coconut	Rum
Maraschino	Yugoslavia	The best is distilled from Marasca cherries, in Dalmatia	Brandy
Parfait Amour	France	Violet colour from violets or pink colour from rose petals	
Southern Comfort	USA	Peach, orange	Bourbon whiskey
Tia Maria	Jamaica	Coffee, spices	Rum
Triple Sec	France	Highly rectified Curaçao	
Van der Hum	S. Africa	Naartjes (species of tangerine), other fruits, herbs and spices	Brandy
La Vieille Cure	France	Roots, herbs	Armagnac and Cognac

Figure 30
APERITIFS

Name	Flavour	Liquid base
Amer Picon	Orange, Gentian, quinine	Wine and Brandy. As an aperitif – mixed with Grenadine and Cassis and diluted with water
Byrrh	Quinine, Brandy	Wine
Campari	Herbs	Grape spirit
Dubonnet	Quinine and Bark. Available as Red and Blonde	Wine
Fernet Branca	Herbs and Barks	Wine
Pernod	Aniseed, herbs	Wine
Pineau des Charentes	Cognac	Fresh pressed grapejuice
Quinquina	Quinine	Fortified wine
St. Raphaël	Quinine. Available as Red and White	Wine
Vermouth	Herbs, spices, orange. Available under many brand names – as White, Red, Rosé and Dry	White wine

aromas, and Angostura bitters adds aroma and flavour and assists in whetting the appetite. Unterberg bitters is made in Germany and is similar to Angostura bitters; Amer Picon and Fernet Branca, although mostly drunk as aperitifs are often used as mild bitters for mixed drinks.

Bitters are used in minute quantities, about 4 drops per 1 dl of a mixed drink being usually sufficient.

MINERAL AND CARBONATED WATERS

The general term mineral waters includes all the natural spring waters bottled and sold commercially for drinking alone or mixing with other drinks. They come from many different countries and many of them are from spas where people go to drink or bathe for medical reasons. They are still or sparkling, alkaline, aperient or sulphurous and all contain certain mineral salts to a greater or lesser degree. They should be chilled before serving.

The best known mineral water in this country is Malvern water; from France the best known are Evian, Perrier, Vichy and Vittel; and from Italy St Pellegrino.

Carbonated waters are commonly referred to as minerals and are used to dilute other drinks or are drunk on their own. They include tonic water, soda water, bitter lemon, dry ginger ale, American ginger ale, cola, ginger beer, lemonade and orangeade, and are available in returnable or non-returnable bottles and cans of 241, 250 and 500 ml.

Other non-alcoholic drinks include squash such as orange, lemon, lime and barley water and natural juices including orange, grapefruit, pineapple and tomato; in high-class establishments the juice served will be freshly pressed from the fruit. Syrups are used in long drinks and in cocktails and include, Cassis – blackcurrant; Cerise – cherry; Citronelle – lemon; Framboise – raspberry; Gomme – plain syrup; Grenadine – pomegranate. Peppermint, lime, banana and mint are others.

BEER

Beer is available in a great many forms and from a number of different breweries which may sell their beers locally or nationally, according to popularity. It is available in bottles, cans and as draught from the cask or keg.

The main types of bottled beer are:
Pale ale or **light ale** which is light in alcoholic strength rather than in colour,
India pale ale which is a pale bitter beer that was once exported to India,
Brown ale which is coloured brown but is light in alcoholic strength,

285

Stout which is very dark in colour and which comes from the well roasted malt it is brewed from; there are several brand names. Guinness is the most famous of these and is noted for its head or foamy top; it must be looked after carefully and stored at 13–16 °C to be in perfect condition.

Draught beers include mild ale, a beer of low alcohol content and which is usually mixed with a stronger beer as either mild and bitter, mild and brown or stout and mild. Bitter is sold on its own but usually with another such as light ale, stout or Guinness; it is a bright beer with a good flavour.

Proprietary beers sold under the names of the big brewers and under well-known brand names are usually dearer than light beers.

Lager beer is available under many brand names, many now being made here and are popular because they are pleasantly pale, cool and refreshing.

Keg beer is sealed in metal containers which guarantees that it will keep in perfect condition. A cylinder of carbon dioxide is connected to the keg through a reducing valve which forces the beer under pressure to the dispenser.

Real ale is delivered in casks and just before leaving the brewery has some finings of isinglass added. In the cellar it is rested on stillions and in a few hours will fall bright and be ready for serving.

CIDER

Cider is made from apples, the juice being allowed to ferment naturally. It is a refreshing drink but can be of high alcoholic strength; because it is cheap it is thought by some people to be innocuous but the dry rough cider can be very strong. Cider can be sold on draught by the measure and by the bottle, and can be still or sparkling, sweet or dry; some is sold as vintage cider.

Perry is not so well known as cider but in the form of a mini-bottle of Babycham it is very popular. Perry is made from pears, in the same way as cider.

CIGARS

The very best cigars come from Cuba and Jamaica and are very expensive because they are made by hand. Good cigars are also manufactured in the USA, Holland and England and a high-class restaurant can thus offer its customers a wide choice.

286

When purchased by the box the colour of the leaf will be stamped on the outside as follows: CCC or Claro means light coloured, CC or Colorado Claro is medium, C or Colorado is the dark and CM or Colorado-Maduro is the darkest.

The size of cigars is related to the name Corona which indicates straight sides and a rounded end. A Très Petit Corona is $1\frac{1}{4}$ in. long, Petit Corona 5 in., Corona $5\frac{1}{2}$ in. and a Corona Corona would be this last size made by the firm of Corona. Other shapes are the Perfecto which has tapering sides and a pointed end, the Panatella which is long and thin, and the Cheroot which is cut straight at both ends.

A nicely presented selection of cigars in a polished Humidor or one with a see-through lid, offered when the coffee is being served and sold at a sensible price gives a restaurant tone and prestige. A Humidor is a specially made case for keeping cigars in the best possible condition. It is made from cedar-wood and must have a very tight fitting lid.

It is unwise to carry excess stock as cigars can deteriorate over a period of time, especially at resort hotels. They must be kept protected from heat, draughts, smells and dampness otherwise they will fail to give the pleasure they promise. The ideal storage is in a cedar-wood cabinet or Humidor at 16-18°C in an atmosphere of 55-60 per cent relative humidity; or in sealed aluminium tubes with a cedar-wood lining.

CLEANING MATERIALS

The Food Hygiene (General) Regulations 1970 have to be obeyed as each offence committed under them carries a maximum penalty of £100 or three month's imprisonment, or both. The environmental health officer will visit premises periodically to carry out an inspection which will be thorough; he will look not only at the general condition but at cooking equipment and utensils, in drawers, even the can opener, to ensure that all are kept in a clean and hygienic condition. For equipment to be clean is not always the same as saying it is hygienic as an item may look clean yet be harbouring unseen bacteria. This means that water alone is not enough to keep everything in a correct condition.

Cleaning materials other than water must therefore be made available to all who need to use them and it is essential to have a separate store to keep them under lock and key as they are expensive items and need to be controlled. Because of their smell they should not be kept in the food store. It is usual to purchase them wholesale from a specialist supplier who deals mainly with the catering industry, the size of pack to be consistent with the normal issue rather than to have to break bulk by refilling bottles or containers.

Stock levels should be set to cover a given period and issues should only be made against authorised documents.

The person in charge of ordering these items needs a knowledge of the many different kinds of cleaning materials available so that he is clear as to where each one should be used and the amount that will be consumed over a given period. A measured amount of a detergent will be more effective in doing a job than by pouring it in extravagantly.

The range of commodities which are usually classed under this heading are:
1. Detergents, soaps, scouring powders, soda, oven cleaners
2. Disinfectants
3. Water softeners which also includes salt
4. Special solvents for use in grease traps, cleaners for air filters
5. Floor and furniture polishes
6. Cleaners for removing stains from silverware
7. Upholstery cleaners
8. Toilet cleaners including air fresheners, toilet rolls
9. Disposable dish cloths, scourers, dusters, rubbish sacks, etc.
10. Small items of equipment including nail brushes, scrubbing brushes, mop heads

Other items normally kept in this store are tapers, matches, light bulbs, rubber gloves, candles for the dining room where featured and candles for use in the event of electricity failure.

STATIONERY AND PAPERWARE

Under this heading is included a wide range of articles that have an important though subsidiary part to play in the efficient operation of a catering department. It includes official stationery items used in the chef's or caterer's office as well as those used in the kitchen and dining room to assist results and enhance presentation. The official documents for use by the catering manager, buying officer, head chef, head waiter and head cellarman are those as authorised by the employer and cover all internal and external correspondence, all ordering on suppliers, all issues within the departments and all control documents in use. Writing implements, waiter's check pads, menu blanks, till rolls, requisition pads, ordering forms, etc. are examples of these important items. They will be kept in the care of the secretary or other responsible person who will be responsible for ordering and issuing.

The other kind of paperware used is also in everyday use but is disposable and in most cases is used once only. The list includes dish papers and d'oyleys, pie collars, cutlet and ham frills, greaseproof paper, kitchen paper, wrapping film, aluminium foil, plastic and foil containers and lids, cocktail sticks, paper

288

table napkins and table mats where used, paper table coverings, menus, wine lists, place cards, balls of string, refuse sacks, etc.

All items of paperware should be kept in a separate storeroom, issued only as authorised and stock levels should be set so that supplies are constant.

9 PROVISIONING II – PURCHASING, STORAGE AND STORES ISSUING

Purchasing – The Buyer – The Principles of Purchasing – Methods of Buying – Standard Purchasing Specifications – Sources of Supply – Receipt of Goods – Storage Siting, Area Allocation, Physical Requirements, Refrigeration, Contamination, Equipment, Stock Rotation, Stock Levels, Control Documents, Stocktaking and Valuation, Issue of Goods – Cellar and Bar Stock Control – Payment of Accounts – Coding Schemes.

PURCHASING

A knowledge of the principles of purchasing and the requirements for storage of the materials used is essential to the efficient operation and successful outcome of any catering business. Purchasing must be carried out in accordance with management's policy and as expressed in the goods offered for sale through the means of the menu and wine list. It is the menu which decides the quality and range of foodstuffs to be purchased, the bar and wine list that decides the contents of the cellar, and it is the person appointed to do the buying who contributes much to the success of the enterprise. In addition to consumable products there is the purchasing of a large number of non-food items such as small kitchen utensils, cleaning equipment, crockery, glassware, linen, paperware and cleaning materials all of which require control of storage and issuing in the same way as consumable items.

THE BUYER

The job of buying goods for a catering establishment is an exacting one that demands a comprehensive knowledge of commodities and the ability to make the best use of the business's funds in buying them so that they will yield maximum profit. In referring to the buyer it has to be recognised that only in a large establishment will there be such a highly qualified person and that in a small firm the buying will be done by the proprietor or manager. In some establishments the catering officer or food and beverage manager is the responsible person; in some hotels the Head Chef buys all perishable commodities for daily use – the decision as to who buys depends on the policy of the particular type of business or operation. A group may have nominated suppliers who give a discount for the business received from the total number of branches, or head office will simply permit the manager of each unit to buy locally from the best source of supply.

The purchase of wine requires a particular and specialised knowledge to ensure that what is decided upon is correct for the type of establishment and customer and that those selected will form a satisfactory wine list. Similarly, policy will decide the contents of the bar list which together with the wine list acts as the blueprint for cellar stock in the same way that the menus do for the food store.

THE PRINCIPLES OF PURCHASING

The person who has the responsibility for buying needs to define the basic principles on which he should work so as to ensure that the decisions he takes are effective; some of these principles are:

1. Buy on quality, not on price alone.
2. Buy goods at the right price at the right time and of the right quality.
3. Know the seasonal availability of goods.

291

4. Foresee market trends so as to avoid possible supply problems.
5. Know the menu and wine list and the pricing policy of the firm.
6. Have more than one supplier for the main commodities.
7. Do not open too many small accounts.
8. Use only reliable suppliers.
9. Know the stores capacity and avoid over-ordering.
10. See that all goods are inspected on delivery.
11. Obtain discounts where possible without this affecting the quality and delivery of goods.
12. Ensure that only one person is responsible for the buying.

The buyer must work closely with the heads of department in order to know their requirements regarding the commodities they use. There is a big difference between the placing of orders and buying goods professionally; merely asking a supplier to deliver certain items without asking the quality, price, source and pack is a negation of his duties and will not gain the respect of the supplier.

METHODS OF BUYING

There are three broad levels at which buying can be carried out, each pertaining to a particular size and volume of business. These are:

1. The Primary Market, where goods are bought at the source of supply be it the grower, producer, manufacturer, or at a central market such as Smithfield or Covent Garden in London. To buy from these sources demands really large orders at regular intervals.
2. The Secondary Market, where goods are bought wholesale from a distributor or middle man; this gives the buyer the advantage of wholesale prices and possible discounts.
3. The Tertiary Market, where buying is from a retailer, or at best from a local cash and carry warehouse, as dealt with further on.

Contract Buying

Under stable financial conditions suppliers are able to agree to supply a large enterprise with its entire requirements of a particular range of commodities at an agreed price for a period of one year, or longer. Inflation and problems with supplies deter firms from tendering for this sort of business unless clauses in the contract allow for price rises at frequent intervals, which rather take away the essence of what contract buying is all about. In the case of the contract with a firm of butchers the price may have to be the one midway between those charged on a certain day at Smithfield and as recorded in a meat trades journal for that particular quality. For vegetables it could be the market price at Covent Garden plus a percentage for handling and delivery. There is a lot of work in making out a contract, there may not then be many firms offering to tender, and there are often questions about quality, price and delivery problems during the life of the contract. The difficulty of foreseeing the possible trend of prices, the increases in wages, and the cost of fuel make this form of buying more hazardous than it used to be.

Some local authorities, or consortiums of several county councils, run central stores depots where every conceivable item of equipment and certain non-perishable commodities are either held in stock or can be supplied by nominated manufacturers or wholesalers and delivered at specified intervals. To house all the goods a warehouse is necessary together with staff to run it and transport lorries to deliver the orders; there are thus several overheads to be added to the price of goods and this may make prices less competitive.

A large user such as a hospital board may deal directly with the manufacturer of a certain range of commodities to supply them with their total requirements for a given period, at one delivery. The price negotiated by the buyer may be keen but there can be overheads of storage for the commodities and delivery costs as it is distributed in small parcels to individual, and probably widely dispersed units. In these two latter cases the goods may well be controlled by computer.

Cash and Carry

This method of purchasing food, drink and minor items of equipment is useful for small firms; the owner can obtain a pass enabling him to buy in what is, in effect, a wholesale supermarket, collecting his requirements, paying by cash or cheque and taking the goods to his own car or small van for transport. To buy at a cash and carry it may be necessary to give a VAT number, or to purchase a minimum amount over a period but in this method of buying goods it is necessary to bear in mind the unseen costs of, (i) the person's time for going to the warehouse and back, (ii) the amount of petrol used, and (iii) running the vehicle. There is also the need to have ready cash to pay for the goods and it is an impersonal way of buying as there are no staff to discuss quality and prices. Discounts are not normally given and it would probably mean purchasing fifty cases of a particular item before being allowed to see the manager to bargain for a better price – then the problem of where to find storage space probably arises.

Market Buying

A very large firm may find it pays it to employ a buyer to go to the main markets each day they are open, to purchase goods actually on display. In Arnold

293

Bennett's *Imperial Palace* there is a description of Jack Craddock buying meat in Smithfield at 5 a.m. for delivery the same day to the hotels he worked for; here the problems and satisfactions of the traditional method of buying are highlighted. The buyer then must be very knowledgeable about his purchases and be able to obtain the exact quality required and to negotiate the keenest possible prices.

It is also possible for a small firm to purchase its requirements in the major London markets by using the services of an agent who will walk through and buy on the caterer's behalf and have it delivered that day by a carrier. He will add a percentage for his services to the prices he has managed to obtain.

STANDARD PURCHASING SPECIFICATIONS

An experienced buyer can sum up the quality of goods delivered by using his own expertise but it is an admission of a lack of liaison between him and his supplier to have to reject an item because it is not of the required standard. It could happen that a substandard item of produce has to be used because there is not time to wait for it to be changed; the expert buyer will seek to avoid such an occurrence by drawing up a standard purchasing specification for practically every commodity he has to order. It requires much thought and the assistance of the chef, or person who uses the goods, to draw up a watertight specification which, once approved, will be referred to every time the item is delivered.

A standard purchasing specification, which will be referred to subsequently as an SPS is a statement of particular criteria related to quality and couched in clearly understood descriptive terms, so that it can act as a common denominator between purchaser and supplier. The use of an SPS should give uniformity of standard and consistency of quality for each commodity it is drawn up for; a copy is sent to relevant suppliers so that each knows what is expected. It may be useful to involve a supplier in the initial stages since the buyer might be asking for the impossible.

The following is a layout example of a typical Standard Purchasing Specification.

SUPPLIER'S QUALITY & PREPARATION SPECIFICATION   No. M10
PRODUCT: Foreribs of Beef
1. No cow or bull meat or meat designated as commercial or manufacturing, will be supplied.
2. Joints to be cut from chilled unfrozen carcasses of English, Scottish or Irish origin. Intervention beef may be supplied if originating from animals that conformed to home killed beef of the same grade.
3. The unfrozen carcass or joints must be stored at approx. 3 °C for eight to ten days prior to delivery.

4. No joints from excessively fat or lean carcasses to be supplied.
5. Joints to be prepared for roasting by removal of the spinal sinew and gristle, the chine bone to be freed and replaced and the rib to be tied.
6. The weight range to be $4\frac{1}{2}$ to $5\frac{1}{2}$ kg.
7. Delivery to be by refrigerated transport during which the temperature of the meat must not reach more than $10°C$.
8. Prepared joints must be wrapped and sealed with the weight noted on each one. They must be delivered in a receptacle of good hygienic standard.
9. No meat supplied shall have been cut from a frozen carcass that has been defrosted for preparation.
10. All products must comply with the provisions of the Food and Drugs Act 1955, the Weights and Measures Act 1963 and 1976 and the Trade's Description Acts 1968 and 1972.

The same use of specifications can apply for chicken – whether needed fresh, chilled or frozen and of a standard weight with perhaps a tolerance of 80 g each way according to size. The weight could be that to yield say four portions if for cooking whole, or smaller if for cutting into two suprêmes. As poulterers can supply birds in rough-plucked, eviscerated untrussed or oven-ready form, the specification could state whether the giblets are required, if the whole leg should be left on or whether Grade A, B, or C chicken are the first choice; and so on according to menu requirements.

Each completed SPS should have an identifying number.

SOURCES OF SUPPLY

Several hundred different commodities are required to fulfil the menu requirements of an establishment that is run on traditional lines and where food is prepared from raw. A fast food snack bar, or other similar place, that runs on a limited choice menu would still need to buy many different commodities divided between perishables, such as rolls and cakes, and the non-perishable items that are issued from stock as required. The major staples of meat, fish and vegetables are usually purchased as required on a daily basis and if the order is fairly substantial two suppliers of each could be used. This entails obtaining a quotation from both in order to obtain the keenest price for a consistent quality.

Some suppliers issue a weekly price list showing what their commodities will cost and what is available; any special offers will be listed. Other suppliers send their representative to see the buyer each week when the market can be discussed and the order taken. Large wholesalers print a price list for distribution to customers to last as long as possible until all-round price rises make it obsolete; individual price increases can be notified weekly.

Provision lists are also issued on a weekly basis and current wholesale prices for categories of commodities are given in the weekly trade journals printed for people concerned with that trade. The catering weeklies include a list of food prices estimated as being those that should prevail during the week, and a monthly food cost index showing on a percentage basis how prices have fluctuated since a certain date.

Sources of supply of wine will be from a shipper if the quantity of wine involved is considerable, or from a local wine merchant who may be an agent for some growers but can obtain steady supplies so that the wine list can remain constant over a period of time.

The supply of stationery and paperware and of cleaning materials would most probably be to cover a lengthy period depending on usage and availability of storage space. There are many firms specialising in the supply of items of paperware for catering establishments, and it is necessary to calculate whether it is more convenient to purchase from one of them or to obtain say paper serviettes and table coverings from a firm that deals in these only. A cook-freeze or cook-chill production unit which uses foil or plastic containers for packing will be able to purchase in bulk from a manufacturer, but again storage space will be required for minimum delivery quantities which could run into tens of thousands of each size.

There is an enormous variety of powders, liquids, creams, sprays and pastes for cleaning purposes and the buyer has to know which of them is the most efficient for the price.

A reserve stock of small utensils is necessary to replace those that get broken or worn out and the buyer must know the catering equipment specialists who can supply good quality professional items.

RECEIPT OF GOODS

Official order forms bearing an order number and printed with the name and address of the establishment will have been used to cover all orders placed on suppliers even though orders may have been telephoned so as to save time. See Fig. 31 for a sample order form. The orders sent to suppliers are their only authority to deliver goods and on which to claim payment for these goods.

With amounts now running up to 50 per cent of sales being spent on the purchase of food it is vital that all goods so ordered are actually received. At the unloading bay or delivery point there must be a foolproof method for inspecting and receiving. Except for mail, all goods must be delivered to this one point and if delivery men in a hurry try to leave goods elsewhere they must be discouraged. There must be a reliable check for quality, quantity and price and no blind receiving without delivery notes. A record of what goes out is also of importance; returnable containers usually carry a substantial deposit and it is necessary to see they are returned promptly in order to be credited. No payment for goods received can be made until the receiving office informs those responsible that it is in order to pay for them.

It is the usual practice to despatch perishable foods directly to the kitchen so that the chef can check their suitability; failure to inspect adequately can lead to higher costs and lower quality and it is important to ensure that the chef can devote adequate time to this aspect of his job.

If, after inspection the goods are found to match the copy order and the SPS if applicable and then meet every requirement, they can be accepted and a signature given; this is usually done by signing a copy of a delivery note or invoice and it is this signed invoice which acts as authority to pay for goods received.

If there are discrepancies between what is written on the invoice and what has actually been received or what was agreed when the order was placed then the invoice must not be signed; it can, however, be annotated that there is some problem which has to be resolved concerning the transaction.

In these days of high delivery costs when the delivery man may not be able to wait whilst a big load involving say a hundred cases of varied items is checked against the delivery note, it is permissible to sign that the total consignment has not been examined; this ensures that any queries can be taken up with the supplier afterwards. This also applies to deliveries that are left after the stores have closed for the day and the van driver leaves the goods in the area in the knowledge that they will be safe until the following morning.

STORAGE

Once goods are received into stock they should be regarded as capital with each item worth a sum of money; in this light the value appears more real than when they are looked upon only as commodities. The storeroom must be regarded as a strong-room for the safe-keeping of valuables that merit every form of protection from misappropriation; this is but one aspect of the storage of goods which covers a wide field, although it all boils down to the need to keep everything under strict control and in perfect condition.

SITING OF STORES AND CELLAR

If possible the food store and the cellar should be on the same level as the kitchen and dining room so that it is not necessary to install a goods lift or to have to haul heavy goods upstairs. The food store will be cool if it is sited to face a northerly direction and the cellar should not have windows so as to exclude the light. Starting at the receiving point for goods, if this is purpose built and for a large establishment, it will allow vans to deliver goods at tail-board level; the buyer's office or the receiving point could be sited to advantage so that it overlooks the delivery point and the distance from there to the actual store should ideally be minimal. Space is required to site a weighing machine and for trucks and trolleys to be parked when not in use. The distance from the store to kitchen and cellar to dispense bar should not be too far.

Automated handling of deliveries by means of an endless belt or overhead rail should be investigated to see if it saves labour. Some wholesalers now put up the complete consignment for an establishment on one of its own delivery trolleys so that the entire load can be wheeled into the stores and avoid double handling.

AREA ALLOCATIONS

The areas allocated to house the commodities purchased should be as extensive as possible within the boundaries set. The amount of storage space has to tie in with the overall type of business being run. A conventional operation because of its preparation of goods from raw will need bulk deliveries on a daily basis and this needs proportionately large storage areas: a fast food operation will require a small store for its limited range and even these may well be held in open storage to be taken as required since control can be so precise.

Non-perishable Goods

With as many as two hundred or more different commodities in canned, bottled or packaged form to be kept in stock, it is this section that takes up so much valuable space. Using the menu as the determinant and knowing the average rate of usage, it becomes feasible to apportion sufficient space for each separate commodity; the rate of issue has an effect on this in that if canned goods are used they may be issued either by the can or by the case; if the latter, they may be stored on slats on the floor whereas individual cans are best arranged on shelves as if on display. Foodstuffs that are packed in sacks may be issued as they are or in smaller amounts in which case they will be emptied into bins to facilitate ease of weighing out as required.

Perishable Foods

This includes fish, meat, poultry, vegetables and fruit, and it is usual for these to be taken into stock by the chef after they have been inspected for weight, price, quality, and suitability.

Wines and other alcoholic drinks are delivered directly to the cellar where items are placed in their respective bins either in readiness for service or, if applicable, to age and mature where space is available.

The total area can be subdivided as required to provide sections that are more suitable for particular commodities. For example, clarets that are going to remain undisturbed for several years until they reach their peak of maturity require a constant temperature and dim lighting regardless of the weather or time of day.

Cleaning materials should not be kept with foodstuffs; some foods even although they are not strong smelling ones have the ability to impart their smell and flavour to others in the near vicinity. Stores layout must be such as to avoid any untoward results and stores operation has to take note of various hygiene regulations.

PHYSICAL REQUIREMENTS OF STORAGE

It is not only the goods in store that have to be considered but also the staff who work there. It is all very well to say that the store should be a cool place but if conditions are too cold this goes against the Shops, Factories and Offices Act which states that working conditions be endurable; staff cannot be expected to work efficiently if the air temperature goes below 6 °C. An ambient temperature of 10 °C is ideal for storage of non-perishable goods but extremes should be eliminated; hot water pipes that run through the store, though not supplying it, may cause localised hot areas and lack of ventilation can give rise to condensation, both of which can affect certain goods such as cereals and canned foods.

Wide fluctuation of temperature should be eliminated as this can also cause spoilage and deterioration; this is not to suggest that the store and cellar be insulated from the surrounding environment, or that they be air conditioned in order to provide ideal conditions. It is a matter of making the best use of the space that has been provided by a knowledge of how different goods behave under certain circumstances.

Humidity is a factor which should be taken into consideration as the amount of water vapour in the air is strictly limited but can increase as the temperature rises. When air that is saturated with water vapour cools it gives up this excess vapour in the form of droplets of water which can cover the floor and walls and make conditions uncomfortable or even dangerous. Relative humidity can be described as the amount of water present in the air, as a percentage of the maximum amount possible at a given temperature.

REFRIGERATION

With few exceptions all perishable commodities need to be kept in cold storage which means having built-in coldrooms or free standing refrigerators. Not so long ago it was the practice to have a general purpose coldroom for keeping practically everything in. This is now frowned on and it is necessary, for example, to keep raw meat in a separate refrigerator from cooked meat and to ensure there is no transfer of smell and taste from one commodity to another because of proximity of storage. The ideal then is to have a series of reach-in refrigerators, one for each separate class of commodities in their raw state and to provide each section of the kitchen with its own place for storing its basic preparations.

The following gives an outline of refrigeration requirements for the various classes of perishable foods.

Meat

Fresh meat in carcass form should if possible be hung in a temperature of 2-4 °C for sufficient time to become more tender; joints and cuts should be spread out on trays on shelves and any drip wiped away regularly. It requires 80 per cent relative humidity. Chilled meat can be stored at −2 °C for up to one month; boneless meat in vacuum packs will keep for several weeks until opened when it must be treated as fresh meat. Frozen meat should be kept in deep freeze at −18 °C.

When meat that has been stored at around 0 °C in the refrigerator is brought out to prepare for cooking, the air surrounding it will be cooled to that of the meat and the moisture content of the air will be condensed onto the surface of the meat thus making it appear to be sweating. This moist surface will encourage the growth of spoilage organisms and this is why meat should not be brought frequently back and forth from the refrigerator for cutting.

Fish

Fresh raw fish may be kept in the open tank of a refrigerator specially designed for this commodity; this allows water to drain away and keeps down any smells. If there is a possibility of desiccation, fish should be covered with crushed ice. Live trout delivered from a fish farm must be put into the water in a fish tank right away. Both raw and cooked shellfish should not be held for any length of time before sending to be cooked; minimal holding periods under refrigeration are permissible only if freshness can be maintained. Fresh fish should be stored at 2 °C and frozen fish at −18 °C; when the latter is required for preparation it needs approximately twenty-four hours in a refrigerator at 6 °C to defrost.

Dairy Produce

All these foods keep better under refrigeration at 5-7°C and it keeps them fresher than under normal storage conditions. Some foods such as eggs and cheese need time to lose their chill before being used so as to obtain best results. If these goods are kept covered the chance of transfer of flavour is lessened.

Vegetables and Fruit

Fresh green vegetables should be treated as perishable and if possible ordered daily for use that same day. When necessary to store overnight they keep fresher in a refrigerator at approximately 6°C. If fruit is to be kept in stock over a period of time it is advisable to keep it in the refrigerator at approximately 8°C but this does not apply to soft fruit which is better kept at about 5°C. Melons will ripen in store when kept at normal temperature of 10°C or more.

Frozen foods

The storage temperatures of any kind of frozen foods whether it is a raw commodity or prepared meals can vary from −18° to −40°C and within this range it will keep in good condition provided it is a fairly constant temperature. Protection against freezer burn or dehydration of outer surfaces by correct wrapping is necessary and there should be a proper rotation of stock as with any other commodity. Frozen foods may be kept in stock for a year without fear of deterioration if well packed, although some smoked foods such as bacon and smoked fish may develop off flavours.

PREVENTION OF CONTAMINATION

The storeroom and cellar must be kept in a clean condition at all times and staff encouraged to be conscious of the need for good hygiene standards. Infestation must not be allowed to develop unchecked. Mice and rats must be prevented from entering under outer doors or by means of drainpipes and vulnerable foods should be kept in rodent-proof containers. Flies can be killed by installing an electrically operated killer; this has an ultra-violet tube which attracts and an electric grill that kills them. Birds, weevils, grain moths, cockroaches, beetles and silver fish are difficult to combat once any has gained a hold on a place. A contract with a firm of pest exterminators will keep pests in check and eventually rid the premises of them; the environmental health officer will advise on protection and decontamination. The best preventative measure is clean orderly storage procedures.

STORES EQUIPMENT

The fitments installed in the store should aim to use the available space to maximum advantage, with shelves of an ideal depth and passage ways that will accommodate a trolley but not be a waste of space.

Shelving

This must be stout enough to take anticipated loads, and capable of being altered should the layout need to be changed at any time. Regulations forbid the storage of opened foods on the floor and the floor space should be used only for storage bins preferably on castors, and for cases of canned foods; but even these ought to be on slats to prevent them getting damp when the floor is washed. Those goods in frequent use should be stored close to the issuing point at a level of approximately one metre high and goods in only occasional demand can be on higher shelves and at a distance from the counter. It is an advantage to know the range and kind of goods and their packing which will be used to produce menus as envisaged, as well as the rate of use and frequency of ordering and delivery; this will decide the amount and type of shelving or cupboards required.

Shelving can be bought in modular form as free-standing and with a load-bearing limit; as wall mounted but adjustable; as self assembly packs; and made in wood, chrome wire, laminated plastic, aluminium alloy or other rustfree metal. Consideration should be given to the possibilities of mobile racking that can double as trolleys for the receipt, storage and delivery of goods to service departments; this applies particularly to vegetables.

Scales

The most important pieces of equipment of the store are the scales required for weighing receipts and issues; a platform scale is required for checking heavy goods on delivery and smaller sets of scales for weighing out goods as requisitioned. It is not advisable to move scales around and to be completely level they must be placed on a firm, even surface at the most useful point. A maintenance contract with the manufacturer will ensure correct issues and receipts.

Other items of equipment required are a desk and chair for use of the storeman, a ladder to reach goods from high shelves; refrigerators; tables; bins; containers; measuring equipment such as scoops and knives, and washing and drying facilities.

ROTATION OF STOCK

A principle of first-in-first-out must be adhered to so that no old stock is allowed to accumulate in the stores. It means juggling with goods on the shelves by putting the fresh delivery behind existing stock and always issuing the goods at the front first. In the case of dry goods such as rice and milk powder stored loose in containers, it is advisable to deplete stock before tipping in the new delivery. Some commodities have a strong smell or ripen during storage which means they must be used before they become over-ripe and obnoxious.

All goods, even canned foods, have an optimum shelf life during which time they are at their best, thereafter they gradually lose quality. If condensation makes the store damp, canned goods may rust and in time the metal will deteriorate and affect the contents. The storeman should have a good working knowledge of the shelf life of commodities, and he should thus be able to prevent anything exceeding its shelf life.

STOCK LEVELS

Not only must there be control over the number of items to be kept in stock to cover all the menu requirements, but there must also be a minimum and maximum stock level for each commodity. The minimum level is decided on with the knowledge of how much time is required to obtain fresh supplies, so that under no circumstances can the store run out of stock. Bearing in mind delivery times, a maximum stock level is decided upon which should cover a given period of time; bin cards showing issues and stock in hand are of great assistance in maintaining these stock levels.

The only time when agreed stock levels may be disregarded is when a supplier offers a greatly reduced price for a bulk order, but before being persuaded into it the buyer must be sure that storage space is available and that the commodity is one that will constantly be used. In many stores there is to be found a stock of items which because of a change of chef or a new menu, no longer get used and slowly gather dust and possibly start to deteriorate. This should not be allowed to happen; notification to the compiler of the menus can usually take care of this problem. The buyer will be given a budget figure showing how much of the firm's capital he may tie up in the form of goods in stock. Money can earn more on deposit with a bank than as shelves full of easily obtainable goods. If, however, the class of business includes the selling of fine wines then stock levels should always be set as high as possible. Not only do fine wines appreciate in value but once sold they are very often impossible to replace with a repeat order.

STORES CONTROL DOCUMENTS

The activities of the stores and cellar need to be carefully controlled and this can be done by a series of forms which act as records of each transaction for the receipt and issue of goods. A document is necessary to authorise every single movement of goods in and out of stock, from when they are ordered through the processes of conversion into meals and drinks which are sold. The following account of the receipt and requisitioning of goods gives samples of the forms in general use; there are several different versions of each of these but in general they provide the same basic details which govern an individual transaction.

Ordering

Orders must be written on an official form in an order book, usually in triplicate, and must be signed only by an authorised person. Some orders are placed by telephone but must still be covered by an official order; all orders will have a number printed on the page. The top copy is sent to the supplier and is his means of obtaining payment for the goods he supplies; the second copy is kept in the store for checking against the delivery note and invoice when the goods arrive, and for entering into the filing system. The third copy remains in the order book for any queries which may arise, and any alterations such as short delivery or non-availability should be noted on it.

Figure 31
SAMPLE ORDER FORM

Universal Hotel Ltd Pondtown Rd., Stornfold.		Order No. 12882	
	Please supply:—	£	p
To: Knightley & Co. Ltd 10–18 Charles Rd, Cross Trading Estate, Bilstown.	20 × 10 litres Bestco frying oil 5 × 2½ litres olive oil 50 kg long grain rice 2 × 1 kg tins ground ginger 10 kg cornflour 18 kg sultanas 18 kg currants 1 case sauerkraut 12 × 300 g jars cafe Hag 10 × 500 g drums grated Parmesan		
Please quote the above order number on your invoice.	Signed: Date:		

Fig. 31 shows a sample order form of the kind printed for use by a group or an authority for ordering supplies. The order can be written or typed in and prices can be entered as agreed by telephone or from the price list as issued by the supplier. The form may be designed for folding and sealing.

Fig. 32 shows a sample order form as sent for supplies ordered under contract.

Figure 32
SAMPLE ORDER FORM FOR USE UNDER CONTRACT

Order Form				No. J 21863 Date:
Universal Hotel, Pondtown Rd.				
Please supply the undermentioned goods:				

Amount	Item	Unit price	Specification no.	Cost
				£ p
180	Lemon sole fillets and bones		35	
2 kg	Peeled prawns, fresh		18	
12 kg	Smoked haddock fillets		3	
10 × 2 kg	Scampi, jumbo		16	
30 kg	Whole cod, headless		28	
6 kg	Kippers		4	

Please see conditions on reverse of form.

To: James Fish Suppliers & Co.,
               Grimsby.

                                                   Signed:
                                                   (Purchasing Officer)

(Reverse of form)

CONDITIONS
1. The specifications regarding quality as laid down by the purchasing officer must be adhered to.
2. A delivery note must be sent with the goods.
3. The amount as indicated must be supplied; no over-supply will be accepted.
4. The prices as set out under contract agreement are not to be increased without notice.

Some wholesalers with a contract to supply all the establishments within a company or authority find it practical to print order forms which list every commodity in use, with a few lines for the buyer to write in items outside the normal range. A pad with a year's supply all correctly dated may be given to each unit; the week's order is written in triplicate and handed to the driver for the following week at the time he delivers the current week's order. The duplicate comes back as the delivery note and the authorisation to pay the account. This system obviates the need to write out official order forms. Figure 33 shows a sample form of this type.

It is common practice for some suppliers to employ sales staff who phone establishments at the same time every so often to solicit orders, to give current prices, make special offers, and to discuss the market situation. Others have a salesman who will make a regular call each week to assist the buyer in making out his order by quoting the supply availability and actual prices as well as any special lines. Some firms send sales/delivery men out with vans loaded with their range of goods for the buyer to decide what is required on the spot. In all these cases it is essential to write out an order form to cover all the items ordered or purchased.

Deliveries

There should always be someone on duty to receive incoming goods and it is always best to check deliveries at the time as they arrive, than for someone to sign the note saying 'unexamined' with the bother of taking up discrepancies on the phone. When goods are delivered they should be accompanied with a delivery note then checked against the order and delivery note for exactness, and weighed or counted and inspected for quality. If standard purchasing specifications are part of the established procedure then the goods need to be carefully checked against these specifications. Where prices appear on the delivery note, they must be compared with the agreed price and any variation taken up with the supplier. The goods must immediately be taken into the stores and not left lying around outside. The various items must be entered into the goods received book if one is kept; if not in the ledger or on the bin cards.

Fig. 34 shows a sample delivery note.

The following points relate to delivery notes.
1. The form of delivery note can vary widely, some firms have every item they supply printed on with only the number of units ordered needing to be entered. Very often prices are not included on the delivery note.
2. The delivery note is often made out in duplicate, one of the signed copies being taken back by the delivery man.
3. Some suppliers use invoices as delivery notes.

Figure 33

COMBINED ORDER FORM, DELIVERY NOTE AND AUTHORISATION
TO PAY

INVOICE ORDER.

To Messrs Gravender & Sharmer, Thalmar House, Charnton, CN1 7RT.

Please supply the goods indicated during the week ending:

To: Foreman Green School.

Signed: E. Gregory.

Date:

Order No. H 0372

Commodity	Unit	Unit No.	Units req.	Unit cost	£	p	Commodity	Unit	Unit No.	Units req.	Unit cost	£	p
Apple, solid pack	A10	6001	6				Currants	3 kg	7001	2			
Apricot pulp	5 kg	6002	3				Dates	5 kg	7002				
Gooseberries	A10	6003					Desiccated coconut	7 lb	7003				
Mandarin oranges	A10	6004	6				Glacé cherries	1 kg	7005	2			
Peach caps	K3	6005					Mixed peel	3 kg	7006				
Pineapple crush	A10	6006	6				Prunes 50/60	12½ kg	7007				
Pineapple rings	A10	6007					Raisins seedless	12½ kg	7008				
Baked beans	A10	8010	18				Sultanas	12½ kg	7009				
Broad beans	A10	8011					Almonds, flaked	500 g	7010				
Celery hearts	A10	8012					Almonds, ground	3 kg	7011				
Carrots, whole	A10	8013	6				Almonds, nibbed	500 g	7012				
Sweetcorn niblets	75 oz	8014	24				Walnuts, shelled	3 kg	7013				
Tomato purée	1 kg	8015					Lemon essence	500 ml	4003	1			
Beans, butter	3 kg	9010	1				Raspberry essence	500 ml	4004				
Beans, haricot	3 kg	9011					Strawberry essence	500 ml	4005				
Lentils	3 kg	9012					Vanilla essence	1 litre	4006				
Peas, yellow split	3 kg	9013											
Pearl barley	7 lb	9014					Sugar, caster	50 kg	3101				
Rice, Japan	25 kg	9015	2				Sugar, Demerara	5 kg	3102	1			

Figure 34
SAMPLE DELIVERY NOTE

DELIVERY NOTE		James Fish Suppliers Grimsby				
To: Universal Hotel, Pondtown Road.						
Your order No: J 21863		Dated:				No. 07351 Date:
		Unit cost.	£	p		
180 2 kg 10 × 2 kg 12 kg 30 kg	fillets lemon sole peeled prawns pkts jumbo scampi fillet smoked had. headless whole cod regret no kippers					Delivery date: Received by:

4. When delivery notes are used, the invoices are usually sent by post at regular intervals.
5. The delivery note should contain sufficient information to indicate to the recipient that the goods delivered conform totally or partially with the original order.

Stock Records – Cards and Files

It is essential to have a system of consolidating the various aspects of stores operation and control. Stock record cards and files can offer an efficient way of doing this. Single stock record cards are simple to use but time-consuming to make-up. The details can be easy to see at a glance and give information regarding dates, receipts, issues, and stock in hand together with its value. See Fig. 35 for an example.

Fig. 36 shows a Bin Card which gives more information. As with the stock card it is kept in the stores or store office and is made up each time a transaction takes place, either by the receipt of a delivery or the issue of stock to any department. It shows both the cost of issues and the value of stock in hand.

Figure 35
EXAMPLE OF STOCK RECORD CARD

STOCK RECORD							
Item: Salad Oil				Minimum stock 30 litres			
				Maximum stock 100 litres			
Date	Stock	Additions	Issues	Balance	Unit price	£	p
15.2.19 ..	30	+ 30	− 10	50	120 p	60	00
22.2.19 ..	50	+ 00	− 10	40		48	00
29.2.19 ..	40	+ 00	− 10	30		36	00
5.3.19 ..	30	+ 30	− 10	50	125 p	62	50

Figure 36
EXAMPLE OF BIN CARD

Item: Spaghetti				Max. stock: 50 pkts.					
Unit: 500 g packs				Min. stock: 10 pkts.					
Price: 25 p			Supplier: Greenleighs						
Received				Issued				In hand		

		Value				Value				Value	
Date	Quantity	£	p	Quantity	£	p	Quantity	£	p
Jan 30							32	8	00
Jan 30				10	2	50	22	5	50
Feb 3				10	2	50	12	3	00
Feb 6	40	10	00				52	13	00
Feb 8				6	1	50	46	11	50
Feb 9				8	2	00	38	9	50

309

A perpetual stock file can give relevant information concerning the complete stock of the store in a single easily available form. It consists of a loose leaf file in which a form for each item is held by ring binders and so arranged that the name of each item is immediately visible on opening the book. The name of the commodity is written on one of the forms and inserted in the file in alphabetic order or in groups according to kind, e.g. flour, baking powder, dried milk, custard powder, cornflour, canned fruit, vegetables. Each day's transactions are entered and the balance should agree with the actual amount in the stores. When one of the forms is filled up a new one can be clipped in. This type of multiple stock sheet is useful for calculating kitchen percentages provided, of course, that accurate records are kept. They are also used for stocktaking at the end of the trading period. Fig. 37 is an example of this type of stock sheet.

Figure 37
EXAMPLE OF A LOOSE LEAF FROM A PERPETUAL STOCK FILE

ITEM: Butter, Salted		Code No. 28		Unit Kg		Min Stock 40 Kg		Max. Stock 100 Kg		
Date 19--	Department Issued to	Quantity			Unit Price		Value			
		Issued	Received	Balance	£	p	Issues £ p	Received £ p	Balance £ p	
June 1	Kitchen	5	20	50	2	00	10 00		100 00	
June 2	Stillroom	4	20	66			8 00	40 00	132 00	
June 3	Kitchen	6		60			12 00		120 00	
June 3	Pastry	4		56			8 00		112 00	
June 3	Dining Room	2		54			4 00		108 00	
June 4	Kitchen	6		48			12 00		96 00	
June 4	Stillroom	4		44			8 00		88 00	

STOCKTAKING AND VALUATION

The physical stocktaking of the contents of store and cellar must be done at regular intervals so as to ensure that these departments are being operated efficiently and that the goods on the stock sheets are actually in hand. Stocktaking can assist in increasing the profitability of a business because (i) it helps in formulating buying policy, (ii) it pinpoints any weaknesses in pricing policy, (iii) it assists in forecasting, (iv) it draws attention to overstocking, (v) it ensures

310

that goods received have been invoiced and accounted for, and (vi) it is a necessary part of budgetary control.

The best system will be a simple one that is tailored to the size of the business. It should not take an undue length of time to carry out and any possible error of calculation should be eliminated or at least reduced to a minimum. Good calibre staff like to know that stocktaking is carried out and will not mistrust it, even although it may sometimes take the form of a spot check. Stocktaking shows store and cellar staff that management is interested in its affairs and wants them to be cost-conscious.

It is possible to put stock and inventory control onto a micro-computer system which will rationalise and possibly reduce unit stock levels, thus improving storage efficiency. The routine clerical functions would be reduced by basing inventory control on minimum stock levels and average usage data, to produce pre-costed re-ordering lists.

SECURITY OF STOCK AND STORES PREMISES

It is very important that stocks of food, drink, cleaning materials and small equipment are kept in safe custody so that no losses occur through break-in. The responsibility for the security of stocks and of the premises where they are kept is vested in the person who is in charge. He must obviously be someone of integrity who will not allow anything dishonest to take place, nor permit any unauthorised person on the premises under his control. Arrangements have to be made regarding the handling of stores keys so that they are not accessible to persons not entitled to use them. All refrigerators and cupboards must be kept locked.

STORES ISSUING

The issue of any of the stock held in the stores or cellar may be done only on presentation of an authentic requisition signed or countersigned by a person who is authorised to do so. No unsigned checks should be honoured and no stores issued on the promise of a requisition to come later. Only if standard issues are in operation should stores be issued automatically without a covering requisition.

It is the responsibility of the stores or cellar assistant to issue only goods as indented, to get someone to counter-check them, and to deliver only to the appropriate section or to the person authorised to collect them. The person in charge of the section should check the goods issued for correctness.

As goods are issued so the amounts should be deducted from bin cards or entered on the file as in Fig. 33. Each requisition will be costed by the storesman

311

so that at the end of each day's business the total value of issues is known; the value of perishable items ordered for the day's menus has to be added in even though they may not have gone through the stores. These figures are required to arrive at the kitchen profit percentage.

A deadline is needed for the submission of requisitions beyond which the stores are closed. This is for stores staff to attend to routine clerical and other matters.

Requisitions

Requisitions can originate from the various departments and sections of the establishment such as the kitchen, stillroom, dining room and dispense bar. In a large kitchen, as an example, each Chef de Partie will look at the menu for the following day and decide the amount and kind of goods required to produce his number of dishes. He will then write out a list, submit it to the Head Chef or Sous Chef for approval and receive the issue first thing in the morning. The chef countersigning the requisition will be experienced enough to judge whether all of the items are actually required and have the authority to delete or diminish any item. All the signed requisitions are sent to the stores and the orders are made up and distributed as required.

Fig. 38 shows an example of a requisition from the fish section for some of the day's stores required to carry out the preparation and cooking of fish as determined by the menu. It is for use in conjunction with the items of fish as supplied from the larder; the fish itself will have been ordered through the normal ordering system.

Figure 38
SAMPLE REQUISITION FORM

UNIVERSAL HOTEL KITCHENS			No. 219	
Stores Requisition				
Dept: Fish			Date:	
Please supply:		Unit	Price	£ p
2 kg	unsalted butter	kg		
60	eggs	doz		
4 litres	double cream	litre		
Signature:			Authorised by:	

312

It is in the larder and fish larder that any preparation is carried out to raw commodities before they are despatched to the kitchen sections for actual cooking, and the cooks in charge of each of these have to ensure they hold sufficient stock to cater for the expected business of the day. In smaller establishments the preparation of meat and fish is carried out in one room with the same person in charge.

The control over this system of issuing is the twice daily stocktaking list of all meat, poultry, game, fish and shellfish, and other important items such as smoked salmon, caviar and foie gras. It is made out at the close of business after each meal and shows the stock in hand from the previous sheet, the day's deliveries and the amounts issued to the kitchen. This list is handed in and the Chef can quickly ascertain that the issues match the day's business and order accordingly. Control can be made by comparing the issues with the number of portions sold. This same method of stocktaking, but on a daily basis only, can be carried out by the vegetable section. Fig. 39 is an example stocksheet of this type.

Figure 39
LARDER STOCK SHEET

Date			Time						
Item	Held over	Received	Issued	In stock	Item	Held over	Received	Issued	In stock
Sirloin	6 kg	$13\frac{1}{2}$ kg	9 kg	$10\frac{1}{2}$ kg	Oysters	240	600	480	360
Entrecotes	52	40	48	44	Smoked salmon	10 kg	–	3 kg	7 kg
Fillet steak	$4\frac{1}{4}$ kg	$8\frac{1}{2}$ kg	$5\frac{1}{4}$ kg	$7\frac{1}{4}$ kg	Smoked trout	31	–	11	20

CELLAR AND BAR STOCK CONTROL

This is carried out on similar lines to other goods, and all the details given for those apply to the control of liquor in the cellar which is in fact a basic holding store, and to the bars which are the selling points. The cellar holds stocks of all the items as shown on the wine and bar lists and according to the expected turnover will keep a sufficient stock of each item to satisfy that demand. See Fig. 40 for a sample Bin Card as used in the cellar for issues of a particular wine.

Each bar will maintain a sufficient stock of every drink on the list to satisfy known demand and send a requisition to the cellar as necessary to keep stock at the appropriate level to fulfil the demand. In some establishments all empty bottles are returned to the cellar for replacement by full ones to bring the stock level back to normal.

Figure 40
EXAMPLE OF A BIN CARD FOR THE CELLAR

Item: Mateus Rosé			Bin No. 36
Supplier: Century Wine Co.			
Date	Received	In hand	Issued
January 19--			
1		50	12
4	120	38	—
6		158	12
7		146	24
10		122	10
16		112	24
18		88	12
22		76	24
27		52	24
30		28	12
31		16	6
February		10	—
2	120	10	24
5		106	12
7		94	12
8		82	24
16		58	12

A dispense bar is the place where drink is kept for serving in the dining room or lounge. It therefore has to carry a stock of every drink that is offered for sale to the establishment's customers. In a residential establishment it supplies guests' requirements in their rooms where this service is offered. Nothing should be served by the dispense barman without a signed check to support the withdrawal from stock. At the end of each service period a consumption sheet is completed and sent for control together with the checks received from waiters to support all the issues.

The person responsible for the food and beverage operation needs a good knowledge of bar work, as only in this way will he know if every drink is served to the required standard and also that no breach of the licensing laws or unacceptable practices take place.

One of the ways by which control can be maintained is by linking the existing optic or other dispensing measures to a micro-processor which will monitor every dispense transaction. This kind of system acts as a control which identifies any shortages between consumption and takings, as well as any surpluses. Some small computers will handle delivery notes, requisitions, stocktakings, stock consumption, cellar receipts and issues and the profitability of each sales outlet; reports can be produced whenever required and for any time period. Ordering can be assisted by identifying slow moving stock and examining stock turnover.

Laying Down Stocks

One of the most important parts of the function of the cellarman lies in the laying down of stocks of wines in order that they mature until the stage of perfection of drinking is reached. At one time most establishments bought wine from the grower or shipper when it was cheap and stored it carefully until it was ready for drinking. This meant that the cellar was the repository of very valuable assets and that the cellarman had to know how to treat the stocks and to monitor their development. Few caterers today can boast about the size and value of their cellar stocks and many are quite happy to leave the wine merchant to hold stocks and supply requirements. The capital tied up in cellar stocks can be put on deposit to earn more than if it was invested in wine, and it is not always easy to provide sufficient space for large stocks nor to have optimum storage facilities. But as previously observed where fine wines are offered for sale, it is wise to hold the maximum possible stocks.

PAYMENT OF ACCOUNTS

Every catering establishment relies on its suppliers to give prompt delivery of goods and in turn the suppliers of commodities need prompt and regular payment of their accounts. The establishment should therefore pass accounts for payment as soon as possible, once they have been checked as being correct. The temptation to delay payment of accounts rendered until the last possible moment so that money can remain in the deposit account accruing interest should not override the requirement to pay within a reasonable length of time after receipt of the invoice. Persistently bad payers may risk not being allowed credit facilities and made to pay in cash for every delivery; suppliers do not like having to affix warning notices onto copy invoices requesting prompt payment. This could cause a supplier to imagine that the caterer's business is not in good health thus deterring him from granting any further credit. Non-payment can cause a supplier to factor his debtors by passing them to a firm which will pay him a percentage of all the money owed, thus providing the necessary cash flow for the firm to continue in business whilst the debts are collected.

Fig. 41 shows a typical invoice; some firms issue a monthly statement showing dates of orders, order number, amount due, any credits allowed, and amount outstanding at the end of each month. It should be remembered that an invoice is a business document that states the price of goods as sold, the terms of payment and the discount, if any; it should be compared with the monthly statement before payment is made. Where goods are delivered incorrectly and in consequence have to be returned to the supplier, they should not be deducted from the delivery note and invoice but accounted for by a supplier's credit note; the amount will appear on the monthly statement.

Figure 41
EXAMPLE OF INVOICE

INVOICE	James Fish Suppliers Ltd, Grimsby.		No. 6070 Date:	
To: Universal Hotel, Pondtown Road.				
Product Code	Quantity	Item	Unit price	Total £ p
10052	180	Lemon sole fillets		
10053	12 kg	Herrings		
13055	20 kg	Coley fillets		
14122	30 kg	Whole cod		
11120	12 kg	Smoked haddock		

CODING SCHEMES

Most retail food and drink packs are now printed with a bar code that is used by supermarkets for the purpose of stock control; at present the code is used on retail packs but could equally be used on catering size products. A central store used as a distribution depot for a large catering firm could use the system for taking stock and the busy store of any large catering establishment would find if possible to save valuable time in their own stocktaking.

The system requires a link at each distribution point that is connected to a computer terminal or a micro-processor. The storeman scans the code on each pack with the 'pick-up' instrument which produces the actual stock situation of each bar immediately as it reads it from the unit data bank.

By pressing the function stock in the computer at any time, an accurate statement of that specific item is obtained from the bar digits, the 'pick-up' operating from the bar reading – an example of which is shown in Fig. 42.

Figure 42
EXAMPLE OF BAR CODING

5 010358 170619

Possible uses of the coding scheme can be in a large meal distribution unit such as an in-flight catering production unit supplying many different kinds of packaged meals for various airlines, and which are supplied by a frozen or chilled meal kitchen producing thousands of meals daily in multi-portion packs. Normally the stocktaking of these meals is carried out inside the deep-freeze store at a temperature of down to $-40\,°C$ and can be a long and uncomfortable job when hundreds of different lines are stored. Staff can spend only a short time inside even though wearing proper protective clothing. The use of a coding system could obviate much of this work.

10 PRODUCTION AND DISTRIBUTION I – ORGANISATION AND OPERATION

Organisation – Types of Authority Relationships – The Kitchen – Kitchen Organisation – Kitchen Routine – Productivity – Continuous Production Techniques – The Dining Room – Staffing of a Dining Room – Food and Beverage Service – Types of Service – Space Requirements – Routine of the Dining Room – The Bars – Ancillary Areas.

A catering operation supplies three things – food, drink and service; in the main the food is produced on the premises from raw materials and it is then distributed to service points for sale to the consumer. Drink is usually dispensed in much the same form as it is purchased, except for hot beverages which are made up on the premises. The third thing, service, is less tangible since it stems from the first two things and exists only in the skill and personality of staff whether they be servery counter hands or head waiters. These three things are produced

318

in the three main areas of the operation – the kitchen, the dining room and the bars which exist as separate units each with its own head person in charge but as they are so closely related it is essential to have one person in overall charge to co-ordinate their functions. The person in charge of the catering department lays down the organisation and routine operation of the three sections and their ancillary areas, and is responsible for the work of all the members of staff under his command and the running of the operation.

ORGANISATION

The term organisation as applied to the management function means the distribution to members of the staff of the tasks necessary to achieve the set objectives, so that each may make an effective contribution to the success of the enterprise. This involves the following:

1. Assessing the component parts of the operation.
2. Determining how these can best be done, without duplication of effort and in the most efficient and economical manner.
3. Assigning the individual tasks which together make up the total operation, to specific persons or teams.
4. Defining the parameters in which the various tasks can be accomplished with minimum effort but maximum efficiency – this may include financial budgets and the need to abide by company codes of ethical practice as, for example, when purchasing materials.
5. Delegating authority so as to ensure that each member of staff clearly understands his responsibilities and accountability. This is particularly important in an enterprise that is organised on departmental lines; without a clearly defined structure of authority a subordinate may be unaware of decision making limits which could lead to a situation of conflict.

TYPES OF AUTHORITY RELATIONSHIPS

Line Management Authority

In line management organisation the lines of authority are clearly defined and there is a direct subordinate/superior relationship. The various aspects of authority rank from the top of the hierarchy down the line with each member aware of to whom he is responsible and those who are accountable to him. The advantages of this are (i) job descriptions can be precise, (ii) decision making is quick, (iii) clear lines of responsibility are shown, (iv) problem areas are easy to identify.

As regards the last point, this may not always be an advantage in that each problem which arises may have to be tackled by the manager without recourse to the specialist; certainly in a large company this will not do and a suitable alternative has to be found.

Functional Authority

In a functional authority organisation each specialist function will be placed under a professionally qualified and experienced head whose parameters of operation would be laid down by the board of directors or general manager. There would be specialists in charge of such areas as Sales and Marketing, Purchasing, Accounting and Control, and Personnel. In each of the individual units of the company, specific areas would be the responsibility of the particular head of department actually working there, the advantage being that each is a specialist and has complete authority over his own area. At head office level there may be an executive or adviser who decides the general policy for the entire company, but in this case there must be a clearly defined structure so as to avoid any possible duplication of effort.

Line and Staff Authority

This type of organisation appears to combine the advantages of both previous styles as it operates partly on functional lines together with a line management approach, so that it retains central control with the specialists having no direct control over individual managers or departmental heads, but helping in an advisory capacity to establish a framework of operations. A major drawback of this type of organisation is that it can be used only by large groups which can afford to employ the necessary range of specialists.

THE ORGANISATION, THE MANAGER, THE MANAGEMENT

The role of the manager should be easy to define because of the known framework but in practice it is somewhat ambiguous since satisfaction with traditionally established practices frequently prevents major reorganisation, with the result that formalised organisation structures have failed to be introduced. It is difficult to know where the fault lies but it appears to be a combination of pride in craft traditions and a misunderstanding of staff development procedures by the major catering groups. The result of this is that the very people who could make a worthwhile contribution to better food and beverage operations, for example, head chefs, are seldom promoted to the post of food and beverage

320

manager, the result being that their specialist knowledge does not become available to bring about any changes in established practices.

It is relevant here to pose the question as to whether a head chef or head waiter is a manager or a head of department. In the organisation of a large establishment they are actually managers who are in charge of major departments that can be virtually self-contained. But there are other instances where the combination of line and staff organisation is in use and there is more central control exerted. A head chef may be given authority to place orders on nominated suppliers who are under contractual agreement negotiated by head office. What happens in such instances is that there are structural guide-lines rather than explicit statements which have to be followed to the letter.

The Managerial Task

The major responsibilities of the line or functional manager are to do the following:

1. Interpret the objectives of the company, or in some cases, to determine the objectives.
2. Plan how these objectives can be achieved.
3. Organise and establish the framework in which these objectives can be achieved efficiently.
4. Monitor, control and co-ordinate progress towards the achievement of objectives.

These responsibilities are all applicable to the persons in charge and responsible for the main departments of a catering operation. In the following pages of this chapter an attempt will be made to show how the techniques of management are related to the practical organisation of the kitchen, dining room and bars and their ancillary departments.

THE KITCHEN

The kitchen is the department where food as a raw material is processed into dishes by a team of cooks working under a head cook or head chef, whose responsibility it is to allocate the work load between the various kitchen sections and to see that the results are of the expected standard. The head cook organises his kitchen on specialisms by assigning particular tasks to specialists in those tasks. This is known as the 'partie' system in which the team of cooks of various grades is divided into separate sections each dealing with a particular aspect of cookery and supplying certain sections of the menu; the term kitchen brigade is

321

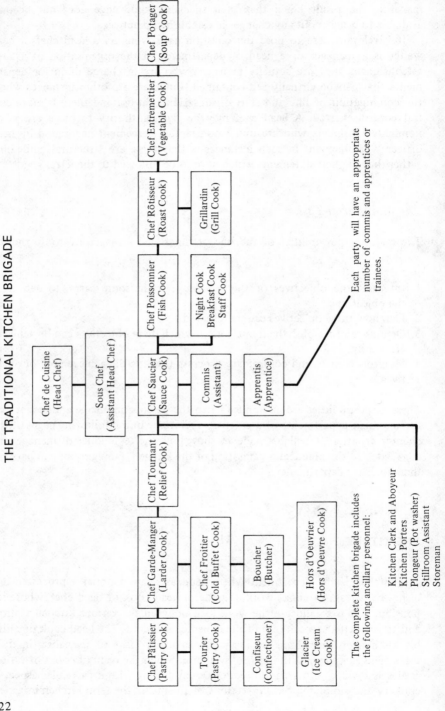

Figure 43
THE TRADITIONAL KITCHEN BRIGADE

Chef Potager
(Soup Cook)

Chef Entremettier
(Vegetable Cook)

Chef Rôtisseur
(Roast Cook)

Grillardin
(Grill Cook)

Chef Poissonnier
(Fish Cook)

Night Cook
Breakfast Cook
Staff Cook

Chef de Cuisine
(Head Chef)

Sous Chef
(Assistant Head Chef)

Chef Saucier
(Sauce Cook)

Commis
(Assistant)

Apprentis
(Apprentice)

Each party will have an appropriate number of commis and apprentices or trainees.

Chef Tournant
(Relief Cook)

Chef Garde-Manger
(Larder Cook)

Chef Froitier
(Cold Buffet Cook)

Boucher
(Butcher)

Hors d'Oeuvrier
(Hors d'Oeuvre Cook)

Chef Pâtissier
(Pastry Cook)

Tourier
(Pastry Cook)

Confiseur
(Confectioner)

Glacier
(Ice Cream Cook)

The complete kitchen brigade includes the following ancillary personnel:

Kitchen Clerk and Aboyeur
Kitchen Porters
Plongeur (Pot washer)
Stillroom Assistant
Storeman

322

sometimes used to describe the full staff of a kitchen. All kitchens of whatever size and in any type of catering operation run on this system, albeit modified or adapted where necessary. It leads to efficient operation and better results when measured against the moving of staff from one task to another during the course of the daily routine. It functions well in all situations from a fast food unit to continuous production cook-freeze or cook-chill operation.

Fig. 43 shows this brigade in the form of a chart and in its most expansive form; it is subject to modification by amalgamating some of the parties according to the type and amount of business, as well as the physical space available in a particular kitchen.

The kitchen of a smaller commercial establishment could be staffed according to the following chart, Fig. 44. Here the Head Chef might actually run one of the sections, either the sauce or the larder and have the assistance overall of one of his Chefs de Partie acting at times as Sous Chef. The Head Chef will therefore take an active part in running his partie as a working Head Chef, then at meal times taking over the service at the hotplate. If administrative duties took up a lot of his time to the detriment of the partie he would need to engage a senior chef to run it, whilst he advised and assisted wherever necessary.

Figure **44**
THE KITCHEN STAFF OF A SMALLER COMMERCIAL ESTABLISHMENT

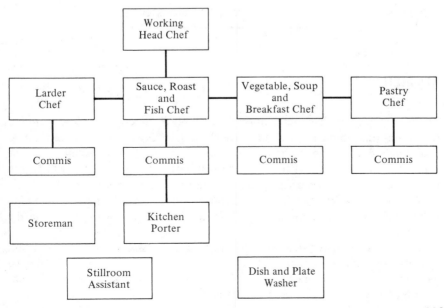

In the kitchen of a large-scale establishment such as a hospital or factory the staffing might follow the chart as set out in Fig. 45. There will be less emphasis on specialisms with every member of staff being capable of carrying out any of the necessary duties. The Head Cook or Kitchen Superintendent would probably run the section producing main meals and carry out such administrative duties as delegated by the caterer. The assistant cooks could move from one section to another on a rota so as to ensure all-round experience.

Figure 45
THE KITCHEN STAFF OF A LARGE-SCALE ESTABLISHMENT

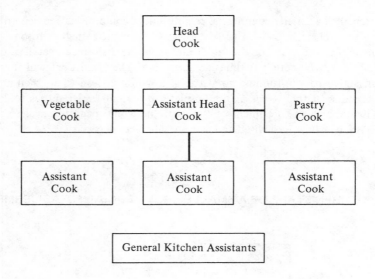

KITCHEN ORGANISATION

The first step in kitchen organisation is to establish the scope, size and nature of the operation. Normally guide-lines will have laid down the objectives, nature and standard of the operation; the more luxurious the establishment is, the higher will be the prices charged and the certainty that the kitchen will be run on related classical lines offering mainly à la Carte dishes with perhaps a Table d'Hôte menu. As far as staffing is concerned a busy establishment of this kind serving say two hundred dinners could well require thirty or more staff in the kitchen.

The organisation requires that the Head Chef breaks down the overall task into its components, grouping these in an orderly sequence of self-contained sections. Precise guide-lines cannot be laid down to cover all types of kitchens but the following are those most usually adhered to.

324

1. The production of a work schedule which indicates exactly what has to be produced for any one meal in accordance with the menu.
2. The purchase of materials according to the requirements by means of the agreed procedures.
3. The issue of these materials for processing.
4. The preparation of meals.
5. The distribution of meals to customers.
6. The organisation of the ancillary support services of washing up and cleaning.
7. The staffing of the kitchen groups and supportive services.

Now that these components have been identified thought must be given to their actual location to enable the progression of activities to proceed in a logical sequence; from these the levels of manning can also be determined.

The sequence of operations in a kitchen of any size can then be shown as in Fig. 46.

Figure 46
SEQUENCE OF OPERATIONS

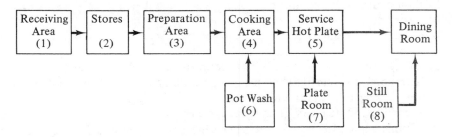

In Fig. 46 the areas 1 to 8 usually all come under the control of the Head Chef and he allocates the number of staff required to operate each, basing it on experience or by an allowance of manpower per customer served according to the type of operation.

Kitchen Staff

The following details cover all the staff who might be employed in the kitchen of a large organisation and give an outline of the duties and responsibilities of each. As previously indicated the actual names, grades and numbers of staff is determined by the operation and can be scaled down to suit all types and sizes of kitchen.

The Head Chef (Chef de Cuisine) The Head Chef holds one of the most important positions in a catering establishment; on his knowledge and expertise depends

325

to a great extent the success or otherwise of the establishment and its reputation. He is responsible for producing or advising on a menu which will satisfy the customer and at the same time provide a satisfactory financial return for the business. He will have to keep abreast of changes in taste and fashion as they arise which can entail interpreting and adapting traditional recipes to the specific need of the clientele.

The Head Chef determines the quality of materials required for his needs and must communicate these by means of purchasing specifications to the store-keeper who places the orders. When compiling menus he must take care to allocate the work evenly amongst the sections of his kitchen and must interpret and communicate his desired standards to his staff. He will be responsible overall for the correct preparation, presentation and qualities of all dishes, both hot and cold, which are served to the customer. To do this efficiently he needs to proceed thus:

1. Keep up-to-date with information on seasonal availability so that he can keep menus fresh and interesting with a suitable variety of items.
2. Note customer's complaints and take immediate action to rectify them, at the same time bringing this to the notice of his staff.
3. Ensure that there is no unnecessary waste and that regular stocktaking is carried out.
4. Maintain the desired kitchen percentage of profit and be good at interpreting figures.
5. Produce the annual budget for his department and operate within it.
6. Be a good disciplinarian and maintain a code of conduct in his staff that is ethical; keep calm under stress.
7. Maintain good standards of safety and hygiene.
8. See that apprentices and trainees are receiving proper tuition.
9. Maintain good relationships with his staff and with other heads of department and management.

The Assistant Head Chef (Sous Chef) A large busy kitchen will need more than one to carry out the volume of work with the most senior acting as the immediate subordinate to the Head Chef. If banqueting is part of the operation then there will be one Sous Chef specifically for this. Others could be related to the early and late shifts. They will all participate in the service on the hotplate. A good Sous Chef needs to have expert knowledge of all sectors of the kitchen. His main duties are related to the following:

1. Relieve the head chef in his absence and assist in day to day administration and organisation of the kitchen.
2. Countersign stores requisitions.
3. Take charge of banqueting work.
4. Arrange duty rotas, days off, holidays.
5. Act as staff manager to the kitchen.
6. Maintain good staff relationships.

326

The Sauce Cook (Chef Saucier) It is generally recognised that the Chef Saucier is the most senior of all the Chefs de Partie and it follows that the sauce section has great demands placed on it in terms of expertise and volume of work. He is responsible for:

1. The cooking of all main meat dishes that are cooked by boiling, stewing braising, poêling, and shallow frying together with their garnishes.
2. The preparation of most hot sauces, for use by himself and the other parties.

The Larder Cook (Chef Garde Manger) The larder is the kitchen storeroom and distribution point for all main perishable commodites. A good larder cook must ensure that all items are properly stored and used fresh and that all usable left-over dishes are reissued so as to avoid waste. In a large busy kitchen the larder cook would be assisted by a butcher to deal with meat, a fishmonger to prepare raw fish, someone to prepare cold buffet work and others to prepare hors-d'oeuvres, salads, the cheese board and fruit baskets. The duties of the larder cook entail responsibility for:

1. The preparation and cutting of meat for cooking.
2. The preparation of poultry and game according to requirements.
3. The cleaning and preparation of fish.
4. The sending of raw prepared commodities for cooking to the correct partie at the right time and in the right quantities.
5. The preparation of hors-d'oeuvre and the presentation of special hors-d'oeuvre such as caviar, smoked salmon and foie gras.
6. The preparation of items for cocktail parties and receptions such as canapés, sandwiches and fillings for bouchées.
7. The preparation of aspic jellies and chaudfroid for use in cold buffet items, and the decoration of these dishes, also galantines, cold pies and pâtés.
8. The preparation of simple and composed salads together with the necessary dressings and cold sauces.
9. The preparation of the cheese board and fruit baskets.
10. The correct storage and control of all items held in the cold store, and the marking of the daily stocksheets showing goods received, issued and in stock.
11. Advising the head chef on suitable items for the menu.

The Pastry Cook (Chef Pâtissier) The pastry department of a large kitchen often runs as a separate entity under the overall direction of a chef who is responsible directly to the Head Chef. This is because of the specialist nature of the work; the staff do not usually move to other parties as do those in the main kitchen. In a large busy pastry there are specialists for the preparation of basic pastes utilised in the making of pastries and sweet dishes. Others are responsible for the making of ice cream, sweets and quite often for the creation of presentation pieces in sugar, gum paste and nougat. The pastry cook is responsible for:

1. The preparation, cooking and serving of all hot and cold sweets on the menu, including ice cream.
2. The preparation of cakes and pastries for afternoon teas and receptions.
3. Preparation of petits-fours; the baking, icing and decorating of birthday and wedding cakes. centre pieces in nougat and chocolate.
4. The preparation of flan cases, vols-au-vent and barquettes for filling with hot or cold mixtures in the main kitchen or larder.
5. The covering of pies and puddings.
6. The making of hot soufflés sometimes including savoury ones.

The Fish Cook (Chef Poissonier) The cooking of fish and its accompanying sauces calls for a high degree of skill, together with a certain feeling for delicacy and elegance. A good palate and a degree of finesse are the two most important attributes required by this job. The fish cook is responsible for:

1. The cooking and presentation of all hot fish and shellfish dishes except those that are deep fried or grilled.
2. The cooking of fish and shellfish for cold presentation by the larder.
3. The preparation of all hot fish sauces plus others such as Hollandaise and Béchamel.

The Roast Cook (Chef Rôtisseur) The roast cook's work is based on three methods of cookery – roasting, grilling and deep frying – and it covers a very wide range of items including fish, meat, poultry, game, potatoes and vegetables. He is also responsible for the production of gravies and some of the sauces that accompany these dishes as well as all the savouries. This job demands sound practical knowledge and experience of one of the basic cooking techniques, namely roasting. In large kitchens a member of this section is responsible as grill cook for all grilled items of food.

The Vegetable Cook (Chef Entremettier) The vegetable cook's responsibility is for the preparation of all vegetables and potatoes that are on the menu and others that are served as a garnish with a main dish. The savoury soufflés are often made to order by this section. Although the position does not enjoy the same status in the hierarchy of the kitchen as perhaps the sauce cook, nevertheless the job calls for a high degree of organisation and attention to detail. Because of the amount of work usually involved in this section it is usually well staffed with assistants. The description Chef Entremettier, which may appear illogical when applied to the vegetable cook, dates from the time when vegetables were served as a dish in their own right and was sandwiched between two other more important courses. In the nineteenth century this course was referred to as Entremets and comprised a selection of sweet and vegetable dishes. Today the word Entremets refers solely to the sweet course.

The Soup Cook (Chef Potager) The preparation of all soups, eggs and farinaceous dishes is the responsibility of the soup cook; his job entails the preparation of special stocks for soups and others for general kitchen use. He is responsible for the egg and farinaceous dishes that feature on the day's menu – usually only for lunch – and receives the sauces to accompany them from either the sauce or fish cook. Only a large busy kitchen would warrant a separate soup section otherwise the work is part of the vegetable cook's responsibilities.

The Relief Cook (Chef Tournant) A relief cook is usually employed only in a large busy kitchen that is open seven days a week. His role is to act as relief for the other chefs de partie when they take their day off during the week or at holiday time. He needs to know the work of each section except perhaps that of the pastry and larder where the first commis usually takes over.

The Breakfast Cook This person usually works to a fixed menu that seldom changes since it covers most customers' requirements. Cooking for this menu calls for some degree of organisation and speed in operation to satisfy the customer in terms of the items of the menu being freshly cooked, but because of the level of culinary skills and experience required it does not rank as a separate partie.

The breakfast cook usually assists on the vegetable section when the breakfast service ends.

The Night Cook (Chef de Nuit) The night cook is engaged in an all night restaurant or hotel offering night floor service. He has to have experience of all the parties since he usually works alone. He may be called on to produce quite elaborate dishes but usually the bulk of his work consists of making sandwiches, serving staff suppers and preparing early breakfasts.

Assistant Cooks (Commis) The commis are the assistants who work under the orders of the Chefs de Partie. They are graded as first, second, and third commis according to length of service and ability with the first Commis being the direct assistant to his Chef de Partie and responsible for directing much of the work of the other commis.

In addition to the above there are the staff employed in the ancillary departments of the kitchen who are dealt with later on in this chapter.

KITCHEN ROUTINE

This relates to the routine or work as carried out in kitchens and how the food is produced by the various members of staff. It is very difficult to describe a pattern of routine which is completely common to all kitchens as the routine

329

varies according to factors such as the type of business, the menu, prices charged, and so on. The common factors, however, are those of ordering, storage and distribution of commodites for their preparation and cooking and according to envisaged numbers of customers; the serving of the prepared food directly to the customer or service staff; the cleaning and hygiene of the kitchens and ancillary departments; and the cleaning and maintenance of equipment. However, it is as well to look at some associated factors and to detail some of the problems peculiar to them.

The length of the working day and the number of days worked each week depends on the type of business; in many instances such as in a hospital the kitchen never closes and there is always someone on duty day and night for every day of the year. In a school the kitchen would be open from 10.00 am to 3.00 pm daily from Monday to Friday only. The dining room connected to every kitchen has to be open for some of the time to serve the food, unless the kitchen is one that runs on continuous production line and deep freezes or chills the meals; here production and distribution are totally divorced.

The routine of any kitchen is based on the menu and the expected number of meals to be prepared. A fairly close estimate of numbers can be based on the figure for the business done on the same day the previous year and/or on the number of bookings; the time of year and the expected weather also have a bearing on estimated business. As to the number of portions of each dish to be produced, this can be gained from records of numbers sold and an estimate of the comparative popularity of dishes. In institutional catering the number of consumers is usually fairly steady. The big decision becomes – How many portions of each menu choice should be produced so that those who come at the last sitting are not disappointed because some dishes are sold out?

In many establishments a combined à la Carte and Table d'Hôte menu is used on which any special dishes, including seasonal items, can also be featured. This conventional type of operation can be very complicated and requires good organisation together with full co-operation between the kitchen and dining room.

An analysis of such an operation would reveal these requirements: (i) the staff of the kitchen must be seen as a whole with each section working in close co-operation with the others to ensure smooth operation, (ii) each member of staff must conscientiously fulfil his role in the organisation, (iii) production must be able to meet demand even though the forecast of business may be faulty, (iv) resources of materials and equipment must be at such a level that they can meet all possible demands, (v) the problem of over-production and subsequent utilisation must be overcome, and (vi) some spare capacity of staff is needed to meet any extraordinary demands of business.

The problem which arises from an à la Carte operation is that of keeping sufficient stocks of perishable items in perfect condition so that customers receive fresh food that has been freshly cooked to order. If some food has to be used up before it starts to deteriorate it should be sold off at a lower price on the Table d'Hôte menu; its profitability, however, as a possible à la Carte dish is of course lost.

330

PRODUCTIVITY

With a called order or à la Carte system where only a certain amount of preparation is carried out beforehand and where all or most of the food is cooked as
required, it is difficult to bring productivity up to a desirable standard. This is
because there is some standing about or wasted time inherent in the system.
Much of the work will come in a rush over a short period of time, passing from
one section of the kitchen to another as the various courses of the meal are
served. It would thus be useful to distinguish between the terms production and
productivity. Production can normally be defined as the transformation of an
item from its raw state into a finished product. Productivity, however, refers to
an outcome of the production process where the product goes through a cycle;
using a system approach the cycle can be presented as in Fig. 47.

Figure 47
PRODUCTION CYCLE

It can be explained as follows:

1. Productivity results when a higher output is achieved from the same input,
   e.g. more portions are obtained from the same weight because of less shrinkage.
2. It can also result when a higher output is achieved from a lower input, e.g.
   fewer man-hours are needed to produce the same number of meals of a
   similar quality.
3. It results when a slight increase in input produces a considerable increase
   in output, e.g. a slightly larger capacity deep fryer may increase the number
   of items considerably over the number previously produced whilst still using
   the same number of man-hours.

Thus in order to remain competitive an organisation must strive continuously
to improve its productivity. In the usual catering business, however, most
attempts to improve the utilisation of resources in the kitchen have met with
little success and batch production on a short-run system generally achieves
good results and thus the necessary customer satisfaction. Most manufacturing
industries operate on a long-run basis of continuous production which permits
of maximum utilisation of the productive resources; this is done mainly by
altering the nature of the operation by utilising a capital intensive method of
production as an alternative to labour intensive methods.

By its nature, catering is a labour intensive industry and any move away from this will need to be prompted by some form of technological innovation. Manufacturers of catering equipment have been as slow as the catering industry itself in introducing new ideas; perhaps the major innovation was the introduction of the cook-freeze system in the early 1960s. A survey at that time indicated that only 35-40 per cent of a cook's time was actually spent on preparing and cooking food, the remainder of his working hours being taken up with routine chores. Obviously a method of continuous production would save much wasted time and increase productivity, also the resources of space, equipment, labour and energy would be more fully utilised by such a system. It would show great savings contrasting sharply with those obtained in traditional methods of food production. It is recognised that the partie system can be wasteful and cause higher prices, because even when every partie works continuously they do not always reach peak efficiency at the same time; inevitably some wasted time and capacity is inbuilt in this system. The big troughs in the daily routine have traditionally been offset by having staff work on split duties but this system, although still widely used, is not popular and enlightened employers offer straight shifts that help with recruitment. This system is not necessarily more expensive to operate since staff who work unsocial hours have to be paid extra.

Another important factor is the non-utilisation of parts of the kitchen area and its facilities during the off-peak periods, which means that rates are being paid on under-used premises – all these drawbacks to efficiency could be overcome if a process of continuous production was to be introduced. Technology might well provide the way although many long cherished traditional rituals and attitudes would have to change.

CONTINUOUS PRODUCTION TECHNIQUES

The systems that provide continuous production are cook-freeze and cook-chill and the way they function is by concentrating on the production of one single item at a time and doing it on a large scale. The item must be produced according to a rigid formula which covers all the various aspects of buying, issuing, cooking, packaging, and preserving – on a large scale like this, there is no room for costly errors. The kitchens must be planned to allow for a good flow line of operations and the fixed equipment must be of a capacity to contain the number of portions being cooked, bearing in mind the economies of scale that have to be produced with production being in the thousands of portions rather than in hundreds. The economies of scale mean that a small number of staff can cope with large numbers of portions and that the facilities are in use throughout the day, giving new meaning to the terms input and output because it is obvious now that production costs per dish can be very low. The problem with continuous production is that of preserving the meals once they have been produced, weighed and packed, and is dependent on the system selected; an account of such systems will be found in Chapter 12.

THE DINING ROOM

There are many different kinds of dining rooms and many different names to describe them accordingly to type and usage; to a certain extent the name used indicate the large-scale type of non-commercial eating place; bistro, brasserie, food and service are offered. Names such as cafeteria, refectory, canteen and hall indicate the large-scale type of non-commercial eating place; bistro brasserie, buttery, trattoria, auberge, snack bar indicate small informal places for meals; espresso bar, coffee shop, tea room, milk bar and ice cream parlour are self explanatory; chop house, grill room, rôtisserie are obviously places that specialise in grills and roasts, while the term restaurant covers a whole range of eating places which serve full meals.

A particular dining room reflects the needs of its customer and the particular character should be obvious in the many forms that each kind can take. The atmosphere plays a part in defining a type of restaurant and its customers. For example, a fast food place usually has almost clinically clean surroundings, bright lighting, straight-backed chairs and no distracting decor so that the whole is conducive to a quick turnover of customers and which allow the fixed costs to be distributed over a large number of consumers. This can be contrasted with a restaurant at the other end of the scale where the atmosphere is restful and discreet and the customer is encouraged to stay in the hope that he will continue spending his money. In the same way that there are many kinds of restaurants and many different ways of running them, there are bound to be many variations to basic organisational and operational techniques, so this account of their function is in general terms.

The Function of the Dining Room

Every dining room through its atmosphere, the food and drink and the people who do the serving should create an experience that is far removed from that of eating a normal meal at home. The background of the room and the pleasant personality of staff must ally intrinsically with the food to make the everyday need to eat a pleasurable occasion. The contribution of staff whether they be silver service waiters or counterhands is of much significance in achieving this. The role played by service staff can be illustrated by another reference to a fast food operation where the accent is on the youth and liveliness of staff that is equal to the customers', and where the uniform they wear is colourful and well designed. In contrast the high-class restaurant may have its waiting staff attired in formal evening dress which suits the atmosphere of leisurely eating, possibly coupled with dancing until the small hours.

STAFFING OF A DINING ROOM

Just as there are many different kinds of dining rooms so are there several different ways of staffing them, usually according to the type of service offered and the prices charged. The traditional hierarchy of a luxury restaurant sets the pattern and can be modified according to varying requirements. This set-up is as illustrated in Fig. 45.

The Restaurant Manager   The restaurant manager is in charge of the entire food service operation. His most important attribute would be a wide knowledge of all aspects of catering. He usually has an ability with languages, is conversant with current affairs and needs to be diplomatic and tactful in his dealings with customers. His personality and appearance should reflect his calling and his customers' expectations. Until fairly recently it was not uncommon for a restaurant manager to create a clientele who would follow him on his taking a new appointment in another establishment. There was often a special rapport between the manager and his customers which suggests that personality often has more pulling power than sumptuous surroundings. The restaurant manager is responsible for:

1. The setting of standards of service in all areas including the bars and reception or foyer.
2. The carrying out of internal training in all the various aspects of food and beverage service.
3. The organisation of an efficient system of table reservations so as to make the proper use of space by combining customers' comfort and maximum occupancy.
4. The organisation of staff rotas to cover days off, sickness, holidays, etc.
5. The arrangements for any special displays.
6. The instruction of staff in the proper knowledge of dishes on the menu and service procedures for them.
7. The demonstration of specialised service techniques including flambé and Guéridon work.
8. The reception of clients on their arrival, the monitoring of their satisfaction during the meal, and bidding them goodbye on leaving.
9. The supervision of the smooth running of the operation and dealing with any problems or complaints that may arise.

The First Head Waiter   He is the deputy to the restaurant manager and he too must have a wide knowledge and experience of catering, be able to converse

334

easily with guests, have an ability with languages and be a good staff manager. His responsibilities will include:

1. Assisting the restaurant manager in his duties.
2. Allocating waiters to stations and rotating staff between stations so as to build up confidence in staff and ensure evenness of duties.
3. Assisting by carrying out specialised carving and guéridon work.
4. Taking charge of the restaurant in the absence of the restaurant manager.

The Reception Head Waiter He should be able to converse well over the telephone, have an ability with languages and have clear, legible handwriting. His duties will entail being responsible for:

1. The taking of reservations, entering them in the reservations diary and keeping this in a correct and proper state of order.
2. Instructing selected staff in the taking of reservations.
3. Conducting customers to their reserved table and assisting in seating.
4. Ensuring that the restaurant is 'dressed' correctly and that customers are accorded the deference due to them.

The Section or Station Head Waiter He should have good organising ability and be able to maintain good relationships with subordinate staff. There could be several Station Head Waiters in a large establishment. He is responsible for:

1. The smooth running of a section of the dining room comprising up to four stations.
2. Ensuring that his section is adequately staffed and briefed.
3. Seeing that the area is clean and tidy.
4. Seeing that the tables are correctly laid and the station carefully stocked.
5. Receiving the guests from the Reception Head Waiter and after assisting them to seat, explain the menu, suggesting dishes and wine and taking the order.
6. Supervising his section during the service and dealing with any incidents or complaints.

The Station Waiter He is in charge of a specific area of the room comprised of from four to six tables seating up to twenty customers and is assisted by a number of Commis Waiters. He is responsible for:

1. The carrying out of the actual service of food to the customers after taking their order or receiving it from his Station Head Waiter.
2. Sending the Commis with the order to the kitchen to collect the food; he must be able to write clearly and correctly.
3. Remembering what each customer has ordered so as to avoid having to ask them who ordered what.
4. Serving his tables in correct order so that no client is kept waiting between courses.

335

5. Having an eye for details so that accompaniments and condiments are offered at the right time.
6. Presenting the bill, taking the money to the cashier and returning with the receipted bill and change; avoiding shortages on the bill.
7. Clearing and relaying the tables.

The Commis Waiter He does the clearing of his station and the lay up of the tables. He is responsible for:

1. Assisting with general preparation, e.g. filling cruets, fetching laundry, etc.
2. Fetching food from the kitchen, assisting with the service, usually vegetables, sauces, etc.; assisting with clearing the table of dirties and carrying soiled crockery and cutlery to the wash up.
3. Assisting with the easier parts of the service, e.g. serving coffee under the supervision of the Station Waiter.

In some restaurants an aspiring commis waiter may be made up to a point midway between a commis and a station waiter and be given a small station to look after.

The young trainee waiter is sometimes known as the Commis Débarrasseur; with his foot on the bottom rung of the ladder he must be of smart appearance, alert and have the ability to get on well with people even though his duties at this stage are concerned only with cleaning up, taking out dirty dishes, bringing in clean plates and perhaps clearing the table.

The Head Wine Waiter The service of drink in a high-class restaurant is operated by separate waiting staff with a sound knowledge of wine and other drinks and their service. These members of staff are called wine waiters and they often wear a badge depicting a bunch of grapes to indicate their role; they may wear the insignia of the Guild of Sommeliers, their own professional body, and often wear a different colour jacket from the ordinary waiters.

The Head Wine Waiter is in charge of all wine waiting staff and is responsible for the service of all wine, spirits and soft drinks sales and service in the dining room. His responsibilities involve:

1. Taking the customers' orders for all drinks except those dispensed by the stillroom, e.g. tea, coffee.
2. Knowing the wine list intimately, being able to describe to customers the characteristic of each in proper terms and advising which wines go best with which food.
3. Knowing about other drinks such as aperitifs, cocktails, non-alcoholic beverages, liqueurs and beers.
4. Knowing when a wine is in poor condition and why.
5. Suggesting additions to the wine list.
6. Being able to open bottles correctly and to decant fine wines.

7. Ensuring that the wines are served at the correct temperature, in the correct type of glass.
8. Instructing his wine waiters and commis in their duties.
9. Ensuring that a liaison is maintained with the cellar regarding stock levels, vintages, etc.
10. Ensuring the correct functioning of the dispense bar and its efficient control, although in some circumstances this responsibility may be that of the head bar-tender.
11. Ensuring that his section makes a significant contribution to the profitability of the operation.

Wine waiters carry out the service of wine for a number of stations working in liaison with the food waiters but coming under the jurisdiction of the head wine waiter.

In addition there are a number of commis wine waiters whose duties would be mainly concerned with bringing the right kind of glasses for different wines.

There are a number of ancillary staff connected with the dining room and they are dealt with further on in this chapter.

FOOD AND BEVERAGE SERVICE

The quality of the food produced must be matched by that of the service and no matter what form it takes it must be carried out correctly so that the customer is not kept waiting because of inattentive staff. Whether it be in a cafeteria, a help-yourself buffet or a dining room using plate service or Geúridon service, the customer must be given full satisfaction.

The job of being a food server is often looked on as a menial one because apart from keeping the customer happy there is no tangible evidence that anything has been produced, but in fact there is a great art in serving food correctly and fine manual skills are a requisite of this job. The laying of a table whether it be in a canteen or in a high-class restaurant must not be looked upon as a daily chore but as an orderly routine which requires a measure of adroitness. Staff engaged in the service of food, again whether they serve from behind a counter or hand things at the table, must be courteous by nature, affable but with a touch of deference and civility as though to imply that the customer is always right; and of course he must be skilled and dexterous.

TYPES OF SERVICE

The type of service adopted by an eating place will vary according to (I) the objectives that establish the framework and the parameters in which it is carried out, (ii) the consumer's needs in terms of the meal experience and food, and the time he has available to eat it in, and (iii) the kind of dining room – ranging from that offering the informal, quick service of a sandwich to the most elaborate, luxury restaurant.

Obviously prices and standard of service should go hand in hand but the spectrum of eating places is so wide that forms of service cannot always be equated with the prices charged. Each establishment is a composite product in which the food is balanced or enhanced by the ambience in which it is served.

There are only two main forms of food service – direct service in which the customer goes to the food himself as in a cafeteria, school meal service or fast food outlet, and indirect service where food is taken to the customer on a plate or served from dishes by a third person in the form of food service personnel who comes between the service point and the customer. The following gives details of the most widely used methods of service.

Plate Service

This method of service was once associated with very modest establishments using unskilled staff, but is now more widely used having been adopted by very high-class establishments. Here the food is arranged on the plate in an artistic and predetermined manner ready to set before the customer. At a more ordinary level the main item of food is placed on the plate and the vegetables in a dish, so that all the server has to do is to place the prepared plate in front of the customer with the dish of vegetables near at hand on the table and to let the customer help himself. This method became popular in the United States in the 1920s and was commonly used in many good class establishments. It was not until the 1950s, however, that caterers in the UK began to question the need to employ highly skilled staff merely to place a plate of food in front of the customer. But plate service should not be considered as an inferior form of presenting food because a good deal of thought is needed to get it right, and it is better to use this method than to risk completely unskilled staff spoiling the work of the cooks by serving the food in an untidy and boorish manner.

Self Service

This form of service was popularised during the Second World War when there was a shortage of labour in the catering industry. It is now the most widely used method not only in industrial and institutional catering but also in fast food operations and all other units where quick service is essential. It is a direct form of service with no one intervening between the server and the consumer. The consumer goes to the counter to help himself or to select what he wants and have the counter hand place it on the plate. Sometimes the form of serving some meals is a combination of this and plate service when the guest serves himself to

338

one of the courses, as in a carvery where he goes to the counter and carves the joint and helps himself to vegetables. A prestigeous form of self service is used for buffets, balls, weddings receptions and cocktail parties where there is a display of hot and cold food to which guests help themselves, often assisted by a number of staff who carve and portion some of the items. Help yourself service, therefore, is not an inferior form of service any more than is plate service; it satisfies a simple but functional need and it requires that food be presented neatly in identifiable portions and in a manner which will allow large numbers to obtain their requirements quickly.

In the industrial version the dining room supervisor will allocate staff to the various service points and the organisation can be expressed as in Fig. 48.

The trolley hands are used to clear the dirty dishes from tables and to keep the dining room tidy; if there is a self-clearing system they wheel the loaded trolleys to the wash up. The runner is needed if there is a distance between dining room and kitchen and commutes backwards and forwards with supplies of food.

Figure 48
STAFFING STRUCTURE OF A SELF-SERVICE OPERATION

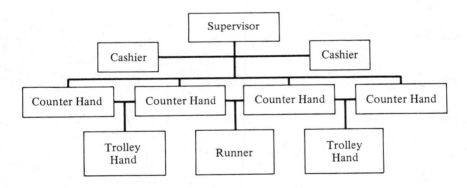

Silver Service

This method of service costs more to operate than others mainly because it requires an adequate number of skilled staff to serve it and expensive equipment on which to display it. The staffing structure for this kind of service is as shown in Fig. 49, the number of each rank being according to the estimated number of customers likely to patronise the restaurant which is, of course, affected by the size of the room, by the prices charged which are a reflection of the standard of the establishment, and to some extent the distance between the room and various service points.

339

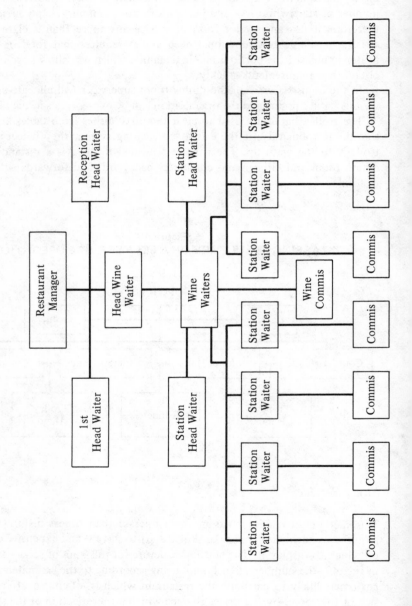

Figure 49

TRADITIONAL STAFFING STRUCTURE OF THE DINING ROOM

Fig. 49 shows only two stations as examples of their size; the number of stations would be in accordance with the size of the room and the level of service offered. It indicates that each station would be staffed by a head waiter, four station waiters and four commis but in addition there could well be a number of assistants for clearing. The number of tables and seats to each station can vary from eight to eighty again according to standard of service and therefore prices charged. The most favoured stations where the important regular customers are seated would have the lesser number of seats so that the service is more attentive than elsewhere in the room. The number of head waiters required depends upon the size of the room and amount of business done; a large brigade would have a staff head waiter whose duties are specifically concerned with staff matters.

The equipment used for silver service may be of stainless steel or electroplated nickel silver but it must be of good quality and kept highly polished. In many instances the silverware is used only as underdishes and covers with the actual food presented on other dishes of the correct size and shape. The waiter is supposed to present the dish for the customer's approval then to transfer it dexterously onto the plate previously placed on the table in front of the guest.

Guéridon Service

This is the same as silver service except that for most of the work the waiter uses a trolley or side table to serve from and a lamp just to put the dishes on for a moment of two to ensure the food is hot; this arrangement of trolley or table and lamp is called the Guéridon. It is supposed to be close to the diners so that not only is the service more direct but for the customer it means more personal contact with his order. This service is perhaps smoother as the waiter can use both hands for serving and can add items to the plate immediately thus obviating any delay. In many dining rooms one of the main dishes, usually the roast, is served from a heated carving trolley which is wheeled to the table for the meat to be carved in view of the client. Otherwise the carving of small items of meat and ducks and chickens is carried out by the station head waiter on the Guéridon.

Flambé Service

Most à la Carte menus feature a small number of dishes that can be actually cooked by the head waiter in front of the guest. They are dishes that can be cooked fairly quickly over a lamp without using over-complicated recipes. Dexterous skills allied to a touch of showmanship are requirements of this style of service, as can be exemplified by the use of spirits and liqueurs and the igniting of these as a flavouring of the dish being prepared. These dishes command a high price for reasons of individual treatment and the cost of the

341

spirit or liqueur used. Correctly speaking, however, so-called Flambé Service really derives from Guéridon Service.

Family Service

This form of service is used on very formal occasions as when royalty is present and at high table in colleges. It is the same as silver service except that guests are proferred the dish containing the food so that they can help themselves to what they need.

SPACE REQUIREMENTS

The various kinds of service have different space requirements per person which means that a dining room has to be planned according to the kind of service it is proposed to offer. The other factors of space allowance are the anticipated number of customers to be catered for at any one sitting and the number of times each seat is to be used during a mealtime. For example, the refectory of an institution catering for 1,000 people need only be large enough to seat 350 at one time if mealtimes can be staggered, so that there are three sittings and the occasion never arises when they all wish to sit down together. In a self service dining room that has tables all of the same size only one-third of the total area need be allocated for circulatory space, just wide enough to allow the movement of the clearing trolley and the area around the serving counter and cash desk.

In the dining room of a restaurant it is necessary to fill the room with as many chairs and tables as the level of comfort will allow, it being estimated that if Silver Service is used approximately 1.5 m^2 per customer is necessary. As an example, in a room that measures say 15 × 11 metres it would be possible to accommodate a hundred customers at ten tables of two, fourteen tables of four and four tables of six which could be divided into five or six stations. The smaller size tables require more space than the larger ones as more circulation space is needed to get around them and the same dining room could accommodate up to 150 persons at larger tables.

THE ROUTINE OF THE DINING ROOM

The daily routine of the dining room starts long before the actual service of the meal. It has to be cleaned, tables laid, glasses polished, cruets filled, table napkins folded, lamps maintained and a hundred and one other duties carried out to ensure that when the service begins, all the preparations have been completed.

The form of routine will vary considerably from one dining room to another and the following details will not necessarily be applicable to them all. This is because there are many patterns of operation, brought about by company policy, type of business, prices charged, staff employed, hours of opening, whether the dining room is open for breakfast and for other meals throughout the day, and so on.

There are, however, three common aspects that apply to all kinds of dining rooms where more than one mealtime per day is offered. These are (i) the preparation period leading to (ii) the service period, followed by (iii) the post-service clearing time with advance preparation for the next meal. The way in which these stages are operated and the times they operate differ considerably from place to place, but for each operation it is important that the main elements are pinpointed so that the operation may be organised around a common pattern of activities.

In Fig. 50 there is an outline of the daily routine and sequence of activities which take place in the average high-class commercial establishment.

THE BARS

The service of drink is a very important and profitable part of a licensed catering establishment and quite often the bar is the first place that the customer encounters on entering a restaurant. The bar should make an impact upon the customer by the way it is decorated and furnished and through the personality of the barman, so that each person immediately feels at ease and has a sense of security and belonging.

The position of barman is one that demands not only a considerable knowledge of all types of drinks and their service, but also the kind of personality that makes him popular with guests because of his pleasant and helpful nature and his ability to please them by his skills at mixing drinks. He should have a good memory for names and faces, and honesty and trustworthiness are essential attributes. The duties and responsibilities of a barman would include:

1. The stocking up of all the drinks required in the bar.
2. The arrangement of the bar in an attractive manner, including such things as nuts, crisps or olives.
3. Maintaining close liaison with the cellar.
4. Ensuring that the bar is run according to the licensing laws and other regulations.
5. Keeping the bar in a state of good hygiene.
6. Seeing that all the necessary equipment is at hand and is in good condition.
7. Knowing the price of each drink; ensuring that money is handled correctly.

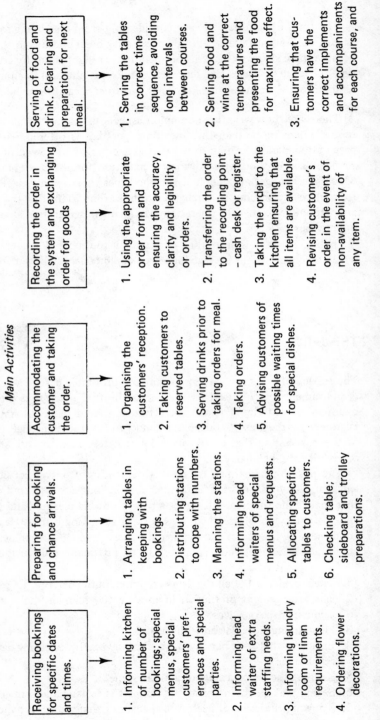

Figure 50
SEQUENCE OF DINING ROOM ACTIVITIES

Main Activities

Receiving bookings for specific dates and times.	Preparing for booking and chance arrivals.	Accommodating the customer and taking the order.	Recording the order in the system and exchanging order for goods	Serving of food and drink. Clearing and preparation for next meal.
1. Informing kitchen of number of bookings; special menus, special customers' preferences and special parties.	1. Arranging tables in keeping with bookings.	1. Organising the customers' reception.	1. Using the appropriate order form and ensuring the accuracy, clarity and legibility or orders.	1. Serving the tables in correct time sequence, avoiding long intervals between courses.
2. Informing head waiter of extra staffing needs.	2. Distributing stations to cope with numbers.	2. Taking customers to reserved tables.	2. Transferring the order to the recording point – cash desk or register.	2. Serving food and wine at the correct temperatures and presenting the food for maximum effect.
3. Informing laundry room of linen requirements.	3. Manning the stations.	3. Serving drinks prior to taking orders for meal.	3. Taking the order to the kitchen ensuring that all items are available.	3. Ensuring that customers have the correct implements and accompaniments for each course, and
4. Ordering flower decorations.	4. Informing head waiters of special menus and requests.	4. Taking orders.	4. Revising customer's order in the event of non-availability of any item.	
	5. Allocating specific tables to customers.	5. Advising customers of possible waiting times for special dishes.		
	6. Checking table; sideboard and trolley preparations.			

344

5. Informing cellar of unusual wine requests.

6. Informing uniformed attendants of special customers.

7. Changing into uniform for service.

5. Collecting items at the appropriate time.

clearing as required during the meal.

4. Ensuring that the customer is billed correctly at the end of the meal and that cash is paid in.

5. Seeing the customer away.

6. After service clearing and preparing for the next meal.

8. Maintaining tight security over stocks and premises.
9. Supervising the work of assistant bar-tenders.
10. Serving drinks at table where necessary.

The dispense bar is usually behind the scenes and does not therefore need any special presentation because customers do not see it. The personality of the dispense barman does not have to be the same as that of the one who is always in contact with the public, unless it is the policy to change staff from one bar to another. In this case, all barman need to be selected on their smartness, pleasant disposition and ability to get on well with people. The dispense bar of a residential establishment is usually open longer than the other bars.

The duties of the dispense barman would be similar to those of the general barman, with the addition of seeing that orders are carried out quickly so that drinks can be brought to the customer as soon as possible, and ensuring that nothing is issued without a proper requisition.

ANCILLARY AREAS

These areas are the stores, stillroom, dish wash and pot wash, all of which play an important role in the total catering operation. The staff who work in these areas often come under the jurisdiction of the chef, even though in some cases the work done in the stillroom and dish wash is more closely concerned with the dining room than with the kitchen. The work of the pot wash and dish wash areas is largely unskilled and repetitive, but provided there is a reliable man in charge, efficiency and some degree of job satisfaction can be obtained, although it must be stressed that the work done in all the ancillary areas is essential to the smooth and efficient running of the whole operation.

The Stores

The importance of well-managed and organised stores cannot be overemphasised. Upon the correct handling and storage of commodities rests so much of the reputation of the establishment. The quality, quantity and availability to the kitchen of food for cooking is a prime responsibility of the stores; not having this quality and quantity available at the right time can have a disastrous effect on the well-ordered operation of the kitchen and can lead to frustration, bad tempers and a general lowering of the standard of cooked dishes. The storeman needs to be technically skilled, highly knowledgeable, honest and trustworthy. The duties and responsibilities of the storeman would include:

1. The ordering of commodities as instructed, and to stock levels.
2. The receipt and safekeeping of goods.

346

3. Protecting foods from contamination and spoilage.
4. The issuing of stores in accordance with requisitions in correct rotation and at the right time.
5. Keeping records as instructed.
7. The safeguarding of stock and premises.
8. Stocktaking as instructed.
9. The care of returnable empties.
10. Acquainting the head chef or person responsible of any goods that require to be used quickly.

The Stillroom

Service from the stillroom is almost entirely to the waiting staff who go there to collect the adjuncts to the meal such as rolls, toast, butter and the beverages such as tea, coffee and fruit juice. The staff come under the orders of the head chef and the cost of running it and of the goods used in it are part of his kitchen costings. It is usual to have a head stillroom person in charge, two if there are two shifts, and a sufficient number of semi-skilled staff to do the routine work of making tea and toast to order, and such things as making butter pats, serving coffee, and squeezing oranges for juice. In some places they prepare the cheese board and fruit basket. In a large-scale establishment the beverage counter is the stillroom. The responsibilities of the head stillroom person would include:

1. Maintaining an adequate stock of fresh beverages, etc. in readiness to serve.
2. Ordering supplies of commodities from the stores.
3. Ensuring that beverages, etc. served are of the desired quality.
4. Issuing goods only against a waiter's check.
5. Making out the duty rosters to ensure the department is always adequately staffed.
6. Maintaining a good standard of hygiene.

Dish-washing Areas

In a large establishment there can be several sections in this area each dealing with a separate category of items namely crockery, cutlery and silverware, and glassware. If housed separately there could be a chargehand in each who works under the direction of a person who is in overall charge.

In a large-scale industrial situation where only crockery and cutlery are handled it is usual to do all the washing up of dining room equipment in one room, using a dish-washing machine that is capable of dealing with large numbers of a restricted range of utensils.

The number of staff required to work in these areas is according to the size of the establishment and amount of business done, also the length of the working

347

day and number of hours of duty worked by staff. In the commerical sector it may be necessary to have two shifts or for staff to work on split duties; some establishments in the welfare sector serve a midday meal only which means that part-time staff can be employed.

A dish-washing machine of a size and capacity to suit the operation helps to lighten the burden of the work in this area and does away with hand washing.

Pot Wash

This area is sometimes referred to as the scullery and is situated in or close to the kitchen whereas the dish-washing areas are more usually adjacent to the dining room. The pot wash does all the kitchen utensils either by hand, mechanical scourer or pot-washing machine and according to the volume of work so there will be one or more persons engaged to do this dirty but important job. It need no longer be considered a degrading and backbreaking job as the use of mechanical aids and detergents has improved its image and made it one that is much easier to carry out and to take pride in its results. The duties of the scullery man would include:

1. Keeping the supply of pots and pans and other kitchen utensils constantly available by washing them up as soon as possible.
2. Ensuring that utensils are thoroughly cleaned and polished.
3. Knowing how to clean the different metals used for pans.
4. Withdrawing from use any utensils which need repairing or refurbishing.
5. Keeping the area in a clean and orderly condition.

In addition to the staff of the dish and pot-washing areas there are others who carry out general cleaning duties. Kitchen porters clean the fixed equipment and other items installed in the kitchen, and keep the floors, walls and the department generally in a good hygienic state. Some of the tasks they carry out have to be done daily but there should also be a planned programme of cleaning and maintenance for those jobs that need to be done periodically. There may be a need to employ a person as a dining room porter whose job is to keep the customer amenities area in clean condition, possibly including the cleanliness of the staff facilities.

A stores porter who works under the orders of the storeman would do the lifting and fetching and carrying of goods, possibly making up the requisitions and delivering them but also keeping the stores and surrounding areas clean. He may also have to keep the rubbish areas in good order of cleanliness. Some establishments find it more desirable to use the services of a firm of industrial cleaners to clean all the areas rather than employing the staff themselves. The advantage is that the cleaning contractor can send in his team at a time when the whole areas are otherwise closed, thus allowing them to do a thorough job without interruption.

348

Customers' Toilets and Cloakrooms

In a large establishment cloakroom attendants will be required to run each of these areas, one for the female side and one for the male side. Their duties would include:

1. Taking charge of customers outdoor apparel, issuing a chit for it, safeguarding it and returning it against presentation of the duplicate chit.
2. Keeping the toilets and wash rooms in a state of perfect hygiene.
3. Maintaining supplies of soap, towels, toilet rolls, etc.
4. Offering simple first aid for such things as headaches or migraine.

11 PRODUCTION AND DISTRIBUTION II – SPECIALISED OPERATIONS

Industrial Catering – Hospital Catering – School Meals Service – College and University Catering – Meals-on-Wheels – Old People's Homes and Day Centres – Vending – Leisure Catering – Motorway Catering – Railway Catering – Catering at Sea – Airline Catering – Catering in HM Forces – Holiday Camps Catering – Kosher Catering – Banqueting – Receptions – Outdoor Catering.

In this chapter is included a brief outline of several of the component areas that go to the making up of the social and welfare sector of the industry and also other catering activities as encountered on motorways, in the air, on the railways, at sea, in the armed services and in catering for special functions.

INDUSTRIAL CATERING

People at work need a break halfway through the working day or shift, and any firm employing more than forty people will have a canteen on the premises where their workers can obtain a meal or refreshments of some kind.

In whatever kind of firm it is, employees feeding is done in one of two ways – either by the firm running the canteen itself, or by having a catering contractor to do it.

The Canteen

In its most basic form a canteen is a room where employees may go to obtain food and drink during authorised breaks. Not a lot of money need be spent on it either for food or equipment and so long as it complies with regulations, and does not cost the firm to much in subsidies, management does not usually mind much whether employees use it or not.

At the other end of the scale the canteen will have a more distinguishing name and reputation and serve very good food for eating in pleasant surroundings and be held in such high esteem that employees regard it as a perk, especially if prices are kept well below those charged in cafés in the vicinity. There are such extremes but there is no reason why a canteen in a factory producing cars should not be as stylish as the cars it produces, or as the one at the head office of a bank or oil company.

There are many reasons for these differences in the way a canteen is run – in some instances the person in charge has many other responsibilities so does not have much time left to look after the canteen – but in the end the reason is usually one of finance. Canteens always have to be subsidised by the firm and this happens whether the staff get their meals for nothing, pay a token sum, or are charged only the costs of food and labour. If the firm tries to make it run like a commercial undertaking, the prices will not then be competitive and employees more likely to go out to get their meals.

This is one of the psychological aspects of staff feeding – when there is a captive clientele who daily face the same surroundings and the same people, no matter how long the menu cycle or how nice the decor, boredom is bound to set in and staff then long for somewhere different for a change. But obviously the idea is to keep them from going out so that the canteen is well patronised and small returns gained from a greater turnover.

Outside competition plays a part in the success of a canteen; if there are no pubs or cafés in the vicinity and no housing estate next to the factory then employees will not go home for lunch because its too far, so business in the canteen should flourish. The canteen manager can tempt customers in by constant menu surprises such as a daily chef's special or a bargain dish – and by catering for all tastes and purses in the range of menus he offers.

Needless to say patronage of canteens by customers varies enormously but few attain 100 per cent and the sad picture is that overall only about a third of those entitled to use the facility offered actually do so. And the reasons why they don't are not concerned solely with the quality of the food and service; psychological factors again, play a large part.

Canteen Operation

The two main ways of operating a canteen are by,

1. **Direct Management** This is where the firm, regardless of what it does or makes, actually runs its own employee feeding facilities. It hires and pays the canteen staff, buys the food and equipment and covers any loss. When refurbishing is necessary it gets it done. The firm has to answer criticism of the way it runs the facility, decide the policy, appoint the catering manager, engage and dismiss staff and become involved in many activities other than those that the company was set up to do. Some firms do all this very successfully and are happy to spend money on keeping staff happy; they have a good image as an employer and can attract and keep good catering staff, even recruiting them from hotels by offering better pay and conditions. It also helps to keep the workforce because it shows concern for their welfare.

2. **Catering Contractors** In contrast, some firms find being directly involved in running their canteen very time consuming and constantly diverting management's attention away from its real job of running the company, so they obtain the services of a catering contractor to come in and run it for them. There are several national and international contractors and hundreds of smaller local ones with the expertise to take over the running of a firm's employee feeding facilities. These firms operate in several different ways but always with the business aim of making a profit; the industrial concern pays for the service offered.

Subsidies

If not all, then nearly every industrial catering unit has to be subsidised irrespective of whether it is carried out by the actual firm or by a catering contractor. Some canteens may make a profit on top of covering the costs of food and labour but this is ignoring the overheads of rates, rent, heating, lighting, equipment, stationery, etc., all of which have to be taken into account in a commercial enterprise. Firms come to accept that employee feeding must be accorded a subsidy but with the expectations of benefit in the form of well-fed staff with a high productivity rate; this may lead to bonus payments but seldom to employees agreeing they can now afford to pay more for meals, thus lowering the subsidy! Another important point is the advantage afforded for social contact in the can-
352

teen during mealtimes, probably the only time during the day for discussion between fellow workers.

Figures gathered by the Industrial Society from their annual surveys indicate that gross profit margins are declining rapidly with costs of consumables and labour rising rapidly while the price of meals has been increased very slowly; the society puts the amount spent on canteen meals at only 2 per cent of gross earnings. The average subsidy is 35 per cent of operating costs and 5.4 per cent of gross profits of the firm.

This system of serving meals at a loss has gone on for so long that it is difficult to reverse it and charge full market prices, yet many staff are happy to be able to leave the work premises for an hour at lunch and pay realistic prices at off-site cafés and public houses. This means they could afford to pay, were the government ever to say to firms that they will no longer be allowed to offset the subsidy against tax.

Effective management does not ignore or undervalue the immense importance of industrial catering so it is certainly here to stay, subsidised or not.

HOSPITAL CATERING

This is one of the few areas where meals are served free of charge to the consumer, a fact which might give the idea that catering for people in hospital is easier than in other areas and that little or no organisational expertise is necessary. In fact the National Health Service expects as much professionalism from its catering officers and kitchen staff as any other employer. Consumer research into patients requirements, together with planning, productivity targets, proper use of manpower and control of resources, are all aspects of the hospital caterer's job just as they are for managers in other sectors of the industry.

Catering for the sick should satisfy three needs – the basic need for safe food that suits the patient's own taste and eating pattern, the medical need as determined by the doctor or dietician (though only one in ten patients in hospital is on a special diet); and the social need of providing him with a wide range of facilities other than that which a bedridden patient must be given. This could include coffee shop; fast food, pub, and gourmet catering so that all needs and tastes are catered for; supplying such needs may not necessarily be as costly as the present traditional arrangement. Here the patient has to choose his meals more than twenty-four hours beforehand during which time his appetite may have altered with a consequent waste of some of the food; or ward staff may over-order meals so as to avoid running short and having to wait for additional ones to be sent up from a distant kitchen.

Staff

Staffing a hospital kitchen means covering a seven day week for fifty-two weeks of the year and covering a fairly long drawn out day from the cooking of breakfast until the despatch of the evening meal. In a large hospital it may be necessary to employ a night cook to feed night duty staff, prepare breakfasts and do general preparation for the next day's meals. Where there is only a small number of night staff the micro-vend system dealt with later on in the chapter will suffice for them to serve themselves.

The minimum number of staff required to run a hospital kitchen where long-stay patients are fed is laid down in the following scale drawn up by the Department of Health and Social Security.

Hospitals under 100 beds	1 staff per 15 persons fed
Hospitals with 100–130 beds	1 staff per 25 persons fed
Hospitals with 300–700 beds	1 staff per 35 persons fed
Hospitals with 700–1000 beds	1 staff per 40 persons fed
Hospitals with over 1000 beds	1 staff per 45 persons fed

Thus a hospital of 1035 beds and with 100 staff could have at least forty-five kitchen staff of which 40 per cent should be of cook and assistant cook grades, and 20 per cent in supervisory grades of assistant head cook and above. This level of staffing allows for providing cooked dishes for breakfasts, lunches and dinners; it covers the length of the working day.

SCHOOL MEALS SERVICE

The Education Act 1980 changed the traditional pattern of school meals service; the old system was costing the country millions of pounds in subsidies each year. Local authorities do not now have a statutory obligation to provide the service but must provide facilities for food to be eaten in school. Even the provision of food to children of parents in receipt of Supplementary Benefit or Family Income Supplement is left to the local authority to be decided as necessary. Many local authorities have closed down their school kitchens, sold the equipment and paid redundancy money to the school meals staff.

Some of the causes of the large subsidy that was being paid by the government were the overheads which in the year 1978-9 amounted to 24.64p for kitchen staff wages, 4.16p for dining room assistants to supervise pupils eating the meal, 1.26p for clerical assistance, 1.00p for administration costs, 6.64p for other overheads with only 16.32p being spent on the actual food. This meant a total cost of 54.02p per meal and a net subsidy of 36.22p per meal.

In February 1980 the price of a school meal was increased to 35p but this still left the sum of £380 millions which had to be paid through rates and taxes;

354

this was 5 per cent of the total education budget. The uptake of meals varied considerably from school to school and according to age and location; in primary schools it was from 53 per cent to 87 per cent and in secondary education from 21 per cent to 70 per cent. There were many free meals – of more than five million meals served in England daily, nearly 1,400,000 were served without payment to pupils of parents on Supplementary Benefit, to kitchen staff and meal service supervisors and to teachers on midday supervisory activities.

Now every local authority can decide for itself on the nature of its meal service in schools. It can continue as before taking into account staff levels and efficient operation; it can run a snack bar operation offering a range of items at various prices; or it need not provide any service at all.

The legislation passed during the last war stated that the school meal be provided on the basis that it was the main meal of the day; thus the portion sizes, recipes, menu balance, and nutritional values always aimed at providing a minimum of one-third of the recommended intake of energy and between a half and a third of the recommended protein intake. In addition, the social aspects of eating in company with other children, a good standard of behaviour at table, a knowledge of balanced meals, and acquaintance with a wide range of meals were meant to induce good eating habits.

The pattern of food as now served in schools where this service continues is that it must be based on popular demand, have good eye appeal, be varied with several choices daily, be self-supporting financially and be nutritionally sound. In this way the overheads of almost 60 per cent can be drastically cut and the pupil obtain sufficient nourishment at a reasonable price; the alternative is a packed lunch provided by the mother so that in no case does the child have reason to leave the school at midday. But local authorities still employ Area School Meals Advisers and School Meals Organisers to be responsible for the efficient day to day operation of the service in those individual schools still operating.

COLLEGE AND UNIVERSITY CATERING

Catering in colleges of further and higher education, and in polytechnics and universities, has to be self-supporting and cover all the operating expenses excepting the rates; it has to satisfy the needs of students and staff at a price which suits their pockets, but at the same time it should seek to broaden the students' knowledge of food and develop his tastes. Students will willingly live on a diet of sausages, hamburg steaks, fried eggs, chips and baked beans with fried fish on Fridays because these are all inexpensive items, but this is to deny them the opportunity to gain an appreciation of good food, and fast food eating denies them the opportunity of social contacts with fellow students at the table.

The menus offered to students should take account of all tastes, including those of overseas students; where service facilities allow, there should be a choice of several menus at varying prices and the cycle of menus should seek to avoid monotony by being changed either term by term, or during the term.

Even with a cafeteria service and in a dining room where students and staff clear away their dirty dishes, staff costs will still be high, running up to 60 per cent of turnover. With a food cost of 40 per cent as in the school meals service there is then no margin left to pay the overheads such as heating, lighting, clerical assistance and telephone charges. There are also the additional headquarter's administrative charges to be paid. Add to this knife-edge situation the fact that in most colleges the academic year is only between thirty and thirty-six weeks long which in turn is diminished by reading weeks, field trips, and examination weeks during which students attend only to sit their exams. The income is thus good for only about twenty-four weeks of the year. Staff, however, have to be retained for the whole year and unless there is some residential accommodation and conference facilities, they go on half pay for some thirteen weeks of the year. When they have to be called in during vacation they receive full pay, or in some areas, time and half. The catering budget is fixed for the financial year and in general the money received cannot be used for purchases, nor may money for academic purposes be transferred to the catering account to balance it, or improve feeding standards.

Universities, polytechnics, and some colleges have the accommodation and facilities in lecture halls and meeting rooms which are ideal for conference use; student halls of residence and catering facilities back these up and with some marketing expertise, a valuable source of income can be obtained during vacations and the profit used to offset losses sustained during term time. Some universities have purpose-built conference facilities with luxury apartments for the organiser and speakers, good public address, translation and video systems and other necessary equipment, plus kitchen and dining room staff capable of producing the requisite standard of meals according to the price being paid.

During term, the universities and halls of residence of colleges afford catering facilities to students. These are on formal lines of dinner served each evening with a special dining-in night once or twice weekly and breakfast and lunch on cafeteria lines; or self-catering with an equipped kitchen for each four to eight students. This accommodation is an important part of conferences as it can save valuable time in transporting delegates from business areas to their sleeping accommodation. Obviously the facilities offered have to be good and money has to be spent on improvements and refurbishing but vacation business is now an important part of the normal running of college catering.

In many colleges the students union likes to run the bar, since if it is well run it will make a considerable profit for the benefit of the union and can be put to sports or social activities. This usually leads to the practice of serving meals at the bar in opposition to the official catering operations, and often at unrealistic prices. The student bar is usually closed during vacation but with an influx of conference delegates who are bound to want bar facilities, the caterer must be able to call in the bar manager to run the bar during opening hours when delegates are on the campus; they can be made temporary members for the duration of the conference.

The new universities have endeavoured to use the better traditions of the old established colleges together with their own less formal approach to running their catering facilities, and some have divided the hall so that those under-graduates who wish may use the cafeteria service while the rest may go into hall where a more formal service is offered. The accommodation is very similar in standard to a 3-star hotel with most of the rooms having their own bathrooms and tea and coffee-making facilities laid on, which makes for ideal facilities for the vacation conference business.

MEALS-ON-WHEELS

This service is operated by the social services departments of local authorities for supplying meals to elderly people who are not really capable of cooking for themselves. It usually operates on four weekdays with the distribution being done by volunteers and by direct council vans or hired transport. The meals can be provided by either a school kitchen, the kitchen of a large local canteen, a day-centre for the elderly, or a purpose-built kitchen that also supplies other local authority food services. The meals can be sent out in any of the following forms, (i) chilled meals delivered twice weekly for reheating in the usual oven, or in a small Regethermic oven, (ii) freshly cooked and portioned and kept hot in charcoal-heated containers, (iii) individual portions of commercially produced food, regenerated, (iv) frozen meals prepared by the authority then reheated and transported in electric hot boxes, or (v) frozen meals as in (iv) but reheated by a microwave oven housed in the van.

The local authorities are aware of the problems of transporting hot meals and the Food Hygiene (General) Regulations 1970 state that food must not be allowed to fall below 62.8 °C during delivery, but there is no legislation which can ensure the person eats it immediately it is delivered.

OLD PEOPLE'S HOMES AND DAY CENTRES

The increased longevity of people has led to a big increase in the need for both private and local authority homes for the aged where they can either live inde-pendently in a warden-guarded flatlet or as a member of the community. When living alone the chore of a pensioner having to cook a meal can be overcome by the provision of a meal-on-wheels service; without this there is the likelihood of the person foregoing proper cooked meals and living on food of poor nutritional

357

value. This can lead to malnutrition making this sector of the population vulnerable to hospitalisation.

Day Centres are set up by local authorities and certain charitable and welfare organisations to get people out of their four walls and spend a day or two each week following various activities and being given a decent midday meal while there. The meal could have been cooked on the premises but is more likely to be a regenerated frozen one, or possibly delivered from a central social services kitchen.

VENDING

Vending machines can fulfil a need in many establishments provided they are carefully sited, properly serviced on a preventive basis with faults quickly rectified, subject to quality control procedures, and kept filled. Vending machines for beverages, snacks and meals offer a service at any time and can serve remote sites; there is no need for fixed break times, they save labour costs, give exact portion control, and can be more profitable than conventional service. The only disadvantages are the loss of personal service and social contact, their inability to cope with masses of people all at once, and sometimes they break down. Staff have to be trained to keep machines clean and to refill them on a regular routine basis. Control is easy because the meter reading will indicate the number of sales made of each item in the machine over a set period; the ingredient cost and the number of portions per pack can be compared with takings to show the gross profit. The time taken by the operators to look after the machine and the rental or leasing cost and maintenance charges are known.

Micro-Vending

Vending machines for the sale of meals to heat in a microwave oven can form the total cafeteria service for a small number of customers, or can be an addition to a traditional service counter. Chilled or frozen meals on plates are placed in the refrigerated vending machine and when the correct money is placed in the slot for a particular meal, it unlocks. The meal is put into the adjacent microwave oven, the time token attached to the plate inserted, and when the oven door is closed the microwave operates for a time related to the meal. Together with a hot and cold beverage vending machine, such a micro-vending unit serves a very useful purpose after the main servery has closed, and for night duty staff.

LEISURE CATERING

At football matches crowds of people are packed into what appears to be an ideal catering situation, but in fact the opportunity to offer food of any sort is limited to the time between the gates opening and the start of the match, and a ten-minute interval. The possible number expected to attend can be judged by the popularity of the teams playing but bad weather can still make a difference to the attendance. A few clubs have a suite of rooms that are suitable for catering purposes and can serve meals; other clubs have fast food bars serving hot dogs, hamburgers, pies, pizzas and drinks and they also serve food from insulated boxes carried by tray boys, and others vend hot tea. Around the ground multi-head dispensing systems for large-scale sale of beer and soft drinks into disposable containers can fill a dozen at one go, and put on the lids.

Catering is normally available in sports and leisure centres and may be run by the local authority itself or on contract by a caterer who has tendered for the catering rights over a given period of time. The service will vary considerably, some centres doing it all by vending machines, others serving full meals and running a licenced bar, but in general a snack bar using the minimum number of staff will be most successful. In many cases there is sufficient accommodation for functions such as banquets, receptions and weddings to be held; the centres can thus become a place of entertainment and for various social functions in fact they can be made into busy multi-purpose places where the caterer helps promote the use of the available facilities.

MOTORWAY CATERING

Catering for people on the move who feel the need to pull up for a drink and a snack and a chance to stretch their legs constitutes an important section of the catering industry, calling for managerial expertise of a high order quite different from that of any other area. Until recently the catering areas were leased under contract from the Ministry of Transport but they have now been sold to the firms operating the sites who in future will have a free hand and not have to pay rent to the government.

Motorway caterers are obviously keen to sell more than just a quick cup of tea and a bun so they offer a range of meals and service to satisfy all income groups, including separate facilities for long-distance lorry drivers who now demand more than a cup of tea and a sandwich.

Motorway service areas are open day and night all the year round, though not all the various restaurants are necessarily open all the time. This means having three shifts of some grades of staff and, since local buses do not run on motorways, a staff minibus to fetch them to and from their homes or central pick-up point. A large part of the staff will be unskilled or semi-skilled counter hands, cleaners and table clearers who require little induction to make them useful. They must be able to cope with peak periods when perhaps a dozen coach-loads of people arrive all at once, or on a sunny bank holiday when thousands of cars crowd the roads and many decide to stop for refreshments.

Managerial staff need to be highly efficient to deal with the many problems that face them in this isolated field of operations for they have many more diffi-culties than the hotel manager - in addition to the problems created by the peak rushes and their effect on supplies of food and availability of staff there are those such as the cleanliness of toilet facilities, rowdiness, the price of petrol, and vending machines out of order.

Motorway establishments are well equipped and quite spacious and vary in size according to the importance of the motorway, and in standards according to the skill of the manager. Often a call-order unit is operated where the cooks prepare grills and fried foods in the servery in view of the customers; convenience foods would be largely used and a lot of bought-in bakery and pastry, either fresh or frozen, would satisfy most customers. Prices charged, however, have to be high to cover the greater amount of overheads which apply to this area of catering.

RAILWAY CATERING

Meals have been served to railway passengers for over a hundred years. At first trains used to coincide a stop at a major station around lunchtime so that passengers could alight and get something to eat in the station buffet; however, in 1879 dining cars were introduced so that meals could be cooked on route. In the 1890s a set lunch of five courses was served for two old shillings and a six-course dinner for three shillings and sixpence; the setting in the first-class dining saloons was opulent with leather, damask, brass, walnut and scrolled iron fittings and there were plenty of stewards to serve the meals.

In 1858 George Pullman, an American, built sleeping cars for leasing to US railway companies for which travellers paid a supplementary fare to enjoy the better facilities they offered. Soon whole trains of Pullman cars were made up and the idea spread to other countries, the first one in Britain being run in 1874 when lunch was served to all the passengers. The Pullman Car Company in the UK maintained its high standard of food and comfort for eighty years, then in 1954 it was taken over by British Rail and no more Pullman cars were built or run after 1966. These days about a thousand trains a day offer either a buffet or restaurant car service with a wide selection of menus to suit most tastes and in addition there are buffets and bars at all main stations.

For many years much of the food preparation was carried out at the main terminus depots then finished on the train so as to be ready for the normal meal times. The foodstuffs now are those that do not require lengthy or complicated

360

preparation and Inter-City trains are equipped with the Mealstream 605 oven which is a combined forced air microwave which cuts conventional cooking times. The kitchen equipment makes it possible for meals to be freshly cooked while being able to serve all those wishing to partake of any of the menus offered.

CATERING AT SEA

Not so many years ago ships sailed the oceans on regular routes taking passengers to set destinations with an occasional round the world cruise. It was the only way to travel between continents and there were many companies competing for the trade. The quality of the food and accommodation rather than the size and speed of the ship was very often the deciding point between selecting one company from another.

There are few passenger liners now sailing regular routes and most companies run their ships for holiday cruises with the entertainment and food marking the difference between companies. These luxury liners are floating hotels or holiday camps and offer such diversion as sports, cinema, discotheques, cabarets, bars and many others as well as sight-seeing trips ashore. This is all in addition to full board and accommodation.

Such voyages afford a very pleasant and popular way of passing any period of time from a few days to several months. Many ships now carry one-class passengers only as against three or four classes in former times. Although the food and service seek to emulate that of the great heyday of ship travel a different class of clientele now means that different tastes have to be catered for.

According to the shipping company and the ship, the catering staff may be British or foreign nationals of the country where the ship is registered. There are as many as 600 catering personnel on a very large liner, consisting of bedroom stewards for both day and night shift, public room stewards and stewardesses, barmen, waiters, wine waiters, chefs, commis and porters – all working under the direction of a manager. Department heads look after the running of their sections; the hours of duty are regulated but catering staff serve one or more sittings at each of the three daily meals whilst at sea. Another form of sea travel comprises the ships and hovercraft that regularly link various countries by short sea routes such as those between the Continent and the UK. Crossings may last only half an hour yet still manage to serve refreshments – others take longer and offer several forms of catering facilities at various levels. There are restaurants with waiter service, self-service buffets, cafeterias, snack bars and bars for drinks. These amenities afford a means of passing the time agreeably so the staff of cooks, stewards and barmen form a large part of the ship's crew and the operation contributes additional revenue. Cabins are available on many crossings and for

those who do not want to go to sleep such forms of entertainment as discotheques, gaming tables, slot machine games and, of course, a queue for duty-free
goods and even a dinner dance all help to smooth the voyage so that some
passengers make the trip without landing abroad.

AIRLINE CATERING

When a passenger buys a ticket to travel with an airline he is paying some of his
money towards the meals served on route; catering plays a big part in the running
of an airline company whether it does it directly, or with a catering firm specialising at in-flight catering. What the airline offers depends upon the company
concerned, the duration of the flight, the type of ticket paid for, and the time
of day. On a very short flight there may be no service, for even on an hour's
journey it would be difficult for the air stewards to serve and clear away a meal,
so the answer is to serve a drink. On a normal flight lasting say six hours a main
meal of three courses, a light meal, and drinks would be served to economy class
passengers, the main meal consisting of an hors-d'oeuvre, a main dish, a sweet
dish, with roll and butter and tea or coffee, quarter bottles of wine would be
available. The complete meals are delivered in closely packed containers and the
hot items are put into an oven to be switched on about twenty minutes before
being served and reheated by forced air. The reheated meal is then put onto the
tray containing any cold items and served to each passenger. The cutlery and
dishes are of good quality designed to be re-used and only cups and glasses are
disposable. On Tri-star the food is delivered from the in-flight kitchen, placed in
a Recon-plus oven and kept chilled until required; the oven is then turned to
regenerate, the timing dial set and in a matter of minutes the hot meals are
ready to serve. The serving trolleys are sent up to the passenger deck by lift and
wheeled along the aisles. Some airlines keep ticket prices low by not including
meals but selling it to passengers willing to pay the extra.

Airline companies are constantly seeking ways to keep down the weight to be
carried on each plane as each kilogram requires so much fuel to convey it
through the sky. This applies to the food and drink which is served in lightweight plastic containers rather than on silver dishes.

There are a number of contractors serving the various airlines, some doing it
on a world-wide basis; major airlines have their own kitchens and all have to
prepare special diets for passengers requesting them, including religious diets.
In addition to the fresh meals put on flights out of the UK thousands of frozen
meals are flown to stations around the world where food of a satisfactory
standard is difficult to obtain locally.

CATERING IN HM FORCES

All the branches of Her Majesty's Forces vie with each other in reaching the highest possible standards in their everyday catering function of feeding their personnel. Their general standards, at home or overseas, is so high that it puts many civilian large-scale efforts to shame and this is not solely because the feeding allowance for the forces is any higher or more generous but mainly because of the excellent spirit of motivation of those entering the catering sections of the different arms, and, naturally, from the exemplary training given at each of the three schools of catering.

When entering the service of his choice the new recruit will be sent to the appropriate training establishment before being sent to work on a station. For subsequent upgrading and promotion he will be sent on a higher level course at his training centre or local technical college and subsequently sit the examination. The level of courses can be equated to City and Guilds examinations for example, the trade standard B2 of the Army Catering Corps is the minimum for direct entry to CG 706/1 Basic Cookery for the Catering Industry; B1 is the trade standard for direct entry to CG 706/2, and A1 is that for CG 706/3-4-5 the most advanced examinations in cookery.

In the Royal Navy a leading cook is qualified for direct entry to CG 706/1 and a Petty Officer Cook to CG 706/2; a Leading Steward is qualified for direct entry to CG 707/1 Food Service, leading to further study for CG 707/2 Advanced Serving Techniques. In the Royal Air Force a Senior Aircraftsman is qualified for direct entry into City and Guilds 706/1, and a Corporal to City and Guilds 706/2. This shows the calibre of the men and women of the services and their ability when applying for a post after leaving the service. On smaller stations or ships, the men's mess offers a good selection of substantial well-cooked meals often featuring Indian, Chinese and salad counters, and the sergeants' and officers' messes would be equally varied and good. Apart from the well-equipped permanent bases the cooks in all three services have to be capable of preparing good meals under primitive conditions and using emergency equipment.

HOLIDAY CAMPS CATERING

A holiday camp is rather like a motel with a central restaurant, a full programme of entertainment and facilities for sports and games. The camp site is in a holiday area and accommodation is in single, double, or family rooms mostly with facilities and, for those who prefer it, a kitchen to do self-catering. The traditional holiday camp charge is an inclusive price for full board including breakfast, lunch and evening meal. These are served by waiting staff who can cope with thirty or more people per station because the food is plated, and as mealtimes are spread over an hour or more this prevents a rush of customers all at once. The dining room has to seat the total number in the camp which can run into as many as a thousand or more persons of all ages, and seating can be at tables to take family parties but not less than four persons. The extent of the service can be judged by the need to lay up several hundred tables with seven items of cutlery per person plus glasses, cruets, paper serviettes, etc. three times a day. The restaurant manager has to produce a foolproof system which ensures that a streamlined service is given by staff working under some tension and serving three meals per day.

The cooking is on a large scale with strict portion control producing relatively simple but attractive looking and substantial dishes. Some choice is offered at each of the three main meals and customers are given the menu to choose from in advance so that the chef will know exactly how many portions of each dish to prepare. Lunch and dinner usually start with soup, then the choice is between two or three main dishes with vegetables followed by a choice of say two sweets, one hot and one ice cream. Full use is made of convenience foods so as to keep the wages bill low.

Some camps offer additional choices to the menu by having fast foods cooked in the restaurant for those who do not fancy anything from the menu. An omelette bar, grill, pizza oven, or some such operation has an appeal as has a few sliced meats and salads, or a counter that offers fish fingers, pies or sausages with baked beans and chips for children. Other areas under the direction of the caterer would be the snack bar, take-away, sundae bar and coffee bar, which would always be open except during mealtimes, as well as vending machines, and licensed bars.

Holiday camps, being mainly seasonal, employ seasonal workers and engage the bulk of them for the peak weeks only, bringing in more as business builds up, and paying off as it tails off. Accommodation on site usually has to be offered for all staff since the day starts at around 7.45 a.m. ending at 7.45 p.m. with short breaks in between. Tipping is not encouraged and a service charge is not usually levied.

The keynote of a holiday camp is its lack of formality as customers do not have to dress up for meals, the staff are friendly, there is some activity going on at all times of the day and there is provision for all sorts of games and sports as well as dancing and cabaret at night; children can be left safely in the play area.

Holiday camps have been in existence now for more than fifty years and form a large part of the total catering industry; the catering policy will be decided at the head offices of the many companies in this business but the day to day operation of buying, cooking and serving will be done at each camp.

364

KOSHER CATERING

When people of the Jewish faith attend a function in a public establishment the catering has to be carried out under religious laws and a member of the Kashrus Commission has to be present to supervise. These laws do not allow dairy products and meat items to be mixed and at a banquet this means that the menu must be based on either meat or milk but cannot contain both. In effect a Kosher menu will usually feature fish as the main course since this means that real cream can be used and milk can be served with the coffee and butter with the roll.

In a Jewish hospital or institution it is usual to have two completely separate kitchens or departments each fully equipped but colour coded so that no equipment can get into the wrong kitchens; only one of the kitchens would be in use at a time. In a hotel doing Kosher banqueting all items for the storage and cooking of each type of food must be kept completely separate and they must all be brand new when applying to the Commission for a licence to do Kosher work. Even the cutlery and crockery has to be duplicated and must be kept in completely separate cupboards.

The expense of having two sets of heavy equipment can be diminished in some areas and although it is essential to install two ovens, as only one can be used on any occasion, only one range is necessary because the food does not actually come into contact with the cooking surface, so only two set of saucepans are needed. One mixing machine but two bowls is acceptable and one slicer is also approved since it will be used only for the meat menu. Working surfaces need not be duplicated as they have to be covered with clean tablecloths or kitchen foil before being used. Cards confirming that the food has been prepared in accordance with the religious laws have to be signed by the Mashgiach and the Rabbi and set before the host before the meal begins. An orthodox Jew will not touch any dairy product for at least six hours after eating a meat meal, and so a caterer cannot serve a late night buffet which includes meat sandwiches at a dinner dance after the guests have partaken of a milk menu. The laws governing Kosher catering are the same as those given to Moses which state that only meat from animals with cloven hooves and which chew the cud are allowed – pigs have cloven feet but do not chew the cud and so are forbidden. In general, game birds, game animals, shellfish and eels are prohibited and only fish with fins and scales may be eaten. Meat, poultry and offal must be freshly slaughtered, soaked in water to remove blood, sprinkled with salt and left for one hour, then rinsed in cold water before being cooked.

BANQUETING

A banquet means a gathering of people who, because of their common interest, meet together as a group for a formal meal. The meal is the same for everyone

365

with the food, speeches, toasts and the reason for the reunion as a common theme, and the price the members pay will reflect the relative importance of the occasion. Any kind of meal can be served as a banquet provided it is ordered for a group – breakfast, lunch, dinner and supper parties can be arranged and any occasion such as a wedding, anniversary, reunion, or conference can be the reason for it.

The business of catering for banquets can be a very lucrative one which brings in additional revenue to a hotel because it uses many facilities which are actually present but under-used. The disadvantage is that it has a busy but short season lasting from autumn to spring with nothing much during the summer months. The usual kitchen staff will prepare the food in addition to the normal restaurant service, and it will be served by a team of people working as 'extras' on a casual basis. A manager or head waiter will be in charge of the arrangements, from dealing with a prospective customer to the actual service of the banquet. There are a number of establishments where the primary business is that of banquets with perhaps a public restaurant open to all and a number of rooms to accommodate different numbers. These can all be served from the one kitchen but with separate serveries.

Selling the Banqueting Facilities

Some companies have a sales manager and sales staff to sell their banqueting facilities and it is their job to approach potential customers and to inform them as to what the company has to offer in the shape of accommodation. The sales people can show photographs, quote room capacities, offer a range of priced menus and suggest other amenities, then if a customer shows interest, invite him to view the premises and offer some hospitality. Then the manager can meet the customer and after discussion give more precise information concerning the proposed function than can the salesman. The manager can discuss the facilities he has to offer, arrange the date and room, explain the menus, show the banqueting bar and wine lists or suggest wines, offer advice on such things as an orchestra or toastmaster, and complete a Banquet Booking Form giving these details, as shown in Fig. 51. This is shown in a simplified form and can be extended in size and scope to include other facilities and information as needed by other departments in the establishment.

From this form, once confirmed by the organiser, the various departments of the establishment will receive the information which concerns them so that all are aware of the event and play their part in making it run smoothly and successfully.

Staffing

A secretary will work under the banquet manager, dealing with enquiries and correspondence. A banqueting head waiter or supervisor in charge of the actual

366

Figure 51
SIMPLIFIED BANQUET BOOKING FORM

Noble Hotel Banquet Department	
Function: Date: Organiser: Firm or Society: Address: Telephone No. office home Room:	No of covers:
Menu **Wines**	Time Departure Toastmaster Orchestra Cabaret Changing rooms Floral arrangements Microphone Seating plan Cash bar Menu cards Place cards VAT

rooms and with his deputy, will arrange the rooms instructing staff on the layout and special requirements. Under him will be the head wine waiter and dispense barman and a small number of full-time waiting staff who will do the laying up of the tables and preparation of mise en place. Banquet waiting staff are nearly always recruited as needed by an establishment, preferring to be self-employed; according to type and tradition of the establishment and the importance of the particular banquet either waitresses or waiters, or both, will be engaged to serve from eight to twelve persons whilst a wine waiter can look after up to twenty five guests according to the number of wines accompanying the food.

RECEPTIONS

This type of function can appear under several different titles although the organisation is much the same for them all. The event could be called a cocktail party or a reception and the reason for this social gathering could be to bring people together for a relatively short space of time for a common purpose such as the launching of a new product, the making of a presentation, or fund raising.

Whatever the reason and at whatever time of day it is held – it can take place in the morning, but more generally in late afternoon leaving time to lay up the room for a banquet that same evening – the food and drink are similar for them all. The only variations to this would be if the sponsor wants to emphasise anything in particular. For example, if he was the commercial attaché of a country he would appreciate the inclusion of some of his native foods or may decide to offer the drinks of his country by providing them.

The first thing is obviously to fill up a booking form for the event as shown for banqueting. The room must be chosen to conform to the number of persons expected to attend; part of the pleasure of such an occasion is to keep guests confined in a limited area so that they can see the guest of honour and rub shoulders with as many of the other guests as possible in the time. The average amount of space to allocate per person attending is 0.5 m^2 excluding the bar and buffet area. If necessary screens could be installed to keep the party as intimate as possible. No chairs or tables other than for the elderly and for the service are needed.

In conjunction with the organiser it is easy to draw up the list of food and drink to be served. The manager will suggest suitable drinks based on his information as to the kind of event and the type of people attending it. It is possible to serve mixed drinks such as cocktails which can be economical to produce as against the more common gin and tonic or whisky and ginger ale. At some functions only wines will be served.

A reception is usually of fairly brief duration lasting less than two hours but the organiser will pay for the hire of the room including the setting up and clearing away, the calculations being based on the size of the room, the time of day, day of the week and sometimes the time of the year. Added to the hire charges and costs of drinks and food will be that of the staff required to operate at the function which may include a master of ceremonies and commissionaire as well as barmen, waiting and portering staff.

OUTDOOR CATERING

This branch of catering presents perhaps more of a challenge to organising ability than any other. It means taking the paraphernalia of the kitchen, servery and dining room to a customer's site, setting up the operation, serving the meal and clearing away so as to leave the site as it was found and transporting staff and equipment back to base; even the swill and other rubbish has to be cleared and taken away. In some instances the catering will be for a private function where all costs having been previously agreed, in others it will be for the general public to pay for what they order. In this last case the caterer needs a wealth of experience so as to estimate how many are likely to attend according to the weather, and thus place orders for goods accordingly.

In many cases these functions are held in a marquee set up in a field and there is a challenge in making it feel like a more permanent setting. Rush matting to cover the grass, coloured drapes to line the walls, floral arrangements, colour schemes with table covering and napkins, a commissionaire at the entrance to greet guests and keep out gate-crashers, and well-dressed staff to serve, are examples of possible attention to good catering practice.

Organisation

The organisation of outdoor catering must be in the hands of experts so that every detail is covered – a missing corkscrew may mean a long and costly journey to the nearest town to purchase one, and to run short of food is more reprehensible than to be left with large stocks of unsold food at the end of the assignment. Not all functions are held in marquees in remote areas; they can be held, for example, on the customer's own premises, in village halls, on river boats, or in factory canteens; certainly the site in these cases will be more easy to work in but generally no use is made of facilities other than power and water supplies and the caterer needs to be self-supporting.

Organisation Check List

The success of any outdoor catering function depends largely upon efficient organisation and careful attention to detail. Among the many and varied points that have to be considered and decided are the following:

1. The name, address and telephone number of the organiser.
2. The type of function; for example, whether a banquet, buffet, catering for a race meeting, reception or tea, etc.
3. The number of persons to be catered for – this can have a bearing on the menu and equipment as well as the number of staff required.
4. The date and time of the function – how long it will take to set up and dismantle the facilities required; whether it is for several days.
5. The exact address of the function and the kind of site to be used.

6. The distance the site is from the caterer's central depot - mileage and travelling time have to be taken into account when quoting for the job.

7. How payment is to be made - whether cash is to be taken at any points or whether the entire bill will be paid by the organiser. The price to be charged per person.

8. The menu - whether it is to be a full meal served by waiting staff, a cold meal served from a buffet, or a combination of menus to suit the particular occasion. The preparation of cold buffets can usually be done better at base than in the confines of a hot marquee on site.

9. The availability of water, gas and electricity supplies - when catering for a hot meal some caterers prefer to cook on site because of the regulations concerning transportation of hot food. Some like to do washing up on site rather than returning dirty dishes to base. Toilet, washing and cloakroom facilities may be required.

10. The size and decoration of marquees if needed and the furniture required - whether the site is likely to become muddy soon after people start walking on it so requiring the need for some form of covering. Space allocation per guest and for food preparation area, bar, etc.

11. The grades of staff required and the number of each; the manager in overall charge, the head chef, head waiter, barmen, waiters and waitresses, porters, and others. Many of the staff will be engaged as extras for this function only and be recruited locally or through a private employment agency. Staff transport facilities and staff changing rooms; details regarding uniform, meals on duty, method of payment all require decisions.

12. The security of premises and equipment, especially if set up overnight, may require the services of guards. It may be necessary to insure the function against loss.

13. Bars: it is usual to serve drink at outdoor functions either as an integral part of the meal or on sale for cash. Accordingly it may be necessary to set up bars, nominate staff, decide on prices to be charged, install cash tills and bar tariffs and so on. Security of stock and reconciliation of takings with quantity sold are important factors. It may be necessary to obtain a licence for the sale of alcoholic drinks.

14. The equipment required, (i) kitchen - stoves, boilers, pans, ovens, canisters of liquid gas, tables, boards, bowls, serving spoons, baths for washing salad, slicing machine, serving dishes, covers, etc., (ii) dining room - cutlery, crockery and glassware in the required numbers; tables, tablecloths, serviettes and teatowels, cruets, ashtrays, baths for cooling white wines, cutlery baskets, floral decorations, (iii) bar - glasses, jugs, optics, and all the paraphernalia of bar service.

15. Commodities. This will include all the necessary foodstuffs and drink necessary for the particular function.

16. Arrangements for disposal of rubbish. This may be done by the local council or privately but it is essential to clear up thoroughly and to leave the site as it was found.

As can be seen from the foregoing details, outdoor catering is a branch of the catering industry which presents perhaps more of a challenge than others but there can be great satisfaction at the successful completion of an ODC job, especially when the facilities have been minimal.

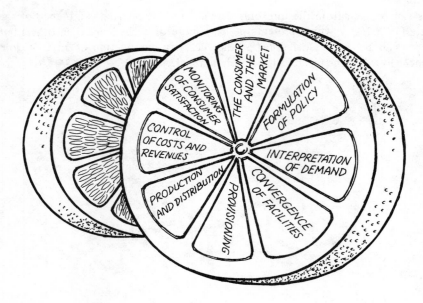

12 PRODUCTION AND DISTRIBUTION III – SYSTEMS AND METHODS

Definition of a System – Characteristics of a System – Types of Systems – Methods – Productive Resources – Implementation of a Production System – Systems for Continuous Production – Large-scale Food Service Systems – Adaptation of Systems.

The aim of every business should be to ensure that all its available resources are used to their fullest possible extent and that the maximum return is obtained from the investment made; in the commercial world there should be a just reward for the entrepreneurial effort involved.

As illustrated in Fig. 1, the Catering Cycle, and by the chapters in this book, every catering business follows an operational cycle and it has also been pointed out that the cycle consists of a series of interdependant activities which are related to those next to it. However, because of the number of sequences involved

372

there is a problem of placing each activity into a context that shows the whole rather than the individual parts. To illustrate this problem, in Chapter 2 there is a description of a social system in which each individual is able to fulfil his own task in the way that his training and ability allows, doing it for the benefit of the community as a whole. In a similar way it is possible to show the relevance of the present chapter by reference to a piece of music in which each individual note as written is an important part of the whole composition, the final effect of which is dependant upon the entire sound rather than each component part. Thus the modern approach to any examination of this industry is through the systems concept. Using the systems approach to analyse a complex sequence of events means adopting a perspective that gives a clear understanding of cause and effect. Within a system each interacting component is given its appropriate value according to its contribution to the whole operation rather than to each separate sequence.

DEFINITION OF A SYSTEM

A system can be defined as a regularly interacting group of activities that are necessary to allow the unified whole to function effectively; a system is seldom comprised of a large number of unrelated activities. But it can comprise a number of subsystems that are necessary for the functioning of the main system as a whole. For example, the sequences of marketing are identification of demand, product development, production planning, advertising strategy and so on which together form the system. In turn, marketing will only be effective if there is a research department that can identify demand, if some advertising is done to increase public awareness, and if a public relations section maintains customer goodwill. So each system has subsections which are essential to the functioning of it as a whole.

Of course, each subsystem must be assessed as to its contribution to the whole; a system of kitchen operation is not comprised of just the number of parties involved but includes the provisioning of those parties and the maintenance of the equipment used by each. Taking the system in its entirety, what is equally vital is that customers are attracted to patronise an establishment, are given a pleasurable meal experience, receive value for money and leave with the feeling that they look forward to a return visit. The fact that some of the food served may not have been cooked on the premises is not the major consideration so long as the objective of the system was achieved.

CHARACTERISTICS OF A SYSTEM

The characteristics of a system can be summed up as follows:

1. **Objective** It is created to achieve a certain goal, needing therefore to be built around the main purpose with each subsection conforming to the main principle.
2. **Concept** It must always be seen as a whole rather than a series of connected parts or sequences.
3. **Input and output modes** The purpose of each system is to affect, convert or transform the nature of what is fed in as production, i.e. input, so that after treatment it results in an affected, converted or transformed output.
4 **Processing and transformation** The nature of the goods or services entering a system should be treated in such a way that they are transformed after having undergone a form of processing.
5. **Monitoring** A system should provide its own self-monitoring and be adaptable to changing needs or changing input. It should thus be able to maintain flexibility and prevent the system from becoming moribund or outdated. Otherwise the end result might be a product that is system derived rather than one optimised by the system to a satisfactory standard of production.

TYPES OF SYSTEMS

There are a number of different systems in existence but there are only two broad based ones that are applicable to a catering situation – these are the Open System and the Closed System.

The Open System

This is where the output responds to the input whilst at the same time the output is isolated and has no influence on the input. When related to an à la Carte restaurant this means that to some extent the type, nature and volume of demand, and from it the type of dish, is totally independent of the number of staff on duty and the amount of stock in store.

The Closed System

This system is influenced by its own behaviour where, if required, corrective action can be taken in the light of system performance. Within it, a balance of input and output can be maintained. Thus a closed system may be used in a catering situation where the production operation is practically a continuous

374

one and a constant effort is made to achieve a balance between the total input or productive resources, and the output or items produced and number of customers served. To a certain extent this can be related to the area of institutional catering in which the number of consumers and time they will take to eat is known fairly precisely in advance and the means are in existence to keep foods both nutritionally and hygienically safe. The major problem encountered in a continuous production system is in keeping the products in the best possible condition until they are required for service, rather than at the initial stages of setting up the production.

A further dimension to this concept of a catering system is one that has been in use for a long time in other industries and that is the Short Run or Long Run production system. The concept of a Short Run is similar to the à la Carte form of operation in which all items are produced to a specific demand. Because that demand cannot always be anticipated either in volume, type or nature some spare production capacity is inevitable which means carrying extra stock and having adequate staff and equipment to cope with all the vagaries of demand.

The Long Run is planned to produce dishes in a continuous flow, so maximising the resources by balancing the needs with the total productive means without interruption and in order to ensure maximum output within a specific parameter.

METHODS

Within each system there are various methods that may be adopted to ensure that its goals are achieved. This implies that a particular form of procedure is adopted within a specific aspect of the system to provide the transformation or services required with maximum efficiency. This has to be, of course, within the limitations imposed by consumer expectations and the provision of productive resources.

Thus a method is a specific approach adopted within the total system to comply with the needs of a specific sequence of events or stage of the operation. This system can be presented in the form of a diagram, see Fig. 52, in which each one of the normal sequences may become a subsystem of its own as, for example, the processing aspect of the partie system; or it could be a method where silver service is a method of distribution.

A subsystem will have to adopt by itself a set of methods or a specific method, but the methods are also closely interlinked with the final product which should be predetermined in its totality at the outset of the operational planning. This involves in the first instance, analysing the system's requirements at the various stages of the operation and from it evolving the most efficient method of carrying out the particular task recognised at that stage.

This analysis normally involves (i) determining the final composition of the

Figure 52
SEQUENCES OF A SYSTEM

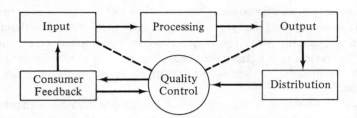

product, its component ingredients, its service and presentation, and the environment in which it should be consumed, (ii) determining the correct state of preparation and readiness in which the various product components should enter the system, (iii) determining the sequence of operation required to modify the materials being used and their addition in readiness for the next stage of the operation, (iv) determining the temperatures to be used at the various stages of production, (v) establishing the procedure of evaluation of quality of all the products before they are served and (vi) determining the means of obtaining a feedback of information from the consumer as to their quality.

At each of these main stages the exact action which contributes towards either the product's state of progressive treatment, or the next step in its movement towards the customer, needs to be clearly identified. This is so that each section can be properly organised in the most efficient manner and provided with the right conditions in which to operate.

Within this framework the concept of method or specific operational procedure can be closely examined in a constructive manner as to its organisational and operational effectiveness. Basically this involves ensuring that each operation in the system is carried out so as to provide optimum productivity and quality standard at that particular level of activity.

In Fig. 52 the diagram is presented in a basic form. The broad functions shown are those found in every system but what is important to understand is that these functions have to be specifically adapted to the needs of a particular system in order that they may contribute to its effectiveness.

By means of analysing a conventional establishment which uses the partie subsystem it is possible to perceive the common features of every system. It begins with the procurement of the raw materials in whatever form is best suited to the system, then goes on to their processing in the various sections in accordance with operational requirements. In other manufacturing industries processing involves the adoption of two main component aspects of production procedures which are (1) Routing – the what and how, and (2) Scheduling – the when and where, of production

Routing

This requires that within the operation the components of each dish are present in their required form and exact quantity and that the operational sequence is properly planned.

Scheduling

This requires that the work is organised in a logical sequence which ensures the involvement of every section and maintains optimum output in accordance with a plan that is compatible with the equipment and staff available.

These two aspects of method fuse together to form a subsystem that is widely used in conventional food production in conjunction with the main principles of catering operation. These are the well-known ones of menu composition, stores requisitioning, preparation, processing, presentation and quality assessment. The guiding principle of this subsystem is that the demand for the finished product is satisfied through the means of a complex network of specialist sections in a logical sequence and each stage of which brings about certain modifications to the original materials. At the same time the value of the goods is increased by means of the labour involved.

To some extent the what and how and the when and where of production are already inbuilt into this subsystem since each commodity moves in a logical sequence from storage to distribution with any additional materials being added to it by the different sections. This is the essence of the partie subsystem where each relevant section makes its contribution towards a completed dish. The total system defines the Product Criteria, its Method of Evaluation in terms of Product Efficiency in relation to Demand, and the Method of Service.

The method of service interacts with this system which means that the appropriate method of conveying food to the consumer has to be included in considerations at the planning stage of the whole operation. The food must reach the consumer in the best possible condition otherwise all the thought and effort that has been given will be for naught.

Forms of operating other than the conventional partie system can be used to satisfy the particular requirements of other types of establishments, but the principles of the system are the same. The more limited the extent of the menu and the easier it is holding food for service so the degree of productivity increases since the various sections of the production line become much more interdependent.

At this stage another differentiation can be made which is that the holding and suspending of prepared foods can be prolonged in a safe manner by various techniques. The technique used whether it be freezing, chilling, irradiation, canning or accelerated freeze-drying, has an influence on the method of production. In general the system involves the individual run of a specific item on a large scale that uses all facilities to their maximum capacity thus giving savings of economy of scale. Work study principles must be observed so as to avoid bottle-necks and ensure maximum output with reasonable effort.

PRODUCTIVE RESOURCES

The productive resources of an organisation are its plant and machinery and its manpower together with the capital used for the purchase of materials for use in the enterprise. In setting up a system to transform raw commodities into finished dishes it is necessary to ensure that maximum efficiency is achieved and the maximum use made of the resources provided. The person who has to plan the operation will need to bear in mind the varied range of products that will be produced and ensure that the equipment installed is of the right nature and capacity. The equipment could be of the kind that can be used for a variety of purposes. thus saving on capital outlay and ensuring maximum usage. The advantages of this system of large-scale production can be lost if the best use of resources is not achieved.

The use of manpower requires that staff are deployed where they can be most effective; it may involve shift duties and the services of a work study expert may be helpful in obtaining the fullest possible return from this resource. The usage of materials also must be optimised; their proper utilisation can be ensured by taking all possible care during preparation and processing and by using up any by-products. The materials must not be permitted to lose their natural qualities or to develop micro-organisms that could cause food poisoning.

IMPLEMENTATION OF A PRODUCTION SYSTEM

The first step in setting up a continuous production system is to determine the product and the necessary technology for its preservation, which is how it is to be kept in perfect condition until required. A knowledge of how materials react to certain processes is also required and it may be necessary to adapt recipes to suit the system but without losing their identity. The system then has to be examined as a complete operation to include the packaging and por-tioning and the means of reconstitution, i.e. its final processing just prior to service and consumption. A centralised production system or commissary can be organised on the lines of Fig. 53.

Within this organisation the **catering manager** will be responsible for everything that is done within the kitchen and its ancillary departments. His duties will include (i) determining production runs, (ii) selecting from several alternatives the best dishes for the purpose required, (iii) investigating through the research and
378

Figure 53
CENTRALISED PRODUCTION SYSTEM

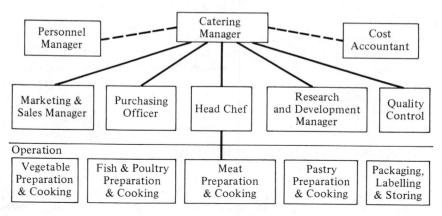

development department the way to standardise the materials and preparation work of each dish, (iv) organising and co-ordinating the total production function and (v) ensuring that the desired standard is maintained throughout.

The function of the **personnel manager** will be to abide by the guide-lines provided by the manager in the selection of applicants with the right attitudes and aptitudes for this kind of work, and will devise induction and training programmes for each member of staff in each of the operational sections.

The **cost accountant** will ensure that the business operates within the budget and that the exact cost of each dish including the proportion of fixed and variable costs, distribution and any bad debt charges, is arrived at. He will organise the method of settling accounts and collecting payments and provide a weekly statement that clearly shows any variances from initial budgets so that any necessary action can be taken to remedy the matter in the quickest possible time.

The function of the **marketing and sales manager** will be to indicate market requirements in terms of product choice, quality and volume. He will establish contact with clients to obtain information on any new products they require and monitor market trends and fluctuations so as to inform the manager of future market changes.

The **purchasing officer** will have to ensure that goods of the correct quality are available at the right time so that there can be no interruption or delay in the production run. He will nominate suppliers who can furnish goods of the required standard at the lowest price compatible with quality. Together with the head chef, standard purchasing specifications will be drawn up for all major commodities. The **head chef** and the production manager may well be one and the same person; his duties will be to organise his staff to run the production line and ensure maximum efficiency. He will be involved in setting up standardised recipes including regeneration instructions, monitoring standards of production and initiating improvements over the entire production field.

379

A **research and development person** will be responsible for the actual standardisation of recipes for continuous production; he will also set up a **quality control** unit to carry out tests on sample dishes so as to get them exactly right before they go into full production. With the head chef he will look at working conditions and levels of performance based on time and motion study.

In the operational section staff work more or less on conventional lines but must be prepared to apply themselves as required to meet the needs of production schedules. It is hardly necessary to emphasise the need for extreme care to be taken when preparing very large numbers of portions for sale to external users.

SYSTEMS FOR CONTINUOUS PRODUCTION

At present there are two main systems of continuous production, these are cookfreeze and cook-chill but there is every possibility that other forms may be developed particularly in the radiation of foods because here the packaging and storage costs are much less costly. The following is an account of the operation of the two most widely used systems.

Cook-Freeze Production

The possibility of preserving foods by deep freezing had been known for over a hundred years before Clarence Birdseye developed it commercially back in the 1920s. He said that if care was taken in the selection of foods for freezing and that they were prepared and transported properly, the result would be equivalent to quality fresh produce. Today many catering operations run entirely on the use of frozen dishes bought from the manufacturer and possibly the back-up of a few freshly prepared items.

The advantages claimed for a cook-freeze system whether it is done with food bought in or prepared on the premises are: (i) it eradicates the peaks and troughs of production that are inherent in a traditional operation; (ii) it divorces production from service so allowing kitchen staff to work without interruptions caused by the daily service periods; (iii) staff can work straight shifts rather than having to be present at all mealtimes; (iv) if necessary, successive shifts may be worked so utilising facilities around the clock, (v) because of large-scale runs, quality control is easier to exert thus ensuring a high standard; (vi) depending on the equipment installed, large-scale production gives lower food, labour and fuel costs; (vii) being a more rationalised system than the traditional one there is greater control over portion sizes; (viii) the use of unskilled staff under limited qualified supervision is possible because of the methods approach; (ix) foods in season at a low price can be bought in bulk quantity and frozen for future use; and (x) according to storage installation, stocks of prepared foods can be built up in advance to cover possible requirements over a given period.

380

An important aspect of a cook-freeze production run is that the process must be completed in the shortest time with the food being prepared, cooked, portioned, blast frozen and stored in one shift so as to ensure no contamination whilst progressing from one stage of production to the next.

Cook-freezing is expensive in the use of fuel as it is essential to bring the temperature of hot prepared dishes from 90 °C down to -20 °C in at most $1\frac{1}{2}$ hours and they must thereafter be stored at -20°C or below. A blast freezer tunnel to accommodate, for example, six trolley loads each of approximately 250 kg requires a loading of 105 kW and a deep freeze store to hold 5,000 meals needs to be 112 m^3 in size and have a 10 kW loading.

Cook-chill Production

Under this system meals can be produced by conventional methods, chilled rapidly and stored at 3 °C for from two to six days. The food can be regenerated, i.e. made ready for service and consumption, in a forced air convection oven, radiant-circulating oven, pressure steamer or microwave oven, or by the Regethermic system (see page 382). The main points to consider about the cook-chill system are, (i) no modifications to recipes are necessary and normal kitchen procedures are followed, (ii) production and service are separated, (iii) production must be for expected demand as an over-run means wasted meals, (iv) it is not appropriate for an unpredictable demand, (v) short production runs are possible so allowing for variation in daily production, (vi) there is no deterioration during the short storage life, (vii) no special equipment is required other than chilling and holding refrigerators, (viii) the energy required to store and regenerate chilled food is much less than that for frozen meals, (ix) better use can be made of manpower resulting in increased production; and (x) the whole range of meals can be produced.

In this system meals can be plated individually or in large containers for a given number of portions. The maximum depth of food should be 5 cm or less if the food is dense in structure. Foil dishes and lids as used in cook-freeze are suitable but any shallow aluminium or stainless steel trays can be used. Each production needs labelling to that there is no doubt as to what the dish is, and by when it has to be consumed. Where chilled meals are distributed to catering units which are not adjacent to its production, it is recommended they be packed into insulated boxes or refrigerated vans and maintained at 3 °C during transit. If sent out reheated the food items must be kept at 62.8 °C in insulated or heat retaining boxes. Small establishments wishing to use this sytem can have blast chillers of 20 kg to 60 kg capacity which are capable of bringing hot food at 65 °C down to 2 °C within the $1\frac{1}{2}$ hours recommended time schedule.

Both these systems allow for extensions to meet various demands and to assist in the saving of labour, as, for example, by balancing the components of a complete main course so that it may be taken from a deep freezer and placed in the regenerating oven with a pre-set disc to govern the timing.

LARGE-SCALE FOOD SERVICE SYSTEMS

There are several large-scale systems of food service in which meals are cooked in the normal manner then portioned either for immediate or subsequent use. They are mainly in use in hospitals and canteens.

Ganymede

When the food is cooked it is put into mobile bain-maries which are then wheeled into position alongside an endless belt. The customer will have previously ticked his requirements on a menu card which is placed on a tray and fulfilled as it progresses along the belt, each member of staff arranging the item he is serving onto the consumer's plate. Hot food is kept warm by means of a metal alloy disc weighing 250 g which has been heated in a special oven to 152 °C and placed into a base container under the plate. It keeps a meal hot for up to forty-five minutes and the plate is made to withstand this heat. Plastic bowls with a vacuum in the base are used for hot liquid foods.

The completed meals are loaded into an unheated trolley and taken to the dining room or ward for distribution. This system ensures each customer gets what he actually ordered. Some of the advantages are: (i) meals are plated by professional servers who have the opportunity to arrange it tastefully on the plate; (ii) nursing and ancillary staff are freed from the task of serving; (iii) the food trolley does not have to be a heated one; (iv) up to ten trays per minute can be serviced; and (v) there is minimal waste as the precise number of meals and portion sizes can be known in advance.

Regethermic

This is a cook-chill system that can be used to serve individual meals or large-scale packs. The food is cooked in the normal manner, placed into trays of twenty portions and then chilled. It is then plated on a porcelain or bright aluminium plate, covered with a stainless steel or black coated aluminium lid, loaded onto a trolley and when required wheeled into a special regenerating cabinet. The infra-red elements in this cabinet re-heat the food to 60-65 °C in twelve minutes, heating only the air chamber under the lid so no further cooking of the meal takes place, nor is there any condensation or evaporation. A trayful of food at 3 °C requires twenty minutes to reach 65 °C – steaks cooked under-done will remain underdone when regenerated and fried eggs or omelettes will still be soft.

A service conveyor belt, blast chillers, portable insulated containers and trolleys that fit the regenerating cabinets, are all part of the complete range of equipment required.

382

Helithermic

This system of food service consists of a fibreglass-polyester tray with indentations into which china plates are fitted. These are filled with the customer's requirements as the tray moves along an endless belt. The plates have a thickened base which when preheated will keep hot food hot; when completed a heat-insulating lid is put on and the tray loaded into an insulated trolley for transporting to service points.

Carousel

While not strictly a food service system this method is very useful for a dining room where there is not enough space for a conventional type of service counter. The servery can be sited in the space between kitchen and dining room in an aperture only two metres wide. Food is either conventional, or regenerated frozen or chilled, which is portioned onto plates in the serving area, these are put into a heated cabinet then onto the Carousel as required.

The Carousel itself is a slowly revolving turntable of which half is in the servery and half in the dining room; it takes a minute to complete one revolution. It has bottom fixed shelves which hold trays and cutlery but the revolving turntable has shelves for plated hot meals and cold meals. As customers take their choice of dish so is it replaced as the shelf reaches the servery.

ADAPTATION OF SYSTEMS

So far the systems described appear more suitable for large-scale catering operations but the system approach has been widely adopted for smaller units such as chain operators and fast food units. An individual unit may be run by a manager directly for a company or by a franchisee who has to operate it in accordance with the franchise company which decides the total package, including the exterior and internal decor and the operational systems. The operation is designed to provide the customer with a satisfactory standard product which never varies, so retaining customer loyalty. The formula for presentation has to be abided by as has the portion size and price. The equipment used is decided by the parent company and strict instructions regarding its operation have to be kept to. Even the packaging and condiments are decided.

Such systemisation covering every possible aspect including staff skills and salaries is the reason for much of their success. Some of these aspects could be adopted by an individual entrepreneur as the know-how is not strictly copyright and the equipment is generally available, but a large world-wide company with resources in research and development has considerable advantages to offer; success as a franchisee is assured.

An individual can move towards a systematic operation by using standardised recipes and by the inclusion of prepared items in his dishes, even by using fully prepared products so minimising resources and space usage. A standardised recipe can provide the following advantages: (i) uniformity of standard with no variation whoever makes the dish; (ii) customer satisfaction every time the dish is featured; (iii) correct portion control; (iv) clarity of instructions make it possible for any semi-skilled employee to carry them out successfully; (v) labour costs are easy to evaluate as they can be timed; (vi) less supervision is needed; and (vii) precise ordering requirements are usually included.

In a small establishment where skilled employees would be too expensive to engage there is an alternative to the conventional system. This is to have a limited core of menu items which can be cooked using the minimum of equipment and which can be backed up by a number of bought in ones which can be quickly regenerated and garnished to order. This reduces stock extent and levels, equipment, personnel and space to a minimum but still provides a high standard of food.

The concept of systems catering must be seen as a whole entity and carried out according to a plan rather than on an ad hoc basis as is frequently the practice. Thus it can be seen that its possibilities are enormous; in application it can offer a flexibility of approach leading to the satisfaction of consumer's needs over a wide spectrum of operations. It can transcend the boundaries of traditional catering and be used in such sectors as transport catering, vending, meals-on-wheels, static and mobile kiosks, and so on. In every situation the important thing to remember is to ensure that with a system the whole operation is properly geared to satisfying the consumer's needs, and that quality control and presentation are an integral part of the operation.

13 CONTROL OF COSTS AND REVENUES

Costing – Catering Costs – Control of Materials – Control of Food Costs – Control of Alcoholic Beverages – Methods of Costing – Costing of Dishes – Limitations of the Gross Profit Method – Pricing by the Unitary Control Method – Labour Costs and Labour Costs Control – Control of Overheads – Control of Revenue – Departmental Control – Analysis of Sales.

The main purpose of financial control is to ensure that an enterprise operates within its budget and, in the case of a commercial undertaking, produces a profit to ensure its further progress and development. Each department must make its contribution towards the financial objectives of the enterprise and every activity that takes place must project the image of the enterprise and seek to enhance it.

The techniques used to ensure that financial control is a working and viable factor in the operation includes forecasting the amount of business that will be done over a period of time, the issuing of budgets for each part of the operation, and having cost control systems to monitor results.

COSTING

In order to control the financial aspect of a catering enterprise it is necessary to know the exact cost of every item produced and served so that both its value and cost to the customer can be assessed. This will enable the customer to receive fair value for his money whilst at the same time sufficient profit should be generated to keep the business financially solvent. Costing is thus a means of control and a technique to ensure the prosperity of the firm both from its own and the customer's interests.

Costing must, however, be the servant and not the master of the control system as it might otherwise exert an adverse effect. It is necessary to know what are each of the charges incurred in the production and service of food and drink to a customer, and it is essential to ensure that they are all passed on to him in the prices charged while still providing good value for money.

CATERING COSTS

There are two broad categories of costs used in the operation of a catering enterprise; the first is usually known as fixed costs or direct costs, and the other as the variable or indirect costs but it is advisable not to categorise them too rigidly as sometimes a more flexible classification may produce better profits. In fact it is possible to put some from both the fixed and variable lists into a third category and label it semi-variable costs, as in practice all of them have similar characteristics in terms of flexibility and inflexibility.

Fixed Costs

Under this heading is generally included loan repayment or interest charges, rent, rates, other local authority charges, water and sewerage, insurance, legal services, advertising costs, maintenance costs, depreciation, and net profit which must be at least comparable to the investment.

Loan repayment and interest The direct purchase of premises is better than renting since over a period of time inbuilt inflation inherent in the system of capitalism reduces the initial proportion of the purchasing cost. If a loan is secured for seven years at the current rate of interest the interest paid is approximately the same as the capital loan repayment. Over a ten-year period there would be a smaller capital loan repayment per annum but a total higher interest paid.

Fig. 54 illustrates how a loan taken out for various periods of time can be repaid; it shows the differences in total repayments.

Figure 54
LOAN REPAYMENT FIGURES

Amount of loan: £100,000
Rate of interest: 15% per annum, constant

No. of years:	7	10	15
Capital loan repayment	£14,285 p.a. × 7 = 100,000	£10,000 p.a. × 10 = 100,000	£ 6,666 p.a. × 15 = 100,000
Interest	£15,000 p.a. × 7 = 105,000	£15,000 p.a. × 10 = 150,000	£15,000 p.a. × 15 = 225,000
Total repayments	£205,000	£250,000	£325,000

Rent   The sum charged to rent a premises is normally dependent on the location and value of the property, the rent being for a fixed period with reviews at set intervals. Renting means that the capital requirement is considerably lessened which offers many advantages over the short term but disadvantages over the long term in that the premises never belong to the operator. The charges increase as the value of the property increases with the owner wanting to increase the rent of a very successful business since it in turn has increased the value of the property.

Rates   The rateable value of property varies according to the locality with high street values generally being rated more than those elsewhere. It should ultimately be remembered that rates tend to rise every year and that their cost has to be borne by customers in the prices charged.

Insurance and Legal Services   The value of the premises and contents need to be fully covered by insurance, also customers and their belongings and any person who enters the premises legally. Insurance is an important fixed cost that needs to be updated with the increase in the value of property and goods.

The services of a solicitor are valuable in dealing with licence applications, unpaid bills and similar problems.

Advertising   The amount of money spent on advertising may not amount to more than 1 per cent of turnover although most restaurateurs do see the need to keep the public aware of the existence of the business. A budget allowance should be made but a feedback of information is necessary to see how effective various means of advertising are.

Maintenance and Repairs   It is usually impossible to predict exactly how much the cost of maintenance and repairs is going to be in any trading period so a specific sum should be set aside for this, the amount expressed as a percentage of turnover probably of the order of $2\frac{1}{2}$ per cent. A planned programme of maintenance with maintenance contracts for all expensive and frequently used equipment is sensible if the size of the business does not allow for the employment of a maintenance engineer or has a works department. It is foolish to neglect the need to budget for these.

Depreciation and Replacement   Utensils and equipment wear out after a time and need to be replaced so an allowance of up to $2\frac{1}{2}$ per cent of turnover should be allocated to this heading. The useful life of fixed equipment and machinery can be estimated and it is necessary to make an allowance for replacement of obsolete items.

Net Profit   It is accepted that the net profit of a commercial undertaking be considered as one of the fixed costs since without any profit the business could not survive. The businessman has to take a salary or living wage as a reward for

388

his efforts. The precise amount of net profit to be expected is related to the amount of capital invested rather than to the turnover of a small firm. The enterprise should yield at least the same gain as if the capital had been invested in bonds, stocks or shares or in a deposit account, after the payment of the entrepreneur's salary. It should be remembered that a catering business tends to be capital intensive and may need premises in a prime location. If it has been purchased by the owner its periodic revaluation will be a form of profit.

The Influence of Turnover on Fixed Costs

Each place allocated for the use of a customer in the dining room costs a certain amount of money to provide and maintain. There is the cost of setting up and equipping the room which as part of the capital expenditure is recouped over a certain number of years. There is also the daily running costs of the room, this being the recurring expenses related to the fixed costs. When added together then divided by the seating capacity and the number of days it operates in figure of the cost of providing each seat can be arrived at. This basic cost has to be recovered from each client who uses the seat.

The occupancy rate will obviously have an effect upon the amount to be recouped from each occupant of the seat, since if the chair is occupied by several customers during the two main meal periods the cost to each would be less than if occupied once only. Thus if the recurring cost is £3.00 per chair per day and it was used by four customers the charge to each would be 75p. This suggests that there is a great advantage to be gained from maximising turnover rather than under-using the resources.

In general this fixed cost per seat is incorporated into the price of the meals and is reflected in the gross profit and the kitchen percentage.

Variable Costs

Under this heading is included the cost of producing items for sale which includes food and drink, labour and energy. They are so called because they show the direct relationship of increased expenditure to additional business.

Semi-variable Costs

Some of the headings from the foregoing lists can be put into this third category because their costs can fluctuate during the financial year; they would include energy, maintenance, and repair and renewals of equipment. Every establishment uses energy regardless of the volume of business; staff have to be kept on duty even at quiet periods and staff meals provided even if the customers' dining room is empty.

389

The three categories of costs can be seen then in the following light – fixed costs tend to remain static over a trading period, the variable costs have a fixed nature up to a certain rate of usage, and the semi-variable costs have a tendency to move in the same direction as the variable ones rather than those of the fixed costs.

CONTROL OF MATERIALS

Until recently the major form of expenditure was accepted as being for materials. It was recognised, however, that the higher the class of establishment, the higher labour costs would be, these then representing the major form of expenditure. But generally speaking, when both food and drink are included under the heading of materials then this certainly constitutes the major form of costs.

The control of materials begins when goods are ordered and continues through the storage and preparation stages. In the latter there are two methods of control – the unitary method and the gross profit method.

Unitary Method of Control

Each item of material is classed as a unit so making it possible to control it by count from the time it arrives to when it is sold. This method is much used in the snack bar, fast food and other similar operations and it can be used with a cyclical Table d'Hôte menu. It is not suitable for the high-class establishment as it tends to restrict choice of foods and methods of cooking and finishing; in these places the gross profit system is widely used.

Gross Profit Method of Control

Under this method the person responsible for the production and finishing of dishes will have received materials to a certain value into his kitchen. He is then expected to achieve a return of monies through sales which will be sufficient to recover the original value of these materials plus a gross profit to pay the fixed and variable costs. This means having to add a figure of from 50 per cent up to 300 per cent or, in other words, multiplying the materials cost by from $1\frac{1}{2}$ to 4 times their value to arrive at the selling price. These percentages are not expressed as an addition on sales but as a fraction of sales returns which represents 100 per cent of revenue.

In some large-scale catering establishments there is a system whereby a total sum of money is allocated to run the operation over the year to cover the cost of food and service for the expected number of customers and at a certain

390

standard. The total sum is divided into the various costs and may not be exceeded; for example, in a hospital the allocation for food may be £1.30 per day per patient which must provide a breakfast, a two course luncheon and a three course evening meal. Labour costs would be under a separate segment of the total budget.

CONTROL OF FOOD COSTS

The problem of keeping strict control over costs by constraint over the usage of materials can be solved by determining the exact number of customers expected on any day and at any meal and by reference to records of past business and other local factors. It is also necessary to forecast fairly accurately the numbers of each item customers will be likely to choose from the day's menu and figures can be obtained from keeping a record of menu item popularity. Together these two will help to prevent over-production and in conjunction with the laying down of production schedules will assist in equating supply to demand.

Records of purchases, performance and sales, together with a cyclical menu and standardised recipes can all help in solving the problem of how many portions to produce; they go a long way in establishing a streamlined organisation which prevents the chances of over- or under-production. The head chef instructs his assistants as to the number of portions to be produced, and a check on numbers as they are being sold will prevent customers from being disappointed by being told a dish is 'off' after having ordered it. With some menu items it is possible to cook more portions if there is an unexpected demand for them, and if the cooking process is not a long one.

In estimating the number of portions there are to be sold it is necessary to evaluate how much of the original amount issued is likely to be lost in the transformatory process from raw to cooked stages. If, for example, roast ribs of beef is being prepared for an estimated eighty portions the figures used by a good class restaurant where the kitchen is run on traditional lines might be:

Allowance of 250 g per portion		
Total weight required 80 × 250 g	=	20 kg – 100%
Preparation loss	=	3 kg – 15%
Cooking loss	=	6 kg – 30%
Bones removed during carving	=	$2\frac{1}{2}$ kg – $12\frac{1}{2}$%
Trimmings during carving	=	500 g – $2\frac{1}{2}$%
Yield of carved meat (80 × 100 g portion)	=	8 kg – 40%

Slow cooking at a low temperature could reduce the cooking loss by 50 per cent thus yielding up to twelve portions more according to the degree of cooking. On a carvery counter where customers carve portions from the joint the number of portions could be less where mainly men serve themselves and averaged out in a dining room patronised equally by both sexes.

The control over a purely à la Carte menu is likely to be less exact than that of a Table d'Hôte one, but as dishes on this side of the menu are more highly priced the return should be better than that for the Table d'Hôte service especially as there is little or no over-production.

One of the secrets of the success of any catering enterprise is said to be the implementation of a very strict system of portion control, preferably on unitary lines. Yet in many cases a certain flexibility in the method of operation may actually prove as profitable, depending on the expertise of the cooks. As illustrated above the buyer will order a certain amount of a commodity based on portion size to serve a certain number of customers, but by careful cooking and carving a greater number of portions can be obtained and in addition there could be a made-up dish from the trimmings. Thus the concept of a precise control with its concomitant standardisation and specification must be seen only as an aid to control, rather than as a strict and undeviating system which could stifle initiative and deter better presentation.

CONTROL OF ALCOHOLIC BEVERAGES

The main differences between the control over food commodities and that of drink lies in the fact that many foodstuffs are of a highly perishable nature in contrast to drink, which in general stores quite well; not all foods lend themselves to unitary control whereas drink is practically all bought in unitary form. All that is required is to know the range of drinks offered for sale, predict the demand for each and set up an operation that establishes stock levels and re-ordering procedures. The stock levels are set to ensure continuity of supply to cover the normal demand plus a reserve to meet a sudden unexpected demand.

To find out how much of each drink to keep in stock it is necessary to know how many of each is likely to be sold each day, how often delivery can be made by the supplier, and add on an amount for a buffer stock to cover any sudden demand. The total value of stock in hand should not exceed the period allowed for payment which is normally twenty-eight days.

The control of wine is quite straightforward and each sale can be accounted for through the checking system used; beer and soft drinks are also easy to control. Other drinks are sold by the measure and yield a certain number of portions per bottle according to contents as shown in Fig. 55. The 'out' measures used indicate the number of portions obtained from 1 gill (5 fl oz or 143 ml). Outage denotes the number of portions obtained from the full bottle.

392

Figure 55
OUTPUT PER BOTTLE

	Bottle size	Measure	Outage	Measure	Outage
Whisky, gin, vodka	$26\frac{2}{3}$ fl oz	5 out	27	6 out	32
Brandy	24 fl oz	5 out	24	6 out	27
Liqueurs	22-27 fl oz	6 out	24-32	—	—
Sherry, port	$26\frac{2}{3}$ fl oz	3 out	16	4 out	21
Vermouth	$26\frac{2}{3}$ fl oz	3 out	16	4 out	21

METHODS OF COSTING

The gross profit method of costing is the one most widely used because it fulfils a twofold function – its simple formula makes it easy to calculate the correct selling price and it ensures that all the costs are recovered from every sale, including the element of profit. The following diagram, Fig. 56 shows an example in a simple form of how the elements of cost are related to sales. Sales are obviously 100 per cent of revenue, costs represent a percentage of sales, these being for materials, labour and the overheads previously mentioned, and when these are subtracted from the selling price what is left is the net profit.

Figure 56
SALES AND RELATED COSTS

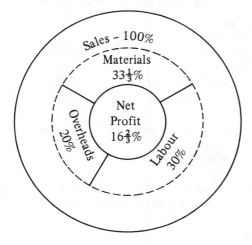

The materials are basically the food and drink with cigars and cigarettes being kept separate – the profit from these is usually 10 per cent which is below that for food and drink. The proportion ascribed to labour includes wages and necessary expenses associated with employment such as National Insurance contributions, pensions, uniform costs and meals on duty. The overheads consist of all the other fixed or semi-variable costs, but to arrive at the figure for gross profit there is only one figure to consider which is the difference between the selling price and the cost of materials as shown in Fig. 57.

Figure 57
SALES AND RELATED GROSS PROFIT

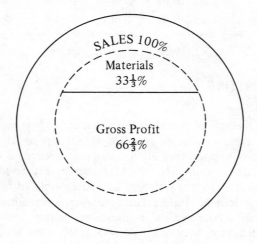

So to arrive at the figure for gross profit all that is necessary is to deduct the cost of materials from the sales; the cost of materials over a trading period is arrived at as in the following example:

		£
	Value of opening stock	1,000
+	purchases during period	10,000
−	value of closing stock	1,500
∴	the cost of materials used equals	9,500
	Sales during the period equals	28,500

The materials cost percentage can thus be expressed as:

$$\frac{\text{Materials}}{\text{Sales}} \times 100 = \text{Materials Cost \%}$$

Then using the above figures, £9,500 for materials and £28,500 for the sales during the same period, the materials percentage becomes

$$\frac{9,500}{28,500} \times \frac{100}{1} = 33\tfrac{1}{3}\%$$

which gives the following percentages:

394

		£		
Sales (Takings)	=	28,500	=	100%
Materials (Goods Consumed)	=	9,500	=	$33\frac{1}{3}\%$
Gross Profit	=	19,000	=	$66\frac{2}{3}\%$

The gross profit percentage representing the kitchen's contribution to the profitability of the business is commonly referred to as the kitchen percentage and this is the figure which shows the chef how efficiently he is running his department. The figures used to arrive at the kitchen percentage must be the costs and sales of food only. Those for drink would be calculated separately.

The formula used for arriving at the kitchen percentage is

$$\frac{\text{Gross Profit}}{\text{Sales}} \times \frac{100}{1} = \text{Gross Profit \% for the kitchen}$$

i.e. the kitchen percentage.

The following example uses the same foregoing figures but related to the costs and sales of food only.

$$\begin{matrix}(\text{Gross Profit})\\(\text{Sales})\end{matrix} \quad \frac{19,000}{28,500} \times \frac{100}{1} = 66\frac{2}{3}\% = \text{Kitchen Percentage}$$

Another way of expressing gross profit is the difference between sales revenue and the cost of materials as in the following example:

	£
Sales	10,000
— cost of materials	3,300
∴ gross profit equals	6,700

To arrive at the figure for net profit it is necessary to deduct from the gross profit the cost of labour and other overheads as previously defined.

Costing of Dishes

To find the cost of a dish accurately before including it on the menu the recipe must be defined precisely as, for example, a Suprême of Chicken Maréchal might have a food cost when cooked of £1.25 which at different gross profits would be:

$$£1.25 \times \frac{100}{40} = £3.12\frac{1}{2} \qquad \text{(gross profit 60\%)}$$

$$£1.25 \times \frac{100}{33\frac{1}{3}} = £3.75 \qquad \text{(gross profit } 66\frac{2}{3}\%\text{)}$$

$$£1.25 \times \frac{100}{30} = £4.17 \qquad \text{(gross profit 70\%)}$$

The quick way to do each of these is to multiply by $2\frac{1}{2}$, 3 and $3\frac{1}{3}$; it is usual to round the figures up to the nearest 5p to give the selling price. A full Table d'Hôte menu can be costed to give the total selling price per meal in a similar manner.

For this system of costing to be an effective means of control it is inadvisable to set a different rate of gross profit for different courses as this would create differing results in the expected return. This applies particularly to drinks as they cannot be separated into various percentage returns unless sales are recorded separately, and variance from expected percentages would occur as drinking patterns change with the seasons. To suggest that beer should yield a lower profit than spirits has some merit but the results in terms of control become unsatisfactory. The average gross return on bar sales is at present approximately 50 per cent as anything higher would have a detrimental effect on sales. The pricing of wine is a different matter and according to quality it can yield a gross profit of 50–75 per cent bearing in mind that there is no processing but simply storage and service.

Limitation of the Gross Profit Method of Pricing

Although this method of pricing is a useful tool of management it must be understood that as a tool of costing it can prove inflexible if complete accuracy is required. In the wrong hands it can cause serious damage to a firm's turnover. One of the hallmarks of good business practice is that it should be both adaptable and flexible – with this system it cannot be so. The accurate and formal application of the gross profit system may be the reason for the disappearance of some of the more expensive items from menus, leading to the conformity of dishes that is noticeable in many catering establishments.

The following examples illustrate this statement but first it is necessary to pose the questions, 'Should a restaurateur expect bigger profits from customers with more sophisticated tastes?' and 'Why should the person wanting an expensive first course pay as much as five times the going rate for the rental of his chair than the one who selects a cheaper one?' This is asked in the knowledge that the restaurateur will not settle the account with his suppliers until well after the foodstuffs are used and he will not be charged any interest on the credit allowed.

EXAMPLE 1. SMOKED SCOTCH SALMON

		FLORIDA COCKTAIL	
1 portion of 70 g @ £6.50 per 500 g =	91p	1 grapefruit	15p
brown bread and butter	5p	$\frac{1}{2}$ orange	5p
lemon, cress	4p	sugar	2p
Cost price	100p	cherry	3p
Selling price @ 65% gross profit	285p	Cost price	25p
Gross profit	£1.85	Selling price @ 65% gross profit	70p
		Gross profit	45p

In this example the cheaper first course is the most labour intensive of the two and yet the profit is only a quarter of that for the expensive item.

This next example shows how inflation can have an effect upon costing and, in turn, competitiveness, because of the method of pricing used.

EXAMPLE 2. GRILLED ENTRECÔTE STEAK

200 g sirloin @ £6.40 per kg =	128p
garnish	12p
Total cost	140p
Selling price @ 66$\frac{2}{3}$% gross profit	£4.20

The following year the sirloin may have increased in price by 20 per cent and other prices by 10 per cent

200 g sirloin @ £8.00 per kg =	154p
garnish	13p
Total cost	167p
Selling price @ 66$\frac{2}{3}$% gross profit	£5.00

The result of inflation shows a rise of 80p in the selling price of this steak and also poses the question as to whether this increase could have an adverse effect upon demand as evinced in the truism, the higher the price the lower will be the demand.

The Pricing of Wine

As previously stated, with a mark up of 50 per cent on a bottle of wine, one that cost £2.00 to buy can be sold for £6.00, but when it is a fine wine that costs £10.00 if it is listed at £30.00 very few bottles are likely to be ordered. It would therefore be advisable to add gross profit on a pro rata scale applied in reverse as follows – 50 per cent gross profit on wines costing up to £5.00 per bottle, 40 per cent on those up to £10 and only 30 per cent on fine ones that cost the firm £20 per bottle.

But it is not necessary to control wine by this method since it is so easy to do it in unit form which also gives flexibility of pricing.

CONTROL AND PRICING BY THE UNITARY CONTROL METHOD

In an establishment that operates on a restricted menu such as a steak house or fast food snack bar this method permits total food control by numbers which means that apart from say chips and ice cream everything is done by count, as shown in Fig. 58.

The left hand side of the form is completed from the purchasing records and the right from sales records or waitress's checks. Rather than having various percentage mark ups for different items a single charge may be made per item sold according to course, e.g. first courses 50p, main course 100p, dessert 50p, thus creating conditions where every customer pays the same amount per chair rent. This is a simple but successful method of operation except that it offers little flexibility and the caterer becomes totally dependent upon portion control lines, for which he probably has to pay more than were he to prepare them himself.

LABOUR COSTS AND LABOUR COST CONTROL

As has been suggested the stage has now been reached when the cost of labour often exceeds that of materials. This may not always be apparent since the major part of labour costs are generated by the kitchen and dining room and may become diffused in the total labour costs of the establishment, whereby the total figure in proportion becomes more acceptable. The cost of serving drinks, for example, may be only $7\frac{1}{2}$ per cent of sales as against labour costs for the kitchen of 35 per cent but it brings down the average to a more acceptable 21 per cent assuming that both sales are equal.

The first task in the control of labour should ideally be by drawing a base-line in relation to turnover of customers and the proposed line of activity; judging the standard against another similar unit may be helpful in deciding on numbers of personnel. It is important that standards are set for each member of staff including managerial, supervisory, skilled and unskilled operatives, and where figures for business turnover exist the best way to obtain a clear perspective is to allocate a specific time to each section in relation to customer numbers, as shown in Fig. 59. This shows a dining room with 200 seats which

398

Figure 58
UNITARY CONTROL STOCK SHEET

Stock Sheet for Week Ending 24.7.1985

Steaks	A Opening stock	B Purchases					Total A + B	Less closing stock	Total usage	Daily usage				
		M	T	W	T	F				M	T	W	T	F
Sirloin 180 g	24			40		50	114	24	90	10	6	18	26	30
Sirloin 250 g	20			30		50	100	23	77	7	6	14	18	32
Rump 180 g	30			30		50	110	26	84	8	7	16	19	34
Rump 250 g	34			30		50	114	42	72	7	7	12	16	30
Porterhouse 550 g	10			20		20	50	7	43	2	6	10	10	15

399

employs the members of staff as shown; assuming it is open for only five days per week and serves 400 customers per day or 2.000 per week the first column shows the total number of hours worked by the staff per week, the second the percentage of time devoted by each group of the total, and the third column shows the time devoted to each customer by each group.

Figure 59

EXAMPLE OF STAFF–CUSTOMER RATIOS IN A RESTAURANT SERVING 400 CUSTOMERS PER DAY OVER A FIVE-DAY WEEK

No. of staff	Total hours per week	% of time devoted to each customer	Minutes devoted to each customer
1 Manager	40	2	1.20
2 Assistant Managers	80	4	2.40
20 Chefs	800	40	24.00
20 Waiters	800	40	24.00
2 Storekeepers	80	4	2.40
2 Stillroom Hands	80	4	2.40
2 Dishwash Hands	80	4	2.40
1 General Porter	40	2	1.20
TOTALS 50	2,000	100%	60.00

Having set the correct hourly manning level, the next stage would be to extend the table to include the wages paid plus employer contributions and staff meals to arrive at the total cost of labour for this establishment.

By clearly establishing manning levels, turnover analysis will indicate more clearly when staff hours increase disproportionately to customer usage but by taking the average labour expense per hour the baseline would clearly indicate how much each customer should pay in what he is charged to cover labour expenses on the average daily usage. Assuming a labour cost of £3.00 per hour then the customer should contribute that amount in his bill. It is important to see that labour costs are kept under control by ensuring that the time allocated per cover or cost per hour does not increase of its own volition, otherwise the figures budgeted become meaningless and there is less net profit at the end. The figures given so far are representative of the higher class of the restaurant business but a similar formula may be used to establish a baseline for other forms of business, although because of large-scale preparation and cafeteria service the amount allocated per customer may be decreased to ten minutes or less of labour hours per customer as illustrated in Fig. 60.

400

Figure 60
EXAMPLE OF STAFF–CUSTOMER RATIOS IN A CANTEEN SERVING
200 MAIN MEALS PER DAY OVER A FIVE DAY WEEK

No. of staff	Total hours per week	% of time devoted to each customer	Minutes devoted to each customer
1 Chef Manager	40	11.11	1.20
2 Chefs	80	22.22	2.40
2 General Assistants	80	22.22	2.40
3 Counter Hands	120	33.33	3.60
1 Cashier	40	11.11	1.20
TOTALS 9	360	99.99%	10.80

Having established the baseline for control over labour costs it is necessary to check that service periods are not allowed to expand with a result that overtime has to be worked. The rate at which staff can be expected to work at because of the skills they possess may be of assistance in saving on numbers employed. Labour saving equipment assists by lessening the burden on staff so allowing them to operate at full efficiency. The use of a proportion of convenience foods will reduce labour requirements by cutting out a lot of preparation work. The application of work study techniques in production practice and the ideal siting of equipment can also contribute to the effective use of labour.

CONTROL OF OVERHEADS

The cost of overheads continues to rise so they all need to be looked at regularly to try to keep them in check. The following points are given as examples of where savings may be made. Savings in the use of energy may be made by creating an awareness in staff of not turning on equipment long before it is required and the need to turn it off when no longer required. A weekly target showing how much less has been used than the previous week, an example of what a particular item of equipment costs to run per hour, and exhortations on the need to conserve sources of energy for future generations are all useful deterrents against waste.

A regular programme of maintenance and repair will save money as minor faults are less costly to put right before they deteriorate further and staff should be encouraged to report defects as soon as they occur. Laundry charges can be reduced by using slip cloths over table cloths and by forbidding the misuse of table napkins, waiter's cloths and teacloths.

CONTROL OF REVENUE

After ensuring that control is maintained all along the line there then comes the final point when the correct amount of money is received for all goods supplied to consumers and is paid into the accounts of the business. There are several methods of revenue control available – manual, mechanical, or electronic installations according to the needs of the establishment. The traditional system of the waiter writing out the customer's order in numbered triplicate – top copy, bottom copy and flimsy copy – and going through the process as illustrated in Fig. 61 is being replaced in many establishments by more sophisticated ordering systems that also act as a means of control.

Figure 61
TRIPLICATE CHECKING METHOD (*Flow Chart*)

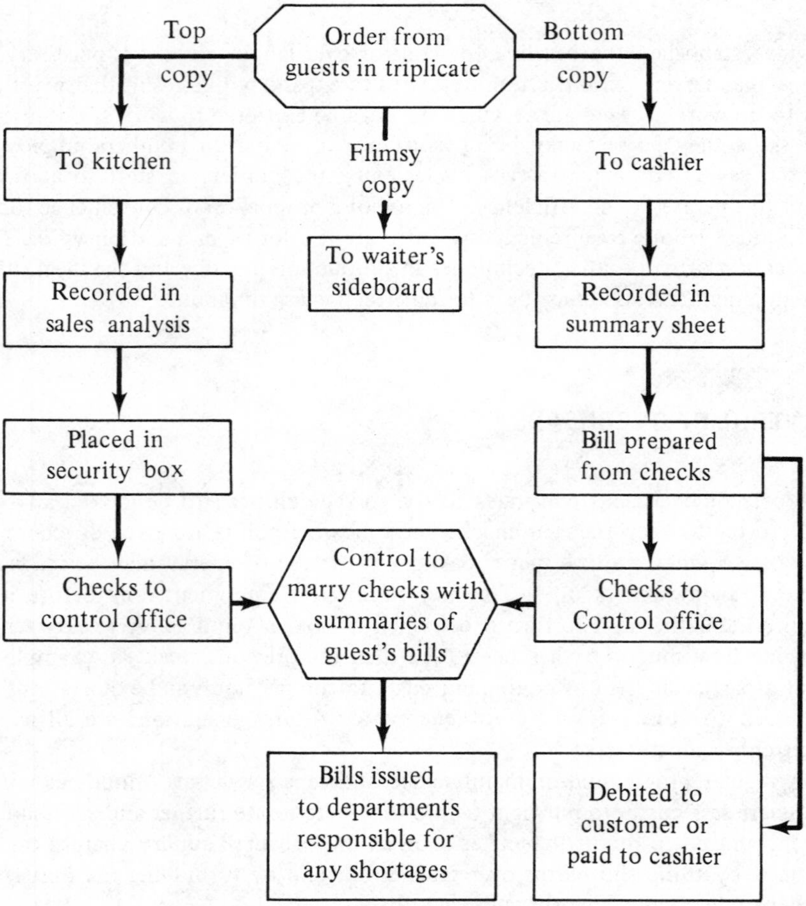

The Waiter Billing Machine

Various billing machines have been introduced to replace the traditional system of waiter's checks. The machine can do away with the need to employ a restaurant cashier and offers a quick analysis of goods sold by means of a memory system. One such machine works by the waiter noting down the customer's order on his pad then going to the machine to insert his own coded key, then entering the order by pressing numbered buttons for each item. This appears in the kitchen in printed form to be announced and when everything is dished up the waiter's number is flashed on a screen in the dining room informing him that the food can be collected. This system saves the need for waiting staff running backwards and forwards between dining room and kitchen unnecessarily.

The waiter then requests the machine to print out the customer's bill which comes out as an easy-to-read list of each item ordered, its cost and the total to be paid plus VAT and service charge. At the conclusion of the service an assistant manager will press each waiter's key to see how much each one has taken and the total business for that session. The total is broken down under food, wine, spirits and any other heading. One of the advantages of such a system is that as the ordering terminals and screen are so very compact they can be placed in between stations as to be available to several waiters. They work very successfully in fast food, pay-as-you-leave, drive-in, and other similar operations but may require further sophistication before they can be used in every class of waiter service establishment.

A similar system can be used in the control of sales and revenue in the bar. A microprocessor connected to the optics and beer engines will record every sale, the monitor being housed in an office away from the bar where usage and income can be checked at the end of each service period and, indeed, at any time in between. When an empty bottle is replaced by a new one this is shown.

It is possible to put control onto a computer – from a bank of dishes with their recipes a complete menu cycle can be programmed giving the precise amount of ingredients to be issued for a given number of portions; it can also show the nutritional value and the cost of the meal. The new microprocessors can handle 300 or more recipes with up to thirty ingredients in each.

DEPARTMENTAL CONTROL

The aim of departmental control should be to provide management with the necessary information as to how each part of the enterprise is fulfilling its role in achieving the anticipated revenue return, so contributing effectively to its overall success. Norms for each department are not easy to establish since it is inevitable that one may contribute to the success of another; for example, a lounge bar obtains most of its income from dining room customers. Yet the fact remains that in this business the profit comes only from the public areas, so each square metre must contribute towards it.

The form taken by control varies from one place to another but certain data must be provided to ensure that profitability is maintained and constantly improved. The data needed by management should show, (i) daily takings, (ii) average spending power per customer, (iii) occupancy rate of the room per meal, per day, and per week, (iv) average spend per customer on (a) food, (b) drink and (v) takings for (a) à la Carte meals, (b) Table d'Hôte meals, (c) drinks. This information can then be extended to provide weekly, monthly and annual reports in conjunction with various cost percentages for departments so that reappraisal can be made an ongoing feature; areas of low revenue or excessive expenditure can be pinpointed, and quiet periods and low operating performance be isolated so that extra resources be allocated there to promote profitability.

ANALYSIS OF SALES

Part of the control of revenue comes from an analysis or summary of daily business as collated by the cashier recording the actual sales of food and drink as taken from waiter's checks. When completed the form is forwarded to the office to be reconciled with the checks received from the kitchen and those from the cashier. This control over the day's business can show how profitable the kitchen or bar has been as well as the sales of each separate department.

From this sheet a daily Comparisons of Business Done can be compiled, but not all the information provided by the summary sheet is necessary to monitor the economic performance of the establishment. All that is required is the essential information about how the unit operates within its stated objectives. The format as shown in Fig. 62 may be used to provide the report on the basis of a 110-seater dining room.

This information is prepared for management perusal each day to provide details of the number of customers served and the occupancy rate, it is calculated by the number of users over the number of available seats. So although the figures in Fig. 62 would appear to be very satisfactory the occupancy rate points to a low level of business at lunchtime, which calls for action. A manager might plot the occupancy rate of the dining room in the form of a graph so as to be able to keep an instant check on the progress of the business, doing it either by number of covers or revenue received. Fig. 63 shows a weekly report which highlights the days of the week when business is slack, a state of affairs which might be improved by means of various marketing methods, such as an advertisement offering some special attraction.

404

Figure 62
DAILY COMPARISONS OF BUSINESS DONE IN A
110-SEATER RESTAURANT

DATE: *Monday 15th Feb. 19. . . .*			*Same day last week*	*Same day last year*
		£	£	£
TAKINGS	– Total	2,500	2,400	2,000
LUNCH	– Table d'Hôte	224	198	250
	– à la Carte	401	402	250
	– Drinks	208	200	167
DINNER	– Table d'Hôte	430	400	400
	– à la Carte	820	800	600
	– Drinks	417	400	333
AVERAGE SPEND				
LUNCH	– Food	7.81	7.05	5.55
	– Drink	2.60	2.35	1.85
DINNER	– Food	12.50	12.00	10.00
	– Drink	4.18	4.09	3.33
NO. OF COVERS				
LUNCH		80	85	90
DINNER		100	100	100
OCCUPANCY RATE				
LUNCH		73%	77%	82%
DINNER		91%	91%	91%

A close look at this report will show that despite the increased takings which could be due to inflation or to higher prices charged, the business performance has not increased very much at dinner while the takings for lunch are down from the previous year. In an establishment that has several dining rooms a comparison between the performance of each can be made.

A trading report to show the profitability of the operation should be kept separate from the business reports as too much information presented at a glance could lose its essential impact. A trading report can be produced weekly, monthly or annually and its format can vary according to the needs of the company. A sample report is shown in Fig. 64 (ASP = Average Spend per Person).

Figure 63
WEEKLY COMPARISONS WITH LAST YEAR OF BUSINESS DONE

WEEK ENDING	MONDAY		TUESDAY		WEDNESDAY		THURSDAY		FRIDAY		SATURDAY		SUNDAY	
May 10th 19 . . .	This year	Last year	This year	Last year	This year	Last year	This year	Last year	This year	Last year	This year	Last year	This year	Last year
TOTAL COVERS	165	160	170	165	175	180	170	165	200	200	220	220		
TOTAL TAKINGS £	1500	1200	1600	1400	1800	1600	1800	1600	2500	2000	2800	2300	CLOSED	
Food £	1000	800	1100	900	1200	1100	1200	1200	1800	1400	2000	1700		
Drink £	500	400	500	500	600	500	600	400	700	600	800	600		
LUNCH Covers	75	80	80	80	80	85	80	85	90	90	90	95		
Food £	333	270	370	300	400	370	400	400	600	550	700	600	CLOSED	
Drink £	150	130	150	150	200	150	200	133	230	200	270	200		
DINNER Covers	90	80	90	85	95	95	90	80	120	110	130	125		
Food £	667	530	730	600	800	730	800	800	1200	850	1300	1100	CLOSED	
Drink £	350	270	350	350	400	350	400	267	470	400	530	400		

TOTAL TAKINGS

For this week: £12,000
For the same week last year: £10,100

Figure 64
DINING ROOM AND BAR
Monthly Trading Report

MONTH ENDING June 30th 19	*No. of covers*	*Sales* £	ASP	*Materials Cost* £	*Materials Cost* % of Sales	*Gross profit* %	*Labour costs* £	*Labour costs* % of Sales	*Operating profit*
DINING ROOM									
Food	10,000	30,000	£3.00	10,000	$33\frac{1}{3}$	$66\frac{2}{3}$	10,000	$33\frac{1}{3}$	$33\frac{1}{3}$
Drink		10,000	£1,00	5,000	50.0	50.0	1,000	10.0	40.0
BAR									
Drink		5,000	£2.50	2,500	50.0	50.0	1,000	20	30.0
Food	2,000	3,000	£1.50	1,000	$33\frac{1}{3}$	$66\frac{2}{3}$	1,000	$33\frac{1}{3}$	$33\frac{1}{3}$
TOTALS	12,000	48,000		18,500			13,000		

On a quarterly report the accrued overheads could be shown by extending the page across.

The purpose of these reports is to provide the manager with sufficient information to take effective decisions in order to maintain the desired business performance. Where a business incorporates several units each possessing a clear identity it becomes important to collect relevant statistics on each so as to point out their performance. In a large establishment with several function rooms it is an equally useful exercise and all that is needed is to add on the figures for the other rooms.

Another report that is of great importance is the one showing occupancy figures over a period of time; it could be an exercise to stimulate a manager to improve his business performance. Fig. 65 illustrates such a report.

Figure 65
MONTHLY OCCUPANCY REPORT

CATERING SECTION

Monthly Occupancy Report

MONTH ENDING 31st March 19....	Seating capacity	Optimum capacity per day	Optimum capacity per month	Actual users	Capacity usage %
RESTAURANT	150	300	7,800	5,200	66
GRILL ROOM	100	200	5,200	5,800	111
COFFEE SHOP	80	400	10,400	10,000	96
BANQUETING SUITE A	100	200	5,200	1,200	23
BANQUETING SUITE B	300	600	15,600	4,800	30

The spare capacity is here highlighted and action is required in some areas as only the grill room is operating to capacity.

The last of these forms of control of a business's performance is the yearly report which can take various forms but should show the information as contained in the following table, Fig. 66.

It should be noted that this is not a financial statement but a managerial report. For this reason VAT and similar service charges are excluded as also are cigarette sales and other services, since the main purpose of the report is to indicate salient points and too much detail would only detract from its relevance.

In this example it can be seen that only the banqueting suites have had an unfavourable trading period as compared to the previous year; unfavourable trends can be given emphasis by the use of either coloured or bold type.

The report can be used for setting up operating budgets; in addition, management has the responsibility of taking action to bring all the areas within a

408

Figure 66

YEARLY TRADING REPORT

YEAR ENDING: *31st Dec. 19 . . . .*

	No. of covers	Revenue excl. VAT £	Materials costs £	%	Labour costs £	%	Operating profits £	%
RESTAURANT								
Food	60,000	600,000	200,000	33⅓	200,000	33⅓	200,000	33⅓
Drink		180,000	90,000	50.0	18,000	10.0	72,000	40.0
GRILL ROOM								
Food	71,000	375,000	125,000	33⅓	100,000	26.6	150,000	40.0
Drink		142,000	70,000	49.2	14,200	10.0	57,800	40.7
COFFEE SHOP								
Sales	120,000	240,000	96,000	40.2	70,000	29.1	74,000	30.8
BANQUETING SUITE A								
Food	7,000	105,000	35,000	33⅓	40,000	38.5	30,000	28.6
Drink		28,000	14,000	50.0	2,500	8.9	11,500	41.0
BANQUETING SUITE B								
Food	30,000	300,000	120,000	40.0	100,000	33⅓	80,000	26.6
Drink		90,000	45,000	50.0	9,000	10.0	36,000	40.0
TOTALS	288,000	2,060,000	795,000		553,700		711,300	

PREVIOUS YEAR

	No. of covers	Revenue excl. VAT £	Materials costs £	%	Labour costs £	%	Operating profits £	%
RESTAURANT								
Food	50,000	450,000	160,000	35.5	180,000	40.0	110,000	24.4
Drink		150,000	75,000	50.0	15,000	10.0	60,000	40.0
GRILL ROOM								
Food	70,000	350,000	115,000	32.8	90,000	25.7	145,000	41.4
Drink		135,000	72,500	53.7	13,800	10.2	48,700	36.0
COFFEE SHOP								
Sales	100,000	190,000	67,000	35⅓	62,000	32.6	61,000	32.1
BANQUETING SUITE A								
Food	10,000	135,000	45,000	33⅓	38,000	28.1	52,000	38.5
Drink		35,000	17,500	50.0	3,600	10.3	13,900	39.7
BANQUETING SUITE B								
Food	28,000	250,000	75,000	30.0	81,000	32.4	94,000	37.6
Drink		70,000	36,000	51.4	7,000	10.0	27,000	38.5
TOTALS	258,000	1,765,000	663,000		490,400		611,600	

UNDISTRIBUTED OVERHEADS

	Current £	%	Previous £	%
Administration	120,000	5.82	112,000	6.34
Heating & Energy	103,000	5.00	98,000	5.55
Repairs & Maintenance	50,000	2.42	44,000	2.49
Replacements	41,200	2.00	30,000	1.70
Advertising	25,000	1.21	24,000	1.35
Total	339,200		308,000	
NET PROFIT BEFORE FIXED COSTS:	372,100		303,600	

desirable course of action. A computer could be used to provide this information, giving updated trading comparisons with previous periods and producing an annual comparison at the end of each month.

In a non-profit making operation the role of reporting would be to monitor costs rather than revenue but otherwise it works as described here.

14 MONITORING OF CONSUMER SATISFACTION

Monitoring of Consumer Satisfaction – Application of Consumer Satisfaction Procedures – Principles of Questionnaire Design – Format of Questionnaires – Evaluation of Questionnaires – Product Evaluation Questionnaires – Food Wastage – Aspects of Quality Control – Budgeting and Management by Objectives – The Budget.

Although each segment of the Catering Cycle indicates the need for good planning and a systemised approach to the operation, each segment must be seen as a dynamic rather than a static process and each must provide means of ensuring that appropriate feedback is received in order to prevent any one stage of the cycle from becoming static. This would lead to it becoming alienated from the original purpose which was based on a specific trend and need when originally planned. It follows that the monitoring of the operation must be comprehensive at all stages, from the identification of demand to the production and distribution of the product, and finally the aspects of consumer satisfaction.

411

To do this it is necessary to monitor the performance of an enterprise from the viewpoint of the customer, from an investigation of the methods of quality control and from the measurement of its financial success. These are the three main sections which together give an overall perspective of the need, the method and the techniques available to monitor the performance of an enterprise; they are dealt with under the following headings, Monitoring of Consumer Satisfaction, Aspects of Quality Control, and Budgeting and Management by Objectives.

MONITORING OF CONSUMER SATISFACTION

As a way of introducing this topic it might be useful to use the analogy of man's bodily mechanism. In the natural course of everyday living, man's conscious and unconscious movements and actions are dependent on obtaining a feedback from the sense organs; this is necessary to adjust muscle contraction or expansion, to maintain bodily posture and to adapt to the various positions demanded by the simplest of tasks. At another level of complexity the bodily mechanism contains certain regulatory processes which permit the maintenance of an almost constant body temperature even when living in such extremes as the Antarctic or the Equator. If man is so dependent on feedback for his survival and wellbeing it follows that each action intentionally undertaken, unless everything remains equal, needs to be continually modified according to changing circumstances or deviation from the intended purpose. Similarly the purpose of monitoring consumer satisfaction is to ensure that what has been set out to achieve is actually fulfilled within the framework established, and that the consumer indicates that his needs and expectations have been met.

Should the means for obtaining feedback in a man fail to function his self-control would be lost, he would cease to exist as a normal healthy person and become dependent upon the care of others. Exactly the same situation will arise in the long term with any enterprise that fails to observe this basic principle of nature, that in order to remain alert to a situation it is necessary to be constantly aware of it by means of a continuous flow of information.

With man the feedback of information is made possible by good dietary practices and healthy habits which maintain regulatory processes in perfect working order. Similarly the enterprise that wishes to maintain a healthy flow of feedback information must create the conditions for it to take place by good organisational procedures. An organisation that does not encourage feedback because of a false sense of security and achievement, or because established procedures are no longer valid in its working atmosphere, is bound to fail in the long run. Only if continuous monitoring is carried out and appropriate action undertaken to interact with changing times and needs can the conditions of continuous growth be maintained.

412

APPLICATION OF CONSUMER SATISFACTION PROCEDURES

The nature of catering has meant that the obtaining of feedback has been carried out in a very informal but effective manner. At its most basic level, custom and courtesy has decreed that the proprietor or head waiter or other person in charge of the dining room asks each customer if he is enjoying his meal; should any sign of dissatisfaction be discerned action to rectify the complaint is taken immediately. It extends beyond an apology to such compensation as a replacement meal with the compliments of the management, a complimentary drink, or a reduction from the bill.

A note would be made of any complaints either in the book kept for this purpose or in the mind of the person in charge, and at intervals a discussion about them would be held between the departmental heads to try to avoid any repetition of such incidents. In this way an approach would have been made to the subject of monitoring consumer satisfaction and a slight attempt made to remedy weaknesses in the system. Unfortunately such an empirical approach fails to reveal consumer dissatisfaction to its fullest extent and a much deeper investigation needs to be taken to discover possible reasons for poor business performance, or any weak links there may be in the catering cycle. It is necessary to trace the sources of consumer dissatisfaction to an earlier stage rather than to allow them to become compounded over several stages and nullifying any efforts made to prevent them arising in the chain of events.

Any investigation at source must start from the premise on which every business is founded, namely the satisfying of an existing demand. Ideally such a provision should be based on a clear understanding of consumer's requirements in terms of choice, quality, quantity and the price they are willing to pay. The system is then based on the product from the acquisition of materials through their processing, distribution and control and should the product become outdated because of a change in eating habits, food fads, or because of competing demands for disposable income, each catering sequence would need to be restructured in order to optimise resources with new product lines. As an example of this it is worthwhile considering the effect upon certain establishments should the hamburger ever go out of fashion. It would have a total effect, as the whole operation is designed around the main product and the introduction of a new product would mean considerable changes to the whole package. It has happened before when some operators have failed to realise that a change was needed and in the end had to go out of business. An operation must be ready to adapt its products to any changes and at times considerably alter the entire concept in order to maintain growth and efficiency. The enterprise must be seen as being dynamic and adaptable; thus it is not only the making of the product which is important but that of supplying a product which is most acceptable in terms of quality and price.

Modern methods of production tend to increase output but constant effort is required to ensure that what the consumer receives is exactly what he requires, as any compromise or adaptation usually leads to loss of business. Catering as a service industry relies on personal contact and the importance of outfront staff and their reaction to consumers must not be overlooked. Consumer satisfaction can stem from the personal contact with staff and eating can be enhanced by personal reassurance and attention. In addition this contact is important in assessing and recording the changes in type of consumer, in eating practices, and in the way in which the product is treated.

An important factor in obtaining consumer feedback at any particular stage of the operation is to design a suitable questionnaire that will result in an unbiased reaction to the questions posed and provide information which will help keep the establishment on the desired course. It should also provide the grounds for any adjustment that may need to be made in order to hold on to the market share, or lay down the premise on which consistent growth can be sustained.

PRINCIPLES OF QUESTIONNAIRE DESIGN

Questionnaires vary according to needs but there are certain principles that may need to be used in all types. These are (i) the format should provide valid and reliable information as to the purpose of the investigation and reveal details of the individual completing it as to age, sex and occupation; it should also deal with prevailing trends which may affect the operation of the establishment; (ii) it should bring out clear indications of the consumer's reactions to the standards and quality of product and service provided yet without causing any embarrassment through including questions that are somewhat personal; (iii) the language used should be clearly understood by all those likely to be asked to answer it; (iv) questions must be framed so that they can be answered in a few words and the whole form be completed in a short time yet still provide the basis for a quick and clear analysis; (v) each question although it may appear open-ended must be capable of being evenly coded; (vi) in the hands of a skilled interviewer the questionnaire should promote rapport with the person being interviewed by avoiding any question that might lead to adverse reaction; this could create a negative attitude which would make it difficult to obtain valid information.

It is not possible to outline the precise design of a questionnaire since much depends upon the scope and purpose of the survey. The scope can include the gathering of information, staff attitudes and taste panels and any other relevant topics.

FORMAT OF QUESTIONNAIRES

When drawing up a questionnaire designed to survey consumer reactions and attitudes, the first part should consist of straightforward questions which help

414

to put the interviewee at ease and at the same time provide a clear profile of the person. This profile is an important factor; for example, consumers under the age of thirty-five would probably express a need for new products and a newer form of service whereas persons of more mature years might prefer established standards. This first part of the questionnaire could then use questions divided into sections so as to obtain a breakdown of relevant information as follows:

Q1 How often do you eat out?   Tick here
                          two or more times weekly   ☐
                          once weekly   ☐
                          once monthly   ☐
                          rarely   ☐

Q2 What is your occupation?   ....

Q3 Are you male   ☐
            female?   ☐

Q4 Which age group do you belong to?
                          under 21   ☐
                          under 31   ☐
                          under 41   ☐
            over 42 but under 60   ☐

Q5 What would you say was a reasonable price to
    pay for a 3 course meal, excluding coffee?
                          less than £5.00   ☐
                          between £5 and £10   ☐
                          between £10 and £15   ☐

Q6 Do you normally take wine with your meal?
                          yes   ☐
                          no   ☐

Questions 7, 8 and 9 would follow a similar pattern.

The next part of a questionnaire should be designed to provide an indication of the quality of services provided. For this a rating scale is best and ideally it should provide an objective assessment of the information being sought. There is, however, a common fault inherent in using a rating scale which is the frequent adoption of a middle tendency. For instance, on a rating scale that runs from superlative to poor the satisfactory or middle point is frequently chosen. Rating on a horizontal line is where the consumer is asked to tick the appropriate reference point that coincides with his opinion or gives his impression of quality of product. The questionnaire could continue:

Q10 Did you book a table in the dining room?   Tick here
                          yes   ☐
                          no   ☐

Q11 When you arrived at the dining room was
the head waiter at the door?

yes ☐

no ☐

Q12 Were you kept waiting for your table?

yes ☐

no ☐

Q13 If you were kept waiting, please say how long for

10 mins ☐

20 mins ☐

30 mins ☐

Q14 Rate how the head waiter received you by ticking
the most appropriate section on this line

Most cordially ⌊8⌋7⌊6⌊5⌊4⌊3⌊2⌊1⌋ Unpleasantly.

Q15 Did you find the menu choice excellent or unsatisfactory?

Excellent ⌊8⌋7⌊6⌊5⌊4⌊3⌊2⌊1⌋ Unsatisfactory.

Q16 Please tell us in terms of value for money if the portion
sizes you received were – Very generous ☐

Generous ☐

Satisfactory ☐

Sufficient ☐

Insufficient ☐

Another means of obtaining direct consumer reaction in a brief space of time is as follows, although this format does not indicate possible causes since it requires only yes or no as answers. Please tick.

	Yes	No
Did you enjoy your visit to our establishment?	☐	☐
Was the price reasonable?	☐	☐
Was a good choice provided?	☐	☐
Was the quality good?	☐	☐
Was the service efficient?	☐	☐
Would you recommend us to your friends?	☐	☐

Yet another way to obtain consumer reaction is by inviting them to write answers to some open-ended questions. Whilst it may be a laborious task to evaluate such answers the exercise could give a valuable insight into the customer's likes and dislikes. The questions must be carefully constructed in order that consumers respond to the particular aspects in which the operator is interested. A short preamble is helpful in obtaining the consumer's interest and involvement as in the following example: Dear Customer, In order to maintain and improve our services we would be very pleased if you could find the time to answer the following questions:

416

Q1 Why did you choose this establishment?
Q2 Did it come up to your expectations? If not, please indicate possible reasons why not.
Q3 What did you think of the choices on our wine list?
Q4 Please tell us your overall impression of the quality of our food.

If all this appears too daunting a task, and remember that there is all the collating to be done, then a complaints book could be kept in a prominent position near the exit for customers to enter any comments before departing. Some people who are loath to complain verbally are often prepared to voice their disappointment in writing.

EVALUATION OF QUESTIONNAIRES

The evaluation of completed questionnaires must be done in a precisely structured manner so that the results can be easily analysed and the information derived therefrom put to effective use. Complaints can be separated into three categories: (1) **Standard** – where complaints are primarily associated with (a) the type of facilities provided, (b) the type of service featured, (c) the hygiene and tidiness of the establishment, (d) the quality of the product offered and its portion size, (e) the consumer's interpretation of value for money. (2) **Psychological** – where complaints are related to (a) aspects of and courtesy of service as when a customer is kept waiting for a table he has previously booked, (b) the quality of the reception, whether accompanied to table, intonation of voice of the head waiter, (c) an interpretation of value for money and pricing policy, (d) undue delay between service of courses, (e) an unfavourable reaction to the shape or colour of food, (f) a negative reaction to the atmosphere of the place, e.g. music played too loudly, excessive clatter, too fast a tempo of activities – all making the customer feel he should eat his meal in a rush and go; there again the decor of the dining room may not be restful, (g) the proliferation of Guéridon lamps leading to fears of the naked flames causing a fire. 3. **Physiological** – where complaints are related to (a) the temperature in the dining room being either too hot or too cold for comfort, (b) poor food combinations or dishes that are, for example, too fatty and cause nausea or over-satiety, (c) the texture of dishes being such that they require painstaking mastication possibly because of poor cooking, (d) food being served at the wrong temperature so detracting from its full enjoyment, (e) an incorrect sequence and balance of menu so detracting from the enjoyment of the meal. Separating the complaints under these headings should facilitate their solution and the people responsible can be made specifically aware of them.

Complaints are an undesirable aspect of any operation but few establishments escape them entirely. It might prove helpful to set negative standards; for

417

example, the acceptance of a toleration level of complaints from 1 per cent to 2 per cent of consumers and when it goes above this level, the setting in motion of an investigation.

PRODUCT EVALUATION QUESTIONNAIRES

In addition to the feedback of information related to the food and service of an existing operation, there is another area of some importance for which valid information is necessary. This is concerned with the evaluating of new products. A different technique is required for validating new dishes before they are featured on the menu, so in this case a selected group consisting of a representative sample of the type of customer who frequents the establishment can act as a taste panel. Its members must be chosen in terms of age, sex, social class and education as closely resembling the clientele and they will need some training and practice on similar lines before undertaking a specific project of quality evaluation.

The main purpose of the taste panel will be to predict consumer reaction to the quality and characteristics of the product in terms of consumer expectation. It is necessary to bear in mind that the pleasure provided by a product is dynamic and that it changes with time and place. This means having realistic surroundings in which the tasting is to take place if valid information is to be obtained.

Having created this atmosphere and laid down the points on which the assessment is to be marked, and which involves the aspects of appearance, texture, aroma and taste, it is then time to bring in the product to be tasted. A scale can be used for marking the product by awarding a specific number on it that ranges from one to nine each having a descriptive value as shown.

Please select the most accurate statement in relation to the product you have just tasted.

Like exceedingly	9
Like considerably	8
Like moderately	7
Like slightly	6
Neither like nor dislike	5
Dislike slightly	4
Dislike partially	3
Dislike considerably	2
Dislike intensely	1

When the panel have made their selection the score can be added together then divided by the number of persons participating, a score above the median number five would indicate a favourable response, whereas one below it would be unfavourable. In the latter case the dish undergoing trial should be modified in order of ascending or descending intensity until the most acceptable formula is found, but it should still be compared with a similar but rival product.

FOOD WASTAGE

A certain amount of waste seems inevitable in any catering operation yet the reasons for its happening do not always receive consideration as a means of monitoring consumer satisfaction. Food waste produced during the various stages of preparing meals can provide an indication of the efficiency of staff, of control over usage as well as highlighting any other inefficient sequences in the cycle of operation.

The basic stages at which wastage can be studied are Storage, Preparation, Cooking, and Plate Waste. A figure of 20 per cent has been quoted as being the maximum acceptable amount but in fact few operations that run on traditional lines manage as low as this, yet it is essential to try to keep the amount down.

Storage Waste

No waste at all should occur in the stores except for a small amount of weight loss through evaporation of perishable foods and a minimal loss of nutritional value in certain goods, but even these can add up to a considerable sum over the year and must be countered. A record should be kept of goods that are lost or have deteriorated during storage and a periodic check made to ascertain possible causes such as excessive stocks being carried, poor ordering procedures, and adherence to old-fashioned practices.

Preparation Waste

The control of food wastage is most important at the preparation stage as here it can be monitored to provide information regarding methods of practice, craft skills and quality of materials purchased. This waste should be kept separate from plate waste and inedible matter. It is even possible to find the exact source, volume and nature of the waste by putting out a number of buckets of different colours in the various preparation areas. The preparation loss of meat and vegetables should not exceed 15 per cent of total purchased weight otherwise the original quality could not have been good; 10 per cent total waste is a realistic figure.

Cooking Waste

Wastage in the cooking process comes from loss through shrinkage; this is usually brought about by overcooking or cooking at too high a temperature which reduces portion size and weight unnecessarily. When food is served hard and dry it is likely to end as plate waste because it is impossible to eat it. Frying oil is frequently wasted through being maintained at too high a temperature which tends to shorten its useful life.

Plate Waste

This stage is the most important as far as consumer satisfaction is concerned. Plate waste should be monitored whenever there is a spate of complaints or when the amount including any bones and skin appears to exceed 10 per cent of what was served. A larger proportion might indicate that (a) the portions served are too large; if kept at an average size the dish could be sold cheaper; (b) the food was not properly trimmed; (c) poor quality food was purchased; (d) the food was unappetisingly served; (e) there were poor meal combinations, and (f) the food was served cold when it should have been hot.

A recent survey on wastage showed the following points: (i) too much sauce is often served; (ii) plated meals produced more waste than served ones, especially of vegetables; (iii) a large amount of toast is made for breakfast and any unused is thrown away; (iv) once dishes on the sweet trolley are started they are discarded as being unfit for the next meal; and (v) when catering staff are working under pressure, presentation suffers and plate waste increases.

ASPECTS OF QUALITY CONTROL

While questionnaires and observation of plate waste provide a feedback of information from the consumer's viewpoint quality control, or quality assurance as it is now called, can be used to monitor the various stages of production from the point of view of management. Procedures of quality assurance have always been used widely in industry, particularly engineering, to isolate and remove batches that are of inferior quality and that could give rise to complaints from customers and so affect the company's reputation. Items having minor defects but still meeting safety standards might be sold as 'seconds' or as 'imperfect', at a cheaper price. At present quality control in catering is used mainly to ensure the chemical and bacteriological safety of continuous production lines from central kitchens, but it should ideally be used at all stages of the production cycle and in all forms of establishments so as to improve standards and give better consumer satisfaction.

420

Purchasing

Quality assurance starts when the menu is analysed to build a list of requirements with information about each in terms of cost, quality, market trends and sources of supply. A standard purchasing specification should be constructed for each to make it clear both to supplier and receiver as to the quality points that are to be checked (see page 294).

Receiving and Produce Inspection

This is a very important aspect of quality assurance that must be properly organised because if uncontrolled it can be a source of considerable loss. The procedure must include delivery times, proper stock rotation and inspection for quality and quantity. Qualitative judgement means that the person responsible for receipt of goods is capable of making an accurate assessment in depth of quality points that relate to touch, vision, smell and taste and into such points as the drained weight of canned and frozen goods. Further extension of this could include where appropriate, measurement of viscosity, density, acidity and alkalinity, using the various pieces of equipment designed to carry out such tests.

Storage Control

Control of goods during storage is necessary to guard against spoilage, shrinkage and change in texture and colour, which means keeping them under conditions where temperature and relative humidity are ideal for each group of commodities.

Food Preparation and Cooking Areas

Quality control in these areas is assisted by the maintenance of a safe environment where productive efforts achieve maximum quality and quantity output within any limitations. This means that lighting, ventilation, temperature and noise levels conform to the requirements of the Health and Safety at Work Act, as well as creating conditions for optimum productivity and job satisfaction. The importance of good hygiene practice cannot be over-emphasised and inspections must be carried out and sample bacteriological checks made to ensure that cleaning procedures are effective. Equipment must be properly maintained so that it functions at the same level of performance as when first installed. The quality of food during the cooking process is determined by temperature, pressure and time, and the measuring aspects of these need to be checked occasionally.

Quality control must ensure that the determined standards are maintained and if possible improved; production must be monitored to provide complete consumer satisfaction as through it the skills and time of staff add value to basic materials all of which is then paid for by the consumer. It can be used to bring about improvements in materials usage and in solving problems by laying down precise instructions of operation; faults in production can be rectified so that they do not recur.

Quality Assurance at the Holding Stage

The holding of food from the time it is cooked until it is served has always been a problem. The texture, flavour and appearance can be damaged and nutritional values lost by prolonged storage at serving temperatures together with the possibility of microbiological spoilage. The answer to this is batch cookery, particularly for vegetables, but this is not possible unless the staff and equipment are available at the right time and place. The higher the holding temperature the quicker deterioration sets in with meat and fish shrinking by evaporation or drying out, battered foods becoming soggy and vegetables discolouring. The optimum holding temperature is from 65–70 °C for both food and serving dishes and a probe could be used to check that it is hot enough to meet consumer approval, but not so that it is causing it to lose its quality.

Work Study in Serving Procedures

The principles of work study can be used to ascertain if the service could be made to run more efficiently. Work study is a technique or methodology that assists in an analytical sequencing approach which may lead to improved performance from established practices.

BUDGETING AND MANAGEMENT BY OBJECTIVES

It has long been recognised that the most important function of the person in charge of a business is to plan it and control it. But the standard to which the business operates should be that of the customer rather than that of the manager, since consumers buy what they can afford within a quality interpretation of value for money. Most success stories in catering are identified with this philosophy of letting the consumer make the total package choice and then providing him with food and drink within that framework and in the most advantageous form. This requires a continuous check to see that the consumer product interpretation does not change over a period of time. If it does then the system will need to be adapted or altered; standards are therefore set by the consumer. Management must thus maintain a framework which ensures that the internal

422

organisation does not conflict with this precept – that what is provided must always be what the consumer wants and is willing to pay for. This calls for ability on the part of management to set precise working procedures which assist in achieving the aims; these procedures should transcend the quality boundaries and take into account the effects of occupancy figures on profitability, which in turn has relevance to the charges made to consumers. The higher the occupancy rate the wider are the fixed costs spread so the more competitive will be the prices charged.

Internal targets of production, revenue and costs can be set for every part of the operation, based on previous performance or that of other similar establishments and closely monitored to ensure they are realistic. Once proven correct they can then form the norm to be achieved. The set objectives become the measure of performance at which the unit should operate. This form of operation and technique of management is known as management by objectives and the way in which it is measured is strictly by numbers with precise target figures being set for each aspect of the operation. This is known as budgeting or budgetary control.

THE BUDGET

A budget is an organised operational plan which monitors and regulates the activities of a business in financial terms. Many claims are made for budgetary control, such as that it sets standards on which an individual's performance can be measured, that it ensures best use of productive resources, that it maximises profitability, that it controls expenditure and promotes cost-consciousness, and that a budget co-ordinates business activities. There is some truth in all of these claims but what is really certain is that a budget maintains awareness of the need to achieve good results. It gives to the persons who plan and implement it a total perspective of the organisation's needs and shows them the interdependence of its commercial activities.

Planning for an Operational Budget

The planning of a budget should be done by a committee composed of management and departmental heads such as food and beverage manager, head chef and head waiter and they may use the pattern as follows: (i) ascertain from previous records the general level of business and possible income; (ii) determine the period to be covered by the budget; (iii) outline the commitments and expectations for the forthcoming period and deal with (a) any variations from set targets in the previous year, (b) any areas requiring special consideration such as wage increases, (c) market interpretations, (d) possible changes in practices such as

Figure 67

BUDGET FOR A COMMERCIAL UNDERTAKING

Projected Budget for Year Ending: 31.12.19 . .

	Jan.	Feb.	Mar.	Apr.	May	June	July	Aug.	Sept.	Oct.	Nov.	Dec.	Totals £
Sales:													
Food	6000	6200	6500	7500	8000	8500	11000	11000	9000	8500	7000	8000	97200
Beverages	3000	3100	3200	3750	4000	4250	6000	7000	4500	4000	3500	4000	50300
Total:	9000	9300	9700	11250	12000	12750	17000	18000	13500	12500	10500	12000	147500
Cost of Sales:													
Food	2000	2100	2200	2500	2700	2850	3700	3700	3000	2700	2400	2600	32450
Beverages	1500	1550	1600	1875	2000	2150	3000	3500	2250	2000	1750	2000	25175
Total:	3500	3650	3800	4375	4700	5000	6700	7200	5250	4700	4150	4600	57625
Gross Profit:	5500	5650	5900	6875	7300	7750	10300	10800	8250	7800	6350	7400	89875
Administration	900	900	900	900	900	900	900	900	900	900	900	900	10800
Labour	2000	2000	2200	2500	3000	3000	4000	4000	3500	3000	2500	3000	34700
Heat & Energy	600	600	500	500	500	600	700	700	600	600	600	600	7100
Repair & Maintenance	300	300	300	300	300	300	300	300	300	300	300	300	3600
Cleaning Materials	200	200	200	300	300	300	300	300	300	300	300	300	3300
Advertising	200	200	200	100	100	100	100	100	100	200	200	200	1800
Printing & Stationery	100	100	100	100	100	100	100	100	100	100	100	100	1200
Telephone & Misc.	100	100	100	100	100	100	100	100	100	100	100	100	1200
Total Controllable Expenses	4400	4400	4500	4800	5300	5400	6500	6500	5900	5500	5000	5500	63700
Operating Profit	1100	1250	1400	2075	2000	2350	3800	4300	2350	2300	1350	1900	26175

methods of service or portion sizes, (e) impending increases in the price of fuel, maintenance contracts, rates, etc., (f) any other useful information bearing on the matter; (iv) give the members of the committee a brief period in which to submit the budget requirements of their department; and (v) discuss the budget and set a precise target for each department.

The total budget should then be compiled by the general manager and accountant and the final version presented to the committee. Once approval for it has been received a period for reviewing performance will be set.

From the main operating budget figure a number of more detailed specialised budgets can be constructed as required to include, for example, a sales budget to show the desirable return from any specific area such as dining room or bar, the desirable mix of sales of food and drink, the nature of food sales in relation to the mealtimes, and ideal figures for lunch and dinner. The idea can be extended to cover any specific area such as labour, purchases or maintenance, but what is of the utmost importance is that the budget be used as a device to monitor financial progress or otherwise of the operation and to adjust relevant factors to emerging situations. This could include adjusting the number of staff employed at periods when business is quiet and increasing it at busy times, and spending more money on advertising at quiet periods and less when business is good. In effect a budget is a form of financial quality control procedure which assists in maintaining the desirable return on investment and ensuring the operating health of the enterprise.

Budgets do not only apply to the commercial sector of the industry, they are extremely important in the industrial and welfare sector. A hospital caterer will be given a budget of a specific amount per person for food and for labour costs. An industrial caterer should know the value of the subsidies he will receive and be able to forecast income from sales for the financial year, and from this to establish an operating budget to guide him through to break even point in the end. An example of a budget for a commercial undertaking is given in Fig. 67.

APPENDICES

A EDUCATION AND TRAINING – OPPORTUNITIES AND CAREER PROSPECTS

The pattern of catering education in this country is both varied and extensive in that it sets out to provide the industry with qualified personnel for all levels of jobs. There are a large number of different courses offered ranging from part-time ones for craftsmen, full-time and sandwich ones at supervisory level, and a wide range of advanced courses leading to managerial positions. The subjects of many of these courses cover quite a wide spectrum so as to allow for flexibility in selecting a job at the end, and to cope with the technological changes that will inevitably be met.

The normal routes through the City and Guilds range of courses are as follows:
Part-time, day release and block release: CG 706/1–CG706/2–CG706/3.
Full-time: CG705, CG707/1 CG706/2, CG707/2 then on to part-time study to CG706/3 or NEBSS (National Examination Board for Supervisory Studies).

The school leaver with four GCE or CSE passes can do the TEC or SCOTEC Diploma in Hotel Catering and Institutional Operations over two years, then proceed to do HCIMA Part B examination after one year full-time industrial experience, or the TEC Higher Diploma in two years.

The school leaver with a minimum of five GCE including one at 'A' level or five SCE including two Highers can do the TEC or SCOTEC Higher Diploma on a three-year sandwich basis.

The City and Guilds of London Institute is an examining body in a wide range of subjects including catering studies; it also runs the Certificate in Supervisory Studies (NEBBS).

The Scottish Technical Education Council is known as SCOTEC. The Technician Education Council known as TEC covers England, Wales and Northern Ireland.

CG705 General Catering Certificate

This is a one-year full-time course in catering subjects which is intended to further the education and development of young people who leave school and wish to follow a career in catering. It is an introductory course that gives guidance as to what particular field of catering a student ultimately may decide to enter.

Colleges are free to accept any likely candidate and there are no required entrance qualifications.

The aims of the course are to introduce students to all the activities of the industry, to give a basic knowledge and skills of the main branches of kitchen, restaurant, housekeeping, reception and maintenance, give an insight into hygiene and safety at work, provide a knowledge of costing and control, help to develop ability in communications and to prepare them for the next level of courses. The examination consists of four papers, two of them being the multiple choice kind – one in food preparation, the second a combined food service, housekeeping and reception paper, the third in communication skills, and the last in numeracy. In addition coursework is assessed.

CG706 Cookery for the Catering Industry

There are actually three different courses under this number, designed as a continuous progress from the very basic to the most advanced state of culinary practice. Each course is numbered as a part of this progression, these are CG706/1, CG706/2 and CG706/3 which has three sections – Kitchen and Larder, Pastry, and Advanced Pastry; the titles of these courses are self-explanatory being Basic Cookery, Cookery, and Advanced Cookery.

The first two courses can be followed by both full-time and part-time students, the third being purely for part-time students, as wider experience is necessary to complete it successfully than may be gained from leaving school and joining a college catering course.

428

The emphasis of the study is on the practical application of cookery with catering theory to support it. In addition food science, costing and control, planning and legal aspects are studied, with General Studies and Communications Skills to complement the technical aspects.

It is also possible to study the CG706/2 as a block release course instead of attending college for one day a week.

Each course has its own separate examination specification with coursework assessment playing a part in each. Part 1 has a multiple choice paper, Part 2 has a multiple choice and a written paper, and Part 3 has a two-hour written paper and a six-hour practical test.

Successful candidates are awarded a joint certificate issued by the City and Guilds of London Institute and the Hotel and Catering Industry Training Board.

City and Guilds 700

There are several courses under this heading, being available for counter service assistance, call order cooks, and room attendants. The course can be held either at a college or an actual place of work where candidates are engaged in the job appertaining to the course; candidates should have had about three months experience. The examination consists of a practical test, a theory paper and coursework assessment. The person running the course should be an HCITB Trainer.

Food and Beverage Service Certificate CG707/1, Advanced Serving Techniques CG707/2, Alcoholic Beverages Certificate CG717

These courses for service staff are taken in progression from the elementary to the advanced, embracing all the attributes and knowledge required by a waiter in the performance of his duties, first as commis then as chef de rang and sommelier.

CG771 Organisation Studies for Catering Supervision

This is the NEBSS course which is a business studies one in all aspects of departmental administration for supervisors engaged in any branch of the industry.

VOCATIONAL PREPARATION

The government finances a number of schemes designed to train young people for a career in the catering and allied industries. The schemes are run by the

Manpower Services Commission which produces a syllabus in conjunction with local employers and technical college and covers all the costs including a weekly grant for each participant. Courses consist of a number of weeks in college and industry with appropriate examinations according to the particular option selected by the trainee.

There are several different training schemes some of which are for mature persons who decide to follow a career in catering after having worked in another industry. The Hotel and Catering Industry Training Board run some of these vocational schemes under the direction of the Manpower Services Commission.

GENERAL CATERING COURSES

When catering education first came into its own in the early 1950s, full-time courses offered by colleges were entirely at craft level. A few colleges began by offering their own college diploma course but by the early 1960s most, including Westminster, were following City and Guilds Certificate syllabuses in cookery and Hotel and Catering Institute in waiting. Mostly they were two-year courses and selection was on the basis of personality rather than GCE certificates. On successful completion of this kind of course a student would possess the CG147 and 151 certificates, the HCI waiting and advanced waiting certificates whilst a girl would also have the HCI housekeeping one. In addition they may have acquired the National Trade Development Association licenced house certificate although the advanced waiting certificate course covered wine, alcoholic and other drinks. Students with an interest in science could gain the HCI Hygiene or Nutrition Certificate.

Full-time college studies offered sheltered conditions and the only realistic practical experience these students obtained was if they were directed to take seasonal employment during the summer vacation. The bias of these courses was toward good class hotels and restaurants and on completion students were often recommended to jobs in the kitchens of particular establishments, very few actually going to work as waiters though at that time it was difficult for a girl to obtain kitchen work.

Recognition of the needs of the welfare sector of the industry was made when City and Guilds designed an alternative course in large-scale industrial and institutional catering at CG151 level, but it did not last many years as even then students working in school meals preferred to take the opportunity of extending their horizons by following the original course. Part-time students went to college for two evenings a week in their own time to gain qualifications, taking two years to attain CG150 which was a general course with a practical cookery core but with some food service, or CG147 Basic Cookery, and another two years to the CG151 examination. Some enlightened employers encouraged the chef to

430

grant time off for trainees to attend college on the basis of one half day which later became one whole day or block release attendance.

The HCI membership examination was for persons at or aspiring to management level positions who could follow a course in their own time either in a college approved by the Institute or by correspondence course. A requirement was that the person held a CG151 certificate. The intermediate examination was in four subjects and the final in six, and it was altogether a very difficult way of becoming professionally qualified.

National Diploma in Hotelkeeping and Catering

This course came into being in 1959 as a means of bringing catering education nearer into line with other fields of study in technical colleges. Applicants had to have five 'O' Level GCE passes to join the course which was a three-year full-time one. The examinations were internally set and externally assessed by a joint committee. On successful completion students were eligible for graduate membership of the Hotel and Catering Institute.

Diploma in Institutional Management

This was an all-girls course and, as the title implied, led them to jobs in the large-scale sector. It included mass production cookery and counter service plus soft furnishing, art and design, housekeeping and physiology.

Ordinary and Higher National Diplomas

After ten years of operating at the National Diploma level, during which time the academic qualifications of entrants rose continuously, it was felt safe to bring in two new courses, one at GCE 'A' level entrance for administrative level jobs and the other with four 'O' levels for departmental head level jobs. This move brought catering education completely into line with other subjects.

Ordinary National Diploma in Hotel and Catering Operations, and Hotel Catering and Institutions Operations

This was two-year full-time, or longer if made into a sandwich course, and designed to educate students up to technician or supervisory level where, after gaining experience, they could aspire to departmental head in their chosen field, be it reception, housekeeping, dining room or kitchen.

Higher National Diploma

This was a three-year sandwich course with two terms being spent in industrial practice. The studies embraced all sections of the industry and some of the work experience could be spent in social and welfare establishments. This experience counted towards the successful completion of the course and students were expected to develop their managerial abilities.

The Joint Committee for National Diplomas in Hotel Catering and Institutional Management governed these two courses and awarded the diplomas.

TECHNICIAN EDUCATION COUNCIL COURSES

The Technician Education Council was set up in 1973 to plan and administer the development of a unified national system of courses and examinations; it works through a programme committee known as C4 which consulted colleges and industry with a view to giving guide-lines for a new scheme to replace the OND and HND. The reason why it was felt necessary to change the OND-HND system was because industry knew where it was with OND students and accepted them readily, whereas holders of HND's were not so warmly welcomed into employment even though they had the benefit of industrial training. In predicting the future, C4's thinking was that this industry will always demand supervisors with sound practical skills, even though much of the food used will be wholly or partially processed and that more technical knowledge will be required than actual craftsmanship.

There are TEC Diplomas, Higher Diplomas, and Certificates and colleges were invited to construct their own programmes without the benefit of a common syllabus and on modular lines.

Since 1980 Scotland has operated a Certificate Course, a Diploma Course, and a Higher Diploma Course under the auspices of its own committee known as SCOTEC, and which offers a common syllabus for these courses. These courses are at supervisory level and offer a sound programme of theory and practice for future supervisors and managers of the catering industry, in a similar fashion to the TEC Diplomas.

The TEC Diploma in hotel and catering is a two-year full-time course for school leavers who wish to gain general education and training as a foundation for a career which will lead to a supervisory or trainee managerial position. Course entry requirements vary with some colleges requiring four 'O' level GCE, or CSE grade 1 passes. The course content may also vary with some colleges placing the emphasis on the non-commercial sector of catering.

The TEC Higher Diploma in hotel and catering is designed to provide the necessary foundations of potential management. It is for post 'A' level students who require a pass at this level together with four 'O' levels or CSE grade 1 passes at A, B or C from a range of selected subjects. It is usually a three-year sandwich course.

TEC Certificates in hotel and catering are for part-time students.

HCIMA COURSES

The Hotel Catering and Institutional Management Association runs professional qualifying examinations that are in two stages. Part A is available in colleges as a part-time or block release course over two years whilst students are working in the industry. It includes food and accommodation studies. Part B is taken on successful completion of Part A or an OND or TEC diploma course. Studies include a compulsory core of management oriented subjects and two elective studies. This part is offered as a full-time, part-time or sandwich course.

DEGREE COURSES

Originally there were two degree courses in catering, one at Strathclyde which was business studies based and the other at Surrey was based more on managerial aspects. Together they supplied the needs of the industry and there was a long waiting list to get onto them. This went on for some years until the advent of the Council for National Academic Awards which was given a charter to approve degree courses in colleges other than universities and to award degrees. The designation in 1970 of 30 polytechnics was the signal for those having departments of catering within them to design a degree course that would satisfy the standards demanded by the CNAA, and to offer such a course alongside an existing HND. Now there are degree courses in various aspects of catering some at ordinary level but mostly at honours. If the course has an engineering or scientific bias it will be offered as a B.Sc. – if it is concerned with business studies or management aspects it will be a B.A. course. Some polytechnics offer a degree course in Institutional Management and there is an honours one at University College Cardiff, the third to be offered by a university.

CAREERS

A person entering the catering industry whether he comes straight from school or from a catering college can be assured of an interesting and worthwhile career. It is one that contributes much to the welfare of his fellow men whilst

433

at the same time holding real prospects of advancement for those who are ambitious, prepared to work often unsocial hours, and study to keep abreast of ever changing developments. There is a career structure which, starting in either the kitchen, dining room or bar, soon leads to promotion through the ranks for those who show ability and have gained the requisite experience.

The commis who starts in the kitchen at the lowest level can expect to get promoted to chef de partie, then to sous chef and finally to the position of head chef. Not all the top positions are filled by chefs from overseas and there is every prospect for the person who learns his trade well, is a good organiser and is prepared to change with the changing times. Commis are also employed in the dining room and the onward path is from that rank to chef de rang; with good ability and the right personality the next step upwards is to head waiter and finally to restaurant manager.

The cellar and bar can likewise offer a good career to the person who takes an interest in the subject of wine and other drinks. Starting as an assistant he can gain promotion to head cellarman, head barman or sommelier. All these career structures offer worthwhile rewards but it must be remembered that catering is a demanding job that can often entail long drawn out hours of duty.

The top position of catering manager is open to a person from any area of catering who wishes to specialise rather than do general management. The title of food and beverage manager indicates that the person must possess a thorough knowledge of all the component sections which would include not only the kitchen, dining room and bar but also the stores, cellar, stillroom, and other ancillary areas. A practical ability gained by actually having worked his way up can be useful.

There are many different titles for this job which include, Catering Manager, Catering Supervisor, Food and Beverage Manager, Catering Officer, Outdoor Catering Manager, Area Catering Manager, Catering Superintendant. In educational establishments the title of the job could be Bursar, Domestic Bursar, Steward, Manciple, or School Meals Organiser. The person in charge of the food production areas can be called by one these titles, Head Chef or Chef de Cuisine, Executive Head Chef, Chef Manager, Kitchen Superintendant.

On the food service side some of the titles are, Restaurant Manager, Head Waiter, Dining Room Supervisor, Refectory Manager, Banquet Manager.

The person in charge of the drinks side could be called the Bars Manager, Head Barman, Cellar Manager, Head Sommelier.

The title Head of Commissariat is sometimes used to denote the food and beverage manager of an in-flight catering department.

On a cruise liner the title of the person in charge of the catering could be Purser or Hotel Manager.

CONTINENTAL EXPERIENCE

It is always useful to see how one's opposite number in a different country goes about his job, and it is possible to obtain a job abroad either by obtaining a work permit, or through an exchange scheme. This is likely to entail hard work at a low salary but the opportunity of widening one's experience, learning a new language, getting to know about another country and forming friendships will always be of use. Some colleges send their students to work abroad during their industrial experience.

The EEC Young Workers Exchange Scheme arranges short courses abroad for experienced personnel between the ages of eighteen and twenty-eight to learn cookery, restaurant service or tourism; a knowledge of French is needed. Employers who allow members of staff to benefit from this scheme can obtain up to 75 per cent of the cost of travel, accommodation, tuition and pocket money.

Both the HCIMA and HCITB offer scholarships to work or travel abroad to gain experience, the latter organisation awarding these to three categories, that for craft, for supervisory, and for managerial career prospects.

APPRENTICESHIPS

Formal indentured and time-serving apprenticeships are no longer fashionable although the HCITB does give its approval to some establishments and registers trainees. The person who does not wish to enter the industry by first following a full-time course in college can still make his way up the ladder by going to work to earn his living and taking a part-time course in his own or employer's time, thus gaining some qualification on paper; the possession of a certificate offers professionalism and can often be a deciding factor for the employer when interviewing for a vacancy. At one time a worker could ask his employer for a reference when leaving that employment but this is not done now and references are taken up by letter or telephone on a personal basis.

B ASPECTS OF THE LAW RELATING TO CATERING

The caterer has a responsibility to himself, the business he works for and to his employees to ensure that each decision taken conforms with established law. Ignorance of the law cannot be used as a defence thus the caterer must make every effort to be familiar with the legal obligation which the job imposes. The following are some of the important laws and regulations directly related to the catering industry but should not be thought of as a comprehensive guide. It is obvious that the caterer will always wish to have professional advice where aspects of law are concerned.

Licenses for Liquor

An on-licence is a licence for the sale by retail of intoxicating liquor for consumption on the premises and there are five different forms of it: (I) intoxicating liquor of all descriptions, (II) beer, cider and wine only, (III) beer and cider only, (IV) wine only, (V) cider only. Conditions can be attached to any of these licences as the Licensing Justices may think proper in the interests of the public.

436

Restaurant Licence

A restaurant licence is granted for premises used or intended for use to provide main meals to persons frequenting it. This licence is subject to the conditions that intoxicating liquor shall not be sold or supplied on the premises other than to persons taking meals at a table there for consumption as an ancillary to the meal.

An application for the granting of this licence may only be refused on certain limited grounds which include: (I) the applicant is under eighteen years, (II) the applicant is not a fit and proper person to hold a licence, (III) the premises are not fully suitable, (IV) a Justice's on-licence has been forefeited within the previous twelve months, (V) the restaurant does not consist solely for the purpose of providing table meals, (VI) the intoxicating liquor is to be sold by 'help yourself service', (VIII) the premises are frequented by persons under the age of eighteen and are not accompanied by adults, (VIII) the police, fire authority, or local authority have tried but been unable to inspect the premises, (IX) non-alcoholic drinks and water are not normally made available.

For a drink to be ancillary to a meal it does not have to be consumed during the meal and the normal kind of drinking before and after it is also included.

Provisional Licence

Where the premises for which an application is required are not yet built, or are in course of being built, or are going to be altered or extended a provisional grant of an on-licence may be made by the Justices. They will have to be satisfied that the detailed plans of the premises show they will be suitable for the kind of licence being applied for.

Applications for Licences

In the case of a new licence the person who proposes to apply for it must notify in writing the clerk to the Licensing Justices, the chief officer of police, the local authority, the fire authority, not less than twenty-one days before the Licensing Sessions. A notice must be displayed on the outside of the premises in a place where it can conveniently be read by the public, not more than twenty-eight days before the Licensing Sessions are to be held; the notice must remain on display for seven days. In addition a notice must be advertised in the local newspaper, not more than twenty-eight days nor less than fourteen days before the date of the Licensing Sessions. The notice must state the name and address of the applicant and his occupation during the preceding six months, the situation of the premises, and the kind of licence for which application is being made. The notice must be signed by the applicant or his authorised agent.

The licensing year runs for twelve months from 5 April in each year; a Justice's licence has effect from the time of the grant until the end of the licensing year or, if granted within the last three months of a licensing year, until the end of the following licensing year. Renewal may be by special forms from the Clerk to the Licensing Justices, or by a letter of application; in general there is no obligation for an applicant for renewal to attend the session.

Transfer of Licences

The Licensing Justices have power to grant a transfer of licence from one person to another, provided they are satisfied that the transferee is a fit and proper person to hold a licence.

Occasional Licences

The holder of an on-licence may apply to the magistrates for the grant of an occasional licence to enable him to sell any intoxicating liquor as under his on-licence, at some other place. A person holding a restaurant licence may make application but the magistrates must be satisfied that the sale of intoxicating liquor is to be ancillary to the provision of substantial refreshment.

Notice of application must be given to the chief police officer at least twenty-four hours before the application is heard and this notice must state the name and address of the applicant, the place and the occasion for which the occasional licence is for, and the period and hours for which the licence is required. A hearing may not be necessary if two copies of the notice are deposited in writing to the Clerk to the Justices at least one month in advance. The clerk will send a copy to the police and they have seven days in which to give written notice of objection.

The premises where intoxicating liquor is sold under an occasional licence are licensed premises and the usual restrictions will apply.

Permitted Hours

It is an offence to sell or supply intoxicating liquor outside permitted hours whether for consumption on or off the premises, or to consume in or take from premises any intoxicating liquor outside these hours. This restriction does not operate in respect of an occasional licence and the consumption of intoxicating liquor on the premises is allowed during the first half hour after the end of permitted hours by persons taking meals there, if the liquor is ancillary to the meals.

438

Supper Hour Certificate

Application can be made to the Licensing Justices for a certificate as for a restaurant licence in which the permitted hours on all days of the week can be extended for luncheon until 3.00 p.m. and until 11.30 p.m. or midnight, depending upon whether the normal permitted hours end at 10.30 p.m. or 11.00 p.m. The intoxicating liquor is to be ancillary to the meal.

Extended Hours Order

An establishment which has a supper hour certificate may apply for an extended hours order where live musical or other entertainment is provided in addition to substantial refreshment. Where this order is granted the permitted hours are extended in this part of the premises until 1.00 a.m. while the entertainment and meals continue to be provided. The Licensing Justices have complete discretion as to the extent of this order and can impose limitations.

Special Hours Certificate

The Licensing Justices may grant a certificate if there is a music and dancing licence in force for the premises, and the whole or part of the premises is intended to be used for the purpose of music, dancing and substantial refreshment to which the sale of intoxicating liquor is ancillary. Where a certificate is granted the permitted hours are 12.30 p.m. to 3.00 p.m. and 6.30 p.m. to 2.00 a.m. (3.00 a.m. in Central London). Where music and dancing ends between midnight and 2.00 a.m., the permitted hours end when the music and dancing end.

Young Persons

It is an offence for the holder of a licence or his servant knowingly to serve intoxicating liquor to a person under eighteen years, or to knowingly allow a person under eighteen to consume it in a bar. It is an offence for any person to attempt to buy intoxicating liquor for consumption in a bar on licensed premises by a person under eighteen. A person who has reached sixteen may be sold beer, porter, cider or perry for consumption at a meal in a part of the premises which is not a bar. It is an offence for a person under eighteen to buy or attempt to buy intoxicating liquor or to consume it in a bar. No person under the age of eighteen may be employed to serve in a bar.

The Food and Drugs Act 1955

This act is the overall enabling and enforcing one relating to the manufacture, storage, preparation, handling, and sale of food and several of its sections are relevant to the catering industry.

Section 1 says it is an offence to add any substance or ingredient to food that would render it injurious to health, or to take away any constituent of a food or subject it to a treatment or process that would render it injurious. It is an offence to sell or possess for sale, any food which has been rendered injurious to health.

Section 2 says a person shall be guilty of an offence if he sells any food which is not of the nature, substance or quality as demanded by the purchaser. The nature of a food means that it is as stated on the menu and a purchaser would be prejudiced if he was served rabbit as chicken. The substance is concerned with foreign objects getting into food, such as a cigarette end in a bread roll. Food not of the quality demanded concerns the giving of a misleading definition, such as saying that free range eggs and stone ground flour are used when in fact ordinary eggs and flour are bought and used.

Under Section 8 it is an offence to sell or possess for the purchase or sale of food that is unfit for human consumption. Unfit food includes putrid or decomposed food, mouldy food, and food which contains extraneous matter such as cockroaches, mice droppings or finger plasters.

Section 9 allows the Environmental Health Officer to examine any food intended for human consumption and if it appears to him to be unfit for human consumption, to sieze it in order to have it dealt with by a Justice of the Peace.

Section 16 is the Registration of Food Premises and the definition of Catering Premises under this Act is where food is prepared or supplied for immediate consumption therein. Such premises must be registered with the local authority but catering premises, schools and clubs are exempted from this requirement.

Sections 26 and 27 make food poisoning a notifiable disease and notice must be given to the local Medical Officer of Health. The medical officer must notify the caterer that he suspects the food and that it may not be used for human consumption until he has completed his investigations.

Section 47 Designation of Cream says that no person shall sell or offer for sale any substance resembling cream which is not real cream, under the description of cream. Reconstituted cream and imitation cream must be identified as such.

The Food Hygiene (General) Regulations 1970

The Regulations apply to any premises in or from which a food business is carried on and it includes canteens, clubs, schools, hospitals or institutions whether run for profit or not, and also any undertaking carried on by a public or local authority.

440

The general requirements cover insanitary premises, risk of contamination, cleanliness of articles and equipment. Food handlers must ensure that all parts of their person liable to come into contact with food are kept as clean as reasonably practical; clothing must be kept as clean as is reasonably practical and protective clothing must be worn by persons handling open food. Food handlers must cover open cuts, wounds or abrasions with suitable waterproof dressings. They must not spit, smoke or take snuff when handling open food or whilst in a room where there is open food.

Persons suffering from certain infections including typhoid, paratyphoid, other salmonella infections, amoebic dysentary, bacillary dysentery, any staphylococcal infection likely to cause food poisoning such as septic cut, boil, spots, burns and throat and nasal infections, must notify their employer who must immediately notify the Medical Officer of Health.

The requirements relating to food premises cover the provision of personal washing facilities for use solely for the personal cleanliness of users with an adequate supply of hot water, soap or detergent, nail brushes and drying facilities, as well as lockers for outdoor clothes, suitable and sufficient lighting, sufficient ventilation, cleanliness and repair of food rooms and the proper accommodation for refuse.

The regulations apply to the temperatures at which certain foods are to be kept. It must be brought to either above 62.7 °C or below 10 °C without unavoidable delay, which means that cooked food must be maintained at serving temperatures of above 62.7 °C or kept cool below 10 °C under hygienic conditions and maintained there until required for serving or further processing.

The Food and Drugs (Control of Food Premises) Act 1976

This act empowers a local authority, under certain circumstances, to apply to a magistrates court for the closure of a food business. Where a person is convicted of an offence under the Food Hygiene (General) Regulations 1970 and the offence included the carrying on of a food business in insanitary premises where food is exposed at risk of contamination, the local authority may make application to a court for an order prohibiting it from continuing to operate.

The Food Labelling Regulations 1980

The law of food labelling is bringing about important changes with special reference to foods delivered to caterers, and the requirements relating to the label state that it must give the name, sufficiently and precisely to inform the purchaser as to its true nature, the list of ingredients given in descending order of weight, and an indication of the shelf life. In addition it must bear the name of the manufacturer and his address, any special storage conditions, and instructions for its use if considered necessary.

The Offices, Shops and Railway Premises Act 1963

This act covers catering premises particularly canteens and dining rooms maintained for the purpose of the sale and supply of food and drink for immediate consumption to persons employed to work in the office or shop, to which the canteen premises are maintained in conjunction.

It covers the cleanliness of premises, including furniture and furnishings, the working temperature, ventilation, lighting and the number of sanitary conveniences, and seeing these are kept clean. It also covers the guarding of catering machinery stating that no person under eighteen may clean or adjust any machinery if this exposes him to risk of injury from a moving part, nor may any person work a machine on the following list unless he has been fully instructed as to the dangers and has received sufficient training in working it, or is under adequate supervision by someone with a thorough knowledge and experience. The Prescribed Dangerous Machines Order 1964 applies to the following power-driven machines: (I) worm-type mincers, (II) rotary knife bowl choppers, (III) dough mixers, (IV) dough brakes, (V) mixing machines when used with the attachments for mincing, slicing, chipping, grating, crumbling, (VI) pie and tart moulders, (VII) vegetable slicers, (VIII) wrapping and packing machines, (IX) circular saw machines, (X) power-driven or hand operated circular knife slicers and potato chippers.

The Health and Safety at Work Act 1974

This Act lays down the responsibility of the employer to his employees to ensure their health, safety and welfare whilst at work. The employer is required to provide and maintain safe systems of working and the information, instruction, training and supervision necessary to ensure this health and safety. An employer having five or more employees must prepare a written statement of policy regarding this matter and what the organisation and arrangements are to be for carrying out that policy. It provides for the appointment of safety representatives and the formation of a safety committee when so requested.

The responsibility of employees is such that an employee must take reasonable care of his and his fellow workers health and safety so that they are not affected by his acts or omissions. Every employee must co-operate with his employer so as to enable him to comply with any duty or requirement of the Act. The employer must nominate a senior person to take responsibility for all aspects of safety and health within the premises.

Not only must the employer have regard for the safety of his own workforce but for guests and also contractors working on the premises.

The enforcement of health and safety legislation in catering premises is the responsibility of the local authority, normally the Environmental Health Officer; inspectors may be authorised to exercise powers to enter a premises and carry

442

out any examination or investigation as may be necessary. An employer must keep a written record of all notifiable accidents and dangerous occurrences.

It is therefore very important that the kitchen floor is kept free from grease and that spillages are cleaned up immediately. Corridors and staircases must not be obstructed and kitchen equipment kept in good order, special attention being given to power-operated machines.

A first aid box must be on hand and where more than 150 staff are working, a member of staff trained in first aid must be nominated.

The 1980 Employment Act

This Act covers the law on unfair dismissals and establishments employing twenty people or less are exempt from the unfair dismissal provisions for any employee who has worked there for less than two years. Thus small firms have two years before which an employee can be fired for any or no reason without the fear of being taken to an industrial tribunal.

The Act also covers trade union ballots and exclusion from trade union membership.

Price Marking (Food and Drink on Premises) Order 1979

Being mainly applicable to the menu and wine list, the details of this order have been dealt with more fully in Chapter 5 (see page 89).

The Price Marking (Drinks on Premises Order) 1975

This order requires the price to be shown for intoxicating and other liquors where they are offered or exposed for sale for consumption on the premises. It requires the quantity being sold to be stated and the indication of prices to be clear and legible so as to be easily read by an intending purchaser.

Racial Discrimination

Under the Race Relations Act 1976 an employer may not discriminate against an applicant for a job on grounds of colour, race, nationality or ethnic religion; the word discrimination meaning the applying of a requirement or condition that a person cannot comply with, or treating a person less favourably than another applicant, on racial grounds. When selecting a person for a job the arrangements for determining who should be selected must be done so that there is no discrimination against any applicant on racial grounds. When an opportunity for promotion or training or other benefit comes up it is neces-

443

sary to give access to existing employees regardless of race. No segregation of employees is allowed on racial grounds as the Act identifies this as treating some less favourably, which amounts to discrimination.

When a particular job in a place providing food and drink requires a person of a particular racial group to fill it for reasons of authenticity this Act is not applicable.

Sex Discrimination

The Sex Discrimination Act 1975 prevents discrimination on the grounds of sex and on the grounds that a person is married, thus employers may not treat a woman less favourably on the ground of her sex than a man, or apply a requirement or condition to a woman which he would also apply to a man but with which the woman cannot comply. It is unlawful to publish an advertisement which indicates an intention to do any act which amounts to unlawful sex discrimination, so to use a word with a sexual connotation would indicate an intention to discriminate. It is unlawful to discriminate against persons when seeking to engage someone for employment on the grounds of sex and also when affording access to promotion, training or other benefits. Sex discrimination is not always against women and men also have protection against discrimination.

Overseas Workers

For employers seeking to engage workers from overseas there are special requirements which apply to senior staff. For a person coming here to fill a position of manager he must be at least twenty-five years old, have had five years high-class experience, and have completed a two-year full-time catering course successfully. For a head chef or sous chef the person must be at least twenty-three years old, have had five years good class experience of which two years must have been in charge of a kitchen, and have a diploma from a two-year full-time catering course in a college. A person coming here as a head waiter must be at least twenty-three years old, be highly skilled, knowledgeable on all aspects of the job and experienced at controlling staff. This should cover five years of which two years spent working as a head waiter.

Persons from EEC countries can come here to work for up to six months; for a longer period a residential permit is required from the Home Office, in which case they may stay for five years.

Overseas students from Commonwealth countries may take up employment which is incidental to their holiday and others may take up employment during vacations from studying, provided they have the consent of the Department of Employment. It must be a supernumerary job and the pay and conditions not less favourable than for the area.

Under the Employment Protection (Consolidation) Act 1978 as amended by the Employment Act 1980, all employees engaged to work for at least sixteen hours per week must be given a statement of the terms and conditions of their employment. It must include details about the rate of pay, hours of duty, holidays, sick pay, pension, length of notice required, job title and disciplinary procedure. This statement must be given to the employee not later than thirteen weeks after he started work.

The Act also covers guarantee payments that must be paid for any workless day and suspension from work on medical grounds by the employer, trade union membership, public duties, redundancy leave and maternity rights.

C HYGIENE

The Food Hygiene (General) Regulations 1970 set out standards which cover food hygiene including food preparation equipment, food containers, temperature requirements and protective clothing. By virtue of the Food and Drugs Act 1955 the Environmental Health Officer is empowered to enter any catering establishment to examine the premises and to take away food samples for inspection. The Prevention of Damage by Pests Act 1949 gives Ministry of Agriculture inspectors right of entry to premises infested by rats, etc., and local authorities have to take steps to see that persons running food businesses take adequate measures to keep premises free from rats, mice and other pests. Under the Food and Drugs (Control of Food Premises) Act 1976 a local authority is empowered under certain circumstances to apply to a magistrates court for the closure of a food business.

There are several aspects of hygiene:
1. The achievement of bacteriological safety of potentially dangerous foods.
2. General hygiene of premises.
3. Cleanliness of equipment.
4. Personal hygiene.

ACHIEVEMENT OF BACTERIOLOGICAL SAFETY OF FOODS

Food hygiene has two main principles the first is to prevent or destroy contamination, the second is to be aware that success in doing it is never certain. Food poisoning can originate in a spotlessly clean kitchen; the dirtiest of kitchens can produce completely safe food. Visible physical cleanliness is an important aspect of good food hygiene but it can be rendered ineffectual by an invisible and unsuspected source of contamination, so methods of handling and storage come into it.

Outbreaks of food poisoning are always caused by bacteria which do not die because they are in a clean kitchen. In a dirty kitchen there is the danger of cross-contamination of prepared food but if it is adequately cooked it is made safe and if eaten promptly then there is no risk.

Most outbreaks originate in meat or poultry which is already infected with salmonella or clostridium welchii when delivered. The salmonella will be destroyed by cooking to the correct internal temperature of 70 °C and so should the clostridia but there is always the chance that some spores will remain to multiply, given the right incubating temperature. To leave foods simmering at a low temperature or to cool down slowly in a warm atmosphere gives the chance for dormant spores to come to life or for the food to become recontaminated.

Any protein food – including dishes containing milk and eggs – left standing about at a temperature within the risk zone of 10 °C–60 °C is at risk, the most dangerous zone lying between 36.1 °C–37.7 °C which is about blood temperature.

Salmonella is found in raw meat, poultry and eggs and its incubation period of twelve to thirty-six hours leads to fever, diarrhoea, vomiting and headache which can last for a week.

Clostridium welchii may be present in raw meat and cause diarrhoea; the incubation period is from eight to twenty-two hours.

The safety of food stems largely from the way it is handled during its stages of production including storage and distribution and staff must be told how they can minimise the opportunities for food poisoning by having an adequate knowledge of hygiene methods.

Cross-contamination often happens in a busy larder where at one minute the chef has to cut raw meat into steaks for the kitchen, then an order for cold meat, which he may cut with the same knife on the same cutting board.

Foods that need especial care are reheated dishes, brawn, bought meat pies. gravy, stock, cream cakes, cooked and raw shellfish and cold meats.

In the event of an outbreak of food poisoning in an establishment the first knowledge of it may come via the local environmental health department which has received a complaint from a customer. When an outbreak is discovered the manager should endeavour to keep some of the suspected food and notify the EHO. No attempt should be made to carry out hurried cleaning and disinfecting nor to throw away dishcloths or teatowels. Up-to-date staff lists must be available and the investigating officer given full co-operation and every facility.

GENERAL HYGIENE OF PREMISES

The busy operation of a kitchen and its ancillary departments that are in operation seven days a week throughout the year make it difficult to clean as thoroughly as one would wish, added to which is the problem of finding and keeping decent kitchen porters who take pride in their job. The cooks have a part to play in maintaining a good standard of hygiene by working cleanly and methodically and not brushing food particles onto the floor; the practice of sprinkling salt or sawdust over spillages may help to prevent accidents but needs to be brushed up before it is trampled all over the kitchen. After brushing, the floor needs to be scrubbed with a floor scrubbing machine but if it doesn't get into the corners this should be done with a deck scrubber. If a contract cleaning company is employed this work can be done during the night or early morning. Walls need regular washing and a periodic wash with a pressurised water-jet is desirable.

Prevention of infestation by any pests is possible by denying them access to premises, keeping foodstuffs covered, working cleanly so that no food crumbs go on the floor and keeping swill and refuse areas scrupulously clean and tidy. Fly killers that operate by ultra-violet fluorescent tubes and an electrocuting grid can be fitted. A contract with a pest control contractor is the best answer to the problem of infestation and the firm should be a member of the British Pest Control Association which is a guarantee that any infestation will be eradicated and premises kept free. Environmental health departments operate a pest control service to rid premises of an infestation but do not carry out regular visits.

CLEANLINESS OF EQUIPMENT

It is the duty of the person in charge of the kitchen to ensure that the standard of cleanliness is kept as high as possible, and to ensure that the same high standards are maintained in all the ancillary areas under his command.

It is in the dishwash area that the obligation of the establishment to serve food on clean dishes is carried out. This means that all serving dishes, plates, cutlery and glassware are washed up correctly so that they are washed and cleaned at the correct high temperature and made sparkling clean for further use. The reputation of an establishment depends to some extent upon the standards of cleanliness and hygiene achieved in this department.

The pots and pans used in the kitchen need to be washed up properly so that there is no chance of cross-contamination caused by food particles left in crevices or corners of these utensils. Whether the washing up is done by hand, by mechanical scourer or by pot-washing machine, the result must be that there is a constant supply of clean saucepans in readiness for use.

Small kitchen utensils such as spoons, whisks, ladles and chopping boards are usually washed up in a separate sink because they do not get so soiled as do saucepans; unless these items are cleaned carefully they can be a source of contamination.

Fixed equipment which includes stoves, steamers, machinery, tables, cupboards, and so on, must be cleaned regularly and kept in perfect order; staff will take greater pride in their working environment if it is kept clinically clean and the results will show up in the quality of their work. To achieve this it is necessary to provide a good supply of hot water and the right kinds of detergents. Wherever possible, equipment should be rinsed in water at 77°C containing a hypochlorate or quaternary ammonia disinfectant after it has been washed as this helps to ensure its hygienic safety. All table surfaces, drawers and chopping boards, should be cleaned and finished with the same type of disinfectant after each period of service.

Service contracts for equipment come in two categories: one firm will contract for the maintenance of say all fixed cooking equipment and come twice a year to take the items to pieces to clean them so as to keep them efficient. A second contract for the same items would cover the cleaning only. Unless the maintenance engineer has his own staff capable of carrying out maintenance and repairs, the sum of contracts can add up to a considerable amount each year.

Cleaning Materials

The choice and use of all kinds of cleaning materials presents a problem as there are so many brands of each item, and as this subject represents a considerable percentage of overhead expenses it is important to get it right. The fact that a dish-washing machine has to be fitted with a detergent and rinse dispenser and this is supplied and maintained free of charge by the same firm that makes the stuff, may decide the choice of supplier since each of them manufacture a range of cleaning materials to cover every cleaning job. The prices of the major items from the main detergent firms may be very similar and appear to be on the high side, but the quality of the service has to be taken into consideration as it is good to know that as soon as something goes wrong the expert can be contacted and the matter put right within a few hours. This, of course, is if the crockery comes out smeary or glasses are not brilliant, not if the machine becomes jammed because a spoon gets jammed in the cogwheel. It is possible to have detergents examined for strength or concentration and to select that which is the stronger, but the human factor often comes into it as to how much is being used per dosage and if the detergent is doing the job. It pays to listen to the sales talk of the various representatives to ascertain the types and uses of their products then to decide which firm to deal with. Washing up liquid is not a general purpose

449

detergent and it is necessary to have products specifically designed for each and every purpose, as the use of the wrong product is merely wasting it.

PERSONAL HYGIENE

Persons employed in the preparation and service of food should be aware of the need for absolute personal cleanliness and hygiene. Training in hygiene should be given where possible and a constant watch kept to ensure that personnel conform to a reasonable standard. The employer must do his share by providing good changing rooms with showers and toilets, adequate facilities for washing the hands and good first aid treatment. A good laundry service for staff to send their own protective clothing or a good linen room service if the firm supplies uniforms is essential; all food handlers except waiters and barmen are required under the 1970 Regulations to wear clean and washable clothing. Nobody is allowed to enter a kitchen unless wearing protective clothing.

Staff are required to play their part by keeping hands and forearms and fingernails thoroughly clean; ornate rings and jewellery that may harbour bacteria may not be worn. The hands must be washed under hot water using soap or a bactericide before commencing work, after going to the toilet, after handling raw food, after disposing of waste and after blowing the nose or touching the nose, mouth, ears or hair. Paper handkerchiefs should be used. Smoking is also prohibited under the Regulations.

Part-time courses in hygiene are operated by local environmental health departments, sometimes jointly with other bodies such as the St John's Ambulance Association, the depth of the course being adapted to the education level and level of responsibility of those taking it, and by the Royal Society of Health and the Royal Institute of Public Health and Hygiene. Staff should be encouraged to sit for the diplomas and certificates awarded and some incentive given to do so.

D PRACTICAL SAFETY PRECAUTIONS

By its nature the work carried out in a catering department can be dangerous if safety regulations are not adhered to. The pressure of business may cause staff to work quickly and under pressure whilst using potentially dangerous equipment and under conditions that are hazardous. Management must make every endeavour to ensure safe working conditions which will help to avoid the possibility of accidents.

It is the duty of the person in charge to note any possible hazard that could cause an accident and take steps to prevent it occurring such as the posting of warning signs about safe working procedures, providing first aid boxes, nominating first aid personnel, siting fire fighting equipment and making known the procedures to be followed in the event of accidents.

The general rules of safety at work include the following points:
1. Know what each type of fire extinguisher is used for.
2. Carry out fire drill regularly. Display clear fire instructions.
3. Show what to do if a person's clothes catch alight.
4. Keep ventilation grilles and ducts free from grease and dust.
5. Use safety guards on all machines.

451

6. Report all accidents and enter details in the official book.
7. Display the procedures for dealing with accidents and how to call an ambulance.
8. Report any suspicious parcels left lying around.
9. Give instructions on how to lift and move heavy goods.
10. Ensure ladders are safe before using.
11. Ensure current safety legislation is understood and carried out.
12. Inform staff they must not run; forbid horseplay on duty.
13. Encourage staff to report unsafe working conditions and to suggest possible solutions.
14. Issue instructions on personal hygiene.
15. Keep trolley wheels oiled and in good working order.
16. Report any signs of infestation.
17. Ensure that detergent and disinfectant containers are labelled.
18. Issue tapers for lighting equipment; forbid the use of paper spills.
19. Keep a record of safety training procedures carried out.
20. Allow only qualified persons to carry out maintenance work.

The Notification of Accidents and Dangerous Occurrences Regulations (1980) which is part of the Health and Safety at Work Act 1974 must be adhered to. This means the keeping of records and details of any accidents or dangerous occurrences as well as notifying these to the persons in charge or having responsibility for departments.

When surveying the various departments many practical situations may be seen to be possible danger points, so it is necessary to bring these to the notice of staff as in the following examples.

Dining Room and Bar

1. Do not use any furniture or fixture which looks unsafe.
2. See that carpets are not torn.
3. Learn to open service doors in the correct manner.
4. Keep floors clean and tidy; pick up anything that gets dropped.
5. Do not overload service trays; load them evenly and carry them with the left hand thus leaving the right hand free for use.
6. Do not use any chipped crockery or glassware.
7. Do not run; work calmly and methodically.
8. Take particular care when using spirit or gas chafing lamps; note the whereabouts of fire-fighting equipment before starting to use them and keep at a distance from customers and curtains.
9. Use a waiter's cloth to pick up hot dishes in case they have just come off the stove or from under the salamander.
10. Remove any chair or table that rocks.
11. Where installed use of hoist or service lift in accordance with instructions.

Kitchen

1. Clean split food or liquid from the floor immediately; warn people whilst it is being done and dry the area thoroughly.
2. Keep passageways clear of debris and anything likely to cause obstruction.
3. Have cleaning equipment immediately available and keep them in good condition.
4. Do not allow glass dishes in the department, if essential ensure safe handling; if broken ensure that all the pieces are cleared up.
5. Give a warning when leaving pans with hot handles on the stove.
6. Do not leave knives in sinks full of water.
7. Light gas equipment according to instruction; turn off if it fails to ignite immediately.
8. Do not insert electric plugs with damp hands; do not overload electrical points.
9. Wear protective clothing and keep it in good condition paying attention to shoes, laces and any tears in clothing. Keep arms and hair covered.
10. Be aware of the dangers when deep frying and be ready to remove the food if it looks as though the fat is going to bubble over. Take note of the whereabouts of fire blankets.
11. Be extra careful when carrying pots full of boiling liquid.
12. Adhere to instructions regarding the operation of new equipment.
13. Do not put hands into mixers whilst the machine is operating.
14. Allow the pressure to subside before opening steamers.
15. Use the plunger to push food through mincer.
16. Do not store liquids, hot or cold, above eye level.
17. Take note of The Prescribed Dangerous Machines Order 1964.

The Health & Safety At Work Act lays down that employees have the right to appoint their own safety representatives or workers inspectors to look at the causes of accidents and above all, potential hazards, and to warn management accordingly. The following are the type of questions which should be asked when the checking or inspecting of premises is carried out by the safety representative.

Lighting Is it good enough to avoid accidents occurring?
Are light fittings cleaned regularly?

Equipment Is it firmly fixed to the floor, table or stand?
If mobile, can it be adequately braked?
Are there long cables stretching across the floor?
Is there a list of operating instructions on each machine?
Are only trained persons permitted to operate machines?
Are only trained persons permitted to clean machines?
Can machines be isolated before being cleaned?

Are power-operated machines fed with proper implements?

Are protective guards always in place on machines?

Are young persons under 18 prevented from the risk of injury from cleaning machines?

Are safety devices on equipment regularly checked – including flame failure detectors?

Are coldrooms fitted with an alarm and inside handles?

Do staff know how to treat a burn?

Is information provided by the supplier on possible hazards and precautions passed on to staff?

Is caustic solution for cleaning stoves and ovens used only by trained employees and are they given protective clothing?

Staff

Are staff made to remove jewellery before starting work?

Are suitable overalls and uniform provided?

Are cloakrooms and locker rooms suitable for staff outdoor clothing and valuables?

Is the name and location of the first aid person widely known by putting on notice boards?

Is somebody responsible for the upkeep of the first aid boxes and has he been trained to render first aid?

Are staff shown the way to shift heavy loads?

Has investigation been done to eliminate or reduce heavy loads?

Are staff made to wear correct footwear?

Premises

Is there a fire certificate for the premises?

Are the fire exits clearly marked?

Are fire drills carried out?

Are there sufficient fire-fighting appliances?

Is the ventilation system efficient and adequate?

Is the kitchen maintained at a satisfactory temperature and humidity?

Are there in and out doors to the restaurant and are they clearly marked?

Are gangways kept clear?

Is the area kept clear at all times of empty crates and boxes and used pans etc.?

Is the floor non-slip?

Is the drainage around wet areas adequate?

Are spillages cleaned immediately and is there a person responsible for doing it?

Is the cause of spillage looked into?

Are floors cleaned correctly, using the right cleaner?

Are floors maintained in good order?

Do doors swing both ways?

Only when all these types of questions can be answered satisfactorily can things be considered as reasonably safe for the efficient operation of the catering department.

E SELECT BIBLIOGRAPHY

The books included in the following lists have been selected in the hope that they will be of assistance to the reader who wishes to make a further study of the topics discussed in this book. They are mostly related to and listed under the chapter headings and appendices of the book, though some will be found useful across a number of chapters because of the wide scope of their contents.

THE CATERING INDUSTRY

BRANDER, M. H. *The Life and Sport of the Inn*, Gentry Books, 1973.
GALLATI, M., *Mario of the Caprice*, Hutchinson, 1960
LUNDBERG, D., *The Hotel and Restaurant Business*, CBI, 1979.
MEDLIK, S., *Profile of the Hotel and Catering Industry*, Heinemann, 1978.
MORRIS, H., *Portrait of a Chef*, Cambridge, 1938.
PRICE, D., *Eating and Drinking in France Today*, Tom Stacey, 1972.
RITZ, M. L., *César Ritz: Host to the World*, Harrap, 1938.
TANNAHILL, R., *Food in History*, Paladin, 1973.
TAYLOR, D., *Fortune, Fame and Folly*, Caterer, 1977.

TAYLOR, D. and BUSH, D., *The Golden Age of British Hotels*, Northwood, 1974.

THALAMAS, P. and HERBODEAU, E., *Georges Auguste Escoffier*, Practical Press, 1955.

WILSON, A., *Food and Drink in Britain*, Constable, 1973.

THE CONSUMER AND THE MARKET

BAKER, M., *Marketing. An Introductory Textbook*, Macmillan, 1979.

BLUM, M., *Psychology and Consumer Affairs*, Harper & Row, 1977.

CAMPBELL-SMITH, G., *Marketing of the Meal Experience*, University of Surrey, 1967.

EHREMBERG, A. and PYATT, F., *Consumer Behaviour*, Penguin Educational, 1967.

KOTAS, R., *Marketing Orientation in the Hotel and Catering Industry*, University of Surrey, 1975.

SHEPHERD, J., *Marketing Practice in the Hotel and Catering Industry*, Batsford, 1982.

WILLIAMS, K., *Behavioural Aspects of Marketing*, Heinemann, 1981.

THE FORMULATION OF POLICY

BUFFA, E., *Modern Production Operations Management*, Wiley, 1975.

DRUCKER, P., *Management: Task and Responsibilities Practices*, Heinemann, 1974.

FEARN, D., *The Practice of General Management – Catering Operations*, Macdonald, 1971.

FEARN, D., *Food and Beverage Management*, Butterworth, 1973.

RYAN, C., *Hotel and Catering Economics*, Stanley Thornes, 1980.

INTERPRETATION OF DEMAND

ATKINSON, D., *Menu French*, Pergamon, 1980.

COMBES, S., *Dictionary of Cuisine French*, Hutchinson, 1980.

COMBES, S., *Restaurant French for Hoteliers*, Hutchinson, 1980.

SEABERG, A., *Menu Design*, Cahners, 1974.

SIMON, A. L., *A Concise Encyclopaedia of Gastronomy*, Collins, 1952.

WENZEL, G.L. Sr, *Menu Maker*, Edwards Bros, 1979.

457

CONVERGENCE OF FACILITIES

COPSON, D., *Microwave Heating*, Avi, 1975.
CUTLIFFE, E. and STRANK, D., *Analysing Catering Operations*, Arnold, 1971.
DOUGLAS, P., *Kitchen Planning and Design*, Blandford, 1979.
FENGLER, M., *Restaurant Architecture and Design*, Hill, 1971.
KORARIAN, E., *Food Service Facilities Planning*, Avi, 1975.
KOTSCHEVAR, L. and TERRILL, M., *Food Service Planning*, Wiley, 1977.
LAWSON, F., *Principles of Catering Design*, Architectural Press, 1978.
MILSOM. A. and KIRK, D., *Principles of Design and Operation of Catering Equipment*, Wiley, 1980.
SENIOR, J., *Work Study in the Kitchen*, Pitman, 1975.
STRANK, D., *Ergonomics: Functional Design for the Hotel and Catering Industry*, Arnold, 1971.
WALLEY, J., *The Kitchen in Catering*, Constable, 1979.
WEST, B., *Food Service in Institutions*, Wiley, 1975.
WILKINSON, J., *The 3 Cs of Atmosphere, Books I & II*, Institutions, 1969.
YOUNG, R., *Modern Cooking Equipment*, Northwood, 1979.

PROVISIONING

AMERINE, M. and ROESSLER, E., *Wines: Their Sensory Evaluation*, Freeman, 1976.
ANDROUET, P., *Guide du Fromage* (English Edition), Aidan Ellis, 1973.
COCKBURN, E., *Portwine and Oporto*, Wine & Spirits Publications.
DAVIDSON, S. *et al.*, *Human Nutrition and Dietetics*, Churchill-Livingstone, 1979.
DAVIS, B., *Food Commodities*, Heinemann, 1978.
DITMER, P. and GRIFFIN, G., *Principles of Food, Beverage and Labour Cost Control*, CBI, 1980.
DOWNEY, W., *Food Quality and Nutrition*, Applied Science, 1978.
FISHER, P. and BENDER, A., *The Value of Food Series*, OUP, 1975.
FORBES, P., *Champagne*, Gollancz, 1979.
JEFFS, J., *Sherry*, Faber, 1970.
JOHNSON, H., *The World Atlas of Wine*, Mitchell Beazley, 1981.
MONTAGNE, P., *Larousse Gastronomique* (French Ed.), Librarie Larousse, 1968.
    Larousse Gastronomique (Eng. Ed.), Hamlyn, 1977.
SOUTHGATE, D. and PAUL, A., *McCance and Widdowson's The Composition of Foods*, HMSO, 1978.
STEEL, J., *Control in Catering*, Barrie & Rockliff, 1968.
STEFANELLY, J., *Purchasing Selection and Procurement, for the Hospitality Industry*, Wiley, 1981.

PRODUCTION AND DISTRIBUTION

BERTRAM, P., *Fast Food Operations*, Barrie & Rockliff, 1975.
BOLTMAN, B., *Cook-Freeze Catering Systems*, Applied Science Pubn., 1978.
BUFFA, A. and TAUBERT, W., *Production – Inventory Systems – Planning and Control*, Irwin, 1979.
FULLER, J., *Modern Restaurant Service*, Hutchinson, 1982.
GLEW, G., *Catering Equipment and System Design*, Applied Science Pubn., 1977.
HOPEMAN, R., *Systems Analysis and Operations Management*, Merrill, 1969.
KOTSCHEVAR, L., *Quantity Food Production*, International Ideas, 1975.
KOTSCHEVAR, L. and KNIGHT, J., *Quantity Food Production – Planning and Maintenance*, CBI, 1979.
PLATT, B. S. *et al.*, *Food in Hospitals*, OUP, 1963.
WARNER, M., *Industrial Food Service and Cafeteria Management*, Cahners, 1973.
WEST, B. *et al.*, *Food Service in Institutions*, Wiley, 1977.
WYCKOFF, D. and SASSER, W., *The Chain-Restaurant Industry*, Heath, 1978.

CONTROL OF COSTS AND REVENUES

ANSOFF, H., *Corporate Strategy*, Penguin, 1980.
BOARDMAN, R., *Hotel and Catering Costing and Budgets*, Heinemann, 1978.
BOYCE, R. and CHRISTIE, N., *Integrated Managerial Controls*, Longman, 1974.
HARRIS, P. and HAZZARD, P., *Accounting and Financial Management in the Hotel and Catering Industry*, Northwood, 1980.
KEISER, R. and KALLIS, E., *Controlling and Analysing Costs in Food Service*, Wiley, 1974.
KOTAS, R. and DAVIS, B., *Food and Beverage Control*, International Textbook, 1981.
KOTAS, R. and DAVIS, B., *Food Cost Control*, International Textbook, 1976.
THORNER, H. and MANNING, P., *Quality Control in Food Service*, Avi, 1976.

MONITORING OF CONSUMER SATISFACTION

JURAH, J., *Quality Control Handbook*, McGraw Hill, 1974.
KRAMER, A. and TWIGG, B., *Quality Control for the Food Industry Vols. I & II*, Avi, 1970 and 1973.
OPPENHEIM, A., *Questionnaire Design and Attitude Measurement*, Heinemann, 1968.

LAW

FIELD, D., *Hotel and Catering Law in Great Britain*, Sweet and Maxwell, 1982.
FIELD, D., *Practical Club Law*, Sweet and Maxwell, 1980.
MITCHELL, E., *The Caterer's Lawyer*, Butterworth, 1976.
RICHARDS, M. and STEWART, S., *Legal Aspects of the Hotel and Catering Industry*, Bell and Hyman, 1979.
UNDERHILL, M., *The New Licensing Guide*, Oyez, 1979.
  ABC of Licensing Laws, NULV, 1980.

HYGIENE

HMSO, *Food Hygiene Regulations*, HMSO, 1976.
HOBBS, B. and GILBERT, R., *Food Poisoning and Food Hygiene*, Arnold, 1978.
PARRY, T. and PAWSEY, R., *Principles of Microbiology*, Hutchinson, 1973.

INDEX

463

466

467